Land Reform:

A World Survey

Westview Advanced Economic Geographies

Land Reform
Russell King

*Agriculture in the Third World:
A Spatial Analysis*
W. B. Morgan

LAND REFORM

A World Survey

Russell King

Routledge
Taylor & Francis Group

LONDON AND NEW YORK

First published 1977 by Westview Press

Published 2018 by Routledge
52 Vanderbilt Avenue, New York, NY 10017
2 Park Square, Milton Park, Abingdon, Oxon OX14 4RN

Routledge is an imprint of the Taylor & Francis Group, an informa business

Library of Congress Cataloging in Publication Data
King, Russell.
    Land reform.
    (Westview advanced economic geography)
    Includes index.
    1. Land reform—Case studies. I. Title.
II. Series.
HD156.K54 1977   333.1   77-24033

ISBN 13: 978-0-367-02205-1 (hbk)
ISBN 13: 978-0-367-17192-6 (pbk)

To
Sue, Zoë and
Alexander Christopher

Contents

Tables

Maps and Diagrams

Preface

The genesis of this book dates back some ten years when, as an undergraduate at the London School of Economics, I first became captivated by the land reform theme whilst pursuing regional courses on Latin America and Mediterranean Europe. My first acknowledgment must, therefore, be accorded to the teachers of those courses, Peter Odell and Dan Sinclair. The latter, together with Professor M. J. Wise, was responsible for guiding my subsequent research at LSE into the Italian land reform. Having completed this 'case-study' I became concerned to look at the issue of land reform systematically and on a world scale. The present book is a result of that effort, spanning, in fact, the past four years.

Conceptually, this book can perhaps be seen to take its cue from a recent paper by Professor Mabogunje which makes a call for geographers to devote more attention to the systematic study of the human and rural environments of the Third World.[1] To date, thematic studies of the development process by geographers have been conspicuously lacking. Recent indications, however, are that this deficiency is about to be remedied; the geography of development is emerging as an important aspect of the current movement of our subject towards greater social relevance.[2] Even so, apart from a few regional case-studies, land reform has been looked at only cursorily by geographers, although a wide historical and social science literature exists on the topic.[3] But land reform is not only a political, economic and social phenomenon; it is very much a spatial process as well. The appeal to the geographer is very plain. Moreover, a change in the distribution of landownership, or of man's rights to use land, often results in more tangible changes in land use, agricultural productivities, settlement patterns and the spatial movements associated with farming. These phenomena also need to be examined. Nevertheless, my plea for geographers to look at land reform should not be allowed to obscure the fact that land reform is a fundamentally mutli-disciplinary topic. I came increasingly to realise this in the course of working on this book. What started out as a well-intentioned geographical account rapidly became a hazardous journey into a no-man's land of interdisciplinary social science investigation. I only hope that my lack of a general social science training does not show through too obviously on the following pages.

Basically, the book has two roles: as a synthesis and as a source-book. Part 1 attempts to lay down some general themes and principles in the study of land reform. The level of generalisation is fairly high, although in Chapter 2 the historical evolution of the concept of land reform is traced in some detail. Parts 2 to 5 constitute a continent-based country-by-country survey of the significant recent reforms in the less developed countries. As far as I know, such a complete survey has not been attempted before in one book. Recent comparative studies by Tuma, Warriner, Tai, Le Coz and Griffin are based on a narrower sample of studies.[4]

I must admit that there were times when I wondered if I had bitten off more than I could chew. I hope this book does not reveal too much evidence of intellectual indigestion, but on occasions I seemed to be writing not one but a dozen or more books. Only my belief in the importance of land reform for many countries, Professor R. O. Buchanan's quiet encouragement and, I guess, my own determination saw the project through.

My debt to the literature will be apparent from the references at the end of each chapter. Keeping abreast of material on land reform has been a major task in itself. Initially I welcomed new material with naive avidness; later, with a sinking feeling in the pit of my stomach, came the realisation that I could not keep up-to-date on *all* major land reforms (indeed, several new ones occurred while I was writing this book), and my visits to the library were made with increasing trepidation. I was, however,

fortunate in having at my disposal a number of useful reference
tools. The FAO *Bibliography on Land Tenure*, issued in 1972, was
my basic collection of sources. This was supplemented by use
of *Geo-Abstracts*, *WAERSA* (World Agricultural Economics and
Rural Sociology Abstracts) and the twice-yearly bibliographic
supplements to FAO's bulletin *Land Reform, Land Settlement and
Co-operatives*. The Agency for International Development's
Spring Review of Land Reform, published in 1970, coincided
happily with my starting this project, and the various country
reports in this monumental survey provided much useful background material. Finally, I must acknowledge a special debt
to the late Doreen Warriner's book *Land Reform in Principle and
Practice*, which was a constant source of interest and inspiration.

Several people have given help and advice at various stages;
their combined efforts have, I am sure, considerably improved
the finished product. Professor R. O. Buchanan went through
the entire manuscript with meticulous care, tidying up my
unwieldy prose; it was largely due to his sterling efforts that a
frighteningly excessive first draft of nearly 200 000 words was
pared down to a length more acceptable to the publisher, and
probably to the reader. In his fifteen years as editor of this series
I doubt if he has spent more time grappling with an author's
manuscript than with mine. It is a great pleasure to acknowledge the assistance of colleagues in the Leicester University
Geography Department with special expertise in various
regions of the world. Iain Buchanan was a prolific source of
information on a number of South East Asian countries, and
he also read and corrected the Asian section of the book; Colin
Crossley provided bibliographic help and advice on Latin
America; and Professor John Paterson read and advised on
Part 1 of the book. A number of other friends and colleagues
elsewhere rendered similar services. Robert Wade of the
Institute of Development Studies, University of Sussex, provided a detailed critique of Chapter 1, and Christine Smith of
the same institution improved the Kenya chapter. Stephanie
Goodenough of the Open University furnished detailed advice
on Mexico and Cuba as well as reading the rest of Part 2,
Keith Sutton of Manchester University gave up-to-date information on the Algerian situation, and Professor W. B. Fisher
of Durham read and commented on the entire Middle East

section. To all these people I extend my thanks, with the usual cautionary caveat that their helpfulness implies no responsibility for what follows. On the technical side I express my thanks to David Orme and Ruth Rowell, departmental cartographers at Leicester, for drawing the maps for this book. Also appreciated were the typing skills of Sue Hollier, Sue Wilson-Jennings and others of the 'Mowsley typing pool'. A word of thanks too to the Inter-Library Loan personnel of Leicester University Library who coped efficiently and uncomplainingly with the reference requests showered upon them. Lastly, I must express heartfelt thanks to my wife who, in addition to her own many and diverse responsibilities, managed to produce two children whilst I was in labour with this book, and who further contributed, by skilful management of young children, in creating regular quiet periods at home.

Leicester   R. K.
February 1976.

REFERENCES

1. A. L. Mabogunje: 'Geography and the problems of the Third World', *International Social Science Journal*, 27 (2), 1975, pp. 287–302.
2. J. Connell: 'The geography of development or the development of geography', *Antipode: A Radical Journal of Geography*, 5 (2), 1973, pp. 27–39.
3. R. L. King: 'Land reform: some general and theoretical considerations', *Norsk Geografisk Tidsskrift*, 25 (1), 1971, pp. 85–97.
4. E. H. Tuma: *Twenty-Six Centuries of Land Reform* (Berkeley, University of California Press, 1965); D. Warriner: *Land Reform in Principle and Practice* (Oxford, Clarendon Press, 1969); H.-C. Tai: *Land Reform and Politics: A Comparative Analysis* (Berkeley, University of California Press, 1974); J. Le Coz: *Les Réformes Agraires: De Zapata à Mao Tse-Toung et la FAO* (Paris, Presses Universitaires de France, 1974); K. Griffin: *Land Concentration and Rural Poverty* (London, Macmillan, 1976).

PART 1

Land Reform: A General Overview

I

The Challenge of Land Reform

Poverty is one of the world's greatest problems. The quest to solve it involves raising the living standards of two-thirds of the world's population. The great majority are rural folk, many of whom are denied the means for self-improvement by restricted access to their most basic need and resource—land. Throughout history there has been a continuous struggle on the part of the poor for land. Land reform has come to be a tremendously popular slogan for redistribution of wealth and promotion of economic development; this has been true in countries with such widely divergent historical, cultural and geographical backgrounds as India, Italy, Bolivia and Japan. One influential writer goes so far as to say that it is the most important social change now taking place in the world.[1]

In fact, arguments for land reform fall under three main heads. The social equity argument is based on the ethical-moral premise that inequality and, worse still, exploitation, are bad things. Secondly, and partly linked to the first argument, land reform has become closely involved with ideological positions and, therefore, with political dogma. Finally, and more recently, land reform has been strongly argued on economic grounds, either for the benefit of the individual farmer, or as part of an overall development policy.

A vast amount has been written about land reform. Three bibliographies on land tenure and land reform, issued in 1955, 1959 and 1972 by FAO, contain between them some 10 000 references.[2] This literature covers a wide range of viewpoints and forms an uncoordinated mass of material. Few attempts have been made to develop general principles or a body of theory, either deductively or based on case studies and historical examples.[3] Perhaps the nature of the topic explains this void, for each land reform has to be tailored to its own situation to be successful, taking particular account of a nation's or region's cultural heritage and economic and political conditions. But, even so, who is best equipped to write about land reform? Land itself is a term of many and varied meanings.[4] In law it is property, in political science it is a source of power and strategy. In economics it is a factor of production and a form of capital. In social psychology it is a personalised guarantor of security; in anthropology an item of culture, and in sociology a part of the social system. In agriculture it means basically the soil. To geographers land can mean most of these things, but most of all perhaps surface land use. Material on the subject of land reform has been produced by scholars and practitioners of many different disciplines, each of whom tends to apply a biased viewpoint derived from the parent discipline.[5] The historical approach is of value in considering the effects of past land reforms and the long term links between agrarian institutional changes and development, but most historians have relatively little knowledge of agriculture. The anthropologist's bias in favour of static descriptive studies is of little use in considerations of policy and development, while agronomists tend to concentrate solely on production aspects. The majority of general economists have traditionally had little to say on land reform, and agricultural economists, strangely, even less. Flores[6] notes that economists react to it 'either as a subject that belongs somewhere in the prosaic underworld of farm management and the applied agricultural sciences, or as a disturbing manœuvre of demagogic or activist intent which anyway would not lend itself to formal analysis.' Economists have neglected the subject because it concerns the institutional framework, which economic analysis tends to accept as given. Recent years, however, have seen a change in this situation. The formulation by the United Nations in 1951 of land tenure as an obstacle to economic development meant that to land reform's original egalitarian motive was added an economic objective. Economists could no longer ignore land reform. Their recent interest in the theme has focused on the central issues of capital formation, employment and investment for economic development, considered at length in Chapter 3. Above all, land reform is a political issue with a perennial fascination for political philosophers. Many so-called economic arguments are really political ones in disguise. Pope John, Mao Tse-Tung, President Truman and Che Guevara have all proposed interpretations of land reform. In Flores's opinion, the best writings of members of this influential group 'display towards the subject . . . sensitivity and sophistication, (and) reveal a thoroughly professional understanding of land reform, both as a supremely effective device to gain and to retain the support of the peasants, and as a deadly weapon against the landed oligarchy.'[7]

To date, however, the subject of land reform has remained an academic no-man's-land. Certainly, with regard to actual implementation, the approach of the land reform planner must be very broad, often based on the investigations of a team of experts comprising economists, agronomists, sociologists, legal experts and the like. Land reform is a thoroughly interdisciplinary topic and cannot be effectively studied by the techniques and approaches of one subject alone. It may well be that in the academic study of land reform the broad view of the geographer, encompassing knowledge and techniques from several fields within a regional framework, will prove the most useful approach.

THE PROBLEM OF DEFINITION

Land reform has come to be a term of a bewildering variety of interpretations. In some cases 'land reform' and 'agrarian reform' are used as straight alternatives; in other cases careful distinctions are drawn. From a purely technical standpoint, almost any programme that leads to change, presumably for the better, in the manner in which land is held or used, might be described as land reform. More precisely and, from the standpoint of this book, more importantly, the different meanings and definitions do appear to have two things in common: land reform is invariably a more or less direct, publicly controlled change in the existing character of land ownership, and it normally attempts a diffusion of wealth, income or productive capacity.[8]

In English, at least, the two alternative terms do have some historical meaning. Land reform, the traditional term, always meant the redistribution of property in land for the benefit of landless workers, tenants and small farmers. But experience of early reforms, in Haiti, Russia and the Philippines for example, showed that land redistribution pure and simple often led to drastic falls in production. The importance was realised of complementary measures such as education, agricultural credit, technical assistance, capital investment in infrastructural works, co-operatives, research and improved methods of processing and marketing. The definition of land reform widened so that it became not so much a concept but more the conception of a policy, and with this broad approach the use of the term 'agrarian reform' came into vogue. Although 'land reform' as a term possibly carries more direct impact, the use of the term *reforma agraria* in Spanish, which language—owing to the continuing debate on agrarian reform in Latin America—accounts for a good proportion of 'reform' literature, has done much to cement the latter term's popularity.

By 'land reform', then, is specifically meant land tenure reform. Land tenure reform is of two main types: land redistribution, which involves the breaking up or combining of existing holdings and leads to a change in scale of ownership; and tenancy reform, which effects improvements in tenancy contracts, with no change in the distribution of ownership. Other forms of land reform are the converting of tenants into owners of previously rented land, and when plots are traded between farmers to consolidate otherwise fragmented holdings. The crucial issue is land redistribution; large-scale programmes of which represent a forceful type of public action designed directly to reduce the political, social and economic power of established landowners. As Warriner explains, this process consists of four stages: expropriation, compensation, exemption and redistribution.[9] Around this 'core' of true land reform lie the more peripheral reforms of the agrarian structure which encounter much less conflict and are therefore manageable by less authoritative governments. In this way Barlowe[10] has separated types of reform into four groups according to their severity. Firstly come mild reforms involving laws governing landlord-tenant relationships, land settlement and land development programmes, agricultural credit facilities and voluntary land consolidation schemes. In making use of such mild measures many countries have prevented their land problems from becoming serious, but these measures are of limited value if offered as a palliative when the real need is for thorough-going land reform. Stronger measures involve 'public controls short of expropriation' and include rent reductions and mandatory consolidation programmes. Thirdly come expropriation and distribution in family plots. This represents a more courageous type of governmental action and often follows, or is designed to prevent, a revolution. Finally there are collectivisation schemes such as those carried out in Russia, China and Cuba. The strength of public action required makes this the most extreme type of land reform.

THE NEED FOR LAND REFORM

Most land reforms occur in situations where great disparities in wealth, income and power exist in agriculture. Proposals for land reform assume that such inequalities are handicaps to progress, and indeed there is some evidence to indicate that extreme inequality acts as a bottleneck to development by depriving both the very rich and the very poor of any real incentive to work for higher productivity. Because there are great inequalities in many underdeveloped countries, because there are many influences tending to make such inequalities cumulative and because the forces opposed to changing this situation are firmly entrenched, there are strong arguments for an egalitarian emphasis as a rough guide to reform policy. Stated in this way, land reform can both have a basic function of providing some measure of social justice, and act to remove barriers to economic development.

Pronounced inequality in the distribution of landownership can come about in a number of ways. The process of economic development itself tends to lead to cumulative concentration of resources, geographically, sectorally and socially, and land is no exception to this general rule. Many countries have witnessed situations whereby large grants of land were made to certain individuals or to organisations such as the church or commercial companies, in return for military service, in order to develop commercial agriculture, in order to foster colonialism, or perhaps as plain gifts. The most important process has been the development of a feudal or quasi-feudal system, most simply characterised by a two-class society and the subjugation of the peasants to the landlords.

The latifundian system, with large estates worked by semi-serf peons, has been a feature common to many underdeveloped areas, especially in Latin America, parts of southern Europe and the Middle East. The most obvious manifestations of this system are the high degree of concentration of landownership in the hands of a few, a large proportion of landless labourers amongst the rural population and insecure tenancy arrangements. In Latin American countries that have not experienced major land reforms, generally about 3–4 per cent of the landowners own 60–80 per cent of the agricultural land. South Asian countries also show substantial degrees of ownership concentration, but ownership is commonly decentralised through tenancy and sharecropping. Comparable figures do not exist for sub-Saharan Africa, and they would have little meaning anyway within the tribal ownership pattern. The most pronounced individual cases of skewed landownership situations come from South America. In pre-reform Chile 4·4 per cent of the landowners monopolised 85 per cent of total farmland. In Brazil over three-quarters of the agricultural population are landless, and 4·5 per cent of the landowners share between them 81 per cent of the farmland. Even in southern Italy before the 1950 reform 3 per cent of the landowners possessed 60 per cent of the land, and there were over two million *braccianti* (landless labourers). In countries such as these, and there are many of them, such is the domination of the landlords and so strong is their monopoly control over land and the supply of capital in agriculture that the possibilities for self-improvement on the part of the peasants are virtually nil. In Egypt, for example, where before the reform 5·8 per cent of the owners claimed 65 per cent of the agricultural land, the capital required to purchase 2 hectares—the size of a typical farm plot— was equivalent in 1947 to an agricultural labourer's wages for sixty years.[11]

In Asia large landholdings have not for the most part been

operated as centrally managed farms, but rented out in small-holdings, usually through intermediaries, to cultivators who paid high rents and had very little security. In India much land was leased through the zamindars, who did almost nothing in return for the fees they received. Before legislation the most common rate of rent was 50 per cent of the gross produce, up to 75 per cent in some cases, the tenant having to bear almost all the costs of cultivation. In Japan 'the landlord was an exalted being. . . . He did not deal with his tenants directly, but through a three-tiered chain of control.'[12] Such outdated and unjust systems of tenancy prevent the adoption of improved production methods and make it practically impossible for the tenant to obtain a better standard of living since, as in the latifundian situation, there is hardly any margin for savings and little incentive for additional effort.

The third type of landownership structure to which land reformers' attention is drawn is the plantation. The plantation estate, common in all three underdeveloped continents, may be run by a company or an individual (either way, often of foreign origin); as a large firm in the economic sense it is capital intensive and centrally managed, with wage labour, often only seasonally employed. Production is frequently for export only, and consists of a single crop such as coffee, sugar or rubber. The main economic (as opposed to political) arguments for land reform in plantation areas are that much labour employment is seasonal, causing great unemployment for part of the year, and that over-specialisation on an export crop limits food production for the home market and renders the whole economy vulnerable to changes in the world market price for one crop. Where plantations are inefficiently operated, as in north-east Brazil, land redistribution could increase employment and production if a more diversified crop system can be substituted by the new owners. If the estates are well managed, on the other hand, their subdivision could well lead to a drop in production. Even if the plantation unit is kept intact with ownership assumed by the state or a co-operative, production may fall if the new management is not as efficient as the old.

No reform can be successful, however, unless it springs from the recognition of its necessity by the peoples concerned. No landlord-dominated government will happily vote itself out of landowning status and various other privileges without strong pressure from other socio-political groups. There must be widespread peasant dissatisfaction with the existing agrarian structure, and the determination and organisation to act upon that dissatisfaction as well as some sort of goal toward which to work. It frequently happens, however, that peasant societies contain within their own structures obstacles to the expression of this collective determination and organisation to effect land reform. Amongst some peasant groups manual labour on the land is despised; the highest aspiration of such societies is to own or control land but not to work it. Several land reforms have shown that some beneficiaries prefer to rent their new holdings out to others, so that they themselves do not have to work the land and can enjoy 'landlord status'. Some anthropologists have pointed out that in backward rural economies which have too many peasants competing for too little land, or where that land is denied them by widespread landlord ownership, any co-operative action on the part of the peasants is extraordinarily hard to stimulate because the peasants are highly suspicious of one another.[13]

Certain social and psychological changes therefore often need to take place. These outlooks and social values are relative; they seem to accompany the spread of ideas that life can be better than it is; they follow contact with cities and importation of political ideas from abroad. The demand for reforms which limit landownership or the rights of landlords is likely to arise when ideas of social justice change more rapidly than the rate at which economic development creates opportunities for parallel advances in income and social status. The process may happen even in the presence of rapid overall economic growth, particularly if the growth is confined to one sector of the country (typically the urban industrial sector) and if population increase prevents a decline in the absolute number of the agricultural population. The premise is of particular significance in some Asian countries where conditions of the mass of the peasantry have not markedly improved despite industrial development and where the mass of the peasantry, although discontented, have not developed a movement, either in the form of political parties or of the tenant unions that existed in pre-war Japan. The existence of strong local peasant organisation is particularly crucial in conditioning the success of legislation governing rent controls and minimum wages. Even when voting is free, it seems that the majority of the South Asian peasantry does not vote in its own interests. Similarly the Charter of Punta del Este and the Alliance for Progress cannot succeed in their efforts to effect structural changes in Latin American agriculture if an organised peasantry which understands the programme's purpose does not exist.

MOTIVES AND OBJECTIVES

Confusion about land reform is not confined to definition but extends also to motivation. Many objectives have been listed in various contexts and opinions differ as to what the ultimate aim of a land reform should be. On the broad view, three motives— the political, the social and the economic—are basic and govern most reforms. Although different objectives are often inter-related and mutually complementary, sometimes the fulfilment of one objective may retard another. The most frequent conflict is seen as that between social equality and economic efficiency. The point is illustrated by India: here the fixing of a 20-acre ceiling on landownership would correspond to an egalitarian motive of enabling every farming household in the country to have a minimum subsistence plot of 2 acres; but the creation of millions of 2-acre plots would adversely affect food production and reduce the marketable surplus, which for India would be disastrous.[14] Nevertheless there is still much discussion as to which of the two principal aims, the economic or the social, should be the dominant consideration in land reform programmes. Many Latin American reforms follow the concept of failure of the 'social function' of landownership as the criterion for expropriation, the idea being that those landowners who fail to bear their social responsibilities to the community adequately, exploiting the peasants who work their land or allowing that land to go to waste, do not deserve to enjoy the privilege of owning land, but the whole concept remains nebulous and therefore easy to evade.

The conception of these two motives as straight alternatives is, however, almost certainly an oversimplification. Countries seldom push a single policy objective to the exclusion of others; usually, multiple objectives are combined in varying arrangements of priority. The achievement of any goal is thus rarely absolute, but a matter of degree. With each objective acting as a constraint on others, the problem of policy formulation is not one of simply arranging a set of objectives in an order of priority, but of deciding how to achieve the optimum combination. Much recent theoretical literature on land reform stresses the view that economic and social objectives do not conflict, that in fact they *must* be welded together in the land reform approach to development. Dorner, for example, explains that the dilemma between distributive justice and economic efficiency is not a real issue. Equity and productivity goals conflict only if the present ownership structure of land and capital is assumed to be fixed. When calculations are based on national account, with all social costs and benefits appraised, the dilemma breaks down.[15]

The political motive is sometimes omitted and often played down in discussion on land reform, yet in the last resort is often the most decisive. It is the balance of political power in a country which ultimately determines the extent of a reform, and political factors help to explain the frequently wide discrepancy between the provisions of a reform law and their eventual practical effects. Many governments use land reform, or the promise of it, to gain or retain power. The political motive in this way is often closely linked with the social motive: the lot of the peasant is improved in an attempt to win his political support. In a strong statement on the political importance of land reforms, Tai[16] demonstrates that in countries like Mexico, Taiwan, Egypt and Iran, where the government has a strong political commitment to carry out reform, and where the ruling elites are separated from the landed class, implementation of needed reform programmes is successful, even if other factors, such as availability of finance and the existence of social problems, are unfavourable. Where sustained political commitment is lacking, as in the Philippines, Pakistan and Colombia, reforms are only partially carried through. Land reform may also be regarded as a political move to avoid impending revolution, perhaps even forced upon an inherently conservative régime otherwise unwilling to enact land reform, because the only alternative is their own ultimate overthrow. Incalculable losses, not only political, occur when a country dissolves into anarchy and revolution. The vital questions of land reform become whether, and how, adjustments can be made within the given structure of politics and administration so that violent revolution is avoided, conflicts are mitigated and the economy is kept functioning as a going concern. A distinction, therefore, is between evolutionary and revolutionary types of land reform. Land reform need not thus always be justified on economic grounds. The relief of social and political tensions can provide a sufficient basis for reform, which may also create, ultimately or incidentally, preconditions for economic development through the formation of new entrepreneurial attitudes.

If political stability is assured, however, attention may be concentrated on measures for increasing agricultural productivity. A land reform which does not increase production merely equalises poverty. In Egypt, for example, the original social impetus of the land reform has been overlain by the drive for economic efficiency. The economic motive reflects the belief that land reform should be instituted to generate a surplus in the agricultural sector to serve as capital for building up industry. The vital contributions that land reform can make towards economic development are analysed in more detail in Chapter 3, but one general aspect of land reform's economic rationale worthy of note here concerns employment. According to Dovring[17] the agricultural population remains stable, or even continues to increase, for some time after the onset of industrialisation in a country. This leads to the conclusion that in most of the less developed countries of today, there is no reason to suppose that numbers employed in agriculture will be greatly reduced in the next few decades. There is tremendous momentum inherent in population increase; the effects of birth-control programmes in underdeveloped countries will not be felt for another twenty years at least due to the delay in the natural life cycle—the future unemployed are already born or about to be born. A goal of maintaining people solidly in agriculture is therefore indicated, particularly when large pools of unemployed labour clustering in shanty towns round the cities of the less developed world indicate the incapability of the urban-industrial sector to absorb excess population. Land reform of itself cannot of course provide the immediate solution to the overpopulation problem which was historically remedied by war and famine. The crucial role of land reform in this context is rather to create additional employment opportunities in the rural sector, holding the agricultural population at an improved standard of living, until industrial development creates the position whereby labour can be moved out of agriculture and perhaps until such time as new cultural attitudes favouring family limitation develop. It may well be that this structural aspect, relating land reform to the short term goal of reducing unemployment and stabilising the agricultural population, and to the long term aim of economic development facilitated by intersectoral shifts of labour, may prove to be the most valuable economic contribution of land reform.

LAND REFORMS AND AGRARIAN REFORMS

At the risk of attempting to be too encyclopædic, this section looks at various kinds of land reform in different situations. The definitional framework established earlier is continued with separation of 'true' land reforms (land redistribution and tenancy reform) from the more peripheral measures affecting parts of the agrarian structure (colonisation, the green revolution, etc.). The term land reform, being a magnetic word in the political lexicon, tends to pick up any and all schemes for rural improvement that are put forward.

LAND REDISTRIBUTION

Land reforms which include redistribution of landownership basically involve expropriation of some or all of the land of the big landowners and its assignment to landless or semi-landless peasants, usually in individually owned small farms, but sometimes, as in the Mexican *ejido*, in communal units. In revolutionary reforms, such as the Bolivian, expropriation may be total, with peasants rushing to occupy estate land, and virtually no compensation paid to the former landlords. Similarly, when the Chinese Communist Party came to power, it expropriated without indemnity all landowners who did not work their land themselves.

Recent land reforms in the North African countries of

Algeria, Tunisia and Libya confiscated foreign-owned land (mostly French and Italian) with little compensation, re-assigning it free of charge to the indigenous rural population. More commonly, however, expropriation is over and above a certain permitted ceiling on private landholding, and some compensation is paid to former owners. The level of the ceiling can vary widely, depending on the severity of the reform legisla-tion and on the intensity of farming practised. In some countries the ceiling is set so high and the legislation is so vague—for example, in western Paraguay there is a 20 000 hectare ceiling on land 'not rationally operated'—that the concept becomes meaningless. Because a simple flat ceiling figure ignores varia-tions in land quality, the principle of measuring land in some kind of productivity units is sometimes used in the implementa-tion. In Taiwan land was classified into 26 productivity grades, and the landlords' retained portion made equivalent to 3 hec-tares of medium-grade paddy land. The notion of the standard acre in India, which chiefly depends on the presence or ab-sence of irrigation, reflects the same principle.

Where land redistribution has been decided in principle but cannot, for political, financial or organisational reasons be organised in one fell swoop over the whole country, the question arises of methods of phasing the operation. Such a selective ap-proach could either involve carrying out the reform only in certain restricted areas (as in Italy) or could operate through a gradual lowering of ceilings (as in Egypt and Cuba). Or the phasing could be qualitative, changing from tenancy regulation initially to redistribution later (for example, Taiwan). The chief merits of a selectively phased reform lie in the possibility of thorough implementation and the scope for correction of early mistakes. On the other hand a phased approach has the disadvantage of creating a state of uncertainty. This could lead in turn to prior sale of expropriable land above the ceiling or to eviction of tenants by landlords in regions due for reform at some future date.

The indemnity payment may take various forms. If the land is purchased at market value—and the market price could well be inflated by the monopolistic control exercised by the big landowners—the land reform becomes a mere real estate trans-action. If the landowners receive cash compensation there is an immediate income redistribution effect only to the extent that the amount paid is inferior to the market price. Generally only the richer countries, such as Venezuela, or countries in which the reform is very small, such as Guatemala, or financed externally (Kenya by Britain, for example), can afford cash compensation to dispossessed landowners. Many schemes provide for the partial repayment of landlords in bonds based on the value at which the land has been returned for taxation. Payment by non-negotiable government bonds forcibly directs landlords' capital into public projects such as state industry and communications, and basing the indemnity value on landlords' tax returns means that those who understated the value of their property for tax evasion purposes are hoist with their own petard. Moreover, experience from Japan and elsewhere shows that if the compensation bonds are long term and low interest, their value is rapidly eroded by the high rates of inflation characteristic of many underdeveloped countries' economies. A further variant is being experimented with in the Philippines where large landowners are paid in the form of unexploited frontier land which it is hoped they will develop.

Most authorities hold that the beneficiaries of land redistribution schemes should be required to pay something for the land they receive, although few would require them to pay the full cost price of the land. Again, the income redistribution effect operates only to the extent that the amount paid by the beneficiaries is less than the full market price. Survey of various countries' experience in beneficiary repayments shows a wide range of situations from Chile (1962), Iran and Spain where assignees in effect pay the full cost of the reform, to South Vietnam and Venezuela where land has been distributed free to the new settlers.[18] Between these extremes a number of arrangements exists whereby beneficiaries pay only part of the total cost, the payment often being directed at a particular sector of expense such as landowner compensation, land improvement or administration.

TENANCY REFORM

Tenancy reform has been most common in Asia where the majority of land is not worked directly but operated by tenant farmers. The defects of tenancy are well known. The tenant has little incentive to invest in and improve the land since he can never be sure of enjoying the fruits of his efforts. If he is a share-cropper he will be reluctant to increase his inputs unless he is convinced that his share of the marginal increase in output will actually augment his income. For example, if the share contract is the classical *métayage* of 50–50 shares, an expenditure of, say, £10 on fertiliser by the share tenant will be worthwhile only if the total increase in output exceeds £20. Where overpopulation leads to keen competition for land and to the tenants having weak bargaining power in relation to that of the landlords, considerable social conflict may be generated by the landlord-tenant relationship. Independence in many newly-decolonised countries of South-east Asia saw increasing pressures put on these old landlord-tenant relationships. Violent encounters took place in Sumatra where feudal-type landowners were massacred and deprived of their land.

The essence of tenancy legislation involves the following considerations: (1) rent levels and form of payment (cash, kind, in advance, etc.); (2) period of tenancy (crop season, calendar year, five years, etc.); (3) basis for renewal of tenancy; (4) grounds for termination of contract and eviction of tenant; (5) restrictions on subletting and 'intermediate' tenancies; (6) right to, and form of, compensation for improvements (irrigation, fertiliser, etc.); and (7) encouragement of eventual ownership by tenant, for example through grant of a right of pre-emption in the case of sale of rented property.[19] The two basic issues are generally rent reduction and security of tenure. In Taiwan, rent was reduced to a maximum of 37·5 per cent of the crop value and security of tenure fixed at six years. In this case ownership rests with the landlords; in cases such as the Gezira scheme in Sudan, it rests with the government. In the big land reforms in Japan and Taiwan tenancy was in fact to a great extent eventually replaced by direct ownership; the percentage of owner-operated to total farmland changed from 54 to 92 in the case of Japan and from 60 to 85 in Taiwan.[20]

Perhaps the most crucial problems facing tenancy reform legislation are the cost and efficiency of the administrative machinery needed for effective implementation. A country with acute landlord-tenant problems is almost always a country whose administrative organs lack the skill, honesty and independence required to perform the task of supervising tenancy laws. The number of still-born tenancy reforms in various parts of the Third World amply testifies to the fact that it is the administration itself which by indifference, collusion and bribery has stultified the effects of tenancy regulations.[21] The prospects for evasion and subversion by the landlords are many and the problem of application can normally only be solved by the existence of a sufficiently cohesive network of peasant organisations at the local level.

LAND TAX REFORM

An approach to agrarian reform currently receiving increased attention is land taxation. There is a body of theory with considerable following amongst economists which holds that land reform could be brought about automatically by indirect methods such as tax reform, thereby avoiding the high costs of conventional land redistribution programmes.[22] In many countries of the world land tax reform is an essential prerequisite for more social justice as well as a necessary accompaniment to land tenure reform. Apart from revenue-raising aspects, important in land reforms which are costly to implement, a progressive land tax would gradually force the owners of large estates either to intensify cultivation or to dispose of part of their holdings. In Latin America it has been said that 'a general land tax alone would be sufficient to sound the death-knell of the latifundia',[23] but to date there are few examples in Latin America of reliance on progressive land taxation as the principal device for financing other agrarian reform measures. Land tax in Latin American countries contributes less than 10 per cent of governmental revenue, the main contributors to the tax mix being customs and excise duties (about 75 per cent) and income tax (about 20 per cent). Even in Mexico, despite the revolution, property tax provides less than 1 per cent of current government revenue, and in Brazil, which has never had a serious land reform, land tax contributes only 0·27 per cent of total revenue.

Like land reform, tax reform is very much a political issue at base. Although the Egyptian landlords in their petition against their government's reform laws in 1952 argued that a higher ceiling would increase the tax revenue, the real point is whether the landlords have enough political power to prevent reform being enacted, or whether they can find means of evasion. While administratively it may be easier to collect taxes from a small number of landlords than from a numerous peasantry, politically just the reverse may be true. What many under-developed countries do not have is the requisite political climate to exploit the considerable capital-forming potential of land taxation; indeed it may only be after a land reform has reduced the political power of the landlords that effective land taxation becomes possible.

CONSOLIDATION

Aside from collectivisation, which is something rather more than a type of land reform and which is dealt with in the next chapter, the other principal kind of land reform is consolidation. While land redistribution reform is applied to agrarian structures which are badly organised with respect to ownership and size of land property, consolidation is concerned with farms which are poorly organised in location and shape—with, that is to say, poor *spatial* organisation of farming. Where the farmers and farms are badly located with respect to their fields, where the fields are inconveniently located with respect to one another (i.e. when the farm is fragmented), or where the fields are an awkward shape for current farming techniques (e.g. in narrow strips or wedge-shaped plots), both the problems and the solutions are basically spatial. Whether the need is to persuade farmers to trade scattered parcels amongst themselves so that a more compact set of farm holdings is arrived at, or whether the consolidation procedure involves reducing the total number of farms to produce larger single farms by combining neighbouring holdings, the employment of traditional cartographic or modern spatial optimising techniques will generally be necessary.[24]

Here, then, we need to recognise two distinct conditions: the division of farm property into undersized units too small for rational exploitation, and the excessive dispersion of the parcels forming parts of a single farm. Rather confusingly, consolidation is the term applied to the remedy for both.[25] Undersized farms constitute an issue of wider ranging implications, being linked often to the problems and objectives of conventional land redistribution, and generally reflecting the condition of overpopulation. Fragmentation of individual farms is a rather separate problem (though the two often co-exist) which can be solved, at least on the theoretical plane, by simple spatial re-organisation of farm holdings by relocating the boundaries.

Although fragmentation of farm holdings into non-contiguous parcels may in some circumstances have a rational basis, to combat soil variations or local climatic hazards for instance, generally the phenomenon, which tends to result from continual splitting up of holdings upon inheritance or when land is freely traded as gifts or dowries, is seen as a great obstacle to farm efficiency. Apart from the obstacles to mechanisation, much time is wasted by the farmer in travelling to and from scattered plots. The problem of fragmentation is present in most old peasant communities throughout the world, and land consolida-tion is an essential part of agrarian policy in many European as well as Latin American and Asian countries. Consolidation of small, far-flung parcels may reduce production costs by a con-siderable amount and even increase by a few per cent the area under cultivation.

Although the importance of the problem of fragmentation is widely recognised, effective legislation is highly developed only in Europe and a few Asian countries (Japan, Pakistan and some Indian states).[26] In northern Europe consolidation programmes started early, in the late eighteenth century in England and Scandinavia, and have since become a permanent feature of agrarian policy, and relatively easy to carry out from the tech-nical point of view. Since 1924 the Dutch government has pursued an active programme of consolidation of scattered strip-holdings; around 1960, during the peak of activity, half the Ministry of Agriculture's expenditure was devoted to this policy. In southern Europe, however, where the fragmentation problem is very serious, relatively little has been done. The Greek government has devoted some attention to consolidation since 1953, and Spain too is making a serious attempt to cope with the problem along similar lines to France, where the fairly old process of *remembrement* (exchanges of land between farmers) has been accelerated through the creation of the SAFERs (*Sociétés d'Aménagement Foncière et d'Établissement Rural*). In Portu-gal, Italy and most of the other Mediterranean countries, al-most nothing has been done to alleviate fragmentation, which now persists as one of the major obstacles to the development of peasant farming. In Malta 112 000 plots belonging to 12 000 separate holdings are still waiting to be consolidated. Examples elsewhere can be even more bizarre. A Punjabi village noted by Spate and Learmonth[27] contains 63 000 fields on its 5300 hectares. In Ceylon the scale of ownership rights extends down to plots of a few square metres[28] Ownership characteristics amongst overpopulated peasant societies may be so fragmented as to involve shares of single trees, or even, in North Africa, the right to use the shade of a particular tree!

The greatest obstacle to consolidation is tradition and the unwillingness of farmers to participate, even when there would appear to be manifest advantages for all concerned. It is often very difficult to persuade a peasant farmer to exchange a plot of land which he has farmed for years, or which has been in the family for generations, for a parcel of someone else's land which lies adjacent to his own. Implementation of consolidation schemes is a crusade against inertia and suspicion. And it is not only in the more backward peasant economies that opposition to consolidation prevails. In England the failure to consolidate fragmented farms in the celebrated Yetminster scheme in Dorset was basically due to the unco-operative nature of local farmers.[29] A recent study by Mayhew[30] on the Moorreim structural reform project in West Germany showed that when it came to the crunch far fewer farmers were willing to be resettled as a result of consolidation than the authorities had originally anticipated; in particular the considerable differences in fertilities between the peat-bog (*Moor*) and river clay (*Marsch*) soils made exchange of parcels very difficult. Aside from certain countries of the Middle East and Mediterranean region such as Spain, Tunisia, Lebanon and Jordan where consolidation is realised to be a necessary accompaniment of irrigation schemes, the only immediate solution to the problem is to impose compulsory reorganisation of holdings. In Switzerland for example the operation becomes mandatory when assented to by at least half the landowners owning at least half the land in a particular locality. Not every government, however, is willing or able to be so authoritative. Even once consolidated, there may be nothing to stop consolidated holdings from undergoing fragmentation anew. Lamartine Yates[31] reports an Austrian village which was consolidated at the turn of the century and is now as fragmented as before. Follow-up legislation is needed to specify minimum farm sizes below which subdivision cannot take place (such provisions exist in Holland, Denmark, Switzerland and Czechoslovakia). Furthermore, policies of encouraging farm enlargement through consolidation run counter to the conventional redistributive function of land reform and, even in some advanced countries, go against the grain of deeply held sentiments in favour of small farm property and a wide distribution of land.

A variant of land consolidation can take place at the 'land use level' without necessarily affecting property rights.[32] One such scheme, based on a three-year crop rotation, has proved successful in the Egyptian land reform. The crop rotation areas are divided into three big lots and each beneficiary gets his land in three parcels, one in each lot. The pattern enables small farms to utilise large-scale machinery efficiently and has resulted in notable increases in productivity over the fragmented farms outside the reform areas. The Sudanese Gezira scheme can likewise be viewed as a giant consolidation scheme at the land use level. Solid blocks of land for cotton cultivation and for the planting of sorghum and fodder crops were created, which economised on water distribution and saved farmers' time in wandering from plot to plot.

COLONISATION SCHEMES

Land settlement and colonisation projects have been among the principal agrarian reform devices in Latin America to increase the number of family farms and to attempt to set up a farming middle class. Certainly Latin America is a part of the world where vast land resources still exist, but their fertility is questionable and their remoteness often extreme. Settlement of such territory has proved very costly. The Italian colonisation agencies of the Fascist period in North Africa encountered similar results: compared to financial outlay, results were meagre. There is no doubt that settlement projects are extraordinarily prone to failure, probably more so than any other agricultural development strategy. Those that are designed as showpieces, with privileged settlers enjoying an artificial existence at the expense of the rest of the farming population, have little value for the development of the country as a whole and in fact may represent a waste of resources. The limiting factor in areas like Latin America is not shortage of land or the under-utilisation of frontier land but rather the monopolistic, inefficient way in which the existing cultivated land is utilised. For potential production increases—the economic motivation of land reform—the already settled areas generally offer better possibilities.

Colonisation schemes are more desirable where the problems of developing uninhabited land are manageable. This is basically where under-utilised land resources offer potentially high returns on investment, as in the Sudanese Gezira scheme; where local population pressure or unemployment can be mitigated by opening up new land—examples of this are the resettling of some excess population from Java as farmers in Sumatra, and the similar government-sponsored migrations from Luzon to Mindinao in the Philippines; and in much of Africa and the Middle East where nomadism leaves certain land resources wasted or underdeveloped.[33] The settlement of nomads and their integration into the life of a nation is a far more complex process than ordinary land settlement schemes; a complete change in values and in mode of existence is required which may take decades to complete. Sedentarisation of nomads may also have a pacification objective, for it can integrate traditionally warlike wandering tribes into the civil and political life of the nation, as well as provide them with educational and health facilities. Results of nomad settlement schemes do, however, vary. While some programmes have met with a measure of success, an account of the Wadi Ca'am project for the settlement of semi-nomadic groups in Libya concluded that landless nomads cannot be settled satisfactorily as independent farmers.[34] Experience from Libya and other oil-rich countries of the Middle East indicates that nomads are more readily attracted to casual labour in the oil industry than to settled farming, partly because the immediate rewards from the former are somewhat greater. This demonstrates that selection of settlers for colonisation schemes is crucial for their success.

Farm settlement schemes may also have a different sort of motivation, that of building up settlement density in certain zones of political stress or strategic importance. In Thailand, for example, 75 000 colonists from other parts of the Kingdom are being settled along the communist-infested border areas.[35] Finally, land settlement projects may be justified in circumstances where wars, natural disasters or construction of dams cause population displacement. Two European countries, Greece and Finland, were faced with a large scale problem of settling refugee populations after war settlements involving boundary changes. Both succeeded in their objectives. In Greece following the 1923 peace treaty, over a million displaced persons were settled, many of them on land requisitioned through a radical reform act which affected 40 per cent of the Greek farmland. After 1945 Finland likewise managed to settle 250 000 refugees from Karelia on 50 000 new holdings.[36]

LAND REFORM AND THE GREEN REVOLUTION[37]

In recent years a major breakthrough has been achieved in the development of new high-yielding varieties of certain crops, especially wheat and rice. The new 'miracle seeds' give yield increases of from 50 to 200 per cent over traditional strains. The tremendous potential for increased food supply for the Third World countries has to a certain extent diverted attention away from land reform, even to the extent that some governments and observers maintain that the green revolution has dispelled the need for land reform.

The history of the green revolution is now well documented. The new seeds have had their greatest impact in certain Asian countries, notably India, Pakistan, the Philippines and Malaysia. In India severe famines following crop failures in the 1960s were a strong fillip to the adoption of the new varieties. In the rest of the Third World, their diffusion outside Mexico has been extremely limited. The first 20 million hectares planted to the new varieties reflected a strongly regionalised pattern even within Asia, with notable successes in, for example, Punjab and very little impact in Bengal. Adoption of the new technology in the second, third and nth blocks of 20 million hectares will be much slower, for these blocks include mostly small peasant farms with limited resources for the necessary fertilisers and irrigation, and physical environments unsuited to the new varieties.[38] The most severe constraint on the spread of the new varieties is availability of abundant yet controlled water supplies. The remarkable diffusion of new wheat varieties over 80 per cent of the wheat land in the Punjab within a few years and the doubling of average yields were largely due to an increase in the number of tube wells from 7000 to 120 000. Some of the highest rice yields in the world have recently been achieved in the Sind province of Pakistan, but this type of irrigated region is relatively limited in South Asia, where two-thirds of the rice land is fed by monsoon and seasonal rain.

It is often said that the new technology is 'scale-neutral', that the new seeds, irrigation, fertilisers and pesticides can be applied with equal success to large and small farms. In practice, however, small farmers are prevented from adopting the new seeds because they lack the finance or the creditworthiness to purchase all the new inputs of the 'package'. The green revolution unleashes a process whereby the larger farmers and richer peasants become better off, and the worse-off farmers, being deprived of the benefits, become even less qualified to receive them. The emergence, through the green revolution, of the modern, capitalist, 'model' farmer in South Asian countries poses a problem for land reform, for no government preoccupied with food shortages is going to legislate against such a progressive character. In many cases, however, large landowners have evicted tenants, increased rents and replaced wage labourers with machines in order to more fully reap the pay-offs of the agrarian technology. Rather than reduce the necessity for land reform, the effects of the green revolution generally work in the opposite direction. The trend is for the concentration of good quality, especially irrigated land in the hands of large modern farmers, while subsistence farmers are relegated to poorer quality dry land. The green revolution is, therefore, no substitute for land reform; indeed land reform becomes even more imperative as the new technology is adopted.

REFERENCES

1. D. Warriner: *Land Reform and Economic Development* (Cairo, National Bank of Egypt, 1955), p. 1.
2. *Bibliography on Land Tenure* (Rome, FAO, 1955, 1959 and 1972).
3. R. L. King: 'Land reform: some general and theoretical considerations', *Norsk Geografisk Tidsskrift*, 25 (1), 1971, pp. 85–97.
4. H. Beers: 'Socio-economic development and man-land relationships', *Sociologia Ruralis*, 18 (3–4), 1968, pp. 330–61.

5. Warriner: *op. cit.*, p. 3.
6. E. Flores: 'The economics of land reform', *International Labour Review*, 92 (1), 1965, pp. 21–34.
7. *Ibid*: p. 28.
8. T. H. Carroll: *The Concept of Land Reform* (Rome, FAO, 1955), p. 35.
9. Warriner: *op. cit.*
10. R. Barlowe: 'Land reform and economic development', *Journal of Farm Economics*, 35 (2), 1953, pp. 173–87.
11. S. M. Gadalla: *Land Reform in Relation to Social Development in Egypt* (Columbia, University of Missouri Press, 1962), p. 13.
12. R. P. Dore: *Land Reform in Japan* (London, Oxford University Press, 1959), p. 34.
13. See, for example, E. C. Banfield: *The Moral Basis of a Backward Society* (Glencoe, Free Press, 1958).
14. R. Krishna: 'Agrarian reform in India: the debate on ceilings', *Economic Development and Cultural Change*, 7 (3) part 1, 1959, pp. 302–17.
15. P. Dorner: *Land Reform and Economic Development* (London, Penguin, 1971), pp. 141–2.
16. H. C. Tai: 'The political process of land reform: a comparative analysis', *Civilisations*, 18 (1), 1968, pp. 61–74.
17. F. Dovring: 'The state of agriculture in a growing population', *FAO Monthly Bulletin of Agricultural Economics and Statistics*, 8 (8–9), 1959, pp. 1–11.
18. H. Meliczek: 'Financing land reform: compensation to landowners and payments by beneficiaries', *Land Reform, Land Settlement and Co-operatives*, 2, 1971, pp. 36–51.
19. E. S. Abensour and P. Moral-Lopez: *Principles of Land Tenancy Legislation* (Rome, FAO Legislative Series 6, 1966), pp. 9, 92.
20. W. Ladejinsky: 'Agrarian reform in Asia', *Foreign Affairs*, 42 (3), 1964, pp. 445–60.
21. E. H. Jacoby: *Man and Land* (London, Deutsch, 1971), pp. 264, 266.
22. See for example R. W. Lindholm: 'Land taxation and economic development', *Land Economics*, 41 (2), 1965, pp. 121–30; and P. Moral-Lopez: 'Tax legislation as an instrument in achieving the economic and social objectives of land reform', *Land Reform, Land Settlement and Co-operatives*, 2, 1965, pp. 2–11. For a rather opposing view see R. P. Dore: 'Sociological aspects of land valuation and land reform', in A. M. Woodruff, J. R. Brown and S. Lin (eds.): *International Seminar on Land Taxation, Land Tenure and Land Reform in Developing Countries* (West Hartford, Lincoln Foundation, 1967), pp. 560–88. Dore maintains (pp. 568–9) that 'land taxation is likely to be a relatively inefficient substitute for land redistribution, *even if* the taxes can be collected.' (Dore's italics).
23. T. Lynn Smith: *Agrarian Reform in Latin America* (New York, Knopf, 1965), p. 61.
24. S. Bonin: 'L'étude de la propriété foncière: un exemple de méthode cartographique', *Études Rurales*, 5–6, 1962, pp. 136–60; J.-P. Ludot: 'Modèle pour l'élaboration d'un projet optimal de remembrement',

Géometre, 12, 1971, pp. 32–45; M. U. Igbozurike: 'Land tenure relations, social relations and the analysis of spatial discontinuity', *Area*, 6 (2), 1974, pp. 132–5.

25. P. Moral-Lopez: *Principles of Land Consolidation Legislation* (Rome, FAO Legislative Series 3, 1962), p. 4.
26. *Ibid*: pp. 127–40.
27. O. H. K. Spate and A. T. A. Learmonth: *India and Pakistan* (London, Methuen, 1967), p. 263.
28. L. C. Arulpragasam: 'A consideration of the problems arising from the size and subdivision of paddy holdings in Ceylon, and the principles and provisions of the Paddy Lands Act pertaining to them', *Ceylon Journal of Historical and Social Studies*, 4 (1), 1961, pp. 59–70.
29. M. Butterwick and E. N. Rolfe: 'Yetminster revised', *Farm Economist*, 10 (11), 1965, pp. 446–57.
30. A. Mayhew: 'Agrarian reform in West Germany: an assessment of the integrated development project Moorreim', *Transactions, Institute of British Geographers*, 52, 1971, pp. 61–76.
31. P. Lamartine Yates: *Food, Land and Manpower in Europe* (London, Macmillan, 1960), p. 176.
32. E. H. Jacoby: *Agrarian Reconstruction* (Rome, FAO Basic Studies 18, 1968), p. 41.
33. For some of the problems and achievements of land settlement see D. Christodoulou: 'Land settlement: some oft-neglected basic issues', *FAO Monthly Bulletin of Agricultural Economics and Statistics*, 14 (10), 1965, pp. 1–6; also Jacoby: *Man and Land, op. cit.*, ch. 9.
34. K. McLachlan: 'The Wadi Ca'am Project: its social and economic aspects', in S. J. Willimott and J. I. Clarke (eds.): *Field Studies in Libya* (Durham, University of Durham Department of Geography Research Papers 4, 1960), pp. 70–6.
35. R. Ng: 'Land settlement projects in Thailand', *Geography*, 53 (2), 1968, pp. 179–82.
36. W. R. Mead: 'The cold farm in Finland: resettlement of Finland's displaced farmers', *Geographical Review*, 41 (4), 1951, pp. 529–43.
37. R. L. King: 'Geographical perspectives on the Green Revolution', *Tijdschrift voor Economische en Sociale Geografie*, 64 (4), 1973, pp. 237–44.
38. W. Falcon: 'The Green Revolution: generations of problems', *American Journal of Agricultural Economics*, 52 (4), 1970, pp. 698–710.

2

Evolution of the Concept

Land reform is a very ancient idea. Reforms of the agrarian structure seem to have been enacted in Biblical times, for there is an Old Testament reference to the redistribution of land every fiftieth year.[1] In ancient China too land reform was a recognised right of the people; every few years the land was redivided and the people set on a new footing of equality. History is full of accounts of peasant revolts, attempts by rural folk to throw off the yoke of slavery or serfdom. Most of the fundamental social changes that have occurred in history—the Fall of the Roman Empire, the American Revolution, the French Revolution and the Russian Revolution, to name a few —have had land reform aspects. This chapter seeks to provide the necessary historical background to the surveys of more recent reforms in the later chapters by tracing through the early evolution of the idea of land reform. Naturally Europe, with its very considerable headstart in development over the rest of the world, experienced land reforms some time ago. It is instructive to look briefly at some of these early European reforms not only because they provide historical background to modern land policy in other parts of the world, but also because some striking parallels emerge in the reasons for the reforms' success or failure. The story starts with two reforms in the classical world.

LAND REFORM IN THE ANCIENT WORLD: GREECE AND ROME

ANCIENT GREECE: SOLON AND PISISTRATUS[2]

The reforms of Solon and Pisistratus in sixth century BC Athens had the objectives of bringing about social and political stability. Background detail to these very early reforms is scanty and difficult to verify but it seems that when Solon came to power in 594 BC land was held in private tenure, in individual operating lots of about 5–20 hectares depending on soil fertility and the crop grown, but with the title vested in the family clan. Social and family status were to a large extent determined by the land tenure system. Many changes were, however, taking place to bring pressure to bear on the existing agrarian structure. The political expansion of Athens in the seventh century BC was accompanied by a growing demand for wine and olive oil, increasing competition from colony-grown cereals, and a switch from barter to a money economy. Money was in demand by the rich to expand their businesses and to indulge in consumption of luxury goods, and by the poorer classes to take advantage of such new farming opportunities as growing grapes and olives. With cash in short supply, the poorer peasants were forced to borrow from the richer landowners. Many became indebted and, having only their labour and their land as security, ended up as virtual slaves (called *hektemors*) working what was once their own land, now marked by *holoi* or 'mortgage-stones'. The *hektemor* worked the land as 'sixth-partner', which meant that he kept only one-sixth of the product of his labour for himself, the rest going to the creditor. As more and more peasant land was seized by the rich, the *hektemors* reacted by demanding a change of government and redistribution of land. The upper classes were aware of the impending revolutionary threat and appealed to Solon to restore peace and calm.

By the *seisachtheia* or 'shaking off of the burdens', as the law came to be known, Solon reformed the debt law drastically. All outstanding debts were cancelled and land that was enserfed was freed. The *holoi* were abolished and *hektemors* restored to their former status. According to Tuma[3] Solon's reform was motivated by three objectives, according to the point of view of the different social groups in the community. The poor believed Solon would quench their grievances against the rich and give them back their mortgaged land; the rich wanted him to restore calm without inflicting any material losses on them; and the general community thought he would create stability, prevent the impending upheaval, and reform the governmental machinery. None of these groups was fully satisfied. The *hektemors* became free but had no land to work because there was no statutory land redistribution; the rich were angry because all debts were cancelled; and for the community at large, although the 'slave revolution' was avoided, great political instability followed.

Thirty years later, Pisistratus continued Solon's original reforming impulse with a land-to-the landless programme which further advanced Solon's attempt to create a class of smallholder farmers. The source was not direct expropriation of the rich landowners but the estates of those of his adversaries who had been killed or forced into exile. Small farmers were also helped by a loans scheme, finance for which was derived from a 10 per cent tax on all agricultural produce. Olive growing was encouraged by the improvement of security in rural areas, and silver mining and temple building programmes expanded employment. Nevertheless, we know little about the scale of reform, except that it was probably small. Since only land of deceased or exiled estate owners was distributed, the number of beneficiaries cannot have been very great. Overall land concentration was thus little affected, and the socio-political structure remained undisturbed. We do not know how much of Pisistratus' legislation survived, or for how long; probably the majority of it was repealed when his opponents overthrew his successors.

ANCIENT ROME: TIBERIUS AND GAIUS GRACCHUS

The Roman land reform, introduced by the Gracchi brothers in the second century BC, dealt with agrarian peasant problems that still persist in some contemporary rural societies. Tuma[4] compares its rapid execution and comprehensive characteristics with those of the recent Japanese and Egyptian reforms. Like the Greek reform it was a response to mounting social tension, it was effected from above and carried out after a period of territorial expansion. Unlike the Greek case, the Roman reform aimed at rehabilitating free people, rather than serfs, by redistributing usurped public land.

Land in Rome was held in private or public tenure. The private land was cultivated either by small farmers, or owned by large landlords who leased it to tenants or operated it directly with slave labour. Part of the public land was allotted to war veterans, to colonists or to creditors in payment of public debts; these allotments became in practice virtually private property, immune from reform whose object was the remaining part of the public domain, some 800 000 hectares. This land was used in two ways. The better quality land was rented to individuals; the lower quality was left for squatting as a means of relieving unemployment, the squatter paying as rent a share of the product (10–20 per cent according to the crop) or a cash fee if pastured.

Two factors led to the increasing concentration of land in the hands of a few people. Although, to encourage smallholder farming and prevent abuse of the public domain, a limit was set on the area an individual could hold, in practice this restriction was easily evaded by counting relatives and friends among the family. Secondly, there was in progress a great transfer of land use from tilled to pasture land. The reasons for this change need not concern us in detail but briefly they involved such factors as competition from imported slave-grown wheat, neglect of home farms, which left them fit only for pasture, the increasing profitability of cattle and sheep farming and the fact that the farmer had no permanent title to public domain land and thus little incentive to invest in long-maturing crops like olives and vines. Grazing, however, required more land, and the effect was for the richer landowners to buy out the peasants, or even simply to seize their land, to set up big livestock farms.

Tiberius Gracchus noted the dangers inherent in the progressive concentration of land and in the decline in peasant farming, particularly for political stability with the possibility of slave uprisings. Legislation for land reform followed his election as tribune in 134 BC. The main points of his *lex agraria* were that no individual should hold more than 500 *iugera* (130 hectares), with an additional 250 *iugera* for each son up to a maximum total holding of 1000, and that land in excess of this ceiling should be surrendered, compensation being rendered for improvements, buildings, etc., and redistributed in lots of 30 *iugera* to peasants. Resistance to the law was strong on the part of the landlords and the Roman senate. Tiberius was murdered and the commission charged with effecting the law threatened to become defunct, but Tiberius' younger brother Gaius revived the reforming impulse when he was elected to the tribunate in 123 BC. Gaius in turn was killed in 121 BC in the continuing civil war and the work of the reform came to an end; a series of reactionary counter-reform measures subsequently passed undid much of what the Gracchi brothers had achieved.

Some information is available as to the effects of the Roman reform. Up to half a million peasants may have benefited from land redistribution. But the fact that the ceiling on individual holdings was set at 500–1000 *iugera* whilst the peasant received only 30 meant that the landlords retained most of their wealth and privileges and the gap between rich and poor remained wide. Even so, in the context of the hostile environment in which the Gracchi brothers had to work, the reform can be considered quite an achievement.

THE FRENCH REVOLUTION AND AFTER

The first big land reform movement of modern times came with the French Revolution. European feudalism, already on its last legs, was becoming increasingly anachronistic. An agrarian system based on an almost total control of land and labour by an exploitative rural oligarchy conflicted with the ideals of man's evolving conception of himself, and proved incapable of expanding production to satisfy increasing demand for food products. In 1789 remaining feudal estates in France were destroyed and the land distributed to the peasants. These simple ideals have since been re-enacted throughout the world in almost every other land reform. They have left an everlasting impress not only because they freed the peasant from his feudal master but also because they institutionalised the small family farm as an ideal agricultural unit.

After the French Revolution various political groups developed ideas and policies on land reform and the ideal agrarian structure. Socialist theory was at first consistent: exploitation of man by man should be abolished; no-one should work for the profit of any other individual, but only for himself and the community at large.[5] The split came when it was found that the theoretical superiority of large scale communal farming was not born out in practice. The strongest element in more conservative circles was the Catholic social programme developed after 1890, which laid strong emphasis on the value of an agrarian structure based on the small family farm. In its ideology the Catholic programme was a cross between the land-to-the-tiller ideals of the physiocrats and the principles of eighteenth century social romanticism which held the farmer as the most essential and stable type of citizen and farming as the most desirable form of occupation.[6] Closely associated with this philosophy, and with similar ideals present in American agrarian thought in the late nineteenth century, was the 'agricultural ladder' concept, whereby the unpaid family worker first became a wage worker for another farmer, then, having saved some money, would become a tenant farmer, and finally, having saved enough, became owner of his own family farm. The automatic assumption that the small-scale landownership incentive was the major factor accounting for rapidly increasing production in the countries of north-west Europe and North America in the nineteenth century was a gross oversimplification; other factors such as technological improvements, extension of cultivation, opening up of overseas territories and rapidly growing demand were at least as important, and it is the neglect of these factors which renders certain aspects of the historical analogy of nineteenth century Europe to the present day Third World countries particularly dangerous.

While the Catholics had to wait until 1950 to put their ideology fully into practice in Italy, other land reform movements had been taking place in Europe in the nineteenth century. Adam Smith had already argued in 1776 in *The Wealth of Nations* that large-scale landowning and servile tenures discouraged progress. The efforts of John Stuart Mill, who formed the Land Tenure Reform Association in 1870, were in part responsible for the English tenancy reform acts of the late nineteenth century. The English pattern was for feudalism to be replaced by tenancy rather than by outright peasant ownership

C

on the French model. In other parts of north-west Europe, such as Sweden and the Low Countries, action was likewise taken to strengthen the position of the tenant rather than effect radical land reforms aimed at full ownership. In the Irish reform of 1881, even though outright ownership was not claimed, the 'three f's'—fixity of tenure, fair rent and free sale—included the essentials of ownership and left the landlords with at best the capitalised value of the fair rent.[7]

In spite of these various land reform movements large estates still persisted in Europe into the present century, especially in eastern and southern Europe. One exception to this regional pattern was Bulgaria, which experienced a remarkably forward-looking land reform during the 1880s. This early reform was extremely well-conceived considering its historical context. Most of the things the United Nations has recommended governments to do during the last twenty years, the Bulgarians had accomplished ninety years ago. They set up co-operative credit societies to break the grip of the moneylenders, they invested pooled savings in processing and canning factories, and they were skilled in intensive farming.[8]

REVOLUTIONARY REFORM IN RUSSIA

Bulgaria apart, the real focal point of radical land reform shifted after the French Revolution to Russia, where emancipation of the serfs had freed them from the landlord but subjected them to the commune. The Stolypin reforms of 1906–11 in turn freed the peasants from the communes but led in practice to sharper differentiation between peasant classes, between the richer peasants—the *kulaks*—and the growing body of the landless. The 1917 revolution and the rise of communism owed a considerable part of their success to this social unrest in the Russian countryside, for peasants had already begun seizing land and liquidating the landlord class when the Soviets took over.

The Soviet reforms abolished the right of private ownership, forbade alienation of land, prohibited tenancy and decreed equalisation of holding, making tilling the land the basis of both the right and size of holding.[9] The measures were unique on several counts. The basic departure from previous reform policy was that the Soviet measures were conceived as part of a national programme. Rather than being an isolated measure of formal tenure reform the plan on which the reform policy was based concerned itself with agricultural production and the development of the economy as a whole, as well as fulfilling the political aspirations of the party in power.

Although the establishment of large co-operative farms was an initial aim in 1917–8, the drive towards collectivisation did not start till the late 1920s. The early 1920s were characterised by the 'New Economic Policy', a transitional phase of retreat from some of the revolution's ideals, carried out to restore the peasants' confidence, increase production and pave the way for ultimate further socialisation of the economy. Severe cutbacks in the sown area and in livestock numbers had resulted from over-zealous application of Soviet reforms during 1918–21, though other factors such as the effect of the First World War and the crop failures in 1920–1 were also partly responsible. The New Economic Policy, by permitting small scale land leasing, tenancy and hiring of labour, and by allowing private market sale of surplus farm produce instead of total state requisition, was designed to cope with the immediate problem of food shortage: it was a short term and necessary modification of soviet policy rather than a fundamental reaction against the revolution. The economic effects of the Policy were dramatic: between 1922 and 1927 the sown area increased from 66 million hectares to 98 million, cattle increased in numbers from 46 to 62 million, sheep and goats from 91 to 123 million and pigs from 12 to 22 million.[10]

By the late 1920s, however, the inherent weaknesses of peasant farming for Soviet economic ambitions were becoming apparent, not to mention the ideological problem of the emergence of class differentiation within the farming population. To facilitate agricultural mechanisation and to support the ambitious industrialisation programme, farming had to be collectivised. The relentless, coercive drive towards collectivisation took about a decade to complete. By 1938 collective farms occupied 85·6 per cent of the sown area, with collective farmers' personal homesteads accounting for another 3·9 per cent; state and co-operative farms covered 9·1 per cent, and individual peasants' land only 0·6 per cent. In 1940 there were 235 500 collectives in Russia, averaging about 1600 hectares and eighty households each.[11]

The social effects of collectivisation are impossible to estimate, particularly the violence and killing that accompanied the early stages of the programme. Economic effects likewise are difficult to ascertain. It is known, for example, that in the short term crop production fell (compounded into a famine which killed perhaps five million people in 1931–2) and livestock numbers were halved. Critics of enforced collectivisation can point to a great deal of human suffering, but to hold collectivisation wholly responsible for the poor performance of Soviet agriculture between 1917 and 1938 is to assume that any other kind of tenure system would have done better, particularly in protecting the peasants, and there is no proof of this. Moreover, because collectivisation itself was not an isolated policy with measurable costs and benefits, it should be viewed within the overall political and economic structure of Soviet society. The disruptive effects of the Second World War, during which some 20 million Russians lost their lives, are another complicating factor. In the absence of reliable data it does seem that collectivisation made possible mechanisation on a very large scale. Machinery and machine parts were initially in very short supply, but recent decades have seen such rapid mechanisation of agriculture that the main problem has now become shortage of technically qualified personnel. Although the use of machinery has in many cases been wasteful and inefficient, labour productivity has risen over the long term (at an annual average rate of 3·1 per cent over the period 1928–57, which compares favourably with the United States figure of 3·4 per cent for the corresponding period), and release of workers, either for industrial employment or opening up new land, has taken place. Collectivised agricultural output showed most dramatic increases in the industrial crops sector (over 300 per cent during the period 1928–57); productivity increases in the livestock sector, at around 50 per cent for the same period, have been much more modest.[12]

The post-1950s rationalisation of Russian agriculture is considered in detail in a recent study by Symons.[13] Briefly, state policy has seen the need to amalgamate collectives into larger units, and the rise of the state farm at the expense of the collective, especially in newly cultivated and marginal areas. By 1969 the number of collectives had been reduced, through amalgamation and conversion to state farms, to 34 900, less than one sixth the number in 1940. State farms increased in number from

6000 in 1958 to over 14 000 in 1969. The doctrinaire interpretation of Soviet state farm policy might lay stress on the fact that state farms are free from any trace of private ownership (whereas the collectives retained their private plots and anyway became rather more liberalised in the 1960s), but another basic reason lay in the necessity for the state to assume the risks inherent in monocrop farming in marginal areas. The rate at which both very prosperous and very poor collective farms are being converted into state farms probably reflects the fact that the state needs the high profits of the former to fulfil its economic obligations to the latter. Initially collectivisation probably caused a depression in peasant living standards, and it is only since the 1950s that real incomes in farming have started to rise.[14]

As a rather drastic form of land reform, Russian collectivisation seems to have fulfilled its original objectives of economic growth through increased agricultural output and industrialisation. The Soviet reforms were probably the first to concentrate on, and achieve, economic as opposed to social aims, but the fact that the whole programme was conceived as part of a great socio-political restructuring means that this is an oversimplification of the true nature of the reform, and furthermore makes it impossible to decide at what social cost these objectives were achieved. These and other reasons, such as the existence of a huge land resource, make the Soviet collective an inappropriate model for most of the developing countries of today to follow. Essentially the success of the system depended upon the gross underpayment of collectivised labour. Although large-scale machinery can increase production by extending the area under cultivation (as in the Virgin lands campaign) and by increasing labour productivity, the advantages of large-scale operation do not necessarily offset lack of personal incentive.[15]

LESSONS FROM EASTERN EUROPE

Meanwhile, land reforms had been enacted in other parts of the world—in Haiti at the time of the French Revolution and in Mexico following the 1911 revolution. The effect was not, however, to stimulate reforms in other Latin American countries. The significant reforms in the interwar period were enacted in Eastern Europe where most of the governments that came to power in 1918 began to introduce land reforms to channel the revolutionary upsurge. In most of these countries (East Germany, Poland, Czechoslovakia and Hungary) the extent of the coverage of the land reform was about 10 per cent of the agricultural area. It would have reached 30 per cent in Rumania had the entire programme been accomplished. In Yugoslavia, already a predominantly small farm country, the figure was about 5 per cent, and in Bulgaria only 2 per cent (this country had already had a land reform forty years earlier).[16] Albania, liberated last, planned a reform with Italian help in 1930, but it was never really implemented, and large estates and the power of the landlords lasted through to the Second World War. As in Mexico, these interwar reforms in Eastern Europe involved little more than land redistribution; no supporting measures for providing credit, technical assistance or marketing facilities were instituted. The reforms grew out of political considerations rather than social and economic policy. As a result production in some cases decreased rather than increased.

In Europe after the Second World War the inherited ideologies of collectivism and Catholic small-farm romanticism still prevailed. A whole constellation of communist governments was now in power in East Europe and land reform laws were quickly passed which made it illegal to hold more than 50 hectares in Czechoslovakia, Poland, Hungary and Rumania; 35 hectares in Yugoslavia and 20 hectares in Bulgaria. In all 12 million hectares were distributed to 3 million peasants. In Bulgaria, Rumania and Yugoslavia the reform had little immediate effect, as most of the landholding units were already below the ceilings set; in East Germany, Poland and Albania about a quarter of the land was distributed, and in Czechoslovakia about half. The most dramatic effects were in Hungary, where land reform touched the bulk of the land, causing a radical switch from large estates to small farms. This redistribution was, it transpired, a temporary measure to win the peasants' confidence; it was a first step along the road to collectivism and the replication of the Soviet policy, albeit more gradually and less violently. For the peasant, land reform is terminal, the ultimate objective; for the socialist it is only the beginning. Confiscation of land and the imposition of production quotas completed what was for former freeholders a rude awakening to the fact of being mere farm hands on collectives, communes and state farms.

As a case study of Eastern European socialised land reform policy the experience of Rumania may be briefly recounted.[17] The 1921 Reform Act expropriated latifundia according to a sliding scale, the ceiling varying between 100 and 500 hectares. By 1929 over 6 million hectares had been assigned to 1 400 000 peasants, 69 per cent of those having a claim, at an average holding of just under 4 hectares. Agricultural production, strangled by the latifundian system, revived somewhat, but there was little consideration whether the reform would support a rational and independent peasant agriculture; the fundamental gaps in the policy were consolidation of tiny peasant holdings, credit and co-operation.

The post-war collectivisation process has passed through a number of stages. Further expropriation programmes in 1945 and 1949 took 2·5 million hectares from remaining large farms and from the richer peasants. Whereas in 1945 the majority of the expropriated land was assigned to some 900 000 landless or semi-landless peasants, the 1949 reform kept most of the land obtained under state control. Jointly used machinery was introduced for ploughing, sowing and harvesting certain crops, such as sugar beet and potatoes. A second and more complex form of co-operation followed, extending this use of machinery to all crops and including some collective management of farming. In a third stage peasants pooled their land and all produce was cultivated and marketed collectively. Initially peasants received payment for their labour contribution with a bonus proportionate to their land contribution, but in the final stage this bonus was abandoned so that land had in effect become communal property with no compensation to former owners. Theoretically, peasants could choose not to join the collective, and individual holdings still exist in small numbers today, but in practice to remain outside the collective involved suffering some discrimination. Hopes that the peasants would enthusiastically welcome the socialist transformation of agriculture were dispelled by the violent encounters of 1949–50, and it is clear that most of the 1029 collectives in existence by the end of 1950 had been forcibly established. The policy was relaxed somewhat in the early and mid 1950s but the collectivisation drive was renewed in 1958 and completed in 1962. More recently still, Rumania has moved to a further stage in collectivised organisation by fostering inter-co-operative co-ordination and investment, and the creation of joint enterprises. By 1971 over 350 of these 'super-co-operatives' were in existence, some of them very large (upwards of 10 000 hectares) and highly intensive, specialising in pigs, poultry and greenhouse produce and with processing plants attached.

State farms in Rumania, far fewer in number (343 in 1967) than collectives (now officially called co-operatives), were created from large private estates confiscated by the state. Through the state farms the state has a measure of control over national agricultural production, and these farms serve as a model to surrounding collectives, demonstrating new techniques, distributing seed and stock. State farms, too, are highly special-ised (one specialising in pig rearing markets 150 000 pigs a year) and operate with hired labour which is rewarded on a bonus scheme if production goals set by the state are met.

The state's demands on the co-operatives are very heavy and the members are left with comparatively little for their own needs; this was especially true in the early 1960s. Yet state in-vestment is not high; agriculture received only 13 per cent of total investment in 1966–70, which increased to 17 per cent during 1971–5. Compared with Rumanian industry, agricul-ture grows slowly. Production has only doubled since 1938, whereas industry registered a seventeen-fold increase during 1938–70. Growth in agricultural production has been greater in recent years however, and is currently about 6 per cent per annum.

RECENT TRENDS: POLAND AND YUGOSLAVIA

Socialisation of the countryside has progressed furthest in Ru-mania and Bulgaria and in these countries collective farm enter-prises are overwhelmingly dominant. But already by the early 1950s an opposite tendency was detectable, with most East European countries experiencing a slowing down and liberalisa-tion of collectivism. In two countries, Poland and Yugoslavia, the deceleration ultimately became reversal. The shift came first in Yugoslavia; the break of relations with the Soviet Union gave the Yugoslav peasants a chance to protest against collec-tivisation. Most of the collectives were disbanded in 1952 or shortly after, and it further transpired that many of the collectives had existed on paper only. Dovring roundly condemns the attempt to collectivise Yugoslavian agriculture as an unqualified mistake.[18] A lowering of the ceiling on private landholding from 20 to 10 hectares in 1953 distributed a further 276 000 hectares to peasants and aimed at making sure that private agriculture would not occur on sufficiently large scale to use hired labour or, for that matter, heavy machinery without co-operative arrangements. The continued existence of some collective and state farms creates a two-sector structure. Official statistics emphasising the greater productivity of the co-operative units are misleading, for they do not reflect the different inputs of special state investment and technology or the fact that such units are on the best land. The inference that peasant farms are probably a better use of scarce land and capital resources is duplicated in Poland, where admission of over-rapid collectivisation in 1952 was followed in the 1960s by statements to the effect that Polish farming must remain structured in small private farms for a long time to come. State farms now account for 13 per cent of Polish agricultural land and collectives only 1 per cent.[19]

Although the opposition of peasant landowners to collectivisation played a crucial role in the decision to abandon it in Poland and Yugoslavia, other factors were important too.[20] Both countries suffered serious shortages of food in the early post-war period, but the expectations of increased output from collective farms were not fulfilled; in Yugoslavia agricultural production actually declined for a time and cereals, traditionally exported, had to be imported. A reassessment of objectives was consequently carried out; the aim of rapid collectivisation was set aside, and peasants allowed to reclaim their private holdings.

In retreating from forced collectivisation, Poland and Yugoslavia have by no means abandoned the socialisation of agriculture as an ultimate objective; they have rather opted to approach it more gradually and by a different route. In both countries the socialised sector of agriculture still covers about 13 per cent of the farmland. Yugoslav policy-makers remain convinced of the merits of large-scale mechanised farming; the Poles, for the time being, rather less so. Current Yugoslav policy encourages private farms to become vertically integrated with the socialised sector by establishing contractual links involving the use of machinery, technical assistance, etc., in return for a supply of produce to a guaranteed market. It is hoped that private farmers will find such contractual relations profitable and that they will be drawn voluntarily into the orbit of the co-operatives so that the socialisation of agriculture will proceed gradually and, most important, on the basis of free will. Poland, on the other hand, prefers a policy of building up the general productive capacity of peasant family farms; large-scale capital intensive collective units are considered premature at the present stage of the country's economic development. In order to strengthen private farm production it was decided to revive the 'agricultural circles', an ancient Polish rural institution founded by the Church and enlightened estate owners in the nineteenth century as a means of educating peasants and encouraging mutual assistance. The purpose of the current agricultural circles is primarily to invest in agricultural machinery for group usage, but they also engage in providing fertiliser, seed and other inputs, and in experimentation. It seems that considerable success has attended these efforts. Financed by members' savings, agricultural circles now affect about a third of the peasant farm sector (1·5 million members) and have brought higher incomes and increased awareness of the need for innovations.

Twenty years after the political upheavals of the early 1950s and the structural modifications of socialist land policy they provoked, three groups of countries in Eastern Europe can be distinguished on the basis of landholding (see Table 1): countries where collectives still dominate (Albania, Bulgaria, Rumania); those with modified forms of collectives (Czechoslovakia, East Germany, Hungary); and those with important owner-occupier sectors (Poland and Yugoslavia). The continued resistance to collectivisation is evident in the considerable amount of time and effort lavished by agricultural workers in Eastern Europe on their small private plots, most of which are less than $\frac{1}{2}$ hectare. Indeed, for the production of such commodities as vegetables, orchard fruits and livestock products, the private plots are of paramount importance. Hungary is the extreme example. Here in 1961 private plots covered less than 4 per cent of total farmland (13 per cent of the arable area) but produced about a third of the total output of wine, fruit and vegetables, 60 per cent of milk, 64 per cent of meat and 90 per cent of eggs. The private plots, in Hungary as elsewhere, stand out as consistent high producers, and although many are probably excessively labour-intensive, increasing the size of private plots would be one of the most effective ways of intensifying Hungarian agriculture.[21]

TABLE I

DISTRIBUTION OF FARM TYPES IN EASTERN EUROPE, *circa* 1961

| | Percentage of total area | | |
	Owner-operated	State farms	Collective farms
Albania	20·0	7·5	72·5
Bulgaria	0·1	6·8	93·1
Czechoslovakia	11·1	21·1	67·8
East Germany	7·4	7·6	85·0
Hungary	3·7	32·6	63·7
Poland	86·0	12·9	1·1
Rumania	4·8	44·0	51·2
Yugoslavia	87·6	6·4	6·0
USSR	0·0	31·0	69·0

Source: World Atlas of Agriculture: Vol. 1, Europe, USSR, Asia Minor (Novara, De Agostini, 1969), p. 8, from Table II.

THE CONTINUING DEBATE IN THE POST-WAR PERIOD

The other prominent agrarian ideology of the immediate post-war period in Europe, the Catholic small farm policy, found its ultimate expression in the Italian land reform of 1950, a direct response to peasant land hunger and to rising communist tendencies in the countryside. The Italian reform was much more than just redistribution of land. Although inspired by political motives, it was a carefully planned and administered programme of socio-economic redemption for certain poverty-stricken areas of the country, chiefly in the south. But by 1960 new perspectives on the land question in Italy had arisen. Agriculture began to suffer rapidly declining numbers and emigration from Italian rural areas grew to flood proportions after the late 1950s. In places the reform administrators were left in the embarrassing position of having land on their hands which no-one wanted:

land which half-starved peasants had been clamouring for only a decade or so previously. The land reform came virtually too late to be of real use.[22]

After the Second World War the real challenge posed by land reform shifted from Europe to Asia and Latin America, although other, rather less underdeveloped countries, such as Tunisia, Egypt and Iraq, revived the European impulse with much-needed land reform programmes based in part on the Italian model. A feature of recent decades is the increasing urgency of land reform in the Third World. Many countries, partly as a result of rapid population growth, have experienced a deterioration in their employment and income situations, and with inequalities in the distribution of land, wealth and income if anything increasing, the net effect is to heighten political and social tensions and to bring forth the demand for land reform.

The end of the Second World War marks the beginning of an era in another sense too. Many states have achieved political independence in the past three decades. Colonialism has crumbled and new nationally minded governments have come to power with internal development as a major priority. Particularly where the new régimes represent departures from the colonial power structure, land reform is often included as a fundamental part of the development strategy.

LAND REFORM AS AN INTERNATIONAL POLITICAL ISSUE

It was after the Second World War also that land reform began to enter the realms of international politics. Perturbed at the way that the communists were gaining power, particularly in Asia, on the promissory note of land reform, the United States began to look for ways of meeting the communist challenge in Asia that would appeal to Asian intellectuals and satisfy the craving of the peasantry for improved standards of living.[23] The ideological conflict with the revolutionary implications of land reform was reconciled by the assumption that short-run stability must sometimes be sacrificed in the interests of long-run democratic equilibrium. Against this background the US army fostered land reform in Japan where absentee landlords as a class disappeared, and in Korea, where a total of 700 000 peasants obtained farms of their own in five months. Official US policy was not made clear until 1950, however, when two undoubted manifestations of the country's intentions were made. One was the support of a Polish resolution on land reform in the United Nations, and the other was a speech by President Truman: 'We know that the peoples of Asia have problems of social injustice to solve. They want their farmers to own their land and to enjoy the fruits of their toil. That is one of our great national principles also. We believe in the family size farm that is the basis for our agriculture and has strongly influenced our form of government.'[24] Family farming through land reform is thus regarded as the necessary basis for free enterprise and political democracy. But in the past, as we have seen, the majority of land reforms were purely or predominantly social in their aims; in Mexico and East Europe between the wars the peasants got the land only, without credit, technical guidance and social infrastructure; post-reform production often dropped as a result. The Americans had seen this for themselves for it also happened following the break-up of the slave-worked cotton plantations in the southern states after 1865. Accordingly the new American conception of land reform went further than just land redistribution, accompanying the social impact with an agrarian policy to increase agricultural productivity.

More recently, Latin America has been the scene of much new land reform activity. The Mexican reform is probably too remote to have been an important influence on current land reform thought in the continent, although legislative changes have been more or less continuous since the original act. After Mexico, and apart from very minor or abortive reforms, the Bolivian land reform of 1953 has been in operation the longest. A true peasant uprising, the land reform was followed by a period of political and economic chaos that, if anything, must have positively discouraged other Latin American governments from land reform. The only other serious movement in the early fifties was in Guatemala where in 1952 the Arbenz government initiated a comprehensive land reform programme. A controversial aspect of the scheme was the expropriation of 16 000 hectares of uncultivated land from the American-owned United Fruit Company. This land reform was washed away in the political events of 1954; rightly or wrongly it is believed that the US reprisal over the reform's action was an important factor in the downfall of the Arbenz régime. The Venezuelan reform, started in 1960, is remarkable for the depth and quality of preliminary study and for its broad coverage, dealing with both land tenure and other aspects of a comprehensive agrarian policy. One fact, however, makes it impracticable for most Latin American countries—its high cost. Instead, it is the Cuban land reform, introduced in 1959 as one of the main props of the revolution, that has, more than anything in the last twenty years, dramatised the necessity of overcoming rural social obstacles to Latin American development. Yet elsewhere in the continent comparatively little has been achieved. The Dominican Republic has a well-conceived but small-scale programme. Some progress has been made in Colombia, in Chile for a time, and most recently in Peru. But in the 1970s it seems unlikely that Castroist or communist methods will be employed in much of Latin America for the purpose of land reform; the reformism of the 1960s has died away.

LAND REFORM AND THE DEVELOPING COUNTRIES: PANACEA OR IRRELEVANCE?

Although the importance of land reform is widely recognised in Latin America, as it is in the world's other underdeveloped agrarian countries, the exact mechanisms which operate to connect land reform, particularly in terms of alternative tenure systems, with economic development, remain something of a mystery. These links form the basis of the next chapter, but a few general remarks at this juncture will serve to smooth the transition from the mainly historical account of the evolution of the concept to the more theoretical consideration of the role of land reform in the developmental process.

THE WORK OF INTERNATIONAL ORGANISATIONS

Much discussion concerning the issue of land reform and economic development is presented in a somewhat negative cast. Defects of land tenure appear as an obstacle to development, the implication being that the problem is resolved when the obstacle is removed. This was the original United Nations approach exemplified in the title of its first document on land reform, *Land Reform: Defects in Agrarian Structure as Obstacles to Economic Development*, published in 1951.[25] Although the United

Nations and its constituent and allied organisations lay great stress on agrarian reform measures as part of official social and economic policy pronouncements, the strength of these recommendations is not really born out in practice. FAO has the most important role to play in land reform but only a small section of its vast Rome bureaucracy is devoted to land reform and allied measures. The United States aid programme to Latin America directed only 10 per cent of its total aid budget towards agriculture during the period 1962–8. Of this 10 per cent, 50 per cent went to schemes benefiting commercial farmers; only 15 per cent was aimed at agrarian reform or the beneficiaries of reform programmes. The experience of these and other aid agencies shows that their operating philosophies are not aligned with their bold official declarations about the crucial importance of land reform; the money often flows in directions quite inconsistent with the reform objectives.[26]

IDEOLOGICAL CONFLICTS

In spite of the work of international agencies, we are not much nearer to a unified approach to land reform. On the one hand many countries recognise land reform as the central issue in their developmental process. On the other hand land reform is denounced as nothing more than an outmoded irrelevance.[27] In many countries, progress in agrarian reform is severely hampered by the ideological conflict between the respective merits of the small family farm and communal or collective units. Although land reform has only relatively recently become an international political issue, the conflict between the ideals of the French and Russian Revolutions has grown to be a major element in the cold war. Because communism and what Warriner calls 'American-way-of-life-ism' are something of rival philosophical systems, the impression is created that they are ideal patterns, that the choice lies between rival models, the American family farm and the Soviet collective.[28] The comprehensive failure of both peasant parcellisation and grandiose collectives in tropical Africa, for example, indicates the fallaciousness of the argument. The American conception of broad 'integral' reform centred round family farming and communist collective agriculture are really no more than by-products of their respective ideologies, the former representing a partial and narrow projection of American institutions, the latter a strategy of socialisation. Both, writes Warriner,[29] require a great expansion of bureaucratic employment and are therefore more attractive to officials than peasants, whose interests rank second to those of the administrators. The basic problem with American integral reform lies in the attempt to transplant agrarian institutions which have been evolved in an advanced country to countries at much more backward stages in the belief that these institutions have been the cause of America's rapid growth, not the outcome of that growth as they in fact are. Integral reform is really social welfare designed to help local pockets of agrarian poverty and backwardness; it worked well in Italy where the problem was local and temporary, but it cannot be used as a general principle underlying large scale reforms in poor countries because of lack of personnel, resources and finance. The collective ideal is negative in that it aims to get more out of peasants at lower prices. Certain aspects of the Russian and Chinese experience may be of relevance to Third World Countries, particularly of course those countries which have already instituted collective agriculture (e.g. North Vietnam and North Korea), and to those countries such as Burma, Egypt, Syria and Tanzania which hope to implement socialist principles, but the current experience of Eastern Europe, where the original application of the Russian model made for concessions to local conditions and where as a result there is considerable groping for new systems and approaches to agriculture, warns against narrow duplication of the Russian or Chinese systems.[30] Complete individualism and total collectivism are not necessarily realistic alternatives for under developed countries. Warriner[31] draws a most illuminating comparison between the political motivations of the post-war reforms in Italy and Yugoslavia, the former following the American family farm model, the latter the collective ideal. Italy aimed at defeating communism, Yugoslavia at demonstrating what communism can do. In Italy the task of turning landless labourers into 'sturdy peasants' running their own holdings, could be achieved only by tight official control on crop rotations, animal husbandry and co-operatives and by providing the beneficiaries with custom-built farmhouses and villages, so that the organisation became virtually that of a state farm. Yugoslavia on the other hand was originally a country of peasant family farmers: the failure of the Yugoslav communists to turn sturdy peasants into labourers on collectives provides an interesting paradox to the Italian failure to turn farm labourers into sturdy peasants. Ultimately, each policy achieved the objective of the other.

Even 'co-operative farming', aimed at by several modern land reforms, has become something of a political slogan. Although group farming theoretically combines the satisfactions of peasant farming with the economies of large-scale operation, the problem is that 'model' forms of tenure like the Israeli *kibbutz* and the Mexican *ejido* are advanced for the social and political values they represent rather than reduced to a neutral, technical means to an end. Certainly with Dorner[32] we must think of new approaches to land reform 'with elements of the private operator system, with its securities and incentives, combined with some aspects of a co-operative or collective system to ensure high quality of management and productivity,' but above all there is a need for dispassionate research into forms of land ownership and farming organisation.

REFERENCES

1. E. Massart: 'Le leggi agrarie nella Bibbia', *Rivista di Diritto Agrario*, 49 (4), 1970, pp. 475–506.
2. Based on E. H. Tuma: *Twenty Six Centuries of Agrarian Reform* (Berkeley, University of California Press, 1965), ch. 3.
3. *Ibid*: p. 24.
4. *Ibid*: ch. 4.
5. F. Dovring: *Land and Labour in Europe* (The Hague, Nijhoff, 1965), p. 235.
6. *Ibid*: p. 236.
7. *Ibid*: p. 241.
8. D. Warriner: *Land Reform and Economic Development* (Cairo, National Bank of Egypt, 1955), ch. 6.
9. Tuma: *op. cit.*, ch. 7.
10. L. Hubbard: *The Economics of Soviet Agriculture* (London, Macmillan, 1950), pp. 82–3.
11. A Baykov: *The Development of the Soviet Economic System* (Cambridge, The University Press, 1950), p. 327.
12. C. Wilber: 'The role of agriculture in Soviet economic development', *Land Economics*, 45 (1), 1969, pp. 87–96.
13. L. Symons: *Russian Agriculture* (London, Bell, 1972), chs. 2, 3, 6.
14. A. Kahan: 'Changes in labour inputs in Soviet agriculture', *Journal of Political Economy*, 67 (5), 1959, pp. 451–62.

15. D. Warriner: *Land Reform in Principle and Practice* (Oxford, Clarendon, 1969), pp. 41–3.
16. Figures from Dovring: *op. cit.*, p. 250.
17. P. Dorner: *Land Reform and Economic Development* (London, Penguin, 1972), pp. 54–5, 62; and D. Turnock: *An Economic Geography of Romania* (London, Bell, 1974), ch. 5.
18. F. Dovring: 'Land reform in Yugoslavia', in Agency for International Development: *Spring Review of Land Reform* (Washington, Department of State, 1970), Vol. 10, p. 53.
19. E. Raszeja-Tobjasz: 'Land policy in Poland', in D. McEntire and D. Agostini (eds.): *Towards Modern Land Policies* (Padua, University of Padua Institute of Agricultural Economics and Policy, 1970), pp. 275–332.
20. D. McEntire and D. Agostini: 'Comparative analysis', in *Ibid*: pp. 474–9.
21. H. D. Clout: *Agriculture* (London, MacMillan Studies in Contemporary Europe, 1971), pp. 31–3.
22. R. L. King: *Land Reform: The Italian Experience* (London, Butterworths, 1973), p. 229.
23. W. Ladejinsky: 'Agrarian reform in Asia', *Foreign Affairs*, 42 (3), 1964, pp. 445–60.
24. C. Senior: *Land Reform and Democracy* (Gainesville, University of Florida Press, 1958), p. 4; J. P. Gittinger: 'United States policy towards agrarian reform in underdeveloped countries', *Land Economics*, 37 (3), 1961, pp. 195–205.
25. United Nations: *Defects in Agrarian Structure as Obstacles to Economic Development* (New York, UN, 1951). As sequels to this document, FAO has issued several progress reports. See *Progress in Land Reform: First Report* (1954); *Second Report* (1956); *Third Report* (1963); *Fourth Report* (1965); *Fifth Report* (1970); *Sixth Report* (1975).
26. Dorner: *op. cit.*, pp. 136–7, 143.
27. G. Hirsch, in R. Weitz (ed.): *Rural Planning in Developing Countries* (Tel Aviv, The Second Rehovoth Conference, 1963), p. 253.
28. Warriner: *Land Reform and Economic Development, op. cit.*, p. 8.
29. Warriner: *Land Reform in Principle and Practice, op. cit.*, pp. 58, 62, 72–3.
30. O. Schiller: 'The agrarian question: communist experience and its implications for developing countries', in W. A. D. Jackson (ed.): *Agrarian Policies and Problems in Communist and Non-Communist Countries* (Seattle, University of Washington Press, 1971), pp. 231–44.
31. Warriner: *Land Reform and Economic Development, op. cit.*, pp. 35–40.
32. P. Dorner: 'Land tenure, income distribution and productivity interaction', *Land Economics*, 40 (3), 1964, pp. 244–54.

3

Land Reform and Development

Economists have generally believed that income redistribution, through land reform or any other means, would act as a brake on development prospects in poor countries, or that redistribution would result only after growth has taken place—views which plainly oppose the argument of this book. Part of the confusion hinges on what exactly is meant by 'development'. Economic literature generally identifies development with, and measures it by, increase in per capita income. Quite apart from ignoring income distribution, such a formulation fails to get to grips with the true nature of development. Development cannot be satisfactorily measured along a one-dimensional scale. Above all it is a human process and due emphasis must be laid on the human factor and on human institutions. Within this broader view, with development considered as a socio-economic, rather than as a purely economic, phenomenon, the importance of land reform is obvious. Another element of confusion results from a misapplication of western, urban, industrial development concepts to the situation of agrarian poverty in the Third World. The relationship between social structure and economic development in the countryside reverses that in the city: in industrial society a more equitable distribution of income is the result of economic growth; in agrarian societies a more equitable distribution of income (through land rights) is the prerequisite for economic growth.

At the simplest level, land tenure is part of a larger institutional system. Without such a system civilisation degenerates chaotically into a condition of war of all against all; life for the individual becomes 'solitary, poor, nasty, brutish and short.'[1] Economic development must, therefore, involve institutional development, and involve the relief of poverty as one of its fundamental objectives. At its best, the land reform approach to development aims at precisely this, by widening the economic opportunities for the mass of the rural people.

Parsons[2] provides a succinct outline of the links between land reform and economic performance through income redistribution. Firstly, in underdeveloped countries high incomes reflect not so much economic ability and skills but privileged access to property, market power and control of labour. Sociologically, landed aristocracies tend to be preservers of a culture whose values are inimical to economic growth; they are concerned with the mastery of men rather than of nature; they uphold a status system which stresses birth rather than achievement.[3] Secondly, under inequitable tenure systems the existing pattern of income distribution distorts and restricts internal demand. Elites demand mostly imported luxury products whilst the peasantry has little or no surplus to demand anything. Rectification of this lop-sided situation results in a more even pattern of demand for consumer products: what might be called the 'more bicycles, fewer Cadillacs, more beer, less scotch' approach. And thirdly, closely allied to the last point, landowning elites save little for investment in productive agriculture and industry, the majority of their income having been spent on luxury products or invested in urban speculative ventures, whereas the peasants have no surplus for productive investment. Redistribution of land and income can, therefore, increase the formation of capital for investment.

THE DEMOGRAPHIC APPROACH

As we saw in the last chapter, land reforms have been enacted and attempted in countries with a wide range of historical backgrounds, environments and population densities. Many of the most crucial land reforms have been carried out in conditions of agricultural overpopulation where not only is the ownership of farmland unevenly distributed, but there is also an overall shortage of land. Generally, this pressure of population is greatest in Asia and least in Africa, with Latin America and the Middle East in intermediate positions. Raup[4] has stated that the man-land ratio is probably the most important variable determining land tenure policy, but we must be clear on the concept of overpopulation before examining the extent to which land reform can respond to such a situation.

OVERPOPULATION DEFINED

There are three situations commonly held to be indicators of overpopulation: (a) surplus labour on the land—this is a static condition; (b) the Malthusian model of falling output per head; (c) falling output per unit area due to failure to maintain soil fertility.

The difficulty with the first measure is that it must always be made within a given technological and economic framework. Various categorical statements made about surplus labour in agriculture appear to conflict. Studies by Warriner[5] on East European countries between the wars revealed that substantial portions of the agricultural population could be drawn off without a drop in production. For southern Italy Dell' Angelo in 1960 calculated that 10 per cent of the agricultural labour force could be immediately withdrawn without reducing output.[6] Also in 1960, the Egyptian First Five-Year Plan estimated that 25 per cent (1·1 million out of 4·4 million) of the male agricultural labour was surplus.[7] Schulz counters all this by stating that there is no evidence from any poor country suggesting that a transfer of some fraction of the existing labour force in agriculture could be made without reducing production.[8] The situation would seem to depend upon the level of technology in agriculture and the value put on leisure, but the static concepts of surplus labour and disguised unemployment are misdirected if the real problem is falling productivity. The third measure, that of declining output per land unit, is by far the most serious condition and in fact represents negative marginal productivity of labour. This situation occurs relatively rarely in the real world, but would tend to happen, for example, if increasing population drove shifting cultivators to re-use their abandoned plots before the natural vegetation had time fully to replenish itself and the soil. Most dynamic analyses of overpopulation in agriculture concentrate on the second index—

falling output per head. Here overpopulation can be defined as the situation in which in underdeveloped countries with conditions of full employment (i.e. implicitly including underemployment) the marginal productivity of labour falls below the minimum subsistence of the worker and approaches zero.

Given that overpopulation, with whatever degree of severity exists, the questions to be asked are: Can land reform help? If so, which approach is best? Although for dynamic purposes the concept of surplus labour on the land is questionable, it is useful when considering demographic changes in relation to an inflexible institutional structure, where type of farming, demand for labour and social system remain constant. Here a land reform of the land redistribution type can theoretically be of great help, for, providing natural conditions are favourable, access to the land for the peasants can promote intensive cultivation and the consequent absorption of some unemployment. It is often said that the task of the tenure system is to put people to work on the land, and it is a fundamental tenet of economic development that no factor of production should remain unnecessarily idle, even if, in overpopulated economies, this means using labour to the point where its marginal productivity becomes zero. Estimates of the increase in employment opportunities for peasants through intensification of agriculture on latifundia expropriated by the Frei régime in Chile are as high as 130 per cent.[9] The Cuban land reform also exhibits an immediate and considerable increase in agricultural employment; from a labour surplus economy, Cuba has become a labour deficit economy.

THE AGRARIANIST DOCTRINE

In conditions of overpopulation in agriculture, labour is the abundant factor and land and capital the scarce ones. New labour saving techniques may reward the profit-seeking landlord, but they will hardly improve the lot of the peasant. To regulate production by individual profit maximisation is probably the worst thing that can happen to an underdeveloped agrarian economy, for it will tend to increase unemployment and unwanted leisure. Owners of large private estates may well maximise their personal incomes by substituting machines for men, particularly if there are government grants for mechanisation and the ready availability of large scale imported machinery, and especially if local labour, although in abundant supply, is governed by minimum wages or is strongly unionised, but these owners generally render a less than useful service to a struggling, low-income, capital scarce economy. Such discrepancies between private and collective benefits are similar to those of a factory prospering at the same time as it incurs social costs by air and water pollution.[10]

Throughout the underdeveloped world urbanisation grows faster than industrialisation; the result of this differential is the growth of shanty-towns round the major cities of the Third World. Shanty-towns probably contain a good half of the underdeveloped world's urban population. In Latin America the shanty-town population is estimated to grow at 15 per cent per year as landless peasants, denied a chance of a viable existence in the countryside, flock in desperation toward the cities. In spite of this rapid rural-urban migration, an annual population growth rate of $2\frac{1}{2}$–$3\frac{1}{2}$ per cent results in continued increase in rural areas. Absolute numbers of rural people decline only in the later stages of development. The inescapable conclusion is that the agricultural sector in less developed countries must continue to provide increased employment opportunities for many years to come.

Given these situations, the agricultural sector must be organised in a different way from the industrial sector; if it were not, the rural overpopulation and employment dilemma would be all but insoluble. In conditions of abundant rural labour and rapid population growth, it is productivity per unit of land, not labour productivity as in industry, which is the most relevant measure for policy, at least for the time being. Georgescu-Roegen[11] has provided an economic rationale for the organisation of the agricultural sector into a framework of small family farms which economise on scarce land and capital resources and which make full use of the labour by employing it beyond the point where marginal productivity is equal to the minimum subsistence. This is the doctrine of agrarianism, characterised by its double negation: not socialism, not capitalism. Under this system the individual working for himself and his family will be motivated not by marginal productivity but by maximising output because as no money wages are paid he will continue to work for very little return, since he places an even lower value on leisure.[24] One of the most powerful arguments for land redistribution is that it can put people to work by reducing enforced leisure. In fact much agricultural capital formation can be explained in this fashion. Livestock care, the repair and maintenance of farm buildings and equipment, and a variety of similar tasks are often accomplished by the farmer in what otherwise might be leisure time. By ensuring that the benefits of such activities accrue solely to the farmer and not to the landlord (in which case they probably would not be accomplished anyway), land reform can exert a strong influence on the use of leisure time. Total national productivity would thus be maximised if an ideal structure were created of small family farms of the size to be farmed intensively by the farmer and his family using no outside labour.

A harsh reality that may have to be faced is that any benefits that result from a land reform, or from any other institutional or technological improvement, may lead to further population increase which swallows up the original benefit. The principle of small farms may not, moreover, create certain important preconditions for rapid economic growth, and if the objectives are dynamic (economic growth through capital formation), the per capita measure is more appropriate than the per acre measure, for only by maximising the former function would maximum capital be generated for reinvestment and growth. Given that splitting up of land on the egalitarian principle can lead to very small farms of sub-optimum size, and given the already acknowledged unsatisfactoriness of large mechanised farms, or retention of some large estates to cope with residual hired labour, some other alternatives must be sought.

BIG FARM vs SMALL FARM AND THE ROLE OF CO-OPERATIVES

The debate on economies of scale in farming has been bedevilled by the influence of political ideology and the lack of empirical study, especially on the relationship between farm size and productivity in underdeveloped countries. It is now widely acknowledged, however, that agriculture and industry are subject to somewhat different economic laws. Scale economies are exhausted at lower levels in agriculture than industry. According to many authors[12] internal economies of scale in agriculture cease to be important beyond a farm size that fully employs the labour of the family. With regard to external economies (large scale machinery, supply of fertilisers and seeds, credit, processing and marketing) the position is different and usually demands some kind of group action.

The arguments conventionally advanced for large-scale farming are that it economises on scarce managerial resources by establishing mass supervision of labour, facilitates mechanisation, planning, irrigation and labour specialisation, and eliminates fragmentation. The difficulty of securing farm products of uniform and high quality from a multitude of peasant-type producers is another argument. Any attempt to work towards a complete structure of equal-sized peasant farms would involve a low ceiling on peasant property; this, it is argued, would constrain ability and enterprise. Yet another argument points out that land reforms should be enacted with reference to future movement of population out of agriculture into a growing industrial sector. Dandekar[13] maintains that creation of new peasant proprietorships would impede such a movement whereas large production units, because they involve looser man-land relationships, facilitate this withdrawal. He argues for the organisation of the agrarian sector into large land-population units, feudal in theory (thus maximising total output with respect to labour), modern in technology and socialistic in purpose.

Such arguments for the large farm structure do have some truth, and can point to some impressive short-run accomplishments. But the distinction is between short-term production effects and laying the foundations for long-term economic growth. In particular, huge-scale units have seldom contributed towards the development of quality in the human resource because individual incentive is lacking. Some have argued that small scale peasant agriculture leads to an excessive accumulation and duplication of capital equipment, but Japan and other countries have demonstrated the efficacy of small scale machinery and 'intermediate' technology in overpopulated economies.[14] The futurity argument of facilitating movement of population out of agriculture is also open to question. In most underdeveloped countries there will not be a movement out of agriculture for some decades to come yet, and although analogy can be misleading, the predominantly family farm structure of Western Europe and North America was not altogether rigid when urban industrial growth began to exert its pull on agricultural labour in the eighteenth and nineteenth centuries. Large-scale farming units do not necessarily hold particular advantages regarding flexibility. In fact technical and managerial mistakes may be magnified. In the Soviet Union, where the average size of many collective and state farms is far larger than can be advocated from the managerial point of view (although this may reflect the necessity to make optimum use of scarce machinery and extension personnel in the 1930s), the question of the optimum size of large-scale farms is now being re-examined. In short, it is difficult to make a case for large-scale, labour extensive units of farming in overpopulated economies at low stages of economic development; the trend toward large farms in economically advanced countries is of limited relevance.

This is not to say that the model of small family farms under peasant ownership should be the sole aim of land reforms. The long run success of a land reform in practice is probably more likely to depend on provisions for flexibility in organisation, size of holdings and administration than on finding the optimum set of arrangements at the outset. In Latin America, which has had a particularly sad history of failed parcellisation schemes, attention has also been focused on schemes which link land reform organisation to communal units. The Mexican *ejido* was the first recognition of this. Similar ideas have proved useful in Africa and the Middle East where communal and tribal characteristics are more strongly developed. In Puerto Rico, Cuba, Algeria and Tunisia, to name a few cases in point, efforts have been made to devise new forms of farm management that make use of existing large farms.

COMMUNAL FARMING: CO-OPERATIVES AND COLLECTIVES

At this point it is necessary to consider the special role that communal organisations have in agrarian reform programmes, and to distinguish co-operatives from collectives. True co-operative farming is something more than the mere use of the co-operative principle in meeting some of the subsidiary needs of the agriculturalist. Situations, present in many countries, whereby certain co-operative organisations provide credit, marketing and machinery hire facilities for small farmers cannot be considered as real co-operative farming. True co-operative farming involves complete pooling of farming resources and reaches its most developed stage in the Israeli *kibbutz*. It is distinguished from the collective farm by three characteristics: membership and withdrawal must be voluntary and free, organisation must be democratic, and the motives for operation must be those of social welfare as well as economic profit. Such differences are greater in practice than in theory. Collectives are subject to a considerable degree of government control, and consist of members who have virtually lost their economic autonomy.[15]

The economic implications of large scale collective farming need brief explanation. Marxist economic doctrine was formulated with respect to industry and industrial workers. How to deal with farmers has been a perennial and thorny problem, not least because Marx had no direct contact with the peasantry. Marx's greatest error was probably his failure to recognise that economic laws apply differently in agriculture and industry; few other theoretical aberrations than the Marxist law of concentration in agriculture have been so comprehensively refuted by historical experience.[16] To fit agriculture into the socialist model it was logically necessary to treat farms as factories and to define workers on the land as members of the proletariat—two transformations which make an awkward fit with reality and which can be achieved only at the risk of considerable socioeconomic upheaval. The socialist condemnation of large landlords was of course attractive to land-hungry peasants—in fact the socialist-communist group has been able to attack the landlords with more success and certainly more zeal than the 'moderate' land reform mongers—but the ultimate socialist objective of abolishing private land ownership and instituting collective farming has proved anathema to the majority of peasants whose aspiration is to own the land they work. Socialist land policy has therefore been put into practice only in those countries whose governments were prepared to force the peasants to accept it, Russia of course being the outstanding case.

Another point about large-scale co-operative or collective units is that the operation of such farms is usually governed by considerations of marginal productivity. The manager of a co-operative farm is usually by background and training a capitalist-entrepreneur type. Once individual holdings are joined together to form co-operatives the important advantage of labour maximisation beyond the marginal rate is lost. Co-operative organisation may thus have the effect of bringing to the surface the unemployment which is otherwise effectively concealed in the sub-marginal self-employment situation. A possible answer to this dilemma is to redirect excess labour time to certain capital works such as irrigation projects and road building which are best undertaken on a large communal scale.[17] This is what the Chinese communes have so successfully done.

Although true co-operative farming is not a common feature outside Israel, the success of a land reform that creates a large number of small owner-operated farms or secure tenancies is to a large extent conditioned by the co-operative provision of supporting measures. Co-operation to reduce the diseconomies of small scale farming is particularly necessary if the dominant farm size, for reasons of equity and population pressure, is very small. Co-operatives for the use of mechanised implements are of particular relevance in this connection, although here the dominant consideration is not so much farm size as plot or field size. If agricultural machinery is used by interfarm co-operation, little additional expense is incurred over the costs of large scale capitalist holdings, providing the parcels are contiguous and can be dealt with one after the other in a single operation. Calculations made in West Germany on the minimum size of plot for efficient use of tractor-based machinery result in a surprisingly low level of 1–3 hectares.[18] In other circumstances it may prove cheaper to adjust the size of machine to the farm rather than the reverse. It is, however, in the provision of more external services that rural co-operatives are particularly important in land reform areas. A co-operative organisation of small farmers can obtain economies by bulk purchase of such inputs as seeds, plants, fertiliser, fodder and poultry; credit will be more easily obtainable for farmers to invest in and improve their holdings; processing, packing and marketing of such pro-

duce as milk, butter, tobacco, coffee and wine can be better organised and executed on a co-operative basis. Irrigation projects
and livestock and crop insurance schemes usually demand co-
operative action. And the co-operative framework can play an
important role in social progress, in the development of a community spirit, in education and training and in the dissemination of new techniques of farming. A point of some ideological
importance concerns the role of compulsion in co-operatives.
Although statutory arrangements to secure entry or prevent
exit cannot result in a true co-operative spirit, some governments have felt that compulsion is necessary in the interests of
beneficiaries, particularly former landless labourers, who are
initially unsuited to the rigours of independent farming. Under
the Italian land reform, for example, ownership of a new holding was made conditional upon the beneficiary joining the co-
operative societies. This element of coercion is in most cases
regarded as a merely transitional phase until the value of co-
operation is fully grasped.

LAND REFORM AND ECONOMIC DEVELOPMENT

Because land reform contributes most directly to agricultural
development, appreciation of the role of land reform in economic development implies a clear understanding of the role of
agriculture in economic development. Johnson and Mellor[19]
summarise the interrelationships between agriculture and development as follows:

(1) Economic development is accompanied by a rapid increase in the demand for agricultural products; failure to expand food supplies in line with this growth in demand can
seriously impede economic growth.

(2) Expanding agricultural exports may be one of the most
promising means of increasing income and foreign exchange
earnings, particularly in the early stages of development.

(3) The labour force for manufacturing and other expanding
sectors of the economy must be drawn mainly from agriculture.

(4) As the dominant sector of an underdeveloped economy
agriculture should make a net contribution to the capital required for overhead investment and growth of industry.

(5) Rising net cash incomes of the farm population may be important as a stimulus to industrial expansion by providing an increase in home market demand.

Although changes in land tenure can affect all these interactions, the two most important links would seem to be land reform's effect on agricultural production and on capital formation.

THE EFFECT OF LAND REFORM ON PRODUCTION AND PRODUCTIVITY

Increases in farm output are important regarding export possibilities and in supplying food to a growing urban industrial sector. Generally a need is felt for tenure systems which facilitate, at early stages of agricultural development, a labour-intensive, capital-saving strategy. There is, however, no single answer to the problem of production and land tenure. If a land reform involves the break-up of fairly efficient estates which further made some contribution to capital, technology and marketing, post-reform marketed production will almost certainly fall in the short term, until and unless such functions can be replaced by the state or co-operatives. Bolivia and Iraq provide examples of this. Even discounting the confusion that destruction of an established agrarian structure by land reform can entail, land redistribution often involves a switch from monocultural cash crops such as wheat, sugar or coffee, to a more diversified but self-sufficient economy, including vegetables, fruits and livestock, which makes fuller use of the family's annual work calendar and provides higher incomes, but which may result in a loss of foreign exchange through reduced exports.

When considering the production effects of a land reform, changes in both output and productivity should be scrutinised. Productivity may be measured for single factors such as labour and land, or for all factors together (gross factor productivity). Gross productivity as an index carries certain conceptual and practical difficulties so that few studies using the measure have been done on land reform situations. Productivity is usually measured with respect to land or labour. Because land is characteristically a scarce resource in overpopulated agrarian economies, the foremost index of productivity is the yield of agricultural products from land in agricultural use; output per worker—labour productivity—may or may not go up in the process, depending on the balance between population growth and the output increase. Land yield is more difficult to measure than would appear at first sight, for it is affected by the land use pattern, particularly the use made of low-intensity marginal land, and there is the crucial problem of finding a standard measure of output. A weight measure ignores the varying values of crops in relation to their weight and bulk (quite apart from livestock produce), but a monetary measure might be difficult to apply in peasant subsistence areas, where a large proportion of the produce is destined for home consumption and thus remains outside the money economy.

From his survey of the economic aspects of the individual country papers in the Agency for International Development's *Spring Review of Land Reform* Dovring[20] reports sudden increases in both output and productivity occurring shortly after the land reforms in Yugoslavia in the 1920s, North Vietnam in the 1950s and Iran in the 1960s, the common factor in all cases being the lifting of burdensome sharecropping arrangements. Decreases in production following smallholder reforms—the standard economic argument against land reform—are usually temporary and traceable to administrative difficulties. There has been much confusion between total production and marketed output; in Bolivia, initial reports of production cutbacks were exaggerated because of the fall in the proportion of total produce that was marketed. Recent output increases in the country have been spectacular. Where production increases are likely to be modest, and where drops may in fact be registered, is where land reform results in the conversion to smallholding peasant property of sub-sectors which were already advanced. The reasons are not hard to see. Foreign estate holdings are often so efficient that it would be difficult to improve upon them, least of all by a revolutionary change involving the sudden exodus of the managerial class. In Kenya transition from large scale British-operated estates in the White Highlands was accomplished more gradually and did not cause any fall in output, but the output increases that were registered were far more modest than those resulting from modernisation of backward traditional villages. The danger of decreases in production and of the destruction of capital that results from dissolution of efficient estates has led many reforms to exempt 'model farms' from expropriation. This may be economically attractive but the practical difficulties of applying a 'model farm clause' where administrative resources are limited and the personnel open to corruption and bribery are often great.

Generally, concludes Dovring,[21] the prevailing impression is that smallholder reforms promote rather than hamper growth in output. Mostly, where output dropped initially it was soon rectified. The advantageous effect of lifting sharecropping obligations is readily identifiable but also rapidly exhausted. The advantage of land redistribution's incentive to intensify agricultural production is of longer duration but is more difficult to trace as a cause-effect process, partly because of the long time-span involved. An interesting theoretical study by Cline[22] on the potential impact of a land reform in Brazil concluded that if all the land were distributed on a regional basis, to form units of uniform size, production increases of the order of 20 per cent could immediately result. A partial land reform, with a ceiling set at 300 hectares, would result in a 6 per cent increase. Predicted production increases do, however, vary according to region and agricultural enterprise. Under total reform, the highest increases, of the order of 60 per cent, obtain for the Minas Gerais cattle sector. In a few sectors, Sao Paulo coffee and Alagoas sugar cane for example, overall production would probably drop. These estimates assume constant technology, crops and labour distribution, and do not take into account the cost of the reform (compensation to landlords, administration). The logical policy outcome is that land redistribution should begin in those sectors showing the highest potential post-reform production increases.

THE EFFECT OF LAND REFORM ON PRIVATE CAPITAL FORMATION

This is the theme examined by most economists interested in land reform. The relevant measures are per capita income and the relative propensities to consume and save. There is reason to believe that there exists an element of capital-forming advantage rooted in the process of extracting a food surplus from the agricultural sector at somewhat less than true opportunity cost. In simple physical terms, this means that agriculture must provide the food for the people who have been released from the agricultural sector and are now engaged in building up capital structures such as factories, roads and schools. Since some of these investments do not have a quick pay-off, agriculture must be required to donate part of this food without an equivalent short-term return.[23] Consequently, where agricultural labour is underrewarded, where food production is an economically second-rank occupation, there has often been rapid industrial growth, accompanied by sustained high rates of capital formation. Conversely, when agricultural labour is paid the same wages as industrial labour, economic development generally tends to lag.[24] This 'double developmental squeeze' on agriculture is, according to Owen,[25] a feature of all developing societies, capitalist or socialist: the difference between the Russian and American approaches to development lies not in the fact that one exacts a special contribution from the farmers and the other does not; rather the difference lies in the way in which the squeeze is applied and in the relative efficiency with which the process operates.

In many underdeveloped countries economic progress has been blocked or hampered by the opposition and inertia of the landlords who are also the political rulers. The big landowners spend conspicuously on luxury products imported from abroad, invest in urban property, or buy more land, thus forcing the price up beyond the peasants' reach. Many economists now agree that a more egalitarian spread of wealth through land redistribution can increase private capital formation and provide a stimulus to demand, particularly for consumer goods. Although evidence on pre- and post-reform income levels is difficult to obtain, a number of case studies support the contention that land reform leads to increased and more evenly distributed beneficiary incomes. Under the Italian reform, beneficiaries enjoyed incomes, on average, of two to three times their previous levels within ten years of assignment.[26] In Egypt reform permitted an annual transfer of £40 million from landowners to beneficiaries during the early post-reform years; because the annual payment made by the beneficiaries for their holdings is less than that which they paid as tenants to the landlords, annual gross incomes increased automatically by 60–70 per cent.[27] Finally, a study by Clark[28] on land reform on the Bolivian *altiplano* revealed that beneficiaries' annual expenditures in real terms

D

had tripled over the period 1950–66. Such evidence, fragmentary though it appears, does show that large scale land reforms can result in substantial income transfers to the rural working classes.

On a more theoretical plane, Raup[29] has outlined an analytical framework which explains why a switch to a system of small farms leads to a process of accretionary capital formation. Capital in small scale farming is spatially dispersed and increases slowly at first, due mainly to the long gestation period characterising agricultural production. A typical process, with the land reform giving security of expectation, would be the incremental private capital formation associated with a shift from a cash-crop economy with a short term investment horizon to the building up of a livestock-feed economy. Given the income redistribution effect, the actual amount of savings available for reinvestment will be influenced by the following factors: propensity to consume, the value put on leisure, the use of credit, and fiscal policy. For capital formation, the first is the most important factor, for every decision to consume is a decision not to invest. In practice, in fact, many beneficiaries show high propensities to consume by spending most of their extra income on food (which will be a productive investment if it enables them to work harder), clothes and household goods. Bicycles and transistor radios are amongst the earliest possessions acquired, and increase in demand for such consumption goods will of course stimulate industrial production. But improved standards of living in the short term mean little capital formation; beneficiaries may, therefore, need encouragement from government agencies to invest at least part of their incomes.

The other major effect of per capita income is on aggregate demand. In an economy with the majority (50–90 per cent in most underdeveloped countries) of the population engaged in agriculture, the per capita income level of this majority is the key factor in determining the level of demand for goods and services. Poor people are poor customers; when desperately poor, they generate very little demand, especially for industrially produced goods. With the internal market for industrial products limited, manufacturing fails to develop, especially where the small size of the country anyway limits possible economies of scale (as in the Central American republics). Income redistribution through land redistribution does not mean that peasants get rich quickly—the overall level of poverty is too great—but if they can receive a little extra income, especially when this is combined with the security that their efforts can yield them more in the future, this can have a significant impact on demand.[30]

An important yet often neglected facet of the theoretical process of land reform's contribution to economic development is what happens to the dispossessed landlords, and in particular what they do with the compensation they receive for the expropriated land. Landowners are often paid in government bonds which in a sense force them to invest in government-owned or sponsored industry or infrastructure, but sometimes part of the compensation is made in cash. Possible outlets for this money include hoarding and luxury consumption (in which case the money will probably go abroad), investment in city houses and urban land speculation, investment in industry, or investment in agricultural improvements (faced with a reduced land area, the expropriated landowner may be forced to intensify cultivation to maintain a satisfactory income). Most important of these is probably investment in industry, for this is typically the important long term growth sector in underdeveloped countries. Although precise data are hard to come by, some redirection of landowners' investment into industry has undoubtedly occurred with many recent reforms. In Mexico, for example, when the land reform was initiated there was a flight of capital in search of security from agriculture to the cities. At first most of this capital was invested in speculative ventures such as urban real estate, but soon it was attracted to the construction industry and from there it spread to other branches of industry.[31] The idea that overall investment increases with such a diversion is, however, a myth.[32] Compensation payments invested by landlords in industry must have come from somewhere, and could therefore have been profitably invested in industry at their source; if such payments came from domestic borrowing or from taxation, for example, all that happens is that landlords become the investing agents for someone else's investible savings. The only way that investment for a given level of income can increase is by depressing average propensity to consume. When diversion into industry of expropriated landlords' investment takes place, it is often the erstwhile agricultural working capital of landlords that is diverted, and this needs to be replaced through government stimulus by co-operatives, credit and banking agencies.

THE HISTORICAL APPROACH

So far the argument has been rather theoretical. An alternative way of demonstrating the relationship between land reform and development is to look for empirical justification of its existence. An immediate problem is to identify cause-effect relationships. In its most precise form the question posed by land reform and productivity is whether the tenure system established by the reform has performed better or worse than the old tenure situation would have done had it been allowed to continue. But other policies which coincide with the implementation of land reform may also effect production, income and employment in agriculture. Some writers have concluded that the effects of land reform stem from the forces that created the reform in the first place rather than from the reform itself. Often broad agrarian reform measures spring from dynamic social and political forces in society which push for modernisation in general. The large output increases in Japan and Taiwan following land reform in fact continued trends already in existence. Agrarian reform may be as much a result of development as a cause of it.[33] Effects of reforms thus are notoriously difficult to measure and empirical evidence on the development effects of land reform is restricted.

From some countries at least, however, the evidence is convincing. In Europe, 'a tremendous outburst of energy' was noted in Denmark after individual holdings were created and bondage abolished in 1788; national crop production rose by 30 per cent almost immediately.[34] When the meaning of land reform is tantamount to the abolition of feudalism like this, the relationship between reform and development seems quite plain. Since then Denmark has been continuously land reforming for nearly two centuries, and it is this constant reappraisal of structural measures and the reciprocal relationship between reform and development that go a long way toward explaining the efficiency of Danish agriculture today. Notable, too, is the concentration of holdings, almost all owner-occupied, in the medium size group; 71 per cent of the farmland in 1961 was under farms of 10–60 hectares. Denmark also belongs to the very small group of countries where the proportion of the labour force engaged in agriculture is matched by the share of agriculture in the gross national product (17 per cent in 1961).[35]

In Japan, the immediate results of transfer of ownership from landlord to tenant were a sharp upswing in the accumulation of rural capital and a marked increase in the real value of total farm production. But land reform in Japan came late in the developmental process. The adjustments incident to the redistribution of property were made easier by the availability of urban industrial occupations, the excellent transport system and the fact that the economy was developing fast anyway. Countries like Japan and Italy which have the political strength, the finance and organisational capacity to carry out a peaceful and orderly reform are just those where the value of a large-scale reform is most in doubt. The 1950 land reform in Italy came so long after the real need was felt that by the time it was completed a decade or so later it was almost an irrelevance.

Having comparatively analysed seventeen land reforms, Tuma[36] tied the most successful reforms to antecedent dynamic social and political movements, and emphasised that in such cases reform was a result of rather than a cause of modernisation and developmental forces. The very real tragedy of land reform is that it is most needed in precisely those countries least able to carry it through. This also indicates the danger of arguing by historical analogy or general theory. Warriner[37] points out that Rostow's development theory is of how growth occurred, not of why it has failed to occur; his interpretation of the process of growth is generalised from past history of advanced countries, and it is a mistake to assume that underdeveloped countries will automatically pass through the same process; if underdevelopment simply meant economic backwardness or an earlier stage of growth, then the poorer countries could get rich simply by imitating the institutions of the developed countries. In reality underdevelopment is a far more complex phenomenon, covering a variety of conditions in different parts of the world. In India underdevelopment means a resource base too small for the burgeoning population, and general and increasing poverty. In Latin America it means the existence of a dual economy, of lop-sided development, where there is a resource base, but a failure to diffuse growth throughout the economy. India is not on a lower rung of the same development ladder as the United States and Europe: it is not on a ladder at all. Latin American countries have one foot high up and the other so low that they cannot climb. The role of land reform differs accordingly: in India it could help a bit; in Latin America it could be decisive.[38]

But this is not to say that land reform is a necessary precondition for economic development. Several countries have achieved rapid growth without land reforms: Italy and Japan between the wars for example. In Latin America, Gautemala, Nicaragua and Ecuador are three countries which have experienced rapid increases in agricultural output without reforming their tenure systems; the increased production has come almost exclusively from the export-oriented plantation sector, with relatively little spread effect to the peasant subsistence sector which produces for the home market.[39] Warriner[40] draws an instructive comparison between Hungary and Bulgaria in the interwar period. Bulgaria had had a land reform in the 1880s when it disposed of the Turkish land system; Hungary had had no reform and presented a quasi-feudal structure, with a small landowning élite controlling the mass of poor peasants. Yet although the average Bulgarian farmer was perhaps more content because there were no extremes of wealth and poverty, Hungary achieved more agricultural development. Output per man was 30 per cent higher in Hungary, even though there was some unemployment. The wealth of the great estate owners had financed industrial development to absorb part of the unemployed labour force in agriculture, whereas Bulgaria's equal-farm policy tended to keep people working on the land and did not promote a high rate of investment. This is not intended as an inclusive argument against land reform, if only because the Hungarian estate owners were more benevolent than their counterparts in other parts of the world, but it does show that if land reform is to contribute to development it is necessary to find types of farming organisation which will mobilise savings and promote progress in agriculture and in industry.

Land reform is thus no panacea. Ultimately much depends on

the intelligence with which, and the conditions under which, the reform is carried out. If the reform is rapidly and efficiently administered, if viable sized units are set up, and if beneficiaries have the right attitudes to owning and farming the land and to learning new techniques, then there is every reason to expect production to increase.[41] On the other hand if there are long delays in the reform's implementation, if reform farm units are economically too small, if the former landlords' functions in the field of credit, expertise etc. are not replaced, and if peasants are alienated from working the land, then production is likely to fall. The relative productive success of the reforms in Japan, Taiwan, Egypt and Italy can be partly adduced to the above-mentioned factors, and to the fact that these countries were already technically advanced. Japan and Taiwan, in particular, were characterised by tenant and sharecropper cultivation, where peasants already had a measure of experience of independent farming, and where services geared to small farm agriculture already existed.[42] Moreover these reforms were partial evolutionary improvements in agrarian structure rather than major revolutionary upheavals. Where reform is total and cataclysmic, followed by political and administrative chaos, where the previous service structure is replaced by nothing in the short run, and where the only beneficiaries are landless labourers devoid of experience of, or even desire for, independent farming, then at least in the short run adverse effects on agricultural output and economic development must be expected: Mexico, Bolivia and Iraq are examples. Revolutionary reforms can get land expropriated but cannot, it seems, carry the administration through to actually implementing a comprehensive assignment and settlement scheme. This incompatibility is perhaps inherent: agriculture demands peaceful continuity, revolution involves violent chaos. The kind of people who make revolutions are not, as a rule, the kind of people who can organise for increased production; nor can landless labourers be transformed into efficient owner-farmers overnight.

Generally the historical approach shows that land reform can make a vital contribution to, but is by no means always an automatic condition of, economic development. Agrarian situations do exist which are beyond the remedy of land reform. Land reform will not solve problems of excessive population pressure; it can only mitigate the problem somewhat. Nor can it solve such economic problems as lack of market outlets for agricultural produce or of adequate supplies of inputs such as fertilisers, machinery and technical knowledge. An unfavourable development in the terms of trade can effectively eliminate the economic benefits derived from land reform; the only consolation is that without the reform, the peasants would have been even worse off. Obstacles such as these can be surmounted only by the diversification of the economy as a whole in the course of a programme of general economic development.

REFERENCES

1. P. Dorner: *The Influence of Land Tenure Institutions on the Economic Development of Agriculture in Less Developed Countries* (Madison, University of Wisconsin Land Tenure Center Paper 55, 1968), pp. 1, 4.
2. K. H. Parsons, in H. M. Southworth and B. F. Johnson (eds.): *Agricultural Development and Economic Growth* (New York, Cornell University Press, 1967), pp. 317-20.
3. R. P. Dore: 'Sociological aspects of land valuation and land reform', in A. M. Woodruff, J. R. Brown and S. Lin (eds.): *International Seminar on Land Taxation, Land Tenure and Land Reform in the Developing Countries* (West Hartford, Lincoln Foundation, 1967), pp. 560-88.
4. P. M. Raup: 'Land reform and agricultural development', in Southworth and Johnson: *op. cit.*, pp. 267-314.
5. D. Warriner: *The Economics of Peasant Farming* (London, Oxford University Press, 1939).
6. G. G. Dell' Angelo: *Note sulla Sottoccupazione nelle Aziende Contadine* (Rome, Svimez, 1960).
7. D. Warriner: 'Employment and income aspects of recent agrarian reforms in the Middle East', *International Labour Review*, 101 (6), 1970, pp. 605-25.
8. T. W. Schulz: 'The role of government in promoting economic growth', in L. White (ed.): *The State of the Social Sciences* (Chicago, University of Chicago Press, 1956), pp. 372-83.
9. M. J. Sternberg: 'Agrarian reform and employment, with special reference to Latin America', *International Labour Review*, 95 (1-2), 1967, pp. 1-26.
10. P. Dorner and D. Kanel: 'The economic case for land reform', in Agency for International Development: *Spring Review of Land Reform* (Washington, Department of State, 1970), Vol. 11, pp. 11, 14-16, 19-20.
11. N. Georgescu-Roegen: 'Economic theory and agrarian economics', *Oxford Economic Papers*, 12 (1), 1960, pp. 1-40.
12. For example E. J. Long: 'The economic basis of land reform in under-

developed countries', *Land Economics*, 38 (2), 1961, pp. 113–23; D. Kanel: 'Size of farm and economic development', *Indian Journal of Agricultural Economics*, 22 (2), 1967, pp. 26–44; and the evidence and studies assembled in Dorner and Kanel: *op. cit.*, pp. 15–31.

13. V. M. Dandekar: 'Economic theory and agrarian reform', *Oxford Economic Papers*, 14 (1), 1962, pp. 69–80.

14. Dorner and Kanel: *op. cit.*, p. 17.

15. O. Schiller: 'A comparison of co-operative and collective farming', in K. H. Parsons, R. J. Penn and P. M. Raup (eds.): *Land Tenure* (Madison, University of Wisconsin Press, 1956), pp. 602–5.

16. Georgescu-Roegen: *op. cit.*, pp. 6, 10.

17. Dandekar: *op. cit.*, pp. 77–8.

18. O. Schiller: 'Co-operative farming and economies of scale', *Land Reform, Land Settlement and Co-operatives*, 2, 1967, pp. 14–18.

19. B. F. Johnson and J. Mellor: 'The role of agriculture in economic development', *American Economic Review*, 51 (4), 1961, pp. 566–93.

20. F. Dovring: 'Economic results of land reform', in Agency for International development: *Spring Review of Land Reform*, *op. cit.*, Vol. 11, pp. 9, 13.

21. *Ibid*: p. 12.

22. W. R. Cline: *Economic Consequences of a Land Reform in Brazil* (Amsterdam, North Holland Contributions to Economic Analysis 67, 1970), pp. 164–5, 179–81.

23. Dorner: *op. cit.*, p. 20.

24. P. M. Raup: 'Land tenure adjustments in industrial-agricultural economies', in H. Halcrow (ed.): *Modern Land Policy* (Urbana, University of Illinois Press, 1960), pp. 311–24.

25. W. Owen: 'The double developmental squeeze on agriculture', *American Economic Review*, 56 (1), 1966, pp. 43–70.

26. R. L. King: 'Italian land reform: critique, effects, evaluation', *Tijdschrift voor Economische en Sociale Geografie*, 62 (6), 1971, pp. 368–82.

27. H. A. Dawood: 'Agrarian reform in Egypt: a case study', *Current History*, 30 (3), 1956, pp. 331–8.

28. R. J. Clark: 'Land reform and peasant market participation in the northern highlands of Bolivia', *Land Economics*, 44 (2), 1968, pp. 153–72.

29. P. M. Raup: 'The contribution of land reforms to agricultural development: an analytical framework', *Economic Development and Cultural Change*, 12 (1), 1963, pp. 1–21.

30. Dorner: *op. cit.*, p. 8.

31. E. Flores: 'Land reform and agricultural development', in Parsons, Penn and Raup: *op. cit.*, pp. 243–6.

32. S. Eddie: *The Simple Economics of Land Reform: the Expropriation Compensation Process and Income Distribution* (Madison, University of Wisconsin Land Tenure Center Paper 75, 1971), pp. 14–15.

33. D. McEntire: 'Land reform goals and economic development', *Land Reform, Land Settlement and Co-operatives*, 1, 1973, pp. 42–9; R. Laptore, J. Petras and J. Rinehart: 'The concept of land reform and its role in

development: some notes on societal cause-effect', *Comparative Studies in Society and History*, 13 (4), 1971, pp. 473-85.

34. F. Skrubbletrang: *Agricultural Development and Rural Reform in Denmark* (Rome, FAO, 1953).

35. D. Warriner: *Land Reform in Principle and Practice* (Oxford, Clarendon, 1969), pp. 392-403.

36. E. H. Tuma: 'Agrarian reform in historical perspective: a comparative study', *Comparative Studies in Society in History*, 6, 1963, pp. 47-75.

37. Warriner: *op. cit.*, pp. 383-4.

38. *Ibid.*

39. P. Dorner: *Land Reform and Economic Development* (London, Penguin, 1972), p. 116.

40. D. Warriner: *Land Reform and Economic Development* (Cairo, National Bank of Egypt, 1955), pp. 6-7.

41. Warriner: *Land Reform in Principle and Practice*, *op. cit.*, pp. 54-55.

42. Dorner: *Land Reform and Economic Development*, *op. cit.*, pp. 110-12.

PART 2

Land Reform in Latin America

Introduction

The choice of Latin America as the first continent is easily justified. Agrarian conditions throughout much of this continent demonstrate, better than in any other part of the world, that landholding patterns cause social injustice and economic stagnation. In most countries here, land distribution is so uneven that distributive reforms could have a major impact on income redistribution and on employment creation. One hundred million poverty-stricken rural people coexist with a concentration of wealth and a relative abundance of natural resources, and this inequality, this inflexible imbalance, causes land tenure to be blamed as the main obstacle to development in Latin America.

On the conventional per capita income criterion, Latin America appears to be quite highly developed compared with Asia or Africa, although far behind North America or Northwest Europe. Nevertheless, most authors place it indubitably in the Third World. The fact is that such generalised indicators as mean per capita income hide many important distinctions, and Latin America is a very heterogeneous continent. Many measures of development show that differences within Latin America are wider than those between the continent's richest nations and the developed nations of the world. Venezuela's per capita income, for example, is similar to that of Ireland or Hungary and above that of Greece or Portugal. Argentina has more doctors per thousand population than either the United States or the United Kingdom. On the other hand Bolivia, Ecuador and Paraguay have measures of development below those of many Asian and

African countries, whilst Haiti is one of the very poorest countries of the world.[1]

Except for the more industrialised nations of Argentina and Uruguay, Latin American countries have 40–70 per cent of their populations living and working in agriculture. The proportion of rural families with no land, or insufficient land for a living, ranges from 55 to 90 per cent; the mean for the continent is 72 per cent. About 40 per cent of all farm families are completely landless, and because the rural labour force grows faster than its access to land, this figure is increasing.[2] The United Nations estimates that 40 per cent of the economically active labour force is underemployed, the equivalent of 25 million jobless, 27 per cent of the active population. Manpower supply grows at a quickening pace—by 2·6 per cent per year in the 1950s, by 2·8 per cent in the 1960s, and by 3·0 per cent in the 1970s. Food supply barely keeps pace with these rates of increase, and some sectors of the rural population are experiencing persistent declines in real income, with 50–75 per cent of income going on food for survival. From 230 million in 1965 the United Nations forecasts a population of 700m by 2000. In rural Brazil and in central Guatemala birth rates are said to be close to the biological maximum. Statements that in Latin America there is no pressure of population, no 'Malthusian underdevelopment', ignore the geographical patterns of population distribution, with particular concentrations in Central America, the Caribbean, North-east Brazil and the Colombian Andean heartland. The crude man-land ratio suggests that there should not be hunger for food or land in this continent, but the area cropped is only 5 per cent of the total area, or 20 per cent of the agricultural area. The agricultural area per head of population—4 hectares (or 1 hectare of cropped land)—is a surprisingly low figure.[3]

Perhaps the most tragic aspect of development in Latin America is the failure to create more jobs and more meaningful employment. In exemplifying this problem Dorner and Felstehausen[4] report that whereas total labour force in Colombia grows by 200 000 annually, modern manufacturing provides only 10 000 new jobs per year. Open unemployment in Latin America is mainly urban; the prime foci of the misery wrought by unemployment are the shanty-towns, whose populations (5 million in 1970) are growing at 15 per cent per year. This forced geographic mobility of the peasantry is a 'protest with the feet' against a deep-seated agrarian malaise—namely that *latifundio* agriculture is unemployment agriculture; it is entirely different from the exodus from the land in Western Europe and North America in the nineteenth and early twentieth centuries; it is not produced by agricultural rationalisation nor does it represent a dynamic peasantry improving its socio-economic status. But for most migrants arrival in the city brings disillusionment. Jobs are scarce and the prospects of integration into the urban community are poor. The villages therefore extend into the cities, and peripheral shanty-towns represent at best a desultory form of 'semi-urbanisation'. The turmoil and rioting in cities like Lima and Caracas represent protest by the displaced peasants for whom there is no room in either village or city. Yet despite massive migration from the countryside Latin America's rural population is increasing by $1\frac{1}{2}$ per cent per year, and absolute numbers in agriculture are forecast to continue rising to at least 1990.[5] Given the demonstrated failure of the urban-industrial sector at present to provide significant employment increases, Thiesenhusen urges a concerted effort, via land reform, to slow down farm-to-city migration until industry can absorb labour more rapidly.[6]

Any brief description of Latin American agrarian structure must suffer from over-generalisation, but it is still meaningful, because of commonly shared historical experiences, institutions and cultures, to enunciate Latin American tenure problems. Before the Iberian conquest some socially advanced types of agriculture existed. The Incas and the Aztecs, for example, produced enough maize, cotton, tobacco, potatoes, beans and other crops to support urban areas and considerable armies. Irrigation and fertilisation techniques and the co-operative organisation of agricultural production were highly developed. The Inca *allyu* system was an early example of planned collective agriculture.[7] Less sophisticated forms of native *comunidad* survive today in Indian areas, notably in the Andes, but only in remote locations, often with poor soils. Apart from the Indian *comunidades* and small to medium family-sized farms (important in Chile, Argentina and southern Brazil), the agrarian structure is dominated by the symbiotic *latifundio-minifundio* complex. Rural Latin America is the classic two-class situation, and it is this 'dismal dichotomy' which sets the stage for agrarian reform.[8]

Basically the *latifundio* system reflects rural social organisation in Spain and Portugal at the time of the conquest and its super-imposition on native cultures through large grants of land and Indians by the Spanish crown to the *conquistadores* for loyal service. The conquerors either enslaved the Indians to work the land for them (the original *encomienda*) or brought in Africans to replace them. These large estates, which for four to five centuries have monopolised much of Latin American agriculture, still hamper the whole continent's economic, social and political development. In Brazil large landholdings and antiquated production methods keep an estimated 40 million people out of the market, with incomes so small that they buy virtually nothing. For the 25 million peasants of North-east Brazil, where the heritage of the slave system is especially marked, the situation is particularly acute.[9]

The *latifundio* pattern has two main variants: the extensively cultivated estate, and the more intensively worked plantation. They create different problems and require different measures of reform. The *latifundio* or traditional *hacienda* typically operates on a cereals-pasture regime with low levels of labour and capital investment. Ownership is usually absentee and labour is supplied by the *colono* (labour tenant) system or one of its variants. Economically, writes Carroll, the *hacienda* is generally a paragon of inefficiency.[10] Sociologically, *latifundismo* is a system of autocratic power.[11] Because of their cultural backgrounds the landlords are not only hostile to change but generally lack understanding of the need for it.[12] Consequently farming stagnates and primitive methods prevail. Indeed in Latin America generally 'at least one half of the agriculturalists are dependent upon methods of extracting a living from the soil that are more primitive, less efficient and more wasteful of human energy than those the Egyptians were using at the dawn of the history.'[13] Although also of colonial origin, the plantation is normally efficiently run, with intensive and closely controlled inputs of labour and high capitalisation, geared to producing large quantities of one product for export. Economic efficiency is, however, achieved by authoritarian management and often foreign control, so that the monopoly element is no better than traditional *haciendas*.

Available data for the continent as a whole show that 90 per cent of the agricultural land belongs to 10 per cent of the owners, and 50 per cent (in estates of over 1000 hectares) is held by 1–2 per cent—a degree of concentration far greater than in any other comparable world region. Locally, more extreme cases exist: in Ecuador 705 *latifundia* (0·17 per cent by number of landholdings) embrace 37 per cent of farmland; in Guatemala 516 farms (0·15 per cent by number) include 41 per cent of agricultural land.[14] Table 2 presents data collected from the seven countries investigated by the Inter-American Committee for Agricultural Development.[15] In two of the countries listed—Chile and Peru—over 80 per cent of farmland is in very large farm units (i.e., with more than 12 permanent workers). In Peru, Guatemala and Ecuador 85–90 per cent of all farms are sub-family units or *minifundia*, mostly tenanted or merely squatter holdings. Actually the concentration of landownership is greater than such data indicate. Firstly, large landowners frequently control several estates (the data are collected by holding size not total ownership size) and under-report the true extent of their properties. Secondly, *latifundia* generally include the best land, whereas most smallholdings are located on poor soils and eroded hillsides. Thirdly, the frequency of underemployment on family-sized units reveals many of them to be really of *minifundio* size. Finally, the conventional method of showing distribution of land only amongst landholders is misleading as it leaves out all the farm people without access to land; if these 40–50 per cent are included (usually their number is under-reported in censuses because so many of this group have no fixed residence) the proportion of *hacendados* of all farm families shrinks still further.

Most large landowners also hold considerable power in the wider economy and society of their countries. Particularly important is their control of market outlets.[16] They have financial and commercial interests in cities, political responsibilities in the capital and cultural interests far removed from the land. With easy access to medical, educational and cultural services in the cities they feel little need to duplicate them in rural communities where they hold their land, even though they are often obliged by law to do so. In Guatemala's central provinces only 5 per cent of the population is literate. Tenants and workers on *haciendas* are often totally dependent upon the *patrón* for employment

TABLE 2
DISTRIBUTION OF FARMLAND IN SEVEN LATIN AMERICAN COUNTRIES,
circa 1960

(Figures represent percentage of country total in each size class)

Country	Sub-family	Family	Multi-family medium	Multi-family large
Argentina				
No. farm units	43·2	48·7	7·3	0·8
Area in farms	3·4	44·7	15·0	36·9
Brazil				
No. farm units	22·5	39·1	33·7	4·7
Area in farms	0·5	6·0	34·0	59·5
Chile				
No. farm units	36·9	40·0	16·2	6·9
Area in farms	0·2	7·1	11·4	81·3
Ecuador				
No. farm units	89·9	8·0	1·7	0·4
Area in farms	16·6	19·0	19·3	45·1
Guatemala				
No. farm units	88·4	9·5	2·0	0·1
Area in farms	14·3	13·4	31·5	40·8
Peru				
No. farm units	88·0	8·5	2·4	1·1
Area in farms	7·4	4·5	5·7	82·4

Notes: Sub-family: farms large enough to provide employment for less than 2 persons (with respect to local and regional income, market and technology levels).

Family: farms large enough to provide employment for 2–4 persons on the assumption that most of the farm work is carried out by members of the farm family.

Multi-family medium: farms large enough to provide employment for 4–12 persons.

Multi-family large: farms large enough to provide employment for over 12 persons.

Source: S. L. Barraclough and A. L. Domike: Agrarian structure in seven Latin American Countries, *Land Economics*, 42 (4), 1966, p. 395.

and a place to live. With the abolition of compulsory servitude during the last century *peones* now have the right to leave the estate, but with little education and few job opportunities elsewhere this is seldom a realistic possibility. Wage and rental agreements favour the landowners, again often in flagrant defiance of the legislation. In Nicaragua rents may be eight times the legal maximum, and in Brazil minimum wage laws are observed in only one of eight states. The minimum wage laid down becomes, in reality, the maximum ever paid. *Haciendas* exist in the Andean region where people have to work without pay on the estate in order to use paths and bridges on it, and corporal punishment is still occasionally encountered.[17]

For agricultural development and employment the most unfortunate characteristic of *latifundia* is their extensive use of land, often the best land in the country for soil quality and accessibility. And yet 43 per cent of all idle land is in *latifundia*. In the seven ICAD countries only one-sixth of *latifundio* land is cropped regularly (and only 4 per cent cropped every year), the rest being pasture and natural vegetation. Even so, in countries for which figures are available, the ratio of arable land to agricultural workers is 9–18 times greater on large estates than on smallholdings.[18]

Minifundia, whether independently owned smallholdings or tenanted plots on the *latifundio*, have a fixed land base and virtually no access to productive factors other than labour. The principal motive for production is survival, and many *minifundistas* are virtually outside the market; they represent neither a productive source of marketable farm produce nor an effective demand for industrial products.

Minifundia origins also date to colonial times, when land was granted in small amounts to low rank soldiers and humble citizens, but fragmentation, uncertain tenure rights and soil erosion have since become grave problems. Population pressure causes subdivision into miniscule plots, in Central America sometimes called *microfincas*. Fragmentation is also acute in the Andean region where holdings are frequently split into 15 or 20 separate plots. Although 5 hectares is often quoted as the upper limit for a *minifundio* (sub-family size) holding, field study evidence indicates 2 hectares to be a more realistic 'break-even' point for family subsistence—most Latin American farmers cannot cultivate more than 5 hectares without hired help or unrealistic investment in mechanical traction.[19] Titleless squatters on public or private land operate many of the smallest units. Squatting dominates tenures in Panama and Paraguay and is widespread too in Venezuela.

The last major feature of the Latin American agrarian structure is the *colono* system (now in fact breaking down), by which
agricultural labour is supplied and contracted to work on large
estates.[20] *Latifundio* workers having the status of *colonos* or tenant
labourers receive temporary or traditional usufruct of a plot of
land in return for a specified number of days' work on the estate
(e.g. four per week), but this is often combined with sharecropping or with cash rent tenancy, and sometimes other customary privileges and obligations as well. *Colonos* carry various
names in Latin America: *yanaconas* in Peru, *inquilinos* in Chile,
huasipungeros in Ecuador and *conuqueros* in Venezuela.

It may seem strange that land reform, except in Mexico, was
so late in coming to this continent, which was, from the structural point of view, 'ripe for reform'. Yet there are reasons. Any
kind of reform is difficult in Latin America because there have
been no preliminary stages, in particular no broad tradition of
small ownership, such as in pre-Revolution Russia, where peasants already owned half the land following serf emancipation
half a century earlier. Articulate demand for land reform, therefore, springs not from these small farmers: they are too weak and
scattered. The significant class division is between big landowners and farm labourers, *colonos* and the like, who have,
nevertheless, been remarkably slow and ineffective in organising
themselves—indeed much of the land reform demand comes
from urban intellectuals.[21]

Apart from the Mexican, Bolivian and Cuban reforms, considered in the next three chapters and representing specific re-
sponses to unique national circumstances, Latin American land
reform has been more fiction than fact, more rhetoric than reality, more hypothesis than truth. Yet in the early 1960s a new
era seemed about to begin. The Cuban land reform (1959) and
the founding of the Alliance for Progress in 1961 set the basis for
a continent-wide land reform movement. Peasant organisations
were at last effectively exerting pressure on their governments to
obtain land.[22] Most countries passed land reform laws and established land reform institutes allegedly to expropriate large estates and redistribute the land to the *campesinos*. By 1970 only El
Salvador had no land reform law.

The Alliance for Progress gave land reform high priority.
Objective 6 of title 1 of the Charter of Punta del Este, signed by

all nations of the continent except Cuba, required 'the effective transformation of unjust structures and systems of land tenure with a view to replacing *latifundia* and dwarf holdings by an equitable system of land tenure'. This shift in US attitudes probably owed as much to Cuba and the shadow of the Cold War over the hemisphere as to fundamental concern to improve *campesino* welfare. Many were sceptical of American sincerity and determination to sponsor social revolutions, and much cynical commentary emphasised confusion of aims and accused Washington of insincerity and opportunism. Two main contradictions were apparent: that of reconciling expropriation with American business interests in Latin America (e.g. banana and sugar plantations) and with the respect for private property that is the foundation of capitalism; and the inapplicability of the American-style family farm, the cornerstone of US tenure policy, to a society lacking tradition in independent family farming.

The Charter was not explicit that Alliance (chiefly United States) aid would be conditional upon land reform, but the text implies this; probably the bilingual ambiguity of exactly what *reforma agraria* meant allowed the signitaries to join the Alliance but opened the door to individual policy interpretations afterwards. In fact, the Charter's enunciation of the transformation of unjust land tenure systems and social structures was politically infeasible, a pious hope. Feder's devastating portrait of the 'counterreform' movement of the 1960s sums up the reality.[23] Partly through fear of peasant uprisings and partly through the need to fulfil ill-defined Charter obligations, most Latin American governments passed complex, mild and procrastinatory land reform laws in the 1960s. Land reform institutes were set up, but starved of real power. The 1964 Peruvian legislation contained 250 articles, many very long and impossible to interpret with certainty; 500 more articles emerged in the following four years. The Brazilian parliament considered dozens of land reform bills during the decade, none of which was effectively implemented; here a major obstacle was the constitution's guarantee of prior payment for expropriated lands. In some countries the introduction of the 'social function of landownership' seemed to be a deliberate obfuscation of the land reform issue. In others the land reform institutes were merely excuses to create centralised bureaucracies providing jobs for the very class supposedly affected by the reform—a built-in sabotage system! In Paraguay, 90 per cent of the staff of the agrarian reform institute work in the central office, leaving a dearth of field staff for actual implementation.[24]

Many countries, notably Chile, Colombia and Venezuela, emphasised colonisation of public land as a surrogate for true land reform, to divert *campesino* pressure for land redistribution.[25] If colonisation is confused with land reform, governments can easily magnify tiny reform achievements by adding-in the peasants settled in colonisation schemes; Columbia, apparently, has spearheaded this trick.[26] Other more complex problems arise. Sometimes the large farm pattern merely emerges again in the newly settled regions, as when large parcels of good quality land are assigned to non-peasant elements such as army officers or former estate foremen. On the more accessible areas of public land planned settlement is often pre-empted by spontaneous or squatter settlements.[27] In Chile and Guatemala colonisation agencies have deliberately formed sub family-scale units, whose operators must seek part-time work on the large farms. Economically, the failure of many Latin American colonisation schemes reflects remoteness and lack of transport (making produce virtually unmarketable), and ignorance of local soil resources. Culturally the Andean Indians are reluctant to move to hotter, more humid environments. Accessible 'virgin' lands requiring only the touch of a human hand to produce wealth do not exist in important amounts; even where there are ample land resources capable of sustaining more profitable use, much is inaccessible without considerable expenditure of financial and technical resources.[28] In fact, by pulling scarce resources away from vital reform activities, colonisation schemes can worsen the overall agrarian situation, and evidence exists that official colonisation schemes compare unfavourably with spontaneous settlement free of government aid.[29]

In general, the episode leaves the landed élite with powers and privileges largely unmolested. Legislation by congresses whose members are mostly big landlords and their friends was approved with the tacit agreement that it would not be rigorously enforced. The peasants have no voice in the reform programmes, and cannot request expropriations in a legal manner. In order to exert pressure on the government they must adopt illegal means, such as invasions of land. The laws allow them no alternative. In such conditions, writes Feder, the peasants are more the victims than the beneficiaries or initiators of land reform.[30]

The break with the Charter expressed itself in two related ways: conceptually, in a progressive de-emphasis of reforms as a pre-requisite for growth; and, practically, in side-stepping reforms as a pre-requisite for aid.[31] The Charter dogma clashed immediately with US business, which considered land reform of any kind a subversive threat to American investments in Latin America. The 'redistributionist' philosophy and the endorsement of land reform in the early Kennedy administration gave way to a 'productionist' tendency favouring technical efficiency on existing holdings for promoting successful development, 'thus bringing US policy more in line with the preferences of the large landowners who are amongst the most reliable political allies of the US.'[32] Increasingly US policy makers think of the Latin American farm problem as one of mere shortage of food, and consequently devise policies to increase food production through improved technology, ignoring the consequences for food distribution or employment and income positions for the rural poor.[33]

Obviously there are fundamental differences among Latin American land reforms. The Mexican, Bolivian and Cuban reforms accompanied revolutionary changes in the wider sociopolitical structure, although the reforms were quite different from one another in impact and final outcome. Such deep structural reforms are easily distinguished from the more conventional 'negotiated' reforms, such as those in Puerto Rico, Venezuela and Chile, which have a limited, but nevertheless significant, impact on agrarian structure. Finally, the 'marginal' reforms, limited to colonisation projects and the occasional purchase and distribution of a few landed estates, do not really affect the agrarian structure at either regional or national levels; most of the recent 'reforms' (*sic*) fall into this category.

REFERENCES

1. A. Gilbert: *Latin American Development: A Geographical Perspective* (London, Penguin, 1974), p. 19.
2. E. Feder: *The Rape of the Peasantry: Latin America's Landholding System* (New York, Doubleday Anchor, 1971), pp. 54, 114.

3. D. Warriner: *Land Reform in Principle and Practice* (Oxford, Clarendon, 1969), p. 219.

4. P. Dorner and H. Felstehausen: 'Agrarian reform and employment: the Colombian case', *International Labour Review*, 102 (3), 1970, pp. 221–40.

5. Feder: *op. cit.*, p. 36.

6. W. C. Thiesenhusen: 'Employment and Latin American development', in P. Dorner (ed.): *Land Reform in Latin America: Issues and Cases* (Madison, University of Wisconsin Press, Land Economics Monographs 3, 1971), pp. 57–76.

7. G. Clawson: *Communal Land Tenure* (Rome, FAO Agricultural Studies 17, 1953), pp. 23–5.

8. Pearse divides Latin American agricultural population into four social groups: estate owners (entrepreneurs or rentiers); an intermediary group of estate administrators and supervisors; smallholders; and landless estate labourers. A. Pearse: 'Agrarian change trends in Latin America', *Latin American Research Review*, 1 (3), 1966, pp. 45–69.

9. R. J. Alexander: 'Agrarian reform in Latin America', *Foreign Affairs*, 41 (1), 1962, pp. 191–207.

10. T. F. Carroll: 'The land reform issue in Latin America', in A. O. Hirschmann (ed.): *Latin American Issues: Essays and Comments* (New York, Twentieth Century Fund, 1961), pp. 161–204.

11. See T. Lynn Smith: *Agrarian Reform in Latin America* (New York, Knopf, 1965), p. 16.

12. A number of recent studies on Latin American *latifundistas* have shown that this group has a large enough share of total income to affect, both directly and indirectly, the level of economic activity of their countries. Traditional expenditure patterns have inhibited economic development as a result of high propensities to consume and low propensities to save and invest. For Colombia Grunig shows that although a few Schumpeterian profit-maximising latifundist entrepreneurs exist, and are increasing in number, traditional *latifundistas* are non-profit maximisers seeking a level of income adequate for their life-style but with minimum managerial effort and investment. This level is generally enough for them to buy or build a fairly elegant house, belong to social clubs and send their children to the best schools and to university, often abroad. Income beyond this level is not too important. More important is a leisurely life and stable investment in real estate or shares. Extensively operated *haciendas* and *estancias* achieve these aspirations perfectly. From a study of Chile, Kaldor concluded that if large property owners reduced the ratio of consumption to gross income to levels found in Great Britain or North America (30 per cent), the resources released would be sufficient to double fixed capital investment and increase the proportion of net national income made up by net investment from 2 to 14 per cent. Forced diversion of this reservoir of potential domestic capital accumulation from its present destination of luxury consumer expenditure through ceiling and expropriation legislation would, therefore, constitute a powerful economic

effect of land reform. See M. J. Sternberg: 'The economic impact of the latifundista', *Land Reform, Land Settlement and Co-operatives*, 2, 1970, pp. 21–34; J. E. Grunig: 'Economic decision-making and entrepreneurship amongst Colombian latifundistas', *Inter-American Economic Affairs*, 23 (1), 1969, p. 21–46; N. Kaldor: 'Problemas económicos de Chile', *El Trimestre Económico*, 26 (102), 1959, pp. 170–221.

13. Lynn Smith: *op. cit.*, p. 40.

14. Carroll: *op. cit.*, p. 163.

15. The seven-volume ICAD studies have recently been published in an abridged English version: S. L. Barraclough and J. C. Collarte: *Agrarian Structure in Latin America* (Lexington, Heath, 1973).

16. A land reform which gives peasants merely land and production power will fail unless they also get more market power. In regions where landlords cannot resist pressure for land redistribution they concentrate instead on monopolising all market outlets: the landlords thus convert themselves to 'business-lords'. G. Fletschner and K. Wierer: 'The role of agricultural marketing in agrarian reform and land settlement projects, based on the experience in Latin America', *Land Reform, Land Settlement and Co-operatives*, 1, 1972, pp 65–71.

17. Barraclough and Collarte: *op. cit.*, pp. 20–1.

18. M. J. Sternberg: 'Agrarian reform and employment, with special reference to Latin America', *International Labour Review*, 95 (1–2), 1967, pp. 1–26.

19. See R. P. Schaedel: 'Land reform studies', *Latin American Research Review*, 1 (1), 1965, pp. 75–122, esp. pp. 87–8, 91–2.

20. S. Schulman: 'The colono system in Latin America', *Rural Sociology*, 20 (1), 1955, pp. 34–40.

21. Warriner: *op. cit.*, pp. 225–6, 231–2.

22. A direct effect of the Cuban revolution was to encourage agitation and the formation of peasant organisations and syndicates of farm workers in Venezuela and Brazil and on the Peruvian Altiplano. Syndicate activities, however, began before the Cuban uprising, in Venezuela in the mid-1940s and in Brazil in the mid-1950s. Moreover, success has not always been due to communist leadership; in Venezuela the Democratic Action Party defeated the Communists for control of the syndicates, and in Brazil a prominent leadership role has been played by radical priests. In Peru, Castroism gave new impetus to a tradition of peasant agitation established soon after the Mexican revolution. Violence in rural areas of Latin America is not something recently introduced by insurgents or revolutionaries; it is something which has existed for decades. Often it is not so much the existence of the traditional latifundian status quo which provokes peasant agitation as the erosion of this accepted situation by further unreasonable and threatening demands by the landlord elite. The traditional *hacienda* is so embedded in the fabric of rural life as not to be identified as a focus of discontent; rather it is the *modernising hacienda*, replacing men by machines, or evicting workers on the pretext of efficiency, which leads to unrest. This happened, for example, in Pernambuco where the *ligas*

camponesas ('peasant leagues') were formed when a landowner decided to annul all tenancy contracts in order to plant sugar on his estate. Once a rudimentary organisation exists, political leaders from urban areas, such as Hugo Blanco in La Convención (Peru) or Francisco Julião in the North-east of Brazil, generally assume overall leadership, helping the movement to gain regional and even national impact. Poverty alone does not suffice to rouse the peasants; they must be made intellectually aware of their unfortunate position *vis-à-vis* the landowners before they can initiate revolutionary change. There is also considerable evidence that where the landholding elites have most violently opposed the legitimate demands of peasant organisations, the *campesinos*, with or without urban support, have later been able to strike back more drastically. The occupation of *haciendas* in Bolivia's Cochabamba valley (1952–3), and to some degree the massive invasions on the Peruvian *altiplano* (1963–4) confirm the hypothesis that it is this 'elite intransigence' which causes or strengthens peasant revolutionary movements. Latin America appears to face the dilemma that land reform, when seriously undertaken, is an unpredictable business, but may be much more explosive if left undone. Rural tensions are likely to intensify as conditions of income and social justice continue to stagnate or decline while the perception of the possibility of change increases. See G. Huizer: 'Peasant organisations and their potential for change in Latin America', *Land Reform, Land Settlement and Co-operatives*, 2, 1971, pp. 1–8; T. F. Carroll: 'Land reform as an explosive force in Latin America', in J. J. TePaske and S. N. Fisher (eds.): *Explosive Forces in Latin America* (Columbus, Ohio State University, Mershon Center for Education in National Security, 1964), pp 84–125.

23. E. Feder: 'Counter-reform', in R. Stavenhagen (ed.): *Agrarian Problems and Peasant Movements in Latin America* (New York, Doubleday Anchor, 1970), pp. 173–223.

24. J. C. Crossley: 'Agrarian reform in Latin America', *Yearbook of World Affairs*, 17, 1963, pp. 123–49.

25. W. C. Thiesenhusen: 'Colonisation: alternative or supplement to agrarian reform in Latin America', in Dorner (ed.): *op. cit.*, pp. 207–25.

26. E. Feder: 'When is land reform a land reform? The Colombian Case', *American Journal of Economics and Sociology*, 24 (2), 1965, pp. 113–33.

27. An illustration of this comes from eastern Nicaragua where the *Instituto Agrário Nacional* sponsored a study of settlement potential in an 'empty' area of 300 000 hectares in Rigoberto Cabezas region. The first discovery of the investigators was that the place was full of people and there was no possibility of fitting in new settlers! J. R. Taylor: *Agricultural Settlement and Development in Eastern Nicaragua* (Madison, University of Wisconsin, Land Tenure Center Research Paper 33, 1969), p. 1.

28. A. L. Domike: 'Colonisation as an alternative to land reform', in Agency for International Development: *Spring Review of Land Reform* (Washington, Department of State, 1970), Vol. 11, pp. 1, 18.

29. As Crossley points out (*op. cit.*, p. 144), this is to an extent a false

comparison. In spontaneous colonisation resourceful colonists are self-selected by the voluntary nature of the process; in planned schemes colonists are selected, for social reasons, often according to their needs rather than their capabilities.

30. E. Feder: 'The campesinos' perspectives in Latin America', *The Developing Economies*, 7 (2), 1969, pp. 233–45.

31. Feder: 'Counter-reform', *op. cit.*, p. 208.

32. J. F. Petras and R. LaPorte: 'Modernisation from above versus reform from below: US policy towards Latin American agricultural development', *Journal of Development Studies*, 6 (3), 1970, pp. 248–66. The 'Declaration of American Presidents', 1967, openly repudiated the original premise of the Alliance for Progress that development and regional integration should follow and not precede land reform.

33. W. C. Thiesenhusen and M. R. Brown: *Survey of the Alliance for Progress: Problems of Agriculture* (Washington, Government Printing Office, 1967), p. 2.

4

Mexico

Now over sixty years old, the Mexican reform represents the only indigenous example of land reform in Latin America, and one of the major reforms in the underdeveloped world. With over 60 million hectares distributed—nearly half the national land area—its scale is exceeded only by Russia and China; and Mexico's land redistribution has not been followed by collectivisation. Other countries have redistributed their land at one point in time; in Mexico redistribution has become a seemingly permanent process. Continued population growth whittles away large estates in an effort to find land for more farmers. The rural population in 1970, 45 million, was double that in 1940. From its inception to the present day, the Mexican land reform's principal aim has been social justice for the peasantry. In consequence it has often been attacked on economic and defended on socio-political grounds. Most recent evidence tends, however, to reverse this judgment. Impressive long-run economic success can now be demonstrated, but as a means of making Mexican society more democratic, its success to date is 'half-way at best, and in many areas problematic'.[1]

Two themes running through Mexican history—cataclysm and regionalism—significantly influenced the course of Mexican agrarian reform.[2] The reform itself, being a principal element in the 1910 revolution, was born of cataclysm. Its implementation has been conditioned by the extraordinary regional diversity within the country. It was a truly revolutionary reform, reversing a four centuries old process in which 'the *hacienda* gradually gained ascendancy and slowly but steadily devoured the village lands and even the villagers themselves'.[3]

TABLE 3

PROGRESS OF LAND REDISTRIBUTION IN MEXICO, BY ADMINISTRATION

Presidents	Years	Land transferred '000 hectares	Average per year '000 hectares
Venustiano Carranza	1915–20	132	27
Adolfo de la Huerta	May–Nov. 1920	34	67
Alvaro Obregón	1920–4	971	243
Plutarco Elías Calles	1924–8	3 088	792
Emilio Portes Gil	1928–30	1 173	1 006
Pasual Ortiz Rubio	1930–2	1 469	551
Abelardo Rodríguez	1932–4	799	351
Lázaro Cárdenas	1934–40	17 890	2 982
Manuel Avila Camacho	1940–6	5 519	920
Miguel Alemán Valdés	1946–52	3 845	641
Adolfo Ruiz Cortines	1952–8	3 199	533
Adolfo López Mateos	1958–64	16 004	2 667
Gustavo Díaz Ortiz	1964–8	10 252	1 709
Total, 1915–68		64 375	1 215

Source: F. Dovring: 'Land reform in Mexico', in Agency for International Development: *Spring Review of Land Reform* (Washington, Department of State, 1970), Vol. 7, p. 19.

The history of Mexican land reform is long and complex, but well documented. Rates of progress have varied according to the commitment of the government of the day. Land redistribution occurred slowly at first (Table 3), but became rapid under Cárdenas with 18 million hectares distributed to 2¼ million beneficiaries during the period from 1935 to 1940. It then slackened until 1958, but again accelerated under the administrations of López Mateos and Díaz Ortiz, when reform turned more towards creating new settlements and reclaiming virgin land. These two presidents dealt with 26 million hectares during 1958–68, but the process is now considered virtually complete and no further fundamental tenure changes are expected.

RURAL LIFE BEFORE 1910

The pre-reform agrarian structure embraced overcrowded

comunidades, traditional under-used *haciendas* and irrigated commercial plantations which developed along with the railways in the nineteenth century. The extraordinary concentration of land in Mexico in 1910—1 per cent of the population owned 97 per cent of the land; 92 per cent of the rural population were landless—was probably then the highest in the world.[4] As elsewhere in Latin America, the *hacienda* evolved out of the earlier *encomienda* system, the concession in trust by the Spanish crown of one or more Indian villages for administration, tax collection and inculcation of Christianity. The accumulating of private holdings which began under Spanish rule accelerated greatly during the later nineteenth century, partly because of misdirected reforms. The 1856 *Leyes de Desamortización* (Law of Expropriation), remodelled in the 1857 Constitution, prohibited ecclesiastical and civic corporations from possessing farmland. Liquidation of the vast church lands, thought in 1850 to comprise half the country's territory, was justified but the various Indian communities, especially numerous in the central *mesa* and in the south, being classified as corporate bodies, also had to break up their *comunidades* into individual holdings. Further laws rescinded communities' rights to use stream water for irrigation, thus rendering much land useless and forcing its abandonment. In this 'rape of the *pueblos*' most Indian land was simply 'absorbed into the great *hacienda* or gobbled up by unscrupulous speculators'; by 1910 90 per cent of the villages and towns on the central Mexican plateau had no communal lands of any kind.[5]

In 1883 a new development greatly intensified concentration of land and dispossession of Indian farms. To encourage development through immigration and colonisation of public land, Porfirio Díaz issued a decree granting 'survey companies' one third of the land they were to develop and authorising them to take possession of titleless small private holdings sited within colonisation areas. Unable to prove ownership of land they held by customary right, thousands of Indians became landless. On one estimate over 54 million hectares, 27 per cent of the national area, were acquired by a few individuals and companies during the thirty-five-year Díaz regime.[6] This upheaval in the land situation has been called the 'New Conquest'.[7]

McBride paints a vivid portrait of the Mexican *hacienda* before 1910[8]. The *hacienda* was not just a large estate: it was a society, under private auspices. Economically self-sufficient with its farms, pastures, woods, streams and sometimes minerals, it was also often a local political unit (*municipio*) with several villages under the control of the *latifundista*, thus promoting *caciquismo*, regional power centres based on large landholdings. With its post office, store, church, cemetery, jail and (less often) school, the *hacienda* also served as a basic community and welfare organisation, but this function, even when it was effective, was at best paternalistic. In North-west Mexico, where land was in greater supply than labour, landowners employed a debt slavery system to control the labour available. *Hacienda* stores, called *tiendas de raya*, gave peasants credit for food, cloth and ceremonial goods, thus binding them into debt. Many landowners forbade their *peones* to plant subsistence plots until all debts were repaid, which made it virtually impossible to become independent of the *tienda de raya*. Peasants endeavouring to escape were pursued by the *sobrasalientes*, the *hacienda* policemen, and brought back to suffer various punishments and indignities. Even more important, the accumulated debt could be passed from father to son, tying families to a *hacienda* for generations. Since frequently peasants were forbidden to move away or buy elsewhere than at the *hacienda* store, little distinguished this life from slavery.[9] Most rural Mexicans found themselves in this situation at the time of the revolution. The 1910 census indicated that 3 million peons were held in service for debt, a figure which represents at least 10 million people, two-thirds of the population. Subsistence peasants, either in Indian communities, or as tenants attached to *haciendas*, numbered only a few hundred thousand.

The Mexican land reform, then, was projected against a backdrop of dispossession of the weak by the powerful. By rigorously exercising their monopoly control the large landowners were able to keep agricultural wages stable while cost of living persistently rose. According to Simpson[10] agricultural wages remained practically stationary during the period from 1792 to 1908. Between 1900 and 1910 peon incomes actually fell 17 per cent whilst the price of corn rose 38 per cent, wheat 42 per cent, beans 58 per cent and sugar 22 per cent. This, and the inequitable landholding pattern, are the crucial factors which made the revolution inevitable. Control of land allowed domination and deprivation of the personal liberties of the peasants; hence, in Mexican eyes, land and liberty were intertwined.

MADERO, ZAPATA AND THE REVOLUTION

Jesus Silva-Herzog attributes the cause of the Mexican revolution to four 'hungers'—hunger for freedom, for food, for land and for justice.[11] Before 1910 the peasant masses, lacking financial support, leaders and any regional organisation outside the confines of single *haciendas*, were in no position to rebel. They were, however, increasingly conscious of their worsening plight, with news of better conditions offered to migrant workers in the United States and of higher wages—up to four times rural levels —in Mexican industry, mining and railway construction.[12] Returning workers from the United States brought back ideas that were revolutionary in the Mexican context. Indeed, it was no accident that many early leaders of the revolution had had experience of the United States.[13]

But the initial leadership for the revolution came actually from a wealthy *hacendado*, Francisco Madero, who challenged Díaz for the presidential election of 1910, incorporating in his election programme a commitment to democratic reform. Having had Madero jailed, Díaz declared himself re-elected, but Madero escaped into Texas, where he declared himself 'provisional president' and issued, with his *Plan de San Luis Potosí*, the call for revolution. The Plan contained only one brief paragraph dealing with land reform, but this did more than any other part of the document to rally rural workers to the cause, once the insurrection started.

The northern state of Chihuahua saw the first armed rebellion, led by Pascual Orozco and Francisco ('Pancho') Villa. Further south, in the state of Morelos, Emiliano Zapata, Mexico's outstanding peasant leader, recruited peons from the sugar estates to rebel against their masters, the 'sugar barons'. Soon, revolt raged in a dozen Mexican states, and the government appeared helpless. Díaz resigned in 1911 and Madero, enjoying widespread popular support, became president.

Madero was the precipitating agent in transforming Zapata's local peasant organisation into a national agrarian movement, but the two revolutionaries soon parted. Madero believed that smallholdings offered the best means of reducing the economic

and social degradation of rural areas. He was unaware that the
Indian had little concept of private land ownership, and neither
he nor his advisors seriously considered the role of the communal holding or *ejido* in an agrarian programme. When Zapata
realised this, he formulated his own *Plan de Ayala* late in 1911.
This demanded more radical land reform measures attuned to
the Indians' real needs and aspirations, acclaimed Orozco as
head of the insurgents instead of Madero, who had 'betrayed into the hands of the *hacendados* and other monopolistic interests'.
Madero was forced from office in 1913 and assassinated soon
after.

Meanwhile the peasant groups continued the guerilla struggle
against the government and the *hacendados*. Each guerilla band
saw the revolution as revenge against the local *hacendado* or
cacique, but Zapata welded these local and regional movements
into a national consciousness. His historic role was to focus the
Mexican revolution on the vital land question. And where he
had control, he distributed land to the peasants. Participation in
Zapatista forces gave peasants a new psychology. Indeed Zapata's
charismatic personality and leadership ability were perhaps the
most important factors in Mexico's agrarian revolution.[14]

In 1915 President Carranza, in order to weaken and win over
the peasant revolutionary forces, which by now practically controlled Mexico City, issued a decree, generally considered the
formal starting point of Mexican land reform, incorporating the
main points of Zapata's programme. The decree contained two
main points: (1) that all alienation of village lands which had
taken place through misapplication of the 1856 law, through
acts of survey companies or through other illegal means be null
and void; and (2) that villages (of specific types) needing lands,
but lacking proof of former titles, qualified to receive lands expropriated from adjacent properties. Unfortunately only certain villages outside of *haciendas* could benefit from the latter
proposal; villages within *haciendas*, even though they had the
greatest needs, were unaffected.[15]

Since, however, the decree got no effective execution, Zapata's groups continued with redistribution and maintained
military control over large areas. Partly through this continued
peasant pressure, the ideas of the *Plan de Ayala* were integrated
into Article 27 of the new Mexican Constitution of 1917. Among

E

other things, Article 27 covered restitution of land to villages which had been illegally dispossessed, granting of land to villages in need of it and creation of new centres of agricultural population.[16] Despite this official ratification, however, effective redistribution still covered only those areas where the peasants were well organised and had arms to combat the 'white guards', the gunmen groups who defended the landlords' interests. Fighting continued till 1920 (Zapata was assassinated in 1919), when Obregón replaced Carranza with the express purpose of carrying out the objectives of the revolution, thereby ending its military phase.

NATURE AND PROGRESS OF MEXICAN LAND REFORM

The Mexican land reform enjoyed a start uncomplicated by international ideological rivalries. Gutelman describes the 'new order' born of the revolution as something 'specifically Mexican'.[17] The resultant pattern of land tenure became an eclectic mixture of private and public, individual and collective ownership. Early on, restitution of Indian lands in communal *ejido* tenure was emphasised. Later, a second method, *dotación* (endowment or grant) dominated land reform (accounting in fact for 79 per cent of the land distributed between 1916 and 1944). This was applied when a village petitioned for land to meet its need rather than for resumption of land formerly utilised.

Obregón's Ejido Law, subsequently incorporated into the Agrarian Regulatory Law of 1922, firmly established the *ejido* as the basic tenure institution of Mexican land reform. The legal processes for villages to petition for restitution or *dotación* were laid down. The size of *ejido* plots was fixed at 4 hectares of irrigated or 8 hectares of unirrigated land.[18] Settlements on abandoned *haciendas* as well as the non-*hacienda* 'free' villages were eligible to secure land, but resident labourers on estates were still excluded.

The law reflected the strong pressures of the *agraristas* of the Zapata tradition on and within the government. Many of these were young agronomists, former university students who had supervised Zapata's distribution of the first estates in 1915. They continuously struggled against the 'men from the north'—Villa, Obregón, Carranza and others—who maintained that individual ownership, not the *ejido*, should be the goal of land reform.[19]

Calles (successor to Obregón) in particular became disenchanted with the *ejido* programme. In 1930 he branded it a failure, and by 1931 *ejido* distribution had petered out in many states, partly because many state governors, closely allied with landowners' interest, were able to obstruct land reform actions. Also around this time the peasant organisations and unions, which had been particularly powerful and successful in states like Morelos, Yucatán and Veracruz, began to be absorbed by the slow-moving central government and taken over by politicians whose interests rarely coincided with the peasants.[20] In 1934 Marjorie Ruth Clark observed that 'agrarianism has become a political game second to no other in Mexico... the peasant is always, either directly or indirectly, under the control of some political faction'.[21] Catholicism was also a generally conservative influence in the land reform context. Economically dependent upon the *hacienda* system, rural priests taught the peasants that land redistribution was contrary to God's will (the priests maintained that the *agraristas* were *agaristas*, robbers) and that the peon owed his *hacendado* implicit obedience. Under such religious guidance many indigenous communities refused ejidal lands offered to them by state governments.[22]

The agrarianists, however, managed to push through the important Agrarian Code of 1934. Besides solidifying and clarifying previous gains of *ejido* policy, this decree accelerated land distribution by enabling village groups to obtain possession of petitioned land within 150 days. The *ejido* programme made its greatest progress between 1934 and 1940, during Cárdenas's presidency, because he shared the *agraristas*' commitment to the *ejido* principle and, unlike Calles, believed in its economic viability. Under Cárdenas 18 million hectares were distributed to 1 million beneficiaries and 10 650 *ejidos* were set up: in all cases these figures represent more than twice the totals for all previous years since 1915. The *ejido* became a pillar of the national farm economy and a greater commitment to rural infrastructure —irrigation, medical services, schools, sanitation—was evident. Land use patterns and the agrarian landscape, as well as rural class relationships, were profoundly modified. By 1945 the area in *ejidal* tenure represented half the total cropland. Co-operative working of *ejidos* was added to simple group ownership; some

500 co-operatively worked *ejidos* (misleadingly called 'collectives') were created where whole *haciendas* were expropriated, often complete with buildings and other farm equipment. The first such new approach was in the rich Laguna region, previously untouched by land reform. Other important communal land reform areas in the Cárdenas era included Yucatán, the Yaqui Valley of Sonora, the Mexicali region of Lower California, Nueva Italia and Nueva Lombardia in Michoacán, and Los Mochis, Sinaloa, although some of these have since replaced their original co-operative organisation by the working of private farms.

Even under Cárdenas, however, a change of policy became evident. At the beginning he gave rifles to 6000 peasants to fight the landlords' white guards, but after 1937 the amount of land distributed declined rapidly, and a firmer commitment to individual ownership became apparent. Small and medium-size private properties grew in number from 610 000 in 1930 to 1 211 000 in 1940.[23] In 1937, to protect the livestock industry, since many cattle ranchers had stopped investing in their enterprises for fear of expropriation, an addition to the 1934 Agrarian Code allowed retention of land sufficient to support 500 adult cattle. This law had an unforeseen effect: it led to the hidden persistence of *latifundia* as simulated cattle-breeding establishments. A new agrarian code of 1940 favoured commercial farming by allowing retention of 300 hectares of irrigated plantation land growing crops such as bananas, coffee and fruit trees.

More important, the Cárdenas period saw the country increasingly unable to feed itself. In productivity, the *ejidos* vegetated. Cárdenas tried to solve the problem by starting new irrigation projects linked to *ejidos* producing industrial crops with processing factories attached. But the weakness of Mexican agriculture became critically apparent with the outbreak of the Second World War and the reduced possibility of importing food.

The main slogan of governments after Cárdenas became increased food output. Two main policies were followed: intensifying production; and extending the area cultivated, particularly by the 'march to the sea'—the opening up of new coastal lands in the humid south and the arid north. Irrigation featured in both policies. *Ejido* land distribution, politically essential, was

still pursued, but less rapidly. In the three presidential administrations following Cárdenas land distribution amounted to
12·5 million hectares (in 18 years) compared to 17·9 million
hectares under Cárdenas's six years. Expansion of the arable area
through irrigation exceeded growth in the ejidal sector so that the
ejido share of total arable land fell from 53 per cent to 40 per cent
between 1940 and 1960. Newly irrigated land, which under
Cárdenas had been granted only to *ejidos*, was distributed to
ejidos and private landowners alike, since new projects had to
pay for themselves quickly. This production-oriented policy
produced faster agricultural growth in Mexico between 1945
and 1960 than in any other Latin American country. Farming
efficiency in the newly irrigated zones was the highest in the
continent.

The main feature of this period was the rise of the 'middle
sector', the private commercial farmers. In 1943 the Agrarian
Code was again adapted to give more protection to this group,
which included *hacendados* with their residual holdings of 100–
300 hectares. The increasing control of the country's economy by
the middle sector at the expense of peasants' interests was particularly evident during the Alemán regime, 1946–52. While
commercial profits were high, the real value of the agricultural
minimum wage fell by 46 per cent between 1940 and 1950.
Landlessness increased. Chevalier indicates that only a few
thousand *ejidatarios*—perhaps 2 or 3 per cent of the total—
benefited from the spectacular agricultural development of
Mexico, which tripled its farm production between 1940 and
1955.[24]

Against this tendency of further peasant exploitation by the
'middle sector', land invasions re-started in the mid-1950s, among the most spectacular being invasions into the lands of the
US Cananea Cattle Group in Sonora. These lands were legally
open to expropriation not only because of their size but also because, according to the Constitution, no foreigners may own
land within 100 kilometres of the national frontier. The local
peasants had long petitioned unsuccessfully for expropriation,
although the government of Adolfo Ruiz Cortines (1952–58)
took initial steps to acquire the 400 000 hectare estates. The lands
of the Cananea Cattle Company were finally expropriated in
1958, heralding the second major wave of Mexican land re-

distribution. López Mateos, president 1958–64, granted 16 million hecares, almost as much as Cárdenas, to the *ejidos*, in response to increasing land hunger and influenced by the Cuban revolution. These figures exaggerate the importance of recent land redistribution, however, because a large proportion of the transferred land was of low productivity and in pastures.

THE EJIDO: PRODIGY OR PROBLEM-CHILD OF MEXICO'S LAND REFORM?

Identification of the land reform with the *ejido* has brought a marked separation of the reform sector from other Mexican agriculture. The *ejido*, championed by the *agraristas*, has its own ideology and its own servicing institutions.[25] Chevalier stresses the antiquity and complexity of the *ejido*;[26] Aztec tenure operated on similar principles. Yet surprisingly little detailed field work has been done on *ejidos*.[27]

In the early post-revolutionary period the *ejido* represented little more than the rejuvenation of traditional village communities which had lost out against nineteenth-century *hacienda* expansion. Groups of *peones acasillados* (workers residing on *haciendas*) could not until 1934 form new centres of population endowed with *ejidos*. It was also not until the Agrarian Code of 1934 that the local government of the *ejido* became formally distinct from that of the village, with the formation of the three-member *ejido* committee (*comisariado ejidal*), which is, together with the 'vigilance teams', still the organisation today.

Both the *ejido* committee and the vigilance committee are elected by all *ejido* members in the *ejido's* general assembly. The *ejido* committee is an executive body to manage the affairs of the *ejido*. The three members serve as chairman, secretary and treasurer, elected for three-year terms. The vigilance committee supervises the work of the *ejido* committee and of individual *ejidatarios*. It is particularly charged with seeing that the land is used in the best possible manner, and that *ejido* investments are sensibly made. General assemblies also elect a 'work-chief' or foreman, and his assistants (warehouseman, herdsman, co-operative store manager etc.). The work-chief is the key man, especially in collectively-run *ejidos*, for he details the work to each member, noting what is assigned and accomplished, and to what weekly compensation members are entitled. He also records daily use of the *ejido's* machinery, animals, fuels and other resources, and maintains close liaison with the Ejidal Bank, established in 1936 as the source of agricultural credit to *ejidatarios*.[28]

The differentiation between 'collective' and 'individual' *ejidos* applies only to crop lands, for all pastures, woodlands and other non-cultivated land (except house plots) are held in common. Collective *ejidos* were mostly set up on plantation lands (such as the henequen estates of Yucatán) or on *haciendas* expropriated as large single units (such as the Laguna cotton farms). Elsewhere *ejidos* chose by majority vote which form they adopted. Workers on a collective *ejido* have a 'certificate of agrarian rights' but no individual land ownership or use rights beyond a house plot; there are no 'private plots' such as have been so important in Russian and Chinese agriculture. Members of an 'individual' *ejido* receive a usufruct title to their land. They cannot sell, lease, rent, mortgage or alienate the land in any way, but the use title is hereditary. Loss of title may occur by non-use for two years or by other irregularities.[29]

Ejido and private tenure are commonly depicted as two independent, geographically separate and mutually exclusive systems. In fact they function side by side, often spatially intertwined in the village landholding patterns (Fig. 1), with *ejidatarios* and smallholders living in the village as neighbours. The total population of an *ejido* may vary from fewer than 100 to several thousand. In the smaller villages where *ejidos* have been established or in newly settled villages resulting directly from the formation of an *ejido*, the *ejido* and the village are virtually coexistent. Larger villages may contain two or more *ejidos*; or the *ejido* population may constitute only a fraction of the total population of a market town. Sometimes the *ejidatario* and the private plotholder are one and the same person, for 18 per cent of *ejidatarios* also own small private plots. The lands of an *ejido* do not necessarily form a contiguous block; often they are interrupted by the remnants of pre-existing *haciendas* and by private smallholdings. As the *hacendado* was allowed to choose which part of his estate he retained as his residual holding, he naturally chose the best parts of his property, which stretched the pattern of the resulting tenure map.[30]

Most *ejidos* are now cultivated as small individual plots; only

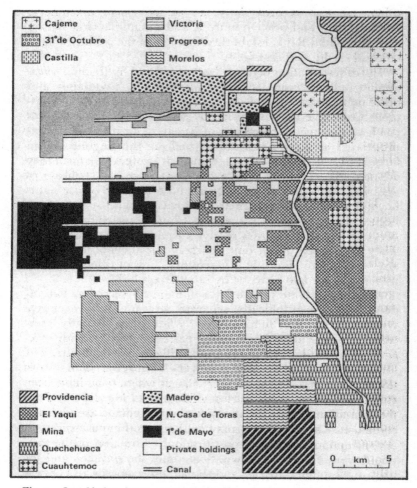

Fig. 1.   Land belonging to 14 *ejidos* in the Yaqui Valley, Mexico. *Source:* N. L. Whetten: *Rural Mexico* (Chicago, University of Chicago Press, 1948), p. 183

2–3 per cent are farmed wholly collectively. Area-wise in 1960 there were 338 621 hectares of communally farmed *ejido* cropland as against 9 990 625 hectares individually farmed. From 700 in the 1940s, collective *ejidos* declined in number to under 200 by the 1960s. Chevalier describes how *ejidatarios* have increasingly approximated to freeholding small farmers.[31] Wherever the *ejidos* have been drawn into a dynamic agricultural or urban economy, some of the *ejidatarios* have become 'little landlords' or 'little capitalists', renting out their land or working with hired labour (even though such practices are illegal). In the Valley of Mexico half the *ejidatarios* rent out or sharecrop their land so that they can work in industry in and around Mexico City. In the Yacqui Valley 38 per cent of the *ejidatarios* rent 30 per cent of *ejidal* land to outside interests. *Ejidatarios* growing cotton hire 85 per cent of their labour requirement. The fathers of the Mexican revolution certainly did not envisage the *ejidatario* as an absentee landlord, but in states like Sonora this is his best chance of sharing in the new prosperity.[32]

The internal politics of the reform have been marred by factionalism. The granting of land not to individuals but to communities in the first instance structured the reform for conflict arising from the allocation of land within the communities.[33] Relations between the government and the *ejidos* are paternalistic and bureaucratic networks have proliferated; only Cárdenas genuinely attempted to make the *ejidos* self-sustaining democratic institutions. *Ejidos* tend socially to be rather closed, immobile institutions; mobility is often achieved only by contravening the *ejido* laws.[34]

Many problems of the *ejido* system stem from the rapid, unco-ordinated nature of the distribution, especially in the late 1930s. In setting general norms for the size of plots assigned, varieties of land quality were ignored, and no attempt was made to organise regional areas into logical producing units or to adapt holding size to the type of crop produced. *Ejido* holdings averaged 27 hectares (but only 7 hectares of cropland). Only 15 per cent of *ejidatarios* received over 10 hectares of cropland (the prescribed minimum), and 44 per cent got less than 4 hectares. In Tlaxcala state, where rural population is acute, most holdings were only 1 hectare. Boundary disputes proliferated. Time for thoroughly investigating all recipients' eligibility to receive land was inadequate. It is generally admitted that errors were made, but, in the fluctuations of Mexican politics, delaying the reform to plan it more thoroughly might have meant that land would never have been assigned.

COLLECTIVE EJIDOS IN LA LAGUNA

Although collectively-run *ejidos* are now a minority, they are conceptually the most interesting feature of Mexican land reform, and they deserve a closer look, if only to explain why they have seemingly failed to 'catch on'. The Laguna region, where the collective ideal has been most severely tested, will get special attention.

La Laguna, an irrigated basin amid the aridity of northern Mexico, is the country's major cotton-producing region. Imported capitalism mated with rural feudalism to produce a hybrid set of socio-economic institutions different from the rest of Mexico. One of the first revolutionary actions of the peasants was to shoot out the church bells because they had been tolled every morning to call them to the day's toil from which they could return only when they tolled again. Yet reform action was delayed. Then, in 45 days in 1936, following a wave of strikes by the *hacienda* workers, Cárdenas expropriated about three-quarters of the irrigated land and one-quarter of the usable unirrigated land in the region. This land, 447 500 hectares, was turned over to 35 000 workers, organised in over 300 communally-run *ejidos*.

A serious problem was the inclusion of seasonal migrant workers amongst those eligible for land. This burdened the *ejidos* with thousands of persons who were not full-time farmers in the area. Beneficiaries received from 4 to 10 hectares but only 1 hectare, on average, was irrigated: the rest was virtual desert. About 7000 peasants, one-sixth of the total legally entitled to receive land, many of them farmers in the area for generations, could not receive *ejido* places. High natural increase exacerbated demographic pressure. La Laguna's population grew at 4·8 per cent per year between 1940 and 1950; the national figure was 2·9 per cent.[36] Moreover, the expropriation procedure denied the *ejidos* the best land, kept by the *hacendados* in their 150 hectare residual plots, top heavy with buildings, equipment and communications. *Ejidatarios*, inheriting only the periphery of formerly efficient economic units, were forced to request the *hacendado* for warehouse space, permission to cross his property for access to market, even drinking water. In 1948 the *ejidos*, with 70 per cent of the land, had only a third of the irrigation wells.[37]

Apart from Cárdenas' commitment to collectively-run *ejidos*, local factors favoured this mode of operation.[38] The region, already farmed in well-organised estates, was of primary importance to the nation's economy. The syndicalist movement, besides being prominent in bringing about the reform, also assisted in persuading the emancipated peasants to adopt the communal system. Many locals were already used to working in specialised teams. Finally, the local irrigation method, flooding large squares of 100 hectares, ruled out individually irrigated smallholdings. Despite initial handicaps, the co-operative *ejido* experiment showed early promise of success. Pre-reform wheat production was already surpassed in 1937-8, and that of cotton in 1941-2, and the upward trend continued. With *ejidatarios* working 232 days per year on average, income per capita also increased, and a healthy co-operative structure was being developed.

This situation was altered by the 1940 presidential change. The collective *ejidos* were disliked on political rather than economic grounds. The Ejido Bank had its funds cut; several important investment projects were curtailed or cancelled. Corruption in the rural sector spread, causing the collapse of many co-operative enterprises. The collective units degenerated into smaller factions or societies organised politically around local leaders or spatially around irrigation wells jointly owned by several families. Little remains of the successful collective *ejidos* of forty years ago. The picture now is one 'of failure, of hopeless stagnation, of chronic problems with no apparent solution'.[39] With less than five years of sustained government support, they were given no chance to prove their worth.

PRESENT AGRARIAN STRUCTURE

Land reform brought a profound change in Mexico's land tenure structure.[40] The predominant *latifundia* have been replaced by a large *ejido* sector with egalitarian distribution of usufruct rights within each community (but not necessarily between *ejidos*). The remaining private farm sector is much less dominated by large units than before; those existing are largely confined to tropical jungle and semi-desert areas. The 900 000 private properties exceeding 100 hectares contain two-thirds of Mexican land, but mostly in extensive grazing incapable of

TABLE 4

MEXICAN LAND TENURE STRUCTURE; 1930, 1940, 1950, 1960

	Private holdings over 5 hectares	Private holdings under 5 hectares	Ejidos
No. of Holdings			
1930	277 473	476 588	4 189
1940	290 336	928 593	14 680
1950	360 798	1 004 835	17 579
1960	447 334	899 108	18 699
Total holding area (m hectares)			
1930	122·4	0·9	8·3
1940	98·7	1·2	28·9
1950	105·3	1·4	38·9
1960	132·3	1·3	44·5
Cropland area (m hectares)			
1930	11·9	0·8	1·9
1940	6·8	1·1	7·0
1950	9·9	1·3	8·8
1960	12·2	1·3	10·3

Source: F. Dovring: 'Land reform in Mexico', in Agency for International Development: *Spring Review of Land Reform* (Washington, Department of State, 1970), Vol. 7, p. 31.

smallholder or *ejido* development. Private farms over 5 hectares have increased in number but declined in average size. The *ejidos* in 1960 held 26 per cent of agriculture and forest land, 43 per cent of the arable land, and 41 per cent of the irrigated land. Table 4 gives more details.

These figures from the 1960 census conceal the dynamics of a changing situation, however. Between 1950 and 1960, reflecting rapid population growth, the agricultural labour force increased by 33 per cent. Over the same period, *ejidatarios* increased by only 9 per cent, and private farmers diminished by almost 5 per cent because of renewed land concentration in the private sector. Landless labourers, consequently, increased by 60 per cent from 2 million to 3·3 million. This swelling pool of agricultural wage-labourers now constitutes over half the rural population but receives only 8 per cent of total agricultural income. Thousands of them are migrant workers, following generally fixed seasonal circuits according to the needs of various crops in different parts of the country. They enjoy limited legal protection; they have no social security, education or medical services; their housing is of the poorest. In Stavenhagen's words, they are Mexico's forgotten class, an incipient proletariat.[41]

The 1960 census recorded 2 321 227 *ejido* families (population 12·3 million), of whom 1 523 796 had land holdings, 738 955 were landless, and 723 536 were 'associated *ejidatarios*'. On the *ejidos*, therefore, live not only plot-holding *ejidatarios*, but also many persons more or less associated with them as relatives or as semi-employed seasonal labourers and migrants. Assertions of ample available and unused land to solve these demographic problems are refuted by elementary arithmetic.[42] Only a modified agrarian policy entailing lowering the ceiling for expropriation could change the nature of the present agrarian problem.

THE PRODUCTIVITY ISSUE

Much debate on Mexican land reform focuses on productivity, but strong ideological positions account for much inconclusiveness. It is in fact difficult to establish criteria and standards by which to judge competing but very different institutions. The productivity objective has been kept decidedly low key; defenders of the reform have been rather apologetic of its short term effects on farm output, emphasising instead the social achievements of providing peasants with land and a minimum assured income. Recent studies (notably by Dovring), however, having analysed long term farm production figures, have shown that land reform has in fact made an important contribution to a rate of growth of agricultural output which was one of the fastest in the world between 1930 and 1960.[43]

Also of interest are the differences, if any, in output performance between the *ejido* and private sectors. Table 5 indicates that between 1940 and 1960 *ejidos* performed creditably, particularly in crop production (a more realistic index since the total agricultural product index includes livestock which is dominated by large privately-owned northern ranches), and particularly from 1950 to 1960. The *ejido* performance is all the more satisfactory considering that *ejidos* have less irrigated area, poorer access to credit (under a quarter of *ejidatarios* received credit in 1968), and are often located on poorer soils. The some-

what larger output increases on the larger private farms than on
ejidos accompanied significantly greater increases in capital inputs. In 1960 *ejidos* (with 45 per cent of the farm labour force,

TABLE 5

CROP INDICES FOR MEXICAN TENURE GROUPS, 1940–50–60

	Total farm output			Crop production		
	1960	*1960*	*1950*	*1960*	*1960*	*1950*
	1940	*1950*	*1940*	*1940*	*1950*	*1940*
Ejidos	210	154	136	223	170	131
Private farms < 5 hectares	142	93	152	168	112	150
Private farms > 5 hectares	364	184	198	323	166	195
Total	256	155	165	262	163	161

Source: F. Dovring: *Land Reform and Productivity: The Mexican Case, Analysis of
Census Data* (Madison, University of Wisconsin, Land Tenure Center Paper
63, 1969), p. 8.

34 per cent of land value and 27 per cent of farm capital) produced 36 per cent of total agricultural output and supplied 34
per cent of all farm products marketed. For every £1000 capital
invested in farming, *ejidos* produce crops to the value of £955,
the private farms of below 5 hectares £698, and the larger
private farms £763.[44] Mueller's study,[45] based on an output
index covering 28 crops, showed production indices of 400 for
private farms (all sizes) for 1960 (1940 = 100), and 242 for
ejidos; but for just the second decade (1950 = 100), performance
is identical at 161. If, further, output is measured against certain
critical aggregated inputs a 'total productivity' index is obtained which incorporates the *ejido* sector's deficiency in strategic capital inputs. The figures then become, for 1960 measured
against 1940, *ejido* sector 133 and private sector 187; and for
1960 measured against 1950, *ejidos* 127, private farms 118.

MEXICAN LAND REFORM: AN INTERPRETATION

Mexico's land reform has not been an integrated policy but
an organic process. Almost any lesson can be derived from this
long and varied experience. Above all it is an argument for
confidence in long-term prospects. According to White[46] the
most remarkable characteristic of the Mexican agrarian revolu-

tion was the completeness with which it overturned not only the land tenure system and the power structure but the value premises supporting the plantation-*hacienda* system. Yet more important to present-day Mexico is the fact that the Mexican revolution, unlike the Russian and Chinese revolutions, did not completely destroy the old power groups. The landowners and their allies—the Church, the bankers, the industrialists—were weakened but lived on. The laissez-faire policy that failed to control the free play of market forces which circumvented the reform laws is mainly responsible for the reappearance of *caciquismo* in the countryside. Mexican economists increasingly realise the need for 'reforming the land reform' in order to free *ejidatarios* and other peasants from the effects of uncontrolled market forces and to give the increasing number of landless labourers a better living. New *latifundia*, particularly in the rich irrigated lands of the north, have been formed by dividing up large landholdings under different registered names. In the Yaqui valley 85 proprietors control 116 800 hectares of the best irrigated land, which are registered under 1191 different names. In reality each landowner possesses 1400 hectares, not 98 hectares as a superficial impression would indicate.[47]

The social depression of low status agricultural workers is accentuated by regional differentiation.[48] Generally land reform has gone farthest on the central plateau, which includes much of the old Indian village areas, and is less comprehensive in the northern states, which have expanded through irrigation-settlement schemes in recent decades. The Gulf region also now ranks high in reform accomplishment. Most states have 35–65 per cent of their total cropland under *ejidos* and smallholdings; the extremes are Morelos (85 per cent) and Quintana Roo (17 per cent). Regional disparities in Mexican agriculture are increasing; farm output per cultivated hectare is three times as high in Sonora as in Oaxaca. Stavenhagen calls this a kind of 'internal colonialism' by which Indian states like Guerrero, Oaxaca and Chiapas are becoming progressively poorer, losing their best human and natural resources under the political and economic domination of the *mestizo* class.[49]

If the social results of Mexican land reform were highly positive initially but are problematic in the long run, economically the reverse holds true. Flores interprets land reform as the key to Mexico's economic success: why Mexico is the sole Latin American country to achieve agricultural self-sufficiency and become a net food exporter.[50] Compensation to expropriated landowners was minimal, thus relieving the government of an important potential burden. The dual farm size and tenure structure that resulted from the land reform has probably served the economic development of the country rather well.

REFERENCES

1. F. Dovring: 'Land Reform in Mexico', in Agency for International Development: *Spring Review of Land Reform* (Washington, Department of State, 1970), Vol. 7, p. 52.
2. F. Tannenbaum: *Mexico: The Struggle for Peace and Bread* (New York, Knopf, 1950), p. 20.
3. N. Whetten: *Rural Mexico* (Chicago, University of Chicago Press, 1948), p. 75.
4. H. C. Tai: *Land Reform and Politics: A Comparative Analysis* (Berkeley, University of California Press, 1974), p. 26.
5. E. N. Simpson: *The Ejido—Mexico's Way Out* (Chapel Hill, University of North Carolina Press, 1937), pp. 25, 29, 31.
6. H. Phipps: *Some Aspects of the Agrarian Question in Mexico: A Historical Study* (Austin, University of Texas Press, 1925), pp. 110–15.
7. The Díaz régime seemed intent on carving the nation into huge principalities. The entire state of Morelos belonged to just 32 people. In the state of Hidalgo the main railway passed through the Escandón estates for 144 km. 78 per cent of Lower California belonged to foreign companies, 17 of whom owned 38 million hectares. Tannenbaum: *op. cit.*, pp. 137–40.
8. G. M. McBride: *The Land Systems of Mexico* (New York, American Geographical Society, 1923).
9. Americans and other industrialists entering Mexico at the turn of the century to build roads and railways and develop mining could secure labour only by 'buying' peons by paying off their debts to *hacendados*. C. B. Parkes: *A History of Mexico* (Boston, Houghton Mifflin, 1960), pp. 305–8.
10. Simpson: *op. cit.*, pp. 37–8.
11. J. Silva-Herzog: *Un Ensayo sobre la Revolución Mexicana* (Mexico, Cuadernos Americanos, 1946), p. 21.
12. Mexican industry was at the height of a wave of prosperity when the revolution came. The national income quintupled under Díaz; this was called the 'Mexican Meiji' period. National prosperity was generated especially by the *científicos*, the new moneyed class of creole 'scientific planners' who became prominent around 1890 and who represented new business and financial interests. If Mexico was pros-

perous, the peasants, however, were not. M. Gutleman: *Réforme et Mystification Agraires en Amérique Latine: Le Cas du Mexique* (Paris, Maspero, 1971), pp. 25, 45.

13. J. Silva-Herzog: *El Agrarismo Mexicano y la Reforma Agraria* (Mexico, Fondo de Cultura Económica, 1959), p. 131.

14. In Emiliano Zapata were all the qualities of the Indian and peasant at their best: dogged determination, ability to sustain suffering, loyalty to his people, a quiet wisdom, a directness and a lack of pretence, a love of the countryside. His peasants could communicate with him, and he understood them. See. R. A. White: 'Mexico: the Zapata movement and the revolution', in H. A. Landsberger (ed.): *Latin American Peasant Movements* (Ithaca, Cornell University Press, 1969), pp. 101–69.

15. Whetten: *op. cit.*, pp. 114–15.

16. See *Ibid*: pp. 117–22, 616–22 for translation and commentary of Article 27.

17. Gutelman: *op. cit.*, p. 22.

18. These levels were increased to 6 hectares irrigated and 12 hectares seasonal in 1943, and to 10 hectares and 20 hectares in 1947, but have rarely been adhered to. Whetten: *op. cit.*, pp. 136–7.

19. When the north was settled in the modern era, small to medium size *mestizo* farms developed, there being few settled Indians. In the twentieth century the north has been a region of sparse settlement, and cattle grazing, with rich nuclei of irrigation farming. It had no history of *ejidos*. The leaders from this zone, being both geographically and intellectually closer to the United States, had little sympathy with communal Indian tenures. They were nationalistic enough, but only marginally were they part of the culture which produced such fierce demands for redistribution of Indian lands. White: *op. cit.*, pp. 117, 163–4.

20. G. Huizer: 'Peasant organisation in agrarian reform in Mexico', in I. L. Horowitz (ed.): *Masses in Latin America* (New York, Oxford University Press, 1970), pp. 445–502.

21. M. R. Clark: *Organised Labour in Mexico* (Chapel Hill, University of North Carolina Press, 1934), pp. 161–2.

22. Huizer: *op. cit.*, pp. 454, 462, 472–3.

23. A fair number of these were, apparently, estate lands divided up amongst family members and others under various pseudonymous evasionary arrangements. Gutelman: *op. cit.*, p. 94.

24. F. Chevalier: 'The *ejido* and political stability in Mexico', in C. Véliz (ed.): *The Politics of Conformity in Latin America* (London, Oxford University Press for the Royal Institute of International Affairs, 1967), pp. 158–91.

25. Within the government, the Department of Agrarian Affairs handles relations with the *ejidos* and the specially created National Bank of Ejidal Credit supplies credit. Both of these are separate from the Secretariat of Agriculture and Livestock and the National Bank of Agricultural Credit, which serve agriculture and farmers generally. Inter-American Committee for Agricultural Development: *Inventory*

of Information Basic to the Planning of Agricultural Development in Latin America: Mexico (Washington, Pan American Union, 1964), pp. 50–7.

26. Chevalier: *op. cit.*, p. 159.

27. Most of this account is from Whetten: *op. cit.*, ch. 9.

28. The Ejidal Bank, set up in 1936, is theoretically the only source of credit to *ejidatarios*, since they cannot offer their credit as mortgage. Credit is available only to co-operative credit societies, not to individuals. Initially Cárdenas saw the bank as a vehicle for social reforms and welfare projects, but this has increasingly conflicted with its primary function of providing credit for agricultural improvement. Huizer: *op. cit.*, pp. 478–9.

29. Whetten: *op. cit.*, pp. 141–2.

30. *Ibid*: pp. 182–93.

31. Chevalier: *op. cit.*, pp. 182–4.

32. D. McEntire and I. McEntire: 'Agrarian reform in Mexico', in D. McEntire and D. Agostini (eds.): *Towards Modern Land Policies* (Padua, University of Padua Institute of Agricultural Economics and Policy, 1971), pp. 229–74, esp. pp. 256–60.

33. *Ibid*: pp. 258, 262.

34. R. Stavenhagen: 'Social aspects of agrarian structure in Mexico', in R. Stavenhagen (ed.): *Agrarian Problems and Peasant Movements in Latin America* (New York, Doubleday Anchor, 1970), pp. 375–406.

35. C. Senior: *Land Reform and Democracy* (Gainesville, University of Florida Press, 1958), pp. 51, 60.

36. *Ibid*: p. 171.

37. *Ibid*: pp. 107, 228; Whetten: *op. cit.*, pp. 212–22.

38. S. Eckstein: 'Collective farming in Mexico: the case of la Laguna', in Stavenhagen: *op.cit.*, pp. 271–99.

39. *Ibid*: p. 276.

40. C. Tello: 'Agricultural development and land tenure in Mexico', *Weltwirtschaftliches Archiv.*, 101 (1), 1968, pp. 21–35.

41. Stavenhagen: *op. cit.*, pp. 242–6, 265.

42. *Ibid*: pp. 246–7.

43. See Dovring: *op. cit.*, pp. 35–43; also by Dovring: 'Land reform and productivity in Mexico', *Land Economics*, 46 (3), 1970, pp. 264–74.

44. D. E. Horton: 'Land reform and economic development in Latin America, the Mexican case', *Illinois Agricultural Economics*, 18 (1), 1968, pp. 9–20.

45. M. W. Mueller: 'Changing patterns of agricultural output and productivity in the private and land reform sectors in Mexico 1940–60', *Economic Development and Cultural Change*, 18 (2), 1970, pp. 252–66.

46. White: *op. cit.*, p. 167.

47. Stavenhagen: *op. cit.*, p. 234.

48. Dovring: 'Land reform in Mexico', *op. cit.*, pp. 32–4, especially the table showing reform activities in each of the 32 states.

49. Stavenhagen: *op. cit.*, pp. 255–6, 267–8.

50. E. Flores: 'From land reform to industrial revolution: the Mexican case', *The Developing Economies*, 7 (1), 1969, pp. 82–95.

5

Bolivia

Land reform in Bolivia, the poorest major Latin American country, has resemblances to that of Mexico, although it came 40 years later. The 1953 Bolivian land reform, like the Mexican, signified the reversal of a long process of land-grabbing from Indians; it also resulted from violent revolution (though the Bolivian revolution, with an estimated 3000 dead as against Mexico's million, was neither so bloody nor so protracted); and it was a genuine peasant uprising, starting in the Cochabamba valley, where *campesinos* drove land-owners off their estates, and ending, as in Mexico, with the government arming the peasants the better to defend their gains. Yet there are also differences.[1] Mexico's reform was a 'blind leap in the dark', with no definite policies for twenty years after its initiation. Bolivia's was initially more broadly conceived and more clearly formulated, even if it deviated subsequently from this ideal. Land reform was closely related to the socio-economic diversification and development of the country as perceived by the MNR (*Movimiento Nacional Revolucionario*) government which seized power in 1952. It was needed to consolidate the revolution, not to start it, as in Mexico.

GEOGRAPHICAL BACKGROUND TO BOLIVIAN LAND REFORM

Land reform had its original focus and greatest effect in the *hacienda*-dominated Bolivian highlands which concentrated 93 per cent of the population on 40 per cent of the nation's territory. The most important upland region, with 60 per cent of the population, is the *altiplano*, 800 km from north to south and

160 km from east to west, at altitudes from 3600 to 4000 metres. Dry and windswept for the most part, with a coarse grass vegetation, this is about the most desolate and inhospitable plateau in the continent. Agriculture and settlement are concentrated in an arc around Lake Titicaca and on the north-east margins of the plateau, where soils are more fertile and rainfall less scanty. Local crops are mostly cold-adapted tubers and grains, notably potatoes and barley. The *altiplano* housed 'the most exploitative peasant-*hacienda* system in the New World'.[2] Large estates contained the best land. Peons had to work 2 to 6 days per week on the *hacienda*, besides providing goods, labour and services of other kinds, in return for a houseplot, additional land for crops, and grazing rights for a few livestock. Seldom were wages paid.

North-east of the *altiplano* stretch the *yungas*, a series of valleys occupied by a sparser population growing subtropical cash crops such as coffee, coca and citrus fruits. With abundant land and labour scarcity, the *hacienda*-system developed differently here, with tenants offered productive cash crop holdings as inducement to work on the large estates.

South of the *yungas* and east of the southern part of the *altiplano* lies the mountain and valley region surrounding the cities of Sucre, Cochabamba and Tarija. Here rugged topography and a variety of microclimatic zones accommodating great crop diversity gave rise to an economically self-contained, inward looking *hacienda*-system in which a hierarchy of tenanting had developed, ranging from *hacendado* through tenant and subtenant to landless labourer. The Cochabamba valley, where population pressure had forced the average *minifundio* below 1 hectare, formed the heart of rural unrest at the time of the revolution. The open-minded Quechua-speaking peasants of this region had a tradition of syndicate and anti-landlord activity, in contrast to the more backward Aymara-speaking Indians of the *altiplano* who were exploited as an almost sub-human caste.[3]

DISTRIBUTION OF LAND BEFORE THE REFORM

The 1950 Agricultural Census revealed that pre-reform Bolivia had probably the most polarised landholding structure in Latin America at that time. Estates of over 500 hectares, 8 per cent by number of all landholdings, occupied 95 per cent of privately held farmland. One-tenth of the area was held by eight landholders. At the other extreme 61 per cent of land-holdings, all below 5 hectares, covered 0·3 per cent of the total area and 8 per cent of the cultivated area. On *latifundia* 8 per cent of the area was cultivated, on smallholdings 50 per cent. The 1950 census also recorded 3783 Indian freeholding villages (where title to the land resides in the community) but not the areas they occupied or cultivated.

Considerable regional variation existed. The degree of land concentration was highest on the *altiplano* and in Cochabamba. In the highlands 90 per cent of large landowners were ab-sentee, living in urban centres or abroad and leaving farm managers to operate their estates. In the sub-tropical Oriente lowlands, in contrast, over 50 per cent of farms were owner-occupied. Highland *haciendas* almost invariably worked on the *colonato* system. So tied to the land were the *colonos* that when properties were sold they were advertised by the number of *colonos* they contained ('*vendo finca con 500 colonos*') rather than by their area.

THE REFORM[4]

The 1953 MNR agrarian reform decree identified different types of holding. All rural properties were to be inspected and categorised to determine liability for expropriation. Detailed limits provided for different categories of property in different parts of the country according to local ecological and geo-graphical conditions. *Latifundia* were subject to total expropria-tion without compensation where the landowner was absentee, forms of agriculture were archaic and the workers abused and exploited. 'Medium-sized properties,' with the owner resident and using some modern farming methods, were subject to partial expropriation if their size exceeded the regional ceiling (6 hectares in the irrigated vineyards of Tarija to 350 hectares on the cold, southern *altiplano*). 'Small properties' were inalienable provided they did not exceed the local maximum (3 hectares in valley vineyards to 35 hectares on the southern *altiplano*). The few estates employing modern methods, the 'agricultural enter-prises', were permitted to retain up to 80 hectares of good quality land (800 hectares on the *altiplano*), the excess to be expropriated, with some compensation (rarely, if ever, in fact paid).

Distribution gave *colonos* immediate ownership of their existing plots, pending distribution of standard holdings to provide a 'vital minimum' size. The *hacienda* land was to be distributed either equally among all the *colonos* on the estate, or so as to 'level up' the smaller holdings. Since land was distributed partly according to area previously occupied, the new holdings naturally varied considerably in size, even within the same region. In the south some peasants received as much as 80 hectares, others 3 hectares or less; in the Cochabamba valley 8000 peasants received holdings of only 1 hectare; and many landless labourers received no land at all. To promote the development of the humid lowlands, the law also awarded every highland peasant the right to 60 hectares on the eastern frontier, over and above whatever he got in his home community. Thousands of peasants, accepting this offer, now commute between the highland and the lowland, and some have permanently settled in the Oriente.[5] Finally, the law reserved 10 per cent of expropriated land for co-operative farming, but the peasants distrusted the new co-operative societies just as they did their old masters. Although, to accelerate co-operative development, 1 million hectares were granted to syndicates in collective ownership (peasants were induced to join the syndicates by the offer of cut-price goods), in practice the peasants invariably divided the land into individual holdings.

Clearly the expropriation-redistribution procedure was complex, and would have become impossibly tedious and expensive. Within two years of the revolution, however, most peasants had independently taken and subdivided the estate land. The work of the land reform service thus became mainly legalising *de facto* situations, surveying properties and issuing titles. By 1975 titles had been confirmed on 18 million hectares of land (under half of it cultivable cropland) distributed to 477 000 beneficiary families, 60–70 per cent of those thought to qualify. Issuing of titles to grantees should finish soon.

THE AFTERMATH

The Bolivian land reform seems to be a case of too much too soon, and too little afterwards. All observers describe the immediate aftermath of revolution and land reform as a period of chaos. Armed peasants occupied estates, chased away landlords and destroyed livestock and capital equipment. Landowners took to urban business and professional occupations; many big *hacendados* fled the country. The first five years suffered political struggles, economic disorganisation and rampant inflation. Estimated mean per capita income fell by 20 per cent between 1952 and 1958. The government lacked the financial resources to administer the land reform effectively, much less to give the peasants the complementary services they so badly needed. In 1959 Dwight Heath, a close observer of Bolivian affairs, wrote that Bolivia's programme of economic development might succeed *in spite of* her thorough-going land reform rather than because of it.[6]

Prime obstacles to carrying out the reform were physical and social problems.[7] Most of the country was unmapped, with physical obstacles combining with sheer distance to make travel and communication difficult. At the time of the reform, Bolivia lacked even the most basic data on soil types and land use. There was no cadastral survey, and land registration and taxation were virtually unknown. Fewer than one-third of the rural population knew Spanish; fewer still were literate. After generations of subservience in a quasi-feudal society, peasants lacked not only formal education but also any understanding of basic legal, political and economic processes surrounding the land reform. Committed personnel to carry out the reform were chronically short. Many peasant syndicate organisers were miners, since no others were trained in union organisation. Galloping inflation, low salaries and political pressures forced many of Bolivia's small class of qualified persons to emigrate; those who remained rarely sympathised with the reform. Many administrative posts were filled by *mestizos*, who were a conservative influence on land reform implementation. Salaries for agrarian reform service employees were scandalously low. Mobile judges working from regional offices received no more than rural schoolteachers, and topographers received little more than half this level.[8] The temptations for supplementing these low incomes by extortion from peasants and accepting bribes were enormous; the surprise, apparently, was that corruption was not more widespread, and that so much was achieved with so few resources.[9]

Agricultural output fell by 1955 to 70–87 per cent of the 1952 level (individual estimates vary) and did not regain the pre-reform amounts until about 1960, and even then much of the increase came from newly developed areas in the Oriente region such as the Santa Cruz rice, sugar and cotton developments, less affected by land reform.[10] Before then, the government had to make emergency imports of corn and potatoes, and wheat imports doubled between 1950 and 1960. Meat shortages were acute in towns as peasants slaughtered estate owners' cattle. Post-reform gross agricultural produce, however, probably differed from the quantities actually marketed; the latter certainly fell, but the former perhaps not. The collapse of marketing, previously done by the landowners, reduced commercial sales until first merchants' lorries from the towns penetrated rural areas, and then the peasants spawned their own marketing facilities. Even produce marketed may have fallen less than indicated, since statistical reporting of produce handled by post-reform marketing channels was inadequate. Inevitably some farmland was actually idled or under-utilised in the turmoil of the takeovers, but the peasants almost certainly worked the remaining lands more intensively than before.[11] For the crops most directly affected by land reform—corn, potatoes and wheat—production was down initially but had mostly recovered by 1958–60. Drought years in the mid-1950s further complicate the evaluation.

CHANGES IN THE SPACIAL ORGANISATION OF RURAL LIFE[12]

Much of rural Bolivia has changed remarkably since 1953, although the changes have varied with the differential regional impact of the reform. Most noticeable in the spatial organisation of the rural landscape are new settlement forms—dispersed farmhouses, roadside hamlets and new market towns. Security of tenure has encouraged the peasant to build a house on his land (before the reform peasants on the estates could seldom build their houses where they wanted) so that dissemination of farm settlement characterises many zones of recently occupied reform land. Often relocation of homes is along a roadway in linear hamlets, improving accessibility to market. Most striking, however, is the creation of new towns of up to 250 dwellings, with churches, schools, markets and service functions.[13] The houses in these towns, built around a square market place, are two-storey structures with windows and corrugated iron roofs, quite unlike the traditional rural windowless adobe and thatch dwellings. The towns' principal function is the disposal of peasant surpluses previously creamed off and disposed of by landlords. The new settlements are particularly frequent north-west of La Paz, on the eastern shores of Lake Titicaca, though examples also exist in the *yungas*. Some houses are occupied permanently by traders and shopkeepers; others, belonging to peasants who prefer or need to live on their holdings, are occupied once a week on market day.

The changes in land use resulting from the land reform are variable: in some regions agriculture has been transformed; in others few modifications are directly attributable to reform. Changes are of two kinds: extension of the cultivated area; intensification of land use. They are most noticeable where peasants obtained access to land, such as former estate pasture, or forest land in the *yungas*, which they were previously forbidden to use. On *altiplano* estates pasture has been ploughed up and sown to wheat and barley; the pasture land is initially very fertile but further intensification is prevented by deficient rainfall and frequent frosts. In the *yungas* coffee, coca and banana cultivation has advanced progressively up the forested slopes. In grazing policy, post-reform peasants are obviously aiming at a higher stocking density than the extensively grazed estates (with consequent danger of overgrazing and erosion). In Cochabamba and below La Paz traditional crops such as maize and potatoes are being replaced by onions, carrots and other vegetable crops, fruit and flowers. It has been estimated that the value of agricultural production in the irrigated lower Cochabamba valley has increased tenfold as a result of these post-reform changes in land use. On one *hacienda* studied peasants market 70 per cent of their agricultural production now, compared to only 10 per cent before the reform.[14]

The long-term effect of the reform on total Bolivian agricultural production, however, has not been large-scale. The most important increases result from the extension and intensification of farming in the tropical lowlands rather than from changes in the highlands. Even in highland Bolivia the land reform affected only those areas with large estates worked in feudal conditions:

a 50-km strip of the *altiplano* east of Lake Titicaca, the *yungas* of La Paz, the Cochabamba basin, and the mountain valleys near Sucre, Potosí, Camargo and Tarija. And here the changes reflected the regional variation in the kind of *hacienda* economy as much as the realisation of the goals of the revolution for the peasantry.[15]

EVALUATION

No other country in Latin America has expropriated and distributed individual land titles to peasant families as widely as Bolivia. By eliminating rent and tribute labour, which had claimed about half the peasants' productive effort, the reform dramatically improved the daily lives of Bolivian peasants. No longer called *Indios* (a word, expunged by the revolution, signifying racially based inferiority) but *campesinos* ('rural folk'), they have a new pride and social status. Geographical evidence of this are the thousands of abandoned manor houses and new peasant homes throughout the landscape today. The great *hacienda* houses, in disrepair and neglect, give parts of the Bolivian countryside an air of decay. Built and maintained by peonage, they are the tombstones of Bolivian feudalism. Peasant buildings now secure labour and materials that once went into *hacienda* buildings: tiles or corrugated tin replace thatch roofs; concrete floors replace beaten earth; windows appear in blank walls.

The fact that most Bolivian peasants now work their own land, with the *hacienda*-system abolished, explains why post-1952 popular movements, such as that created by Ernesto ('Che') Guevara, found little response amongst the Bolivian peasantry. On the other hand, new peasant-landlord conflicts show a recent trend towards reassertion of landlord power. The 1971 right-wing coup had its power base in the eastern lowlands where landholdings had remained large. Where peasant organisations are weak, landlords have even resumed control of all or part of their lands; in other cases they have persuaded peasants still waiting for title ratification to work the land as share-croppers or have sold them spurious titles.[16] Before 1971 the Bolivian peasantry had rapidly evolved from a position of oppression to one of close integration into the government; since 1971 landowners, allied to the new military régime, have gained influence.

Economically, the reform's major aspect was the restructuring of market systems.[17] Peasant trading is immensely more widespread. Pre-reform tenures forced the peasant to produce largely for himself and to consume few goods not produced on his own lands; his participation in the money and market economy was minimal. With redistribution providing opportunities to earn a cash income from the land, regional and national markets have arisen. Evidence of improved living standards comes from local case-studies. Clark, for example, noted that in the 1950s the 200 families of a typical *ex-hacienda* had contained only one house with a tin roof, one bicycle, one radio and seven sewing machines; by 1966 the figures were, respectively, 40, 80, 100, 120. Amounts spent on consumption goods tripled between 1952 and 1966.[18] Even for Pairumani, a poor, remote *altiplano* community, 'land reform produced changes in attitudes which make innovation and initiative possible, opening the way to a search for achievement rather than a resignation to fate'.[19]

Nationally, however, the reform leaves much still to be done. Bolivian land reform administrators speak of two stages.[20] The first, distribution of land, is now virtually complete. The second must provide the *campesinos* with the means for developing the land and involves such vital but costly inputs as tools, credit and extension. This stage has hardly begun. No well-co-ordinated co-operative movement exists for beneficiaries. Complementary services that have been introduced, often assisted by foreign aid projects, have largely by-passed the land reform sector and been applied to the commercial development of the Oriente region. The Bolivian experience shows that land reform—even if well conceived—cannot become a dynamic force if the state does not support it fully through all of its resources and extension efforts.[21] Agricultural growth slipped from 2 per cent per year in the early 1960s to almost zero by 1970, and was primarily responsible for the failure of the 1962–71 Ten-Year Development Plan to achieve its target GNP. While the reform has enabled the land to accommodate the estimated 25 per cent increase in rural population since 1952, as well as feed the urban sector, there are limits to this kind of achievement. There is evidence that the reform has stimulated an increase in population growth rate.[22] From 1·7 per cent annual increase in 1950, annual rural demographic growth rate is now 2·7 per cent largely because better diets and easier access to medical services have lowered the rate of rural infant mortality.

If the inequality between landlord and peasant has gone, the inequality in the size of individual landholdings which separated the poor from the not-so-poor peasant in pre-reform days remains. If anything it is more acute, since comparatively well-to-do peasants could better afford the costs of claim presentation. The amount of land titled to the *ex-hacendados* also varies greatly, ranging from nothing to thousands of hectares. Much of this disparity originates in the way the regional agrarian reform judges classified properties. Despite its radical nature, the reform has still suffered from ex-landlords exercising their pre-1952 social prerogatives, particularly in regional towns, where they still largely constitute the administrative and professional class.[23] Land reform also ignored the problem of future land shortages arising from subdivision upon inheritance of reform holdings. The small plots of assignees in densely-peopled parts of the highlands deny succeeding generations any room for expansion, let alone mechanisation. In the Cochabamba valley fragmentation and inheritance pressures are 'the knot which strangles the rural economy of the country's best agricultural land'.[24] Only state remodelling of the millimetric landholding structure will help. Finally the freeholding communities, unaffected by the reform, need urgent attention. With their inferior land and higher population densities, these custom-holding groups have a dire need for greater security of tenure and for extension and other reform benefits.[25]

REFERENCES

1. D. Warriner: *Land Reform in Principle and Practice* (Oxford, Clarendon, 1969), pp. 241–8.
2. See P. De Shazo: *The Colonato System on the Bolivian Altiplano from Colonial Times to 1952* (Madison, University of Wisconsin, Land Tenure Center Paper 83, 1972); F. L. Keller: 'Finca Ingavi—a medieval survival on the Bolivian altiplano', *Economic Geography*, 26 (1), 1950, pp. 37–50.
3. W. E. Carter: 'Revolution and the agrarian sector', in J. M. Malloy and R. S. Thorn (eds.): *Beyond the Revolution, Bolivia since 1952* (Pittsburg, University of Pittsburg Press, 1971), pp. 233–68.
4. For a detailed discussion of the law see D. B. Heath, C. J. Erasmus and H. C. Buechler: *Land Reform and Social Revolution in Bolivia* (New York,

Praeger, 1969), pp. 49–59; an annotated translation of the reform decree is on pp. 401–36.

5. Carter: *op. cit.*, p. 244.

6. D. B. Heath: 'Land reform in Bolivia', *Inter-American Economic Affairs*, 12 (4), 1959, pp. 3–27.

7. Heath, Erasmus and Buechler: *op. cit.*, pp. 51–9.

8. Carter: *op. cit.*, p. 245.

9. Heath, Erasmus and Buechler: *op. cit.*, pp. 52, 59.

10. J. C. Crossley: 'Santa Cruz at the crossroads: a study of development in eastern Bolivia', *Tijdschrift voor Economische en Social Geografie*, 52, 1961, pp. 197–206, 230–41.

11. R. J. Clark: 'Land reform in Bolivia', in Agency for International Development: *Spring Review of Land Reform* (Washington, Department of State, 1970), Vol. 6, pp. 52–63. Clark points out that any decline in agricultural output was not a strict result of land reform (subdivision of estates into small peasant holdings) but of the general revolutionary situation which pre-dated the land reform.

12. D. A. Preston: 'The revolutionary landscape of highland Bolivia', *Geographical Journal*, 135 (1), 1969, pp. 1–16.

13. D. A. Preston: 'New towns, a major element in the settlement pattern in highland Bolivia', *Journal of Latin American Studies*, 2 (1), 1970, pp. 1–27; K. Barnes de Marschall: 'La formación de nuevos pueblos en Bolivia: proceso e implicaciones', *Estudios Andinos*, 1 (3), 1970, pp. 23–37.

14. C. Camacho Saa: *Minifundia, Productivity and Land Reform in Cochabamba* (Madison, University of Wisconsin, Land Tenure Center Research Paper 21, 1966), p. 15; M. Peinado Sotomayor: *Land Reform in Three Communities of Cochabamba, Bolivia* (Madison, University of Wisconsin, Land Tenure Center Research Paper 44, 1971), p. 79.

15. Heyduk has deftly demonstrated how geographical conditions and the type of *hacienda* tenure existing before the reform have influenced the course of post-reform progress. In the south-east around Sucre, for example, where a hierarchical tenure system had developed, removal of the topmost member of the structure (the *hacendado*) only meant continuance of the truncated hierarchy, with the former tenant as a kind of new reform-created small-scale landlord, and with very little land available for redistribution. As a result this region has changed little from its pre-reform condition. In Cochabamba, original hotbed of the land reform movement, pressure of population and shortage of land for redistribution again meant that peasants have benefited less from reform than those in other highland regions. The *yungas*, by contrast, has experienced rapid socio-economic progress since the reform. New settlements are conspicuous, the social structure is more fluid and a growing emphasis on possession of manufactured goods is evident. These developments are all consistent with pre-reform patterns. The reform merely gave the *yungas* a greater potential for an existing pattern of commercial coffee and fruit production. The social structure had also been more open before the reform than, for example, on the

altiplano or in southern Bolivia. See D. Heyduk: 'The *hacienda* system and agrarian reform in highland Bolivia: a re-evaluation', *Ethnology*, 13 (1), 1974, pp. 1–11.

16. R. J. Clark: 'Problems and conflicts over land ownership in Bolivia', *Inter-American Economic Affairs*, 22 (4), 1969, pp. 3–18.

17. R. J. Clark: 'Land reform and peasant market participation on the northern highlands of Bolivia', *Land Economics*, 44 (2), 1968, pp. 153–72.

18. *Ibid*: pp. 169–70.

19. R. Patch: 'Change on the Bolivian altiplano', *Land Tenure Center Newsletter*, 25, 1966–7, pp. 21–4.

20. Heath, Erasmus and Buechler: *op. cit.*, pp. 58–9.

21. A. García: 'Agrarian reform and social development in Bolivia', in R. Stavenhagen (ed.): *Agrarian Problems and Peasant Movements in Latin America* (New York, Doubleday Anchor, 1970), pp. 301–46.

22. Clark: 'Land reform in Bolivia', *op. cit.*, pp. 64–5.

23. *Ibid*: p. 88.

24. García: *op. cit.*, 323–4.

25. D. A. Preston: 'Freeholding communities and rural development: the case of Bolivia', *Revista Geográfica*, 73, 1970, pp. 29–41.

6

Cuba

Discussion of land reform in Latin America must include some account of Cuba, even though accurate evaluation is difficult for lack of reliable and recent information. Of the three revolutionary reforms bringing radical agrarian change to the continent, Cuba's was the most drastic and far-reaching. For the first time a truly socialist agricultural economy functions in Latin America, albeit with a private sector which still controls nearly a third of the land and the farm population. Cuba carried revolutionary socialism to the New World, thus acquiring truly world-historic significance. The immediate impact was electrifying: it seemed to mark the beginning of a vast reform movement on the entire continent. The young bearded men who came down from the Sierra Maestra to topple Fulgencio Batista's corrupt régime have inspired peasants and agricultural workers the world over. The political changes, too, have been profound, for Cuba has severed most of its ties with nations of the Western Hemisphere, except for diplomatic relations with Mexico, while establishing close bonds with the socialist bloc and with newly-liberated countries like Algeria and Portugal. Cuba, in short, is different: different as an underdeveloped country, as a socialist country, as a land reform. It is the only major exporter of primary produce to have embraced highly centralised planning. The accent is on youth, and on the countryside.

Contrasting with the simple land-to-the-tiller reforms of Mexico and Bolivia, the Cuban government collectivised the expropriated estates rather than divide them among the workers. Most are now state farms. Cuban land reform was part of a much wider political and ideological programme. One aspect of this policy was diversification, to increase production of crops other than sugar, upon which the economy was, and is, highly dependent. This policy, designed to reduce dependence on the United States, was perhaps more political than agricultural; but, since more food could have been produced on idle estate land, it was sound enough. In practice, however, it caused a decline in sugar production far greater than anticipated; and the policy was subsequently condemned as one of many 'mistakes'.

The second plank in post-revolutionary reform policy was the all-out attempt to correct the spatial distortion of Havana's economic and political overwhelming dominance. This geographical objective of the revolutionary government has been far more successful. Havana is now being deliberately run down: decaying but no longer decadent. To understand what is really happening in Cuba now, one must go into the countryside, in all its rich variety: to the Sierra Maestra mountains of the extreme south-east, whence Castro launched his attack on Batista in 1957–8; to the Escambray mountains of the south, centre of counter-revolutionary activity in 1960–1; to the coastal swamps south-east of Havana, site of the abortive Bay of Pigs invasion of exile forces in April 1961; to the rich, flat sugar lands of the east; and to the tobacco landscapes of the westernmost province, Piñar del Rio.

THE PRE-REVOLUTIONARY BACKGROUND[1]

Cuba's pre-revolutionary situation differed from that of other Latin American countries. Cuban income and literacy figures were high for the continent. The rural labour force was no isolated and impoverished peasantry; indeed Castro himself said that they earned the highest wages in Latin America. Unlike pre-revolutionary agriculture in Mexico and Bolivia, which still followed the Spanish colonial pattern, Cuban agriculture was largely commercial. Nor was concentration of land in large estates as extreme in Cuba. In 1946, 8 per cent of the holdings accounted for 70 per cent of the farmland, whilst 80 per cent of the holdings, mostly less than 25 hectares, shared under one-fifth of the agricultural land. The need for land reform arose less from land concentration as from the domination of the national economy by sugar, production of which was largely in foreign hands.

Cuba's economic history is largely that of Cuban agriculture, and over the last century or so, that of sugar. Foreign appreciation of Cuban sugar had begun by the close of the eighteenth century. Later the application of steam power led to mill mechanisation. Railways linking the cane fields to the new and larger mills (*centrales*) enabled sugar output to increase 50 per cent between 1890 and 1894. But the great sugar boom, lasting for two decades after the launching of the Cuban republic in 1902, was still to come. Cuban sugar enjoyed preferential treatment on the American market, where consumption was rising sharply; US capital poured into Cuba in massive amounts, helping to finance the building of modern *centrales* and the purchase of vast tracts of land. World War One generated further demand, intensified by the post-1918 slump in the European beet industry.

These developments considerably influenced the landholding structure, promoting particularly its concentration in progressively fewer hands. Up to the 1870s sugar had been grown primarily on small and medium-sized owner-operated farms, cane being sold competitively to numerous small mills; the area served economically by the mills was limited by ox-cart transport for the cane and for the timber to fuel the mills. The rail network enabled the mills to serve much larger areas, and, moreover, made it profitable for the sugar companies to own the surrounding land to ensure adequate supplies of cane for their mills, now bigger and more efficient. The small independent cane growers and mill owners were bought out. Mills declined from 1190 in 1876 to only 207 in 1899, though both amount produced and area cultivated increased. Sugar industry rationalisation during the inter-war slump further accentuated concentration. By 1926 only 171 mills were operating, but they controlled 18 per cent of the country's land. Foreign-owned mills ground over 90 per cent of the island's cane. Many mills were owned by one company; four American companies owned a quarter of the *centrales* at this time. During the early 1920s Cuba produced over a fifth of world production of sugar; it was the classic example of a one-crop, export-oriented economy. In 1959, immediately prior to the revolution, 22 of the most important sugar companies owned 1·8 million hectares of land, and 13 of them, all American-owned, accounted for 1·2 million hectares, with an average size,

F

therefore, of 90 000 hectares. Sugar occupied over half the island's cultivated area, producing 25 per cent of national, 40 per cent of farm sector income and up to 85 per cent of export revenue.

During the sugar boom most mills ground 'administration cane': the mills themselves grew the cane, using hired, wage-earning, landless labourers. Some of the cane, however, was cultivated by *colonos*, independent farmers growing cane on land leased from the *centrales*. The *colonos* hired labour for their harvests, but were themselves dependent upon the mill for land, credit and processing—the 'triple bond' which tied the *colono* to the mill. The *colono* was obviously vulnerable against arbitrary action by sugar mill landowners, but his status improved after the collapse of the sugar market in the early 1930s, and in 1937 the *Ley de Co-ordinación Azucarera* regulated his rights and obligations in detail.

Rural wage workers were less well cared for. Numbering 400 000 at the 1946 census, their annual income was under a quarter of the national average. Their problem was the seasonality of sugar farming and the lack of alternative employment in the protracted *tiempo muerto* (dead season). Over half of them worked for less than four months per year; only 6 per cent found work for nine months or longer. Rural unemployment was all the more unfortunate considering the amount of cultivable land left idle. Half of this 'unproductive' land was in estates of over 1000 hectares. Sugar holdings planted only half their area to cane, keeping the rest 'in reserve', generally as rough cattle grazing. This extensive land use served several purposes. Land being the cheapest and most abundant factor of production, economic rationality recommended keeping some uncultivated to cater for a market characterised by wide periodic fluctuations. More insidious, however, was the mills' monopoly of idle land to prevent sugar workers from getting at it. The sugar companies had an interest in maintaining high levels of unemployment to preserve a reservoir of uncommitted labour for the cane-cutting season.[2]

The great estate owners could pursue this policy because of United States support via the international quota system, by which the landowners were guaranteed a fixed minimum price for a certain amount of sugar, besides a profit on the shipping costs. Cuba was an economic colony of her large neighbour. In the early 1950s the US had more capital invested in Cuba than in any other country in Latin America, controlling 40 per cent of Cuba's sugar industry, 90 per cent of power and telephone services and 50 per cent of the railways. The US provided 70–80 per cent of Cuba's imports and absorbed 58 per cent of exports. Under American economic dominance and with upper class urban dwellers emulating American standards and styles of living, Cuba's surplus investment capital flowed abroad and Cuban enterprises suffered. Agriculture was so distorted that during the 1950s the country had to import £60–70 million worth of foodstuffs per year (a quarter of total import values), because land was not used to supply domestic needs. Over 60 per cent of these foodstuffs could have been produced locally.[3]

The crux of the agricultural problem before 1959 was that no structural transformation took place to mitigate the effects of the inter-war sugar slump. 'High level stagnation' was one description of the old Cuban social economy: its fundamental causes were political and market disorganisation.[4] Economic stagnation was greater and lasted longer than anywhere else in Latin America, except, possibly, Haiti and Bolivia. The situation was worsened by the sugar companies' insistence on refining most of their product overseas, and by customs preferences on US manufactured goods, which strangled the establishment of Cuban industry (just when basic metal and engineering industries were being established in Venezuela, Chile, Colombia and Mexico). True, some crop diversification—into coffee, rice, tobacco and citrus fruits—took place but it was insufficient: a failing and an ailing monoculture still dominated the economy. In 1950 Lowry Nelson wrote that the land was rich yet the people poor.[5] While Havana became the Caribbean fun city, a veritable caricature of capitalism, the rural population languished: 45 per cent illiterate, 75 per cent in wood and thatch huts with earth floors, 90 per cent without proper water or toilet facilities, 75 per cent of their diet composed of rice, beans, tubers and plantain bananas. Absentee landownership was common on the extensively-run cattle ranches, sharecropping on the intensive tobacco farms. Finally, squatters (*precaristas*), 84 per cent of them concentrated in the south-eastern Oriente province, held 9 per cent of the farms.

In summary, five socio-economic problems afflicted Cuba on the eve of the revolution: overall economic stagnation; over-reliance on sugar as the basis of the economy; overdependence upon the United States for trade and capital; high unemployment; and the geographic dualism between metropolitan and rural Cuba.[6]

REVOLUTION, THE AGRARIAN SECTOR AND
TWO STAGES OF LAND REFORM

Although the peasantry's role in the Cuban revolution remains enigmatic, Castor's continued espousal of agrarian reform (expressed as early as 1953 in his famous 'History will absolve me' speech) indicates close peasant involvement with the revolt. If the revolution initially had a 'classless' character, the early illusory unity soon disappeared with the advocacy of land reform. In fact some land had already been distributed in 1957 and 1958 to tenant coffee growers and subsistence farmers in those parts of the Sierra Maestra occupied by Castro's rebel army. In October 1958, three months before Batista's collapse, the revolutionary leaders prepared a provisional land reform law (the Sierra Maestra law), and in May 1959 its provisions were incorporated into the basic Law of Agrarian Reform, the first stage of Cuban land reform.

The first agrarian reform was radical but outwardly conventional, being mostly within the powers of the state under the 1940 constitution. The law decreed: (1) expropriation of estates over 30 *caballerías* (403 hectares) with possible exemption up to 100 *caballerías* (1342 hectares) for exceptionally productive rice and sugar holdings with yields of at least 50 per cent above the national average; compensation, based on assessed tax values, to be paid in 20-year $4\frac{1}{2}$ per cent bonds; (2) expropriation of all foreign-owned properties; (3) land redistribution to small tenant farmers, including squatters, the basic entitlement being 2 *caballerías* (27 hectares) free of charge, with the option of a further 3 *caballerías* at a low price; (4) abolition of tenancy, tenant farmers becoming automatic owners of the land they rented; (5) creation of the National Institute of Agrarian Reform (INRA) to execute the reform; and (6) formation of co-operatives under the auspices of INRA; land and tools being owned collectively by the members, who would jointly farm the land

and share the profits.[7] This last provision, a late addition by Castro, clearly opposes the spirit of the earlier clauses and subsequently transformed the reform from an instrument of land redistribution into a policy of collectivisation. Superficially, the 1959 law was a reformist law, with especially generous terms for the retention of land. At this time most of the population, including some of the bourgeoisie, were still 'Fidelist'. Castro himself at this stage did not want to antagonise the United States, for Cuba still depended on her neighbour for imports and exports. But in August 1960 Castro declared the agrarian reform over; the agrarian revolution had begun. The indemnities would never be paid.

INRA, the land reform organisation, became the revolutionary government's most important organ, a virtual state within the State. Completely overshadowing the Ministry of Agriculture (which was abolished in 1960), INRA focused centralisation even more when the revolutionary leaders created within it, or dependent upon it, all the revolution's new institutions, the Department of Industries, the Cuban Petroleum Institute, the Rural Housing Department, the Bank of Agricultural and Industrial Development and others. Contrasting strongly with the generally weak, under-staffed, under-financed reform institutes of other Latin American countries, INRA has become a strong, autonomous agency for planning virtually the whole of national farm policy. It also divided Cuba into 28 'agrarian development zones', superseding the existing political division into provinces and municipalities, thereby changing the whole administrative geography of the country. These zones provided the regional framework for executing the reform. Under a chief named by INRA (usually a military man) they were the links between the bureaucracy and the peasantry, organising co-operatives, granting credit, opening roads, carrying out technical assistance, educational, health, sanitation and housing projects.

US hostility to the early revolutionary events in Cuba was partly responsible via a chain of events for hardening the commitment to a more radical land reform. Light military action culminated in the Bay of Pigs invasion of 1961. In July 1960 the US abolished the sugar quota. In response Cuba passed Law 851 of Nationalisation, siezing all foreign-owned agricultural enterprises, including sugar mills and their attendant lands; of the 165 existing mills, 61 were American, handling half the annual sugar production. Land redistribution was further hastened by Law 890 of October 1960, which nationalised industry and its attendant land. About half (2 172 134 hectares) of the redistribution effected by early 1961 (4 438 879 hectares—roughly half of Cuban agricultural land) emanated from these two decrees. Only 27 per cent (1 199 184 hectares) resulted from the original reform law, even though it was applied down to a limit of 50 *caballerías*, not the 100 *caballerías* prescribed by the law. Strict application of the 1959 law's tenancy clause could have affected a further 2 million hectares (nearly 20 per cent of Cuban farmland) and 28 000 medium landowners (half the island's landowners), but little was done for fear of jeopardising the future of the revolution.[8]

To be effective, land reform has to be quick. Special provisions streamlining the 1959 law ensured rapid implementation, so that Cuba did not repeat the course of other Latin American reforms, which have been confounded by juridicial sabotage. After a somewhat cautious start, in early 1960 the pace of Cuban land reform suddenly accelerated when the central and eastern estates, which included many cattle ranches, were confiscated. More than 600 000 hectares were expropriated in one week in January 1960, and by mid-1961 101 000 peasants had obtained titles to 2 725 000 hectares.[9]

Although the prime purpose of the 1959 law was to create and strengthen a peasant bourgeoisie, from the earliest days of the revolution Castro clearly wanted, for both practical and ideological reasons, to redistribute the least possible land in individual titles. Carlos Rafael Rodríguez, president of INRA, maintained that their background as plantation wage-workers gave rural dwellers in Cuba little desire for plots of land.[10] Although the promise of land redistribution had gained considerable rural support for the revolution, Castro was worried that 'after one piece of land the peasant would want another'. In collectivising immediately, he left the orthodox communist path of redistribution first, then collectivisation. Omitting the interim stage was also practical because, quite simply, preserving the large units intact was easier than breaking them up only to reconstitute them subsequently. Farm workers' support could be won more quickly by paying higher wages than by distributing land. Production would have fallen had the estates been fragmented.[11]

Late 1960 marks the end of the first phase of agrarian reform, in which institutional changes occurred rapidly, reflecting primarily the progressive radicalisation of the Castro regime and the deterioration of Cuban-American relations. The organisation of a more socialist agriculture from early 1961 introduces the second phase; this involved the politically-motivated confiscation of lands from counter-revolutionary sympathisers following the Bay of Pigs landing, the increasing reliance on state farms, and finally the lowering of the ceiling on private property to 5 *caballerías* (67 hectares) in 1963. The 1963 law—'Cuba's final land reform' in Castro's words—authorised expropriation of another 1·8 million hectares from 9825 owners. This sequence of events is best looked at against the complex changing institutional framework of Cuban agriculture in the 1960s.

CHANGES IN THE INSTITUTIONAL STRUCTURE OF CUBAN
AGRICULTURE[12]

During the reform's first phase, 1959–61, INRA organised three types of agricultural enterprise: 'co-operatives', 'sugar co-operatives', and 'farms under direct administration'. The term 'co-operative' was a misnomer for the first type; mostly these were the former large specialised holdings (producing crops like tomatoes and sisal), which were given INRA administrators, generally rebel army soldiers. These 'co-operatives' were created from the double need of maintaining and increasing production of these specialised crops, and quickly giving work to the unemployed. Numbering 881 in May 1960, they were the first absorbed by the larger state farms in 1961. The 'direct administration farms' represented essentially former cattle ranches, plus a few rice estates. Given the way the land was acquired, the type of organisation (direct INRA control) and the fact that the workers were wage labourers, these units rank as the first true state farms. In May 1960 they numbered about 500, covering 845 460 hectares, and including 605 000 head of cattle; their numbers increased when the nationalisation acts were passed later in the year. The 'sugar co-operatives' also resulted from the massive confiscations of late 1960. They occupied land which had grown administration cane and also the nationalised properties of the larger *colonos*. The smaller cane-growers were not brought into the sugar co-operatives until 1963 even though they produced a quarter of all cane grown in Cuba.

At least on paper the sugar co-operatives were more authentically co-operative than the others. A general assembly of all workers elected a board of directors headed by a 'co-ordinator'. Each permanent member of the cane co-operative received a daily wage, plus supplements proportional to the resulting profits. Temporary workers received higher wages but no share in the profits. In practice, however, the sugar co-operative was far from being an autonomous democratic body. The 'co-ordinator' had to work with an 'administrator', state appointed, who received and implemented instructions from INRA. This two-headed management inevitably created difficulties and conflicts. The system in fact transferred effective power from the co-ordinator to the administrator; the sugar co-operatives thus changed from the virtually true co-operatives they initially were to state enterprises dominated by INRA management.[13]

Centralisation of farm administration intensified after June 1961 with the decision to create *granjas del pueblo* or 'people's farms'. Initially the *granja* (comparable with the Soviet *sovkhoz*) represented the simple geographical fusion of direct administration farms and the non-sugar co-operatives. Each people's farm was headed by an administrative council and an administrator appointed by INRA. The state owned the land; labour was paid wages, with no share in profits, all of which accrued to INRA. All investments, working capital and social funds were financed from INRA's general budget. The reason for the transformation was principally to effect the dramatic plans for agricultural diversification which ruled economic policy immediately after the revolution. When in April 1961 the revolution was officially declared socialist, ideological factors became increasingly important. Workers on people's farms were—and are—salaried state employees, entitled to free housing, education, medical care and recreation facilities. All were formerly landless members of the rural proletariat.

In August 1962 the 'sugar co-operatives' were converted into 'sugar farms' (i.e. state farms), a legal transformation which merely confirmed a *de facto* situation; 90 per cent of the sugar co-operative delegates voted for this move, largely because state farm workers on the *granjas*, with their higher wages and numerous benefits, were much better-off than the sugar co-operative workers. The two-headed power structure was eliminated, only the administrator remaining. In late 1962 (approximate figures) 600 sugar farms covered 900 000 hectares and employed 120 000 permanent workers; 280 people's farms covered 2 844 000 hectares and embraced 200 000 workers. The land use differences between the people's farms and the sugar farms were gradually eliminated as sugar farms were asked to plant other crops to support the drive towards diversification. In 1963 all differences were abolished and both are now called 'state farms' (*granjas estatales*). At the same time they were grouped into large regional administrative units called *agrupaciones*, strong federal organisations to aid the mid-1960s move towards decentralisation. In 1966 575 state farms were grouped into 58 *agrupaciones*, whose areas ranged from 13 000 to 100 000 hectares. No major changes in the structure of tenure and agricultural organisation have since occurred. The 1963 reform, which confiscated land from the medium size farm group (67–403 hectares), left only 155 000 small farmers with control over less than a quarter of the arable land.[14] The state then owned over 70 per cent of the country's land: the highest degree of collectivisation in the world. Remaining peasant farmers are nearly all members of ANAP (National Association of Small Farmers), created in 1961 as a 'first step towards socialism' for this group. ANAP's main fields of activity are co-operatives for credit, agricultural services and some aspects of agricultural production; its ulterior motives are to orient private production according to the national policy of the day, and to foster in small private farmers the spirit of collectivism.

ECONOMIC PERFORMANCE

Cuban agricultural performance since 1959 should be judged against the relatively fast increase in output that was physically manageable.[15] The output of several farm products increased in the first phase of the land reform (1959–61). Official publicity claimed that only the Cuban land reform had immediately yielded markedly increased production. This was also the view of Antonio Núñez Jiménez, former professor of geography and first president of INRA. Output of most crops was maintained during 1959 and 1960, and a big increase was obtained in 1961, with total crop output about 12 per cent higher than the 1957–58 average. Tobacco, rice, corn, potatoes, henequen and beans all improved. The chief reason was the use of empty cattle land for crops for domestic consumption, but other factors also played a role. Increased employment stimulated demand. Although INRA delegates and co-operative managers promised impossibly high output targets, in striving for these levels land was cleared and ploughed, fertilisers applied, machinery fully used, slack labour fully employed, and farm output boosted. Sugar production also increased, by about 20 per cent from 1958 to 1961, although this partly reflects pre-revolution plantings (the estates anyway were not taken over until late 1960). Gayoso opined that the agricultural production increases verified during these first two years were a function of the surprise redirectioning of the revolution.[16] Few realised that the 1959 law was only a preamble to collectivisation, and so many planted hurriedly to invoke the high yield exemption clause. So the government got intensively cultivated farms instead of, as commonly, sabotaged ones.

The bonanza was short-lived. A composite agricultural product index (1952–5 = 100), which reached 133 in 1960–1, fell in successive crop years to 101, 84 and 77.[17] Meat output was falling as early as 1960, through overslaughtering the previous year. Most serious, sugar output plummeted from the record 6·8 million tons in 1961 to 4·8 million in 1962 and 3·8 million in 1963, levels which could not even fulfil international trading commitments. Official explanation was 'shortage of workers', many of whom had been enlisted into the armed forces to suppress counter-revolutionary movements. Others left the sugar estates of their own accord, mostly for Havana. 1961 was a dry year, affecting the poor harvest of 1962. In 1963 Hurricane Flora caused widespread disruption in Oriente province, Cuba's foremost agricultural region. But the fundamental reason for the sugar crisis was the economic and organisational policies of the régime. The revolutionaries, biased by their guerilla mentality, undervalued technical expertise and economic rationality and opposed any form of bureaucracy.[18] Qualified personnel were allowed to leave the country (most did) instead of being encouraged to stay and work with the revolution (only in 1971 was emigration restricted). The anti-sugar cane diversification policy inevitably subtracted resources from sugar production; 130 000 hectares of cane land (nearly 10 per cent of the sugar area and including some of the best land) were uprooted following the 1961 harvest for planting to other crops. This disastrous decision was perhaps the great error of agricultural policy since the revolution, for output could not be intensified on the remaining sugar land, and in 1963 200 000 hectares were replanted to sugar in a dramatic reversal of policy. The wage system on sugar co-operatives and state farms—a flat hourly rate regardless of output—also contributed to the production shortfalls. Workers lacked incentive to work harder or longer.[19] Still today, some cut cane until they have enough to buy their food ration and then, because they can buy no more in a heavily rationed economy, stop work. Absenteeism has emerged as a serious problem.[20] Volunteer brigades, composed of women, children, urban and office workers, are no solution because of their low efficiency; cane-cutting is a skilled business learnt by experience.[21] In September 1963 René Dumont reported to INRA that the agricultural situation was serious and potentially catastrophic.[22] Seemingly unconcerned about costs, almost all state farms were in debt; rural workers produced on average little more than half of what they were paid (productivity, therefore, had dropped by about 50 per cent since 1958); yields and production had gone down.

The post-1962 reappraisal of agricultural policy strongly attacked what Castro called 'subjectivism' in planning; the result was a long-overdue stress on realistic assessment of production possibilities, with a vigorous drive towards securing reliable statistical information. Efforts were made to raise farm productivity by concentrating on cost-effectiveness. The appointment of Rodríguez as president of INRA shifted the emphasis from the grandiose to the feasible. The emphasis on sugar cane production increased, although diversification remains the long-run target.

After 1964 a supreme effort was made to increase agricultural production, especially sugar, to meet the new quota agreements (7 million tons of sugar annually) with Russia and Eastern Europe. New methods gave special attention to mechanisation, irrigation and fertilisers. The labour force were urged to participate in voluntary labour and other unpaid work. A solid rural infrastructure was created, with lavish expenditure on roads. The 1965–70 sugar plan aimed at 46 million tons overall, culminating in the much-publicised *Zafra de los Diez Milliones*, the 10-million-ton target for the 1970 harvest. The impressive investment of the late 1960s brought austerity and diminished consumer goods. Ration queues grew longer. Gross investment increased from 1964 to 1968, while GNP fell. Between 1965 and 1967 agricultural production grew steadily, but then relapsed, and the failure, by 1·5 million tons, to achieve the 10-million-ton *zafra* of 1970 was a political and psychological, as well as an economic, setback.

René Dumont, after criticising the diversification policy, said that the swing to monoculture, correct in principle, had been too extreme.[23] Undoubtedly the area of cultivated land has been increased, and agriculture has advanced significantly in mechanisation, fertilisation, and irrigation (e.g. the Carlos Manuel Cespedes dam, which irrigates over 50 000 hectares of rice and sugar land in Oriente province). After his 1969 visit, Dumont wrote that Cuba promised considerable agricultural progress, and instanced irrigation, cattle breeding research, new strains of rice, pangola and guinea grass for grazing, and new plantings of crops like citrus, coffee and pineapples, although not all had been efficiently done.[24] The main current problems seem to be the frequent policy shifts (partly from the excessive concentration of power in one man's hands), the grandiose targets requiring great efforts and sacrifices and generally ending in disappointment, and the lack of efficiency and productivity resulting from naïve economic perspectives, poor management and lack of proper incentives.

CONCLUSION

Consistency in economic policy has not been a virtue of the Castro régime. Castro reasons politically, sentimentally, passionately, and now technically, but still not economically.[25] Geographically the most interesting aspect of post-revolutionary Cuban planning has been the attempt to eliminate the spatial distortion the dualistic pre-revolutionary economy had produced.[26] The cheap cost-price goods available from the rural *tiendas del pueblo* (people's stores) on the one hand, and the rationing and queueing for goods in Havana on the other flow essentially from the attempt to correct spatially distorted patterns of income distribution, of flows of goods and services and of other inequities. In this respect, land reform, by nourishing the Cuban countryside and by rewarding rural workers more like their urban counterparts, has succeeded. Havana's population has stabilised since 1965 at 1·7 million (cf. 1·2 million in 1953) and its relative importance has diminished as the total population has grown. New 'intermediate'-sized towns have generated regionally balanced growth. Oriente province, traditionally most 'exploited' by metropolitan Cuba, now has a population proportionate to its land area (one-third of the country). The *agrupaciones* introduced a new form of socialist regional economic planning. Unlike the unco-ordinated spatial dispersion of effort in the early diversification drive, regional specialisation is now emphasised, though each region must produce basic foodstuffs to avoid wasteful intra-island transport of produce and labour.

The spatial *organisation* of agriculture has been transformed by central planning, but land reform has not caused any remarkable changes in the physiognomy of the agricultural landscape, for large units (producing cattle, sugar, rice mainly) are still juxtaposed with small peasant holdings (dominant especially in the tobacco sector).[27] The result of the Cuban land reform differs from its initial aims in that medium-size farms are now rare and large estates still predominate, the state having replaced the former individual or company landlord. Consequently landless farmworkers are still the majority, while newly-created small peasant farms are few.

Logic suggests that the private sector will soon be eliminated. Politically and economically these peasants are already neutralised since no free market now operates on the island: they sell to the state monopsony. There are already reports of a 'third land reform', whereby private farmers are very strongly encouraged to cede their land to the nearest state farm in return for certain benefits and guarantees (which, apparently, do not always materialise).[28] In any case, since the Cuban revolution has been diligently converting the young and is gradually narrowing the income gap between rural workers and peasant farmers, the landowning peasant class will probably disappear of its own accord within a generation.

Despite economic problems the land reform's numerous strong points need emphasising. It, almost alone among land reforms, communist or other, gives the benefits mainly to farm workers as opposed to landowning or renting peasants. Agricultural workers, who outnumbered the *colonos* by about five to one before the reform, became the revolution's favoured class.[29] The lavish social benefits—housing, education, cheap food and clothing—given to state farm workers surprised many commentators. Dumont wrote that if Russia exploits the peasants, Cuba spoils hers too much.[30] The average Cuban wage rose 56 per cent between 1958 and 1970, with higher percentage increases in jobs traditionally poorly paid.[31] Since 1965, when Castro himself assumed the direction of agriculture, production has increased in both crops and livestock; the emphasis on scientific agricultural research, technical progress and investment in agriculture (especially irrigation and fertiliser) is an example to other Latin American countries.

Jacoby notes a fundamental characteristic distinguishing Cuba from other underdeveloped countries: it has no unemployment problem.[32] On the contrary, it has a chronic labour shortage. Particularly in agriculture job openings outnumber people entering the labour force. In 1972 it was estimated that the economy could rapidly absorb 450 000 new workers.[33] This strange situation reflects abolition of child labour by compulsory education; introduction of a regular 8 hour work day; expansion and intensification of agriculture; increased industrialisation; building of roads, dams and other public works; and heavy absorption of workers into military service. The situation may, in fact, be less simple than this, for, as already noted, part of the rural labour shortage derives from absenteeism, which necessitates temporary geographical shifts of labour from the oversubscribed urban sector. Such a remedy depends upon an increasing appeal to people's 'revolutionary awareness' and, in the face of increasing discipline problems, an increasingly military attitude to labour management. As Castro lamented in 1968, the Cuban people are willing to fight for the revolution, even die for it, but not to work for it.

Castro's revolution, and the agrarian structure it has created, will be most remembered for its ideology. Eschewing orthodox socialist tenets, Fidel promulgated his own brand of land reform;

it may not initially have been well thought out, but in general the land distribution aspects of his agrarian policy have been bold yet sound. But this is not all. By rubbing people's noses in the countryside, Castro is smashing the traditional class distinctions and social relations of what was once a very Latin society. In all Latin America, only in Cuba are boots, dirty clothes, rough hands and agricultural talk hallmarks of honour and status. Castro's is a vision of optimism, with strong overtones of utopianism. Mistakes abound, but so do new ideas. The Cuban agrarian reform, moreover, is only fifteen years old and is still adapting itself to the socio-economic changes caused by the 1959 revolution. The future course of the land situation will be interesting to watch and a challenge to geographers and social scientists for decades ahead. It is, in the whole ex-colonial world, unique.

REFERENCES

1. Mostly based on A. Bianchi: 'Agriculture: the pre-revolutionary background', in D. Seers (ed.): *Cuba, The Economic and Social Revolution* (Chapel Hill, University of North Carolina Press, 1964), pp. 65–99.

2. E. Boorstein: *The Economic Transformation of Cuba* (New York, Modern Reader Paperbacks, 1968), p. 4.

3. A. Gayoso: 'Land reform in Cuba', in Agency for International Development: *Spring Review of Land Reform* (Washington, Department of State, 1970), Vol. 7, pp. 22–3.

4. J. O'Connor: 'Cuba: its political economy', in R. E. Bonachea and N. P. Valdés (eds.): *Cuba in Revolution* (New York, Doubleday Anchor, 1972), pp. 52–81.

5. L. Nelson: *Rural Cuba* (Minneapolis, University of Minnesota Press, 1950). The figures which follow are mostly from Nelson's survey, the classic work on pre-revolutionary rural Cuba.

6. C. Mesa-Lago: 'Economic policies and growth', in C. Mesa-Lago (ed.): *Revolutionary Change in Cuba* (Pittsburg, University of Pittsburg Press, 1971), pp. 277–338.

7. Fuller details of the 1959 reform are set out in Gayoso: *op. cit.*, pp. 42–6. The full Spanish text is in M. A. Durán: 'La reforma agraria cubana', *El Trimestre Económico*, 27 (107), 1960, pp. 410–69.

8. J. O'Connor: 'Agrarian reforms in Cuba 1959–1963', *Science and Society*, 32 (2), 1968, pp. 169–217.

9. M. Gutelman: 'Socialisation of the means of production in Cuba', in Bonachea and Valdés: *op. cit.*, pp. 238–60.

10. C. R. Rodríguez: 'The Cuban revolution and the peasantry', *World Marxist Review*, 8 (10), 1965, pp. 12–20.

11. D. Warriner: *Land Reform in Principle and Practice* (Oxford, Clarendon,

1969), pp. 240–2. A few years later Algeria followed Cuba's example by preserving intact the estates of the French colonials.

12. This section is based largely on A. Bianchi: 'Agriculture—post-revolutionary development', in Seers: *op. cit.*, pp. 100–57; O'Connor: 'Agrarian reforms in Cuba', *op. cit.*, pp. 170–84, 187–207.

13. René Dumont, who was involved with the Cuban land reform in the early years as Castro's personal adviser, regretted this tendency bitterly. He wrote that departure from the co-operative formula was the basic error of the Cuban leaders, but his plea for genuine producers' co-operatives went unheeded. R. Dumont: *Cuba: Socialism and Development* (New York, Grove Press, 1970), p. 53.

14. The motivation for the 1963 reform law lay in the strategic and economic relations between state agriculture and the 'middle sector' (those farms with between 5 and 30 *caballerías*). Much of Cuba's domestic food production, besides nearly 25 per cent of sugar cane, was produced by this group. The division particularly of the cane fields between public and private ownership constituted a serious obstacle to physical planning (of labour, irrigation, harvesting, etc.). With few incentives to reinvest current earnings the middle *colonos* were able to bid labour away from the state-owned farms. Once the government had committed itself to socialist planning, it was only a matter of time before it moved against the *kulaks* of Cuba. O'Connor: 'Agrarian reforms in Cuba', *op. cit.*, pp. 189–90.

15. Cuba began her revolutionary programme with advantages other socialist or less developed countries lacked. Unlike their Mexican and Bolivian forerunners, the Cuban revolutionaries did not have to grapple with a country split by distance and national boundaries into numerous diverse regions. Cuba was already integrated geographically, culturally and racially. Much of the rural labour force were accustomed to working in an organised and disciplined fashion. A telecommunications network facilitated dissemination of new policies. Castro projected both his doctrine and his charisma to every corner of the country, an advantage which perhaps no other revolutionary leader has enjoyed. By 1959 other socialist bloc countries, notably Russia, were economically strong enough to provide aid and a guaranteed market for Cuban export produce. D. Seers: 'The economic and social background', in Seers (ed.): *op. cit.*, pp. 3–61.

16. Gayoso: *op. cit.*, p. 75.

17. *Ibid*: p. 74.

18. Mesa-Lago: *op. cit.*, pp. 281–2.

19. The problem of incentives and rewards in Cuba is very delicate and a number of approaches have been tried. In the mid-1960s the system of economic incentives (production bonuses, better housing, prizes of holidays, cycles, refrigerators, etc.) was replaced by one of moral incentives (flags, medals, honourable mentions of 'vanguard worker', 'hero of production', etc.), but only a minority of workers participated in the emulation campaign. In 1967 peasants on state farms lost their garden plots. In the late 1960s the rural labour force was increasingly

militarised. Workers were encouraged to 'wage a war against nature'. None of these measures has effectively stemmed falling productivity of labour. C. Mesa-Lago: *The Labour Sector and Socialist Distribution in Cuba* (New York, Praeger, 1968).

20. Absenteeism emerged as a serious problem as early as 1962 and has plagued state-run farming ever since. Until recently (on Castro's own admission) workers on state farms worked an average of 4–5 hours per day and got paid for 8. In the sugar industry 77 per cent of the labour force is still effectively seasonally unemployed, and in tobacco 47 per cent work only 6 months of the year yet get paid for 12. Graduated punishments for absenteeism have done little to ease the problem. Bonachea and Valdés: *op. cit.*, pp. 358, 370, 377.

21. Five types of unpaid labour may be distinguished in Cuban agriculture: (1) work performed by employed workers outside of regular working time; (2) work done by unemployed women; (3) work performed by students as part of their 'socialist education'; (4) work accomplished by politico-administrative prisoners as a means of 'social rehabilitation'; and (5) work included as part of compulsory military service. Unpaid labour performed by employed male and female workers is usually called 'voluntary work'. It is performed beyond regular work hours in one of four ways: as overtime subsequent to the regular workday (often as night work); at weekends; during annual holidays; or for a longer period of one or more months (often for the sugar harvest). It should be noted that the sectors furnishing voluntary workers are mainly those suffering from disguised unemployment (mostly service jobs in administration, trade, construction, etc.). The idea of having civil service workers, students, salesgirls, etc., participate in agricultural work seems a good one. This by and large petit-bourgeois mass has an exaggerated tendency to disdain manual labour, particularly in the fields, and those who engage in it. Similarly, 'the schools to the countryside' movement is designed to instil in students a respect for physical labour as well as some basic knowledge of farming. In 1967 volunteer labour represented about 10 per cent of total labour time, although its productivity is much lower than the average. There is no unanimity even amongst Cubans on whether the principal advantage of voluntary labour is economic or ideological. Mesa-Lago calculated an annual wage saving (1962–7) of over £20 million (1·4 per cent of Cuban national income) due to unpaid labour (but this says nothing of the productivity of that labour, or its deleterious effect on urban production, administration or services). C. Mesa-Lago: 'Economic significance of unpaid labour in socialist Cuba', *Industrial and Labor Relations*, 22 (3), 1969, pp. 339–57.

22. R. Dumont: *Is Cuba Socialist?* (London, Deutsch, 1974), p. 29.

23. *Ibid*: p. 74.

24. *Ibid*: pp. 41–7, 61, 75–83, 88–91.

25. *Ibid*: p. 143.

26. P. Susman: 'Cuba: from dualism to integration', *Antipode, A Radical Journal of Geography*, 6 (3), 1974, pp. 10–29.

27. H. Blume: 'Agrarlandschaft and Agrarreform in Kuba', *Geographische Zeitschrift*, 56 (1), 1968, pp. 1–17.
28. Dumont: *Is Cuba Socialist? op. cit.*, pp. 64–6.
29. E. H. Jacoby: 'Cuba: the real winner is the agricultural worker', *Ceres*, 2 (4), 1969, pp. 29–33.
30. Dumont: *Cuba: Socialism and Development, op. cit.*, p. 47.
31. Bonachea and Valdés: *op. cit.*, p. 361.
32. E. H. Jacoby: *Man and Land* (London, Deutsch, 1971), p. 30.
33. Bonachea and Valdés: *op. cit.*, p. 359.

7

Other Countries

VENEZUELA

The Venezuelan reform is the most extensive non-violent Latin American land reform, introduced democratically and, more significantly, with the active participation of peasants, united in the 500 000 member *Federación Campesina de Venezuela* (FCV), perhaps the most powerful peasant movement in Latin America. Economically the Venezuelan land reform faces conditions very different from those in most other Latin American or underdeveloped countries, although parallels with Iraq have been suggested.[1] Since the 1920s, when oil replaced coffee and cacao as the backbone of the economy, the country has not been dependent upon agriculture to earn foreign exchange, accumulate savings or even feed the population. Financial resources have not seriously constrained the development of land reform. Nor, indeed, have land resources, with large areas said to be potentially cultivable, both in the underpopulated Llanos and in the coastal Valencia and Lake Maracaibo basins. Finally, the *latifundio* system has never been so extreme as elsewhere in the continent; the absentee landowner investing little or none of his earnings on his estates has been much less evident.

EVOLUTION OF THE AGRICULTURAL SITUATION IN VENEZUELA

The background to the 1960 land reform lies in the economic and political developments of the past 40 years when substantial oil revenues have transformed a poor, backward agricultural country into a rich industrial country. The economic growth rate is now the fastest in the continent; per capita income is second only to Argentina's. Population growth (nearly 4 per cent per annum) is absorbed entirely by the urban and industrial sectors, so that rural numbers will probably decline in the foreseeable future. Political and economic power are far less rooted in agriculture than in most Third World countries. In 1960 agriculture contributed only 6 per cent of GNP (22 per cent in 1937), even though employing over a third of the population (2·7 million out of 7·5 million). Herein lies part of the Venezuelan dilemma, because the tremendous growth of urban industry has shifted attention and resources from agriculture, which has languished. Venezuela's problem in 1960 was essentially structural. Oil employed 2 per cent of the active population, yet provided 25 per cent of GNP and 90 per cent of export revenue; unemployment increased from 6 per cent in 1950 to 13 per cent in 1960. Celso Furtado called Venezuela the underdeveloped country with the highest per capita income in the world: meaning that the income figure conceals problems of structural underdevelopment (economic dualism, poverty, illiteracy, low productivity of the mass of the population, etc.), which are, if anything, worse than in many other Latin American countries with lower income indices.[2]

The erosion of agriculture caused by the easy flow of 'black gold' worsened conditions for at least 75 per cent of the rural population and created rural unrest and occasional violence. From this conflict emerged peasant syndicates, wedded by Rómulo Betancourt into an alliance with his Democratic Action Party. This marriage of politics and peasant activism became the driving force behind the land reform movement. The three year rule of Betancourt's *Acción Democrática* junta (1945–8) saw a marked change in the control of land and power, with peasant syndicates securing widespread land transfers and other privileges from large landowners. By 1948 the union leader had displaced the landlord in control of the social and political forces affecting the lives and fortunes of the peasant masses. In three years the reform programme had leased 125 000 hectares to some 73 000 members of the 500 peasant syndicates. Powell, a meticulous student of rural Venezuela, considers this little known 1945–8 *de facto* reform the real impetus to agrarian change in Venezuela.[3] It initiated changes which, after the interregnum of the Pérez Jiménez dictatorship (when 96 per cent of the beneficiaries were dislodged from their plots and many peasant union leaders imprisoned), re-emerged in the post-1958 *de jure* land reform.

THE 1960 LAW

Returned to power in 1958, Betancourt appointed a land reform commission whose four subcommittees dealt respectively with legal, social, economic and agro-technical aspects. Considerable research and discussion went into the resulting law, which was passed by the Venezuelan congress with few modifications. The 1960 law is notable for its broad coverage, surrounding land tenure reform with other aspects of an 'integrated' approach. Under the concept of the 'social function of landed property', three kinds of land are subject to expropriation: uncultivated land; estates worked indirectly through renters, sharecroppers and other intermediaries; and land kept in natural pasture but suited to cultivation. Private land may be expropriated only if no publicly owned land is available in the vicinity, and then only from properties exceeding certain size limits (except in circumstances of extreme social pressure). These limits are 150 hectares of irrigated or good humid agricultural land, 300 hectares of dry agricultural land, 5000 hectares of improved grazing land, and 21 000 hectares of natural pasture. In addition, lands growing certain specialised market crops such as sugar, coffee, rice and wheat, were exempt in order to maintain their production at full capacity. Thus, although the land reform was the main social policy for assisting a peasantry stranded by the uneven process of national modernisation, economic and production motives were clearly important, too.[4]

Land expropriated is paid for in cash, at current market value, up to about £13 000; above this, payment is partly in bonds according to a sliding scale. Such generous compensation procedures brought accusations of a sell-out to landlords, but, with capital to spare the government's aim was to effect land transfers amicably. It is true, however, that landlords encouraged some peasant land invasions and petitions in the early 1960s because subsequent indemnity for the land showed a profit; compensation for 'expropriated' land was so favourable that the reform agency has had to limit the number of farms purchased.[5]

Priority in selecting beneficiaries goes to those actually cultivating the land. Repayments for the land are spread over 20–30
years, but in special circumstances distribution can be free.
Petitions for land assignment were granted as *asentamientos* (settlements) to individuals or groups. Plots awarded varied in size
according to land quality, family size and other factors; half
were 5–15 hectares.

Besides these basic land redistribution measures the law provides for credit, marketing, extension services, co-operatives,
land development and graduated land taxes to force further sale
(or intensification) of large properties. Land, credit and technical assistance, the 'three rights', were the fundamental means of
socio-economic improvement for previously landless assignees.[6]
Three institutions were accordingly established: the *Instituto
Agrario Nacional* (the land redistribution agency); *Banco Agrícola y Pecuario* (for credit); and the already existing *Ministerio de
Agricultura* (for extension and technical assistance services).

About 2500 farms (comprising 15 million hectares, half the
land in farms in the country) exceeded the legal limits and were
therefore technically available for expropriation. The announced objective of the reform was to benefit 300 000 rural families
within ten years, covering nearly all the landless and needy
families in the agricultural sector. Achievement has fallen well
short of this. By 1971 nearly 120 000 peasant families had received land totalling 4·6 million hectares (2·8 million public
land, 1·8 million hectares private). The beneficiaries are organised into about 1000 *asentamientos* or agrarian reform settlements.

From the 1945–8 procedure of leasing land to peasant groups,
emphasis has shifted since 1960 to establishing a new class of
peasant smallholders. Initially (1960–2) there was a good deal
of peasant occupation of land; this was largely repossession of
land awarded in 1945–8 but taken away by the Pérez Jiménez
régime. The government soon split over the direction of the reform. Ramón Quijada, the principal peasant leader, wanted
faster expropriation of privately-owned holdings, including those
protected by law as efficient specialist estates; Betancourt and
the Democratic Action Party moderates emphasised colonisation of public land, with expropriation of private land limited
to underutilised areas not fulfilling a 'social function'. Segnini,
president of the reform institute, wanted caution in the distribu-

tion of land, supplying new owners with all the services needed to make farming efficient. Quijada demanded immediate redistribution but proposals to accelerate the reform drastically were defeated in congress, largely through the economic arguments of the commercial farmers, and Quijada was ejected from the official reform movement in 1962. Nevertheless, after the lull in reform activity in 1961–3 due to budgetary restrictions and preparations for the 1963 elections, speed of redistribution did accelerate, although the balance shifted markedly from private land expropriation to allocation of public lands. A 1964 decree gave all public land (7 million hectares) to the *Instituto Agrario Nacional* for distribution.

SETTLEMENT CHANGES

The land reform was reinforced by a massive housing programme. During the decade 1960–70 some 100 000 rural housing units were constructed, mostly in hamlets and small villages. These *asentamientos* are the reform's principal effect on the visible landscape. Indeed nowhere else in Latin America has land reform wrought such remarkable changes in rural settlement.[7] A distinction, however, must be made between the pre-1960 settlements established for large scale irrigation projects, and the smaller post-1960 group settlements, mostly independent of irrigation projects.

Large scale colonisation schemes were given greatest impetus in the early 1950s, under Pérez Jiménez. About 1500 families, a third of them European immigrants, were settled between 1950 and 1957. The largest schemes were Turén (700 families) and Guárico (500). Mean holding size was 200 hectares. This policy was commercially oriented, aimed at reducing Venezuela's dependence on foreign food supplies, rather than at benefiting the peasantry. Despite lavish finance, results were generally poor. The World Bank Mission to Venezuela judged that giving some benefit to many farmers would have been better, economically and politically, than providing everything for a few.[8]

Further large scale irrigation-colonisation projects were established after Pérez Jiménez's fall but these ones were intended primarily for landless and small peasants, and the assigned plots were much smaller. On the Centro-Occidente de Cojedes scheme, started in 1959, 1170 *microparcelas* were established on

26 300 hectares organised in 11 settlements, although 34 310 hectares were still reserved for a much smaller number of large and medium-sized farms. After 1960, with increased oil revenues, commitment to helping Venezuela's landless strengthened. Israeli settlement experts helped to plan the 30 000 hectares settlement complex of Las Majaguas during 1963–6; five co-operative *moshavim* settlements (80 farms each) are provided with carefully planned services. A 60 000 hectares extension of Las Majaguas, connecting with the Turén scheme to the south, is scheduled for the 1970s. Two other newly started large developments are the Orinoco Delta scheme, which will develop half the area of Delta Amacuro territory, and Sur del Lago, south of Lake Maracaibo. Since the mid-1960s, however, the government has concentrated on smaller, cheaper irrigation schemes to support the *Instituto Agrario Nacional*'s land redistribution efforts.[9] Figure 2 shows the location of both types of irrigation projects.

Asentamientos rurales are the smaller group settlements established by the land reform on petitioned land. Like the smaller-scale irrigation projects they are fairly evenly dispersed throughout the country, but relatively concentrated west of Caracas. Early concentration on developing the western *llanos* (partly because of uncontrolled immigration of Colombians across the border) has now shifted to the east, especially to the Orinoco Delta region, thus making the programme truly national in scope. Most *asentamientos* have approximately 100 families; the average lot size is 10 hectares. In 1974 1000 *asentamientos* housed half a million people. Settlers attend agricultural schools, to learn elements of crop raising, irrigation and livestock husbandry. University-trained female social workers instruct peasant women in hygiene, health, cooking and family care. Many *asentamientos* follow the Israeli *moshav shitufi* model (communal planning with individual cultivation): a blending of Old and New World rural cultural geography. Most reform settlements are advantageously located along good roads, assuring market accessibility. In form, they tend towards a linear shape (as opposed to the traditional |Latin American rectangular plaza nucleus); this facilitates expansion and accommodates the growing emphasis on horticulture and poultry production.

The *Instituto Agrario Nacional* claims that a third of the farm

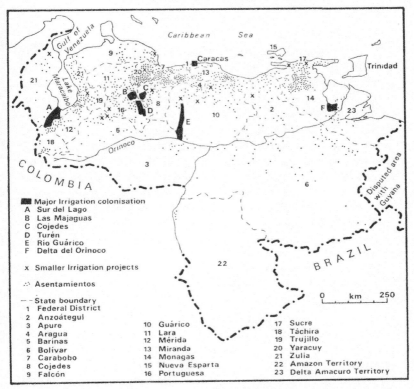

Fig. 2. Agrarian reform activities in Venezuela: *asentamientos* (reform villages) and irrigation schemes. *Source:* R. C. Eidt: 'Agrarian reform and the growth of new rural settlements in Venezuela', *Erdkunde*, 29 (2), 1975, pp. 131–2

population have markedly improved living standards through the *asentamiento* programme. The social benefits of health, comfort, morale and education for former landless peasants have been considerable, though income gains are more modest. Commercial production is rising significantly. Since 1970 the new settlements have made Venezuela self-sufficient in rice, sugar, manioc, beans, sesame and some other crops; between 30 and 50 per cent of the production of these important commodities comes from reform settlements. The impact on the livestock sector has, however, been slight.

CONCLUSION

Warriner rightly questions whether this has been a genuine reform.[10] It has been made possible only by abundant funds. Real redistribution effects are hardly evident: the landowners have gained as much as the *campesinos*. In 1969, 7 per cent of private, and 42 per cent of public land was in land reform assignees' hands. The reform's shortcomings mostly reflect the fact that many peasants got too little land, and that co-ordination in implementation was lacking.[11] Half the beneficiaries received less than 10 hectares—the size generally considered the minimum viable unit in Venezuela—and in the mountain zones 72 per cent. Abandonment is a serious problem. During 1960–70 land was awarded to 171 500 assignees, but 64 000, over a third, left their plots, ceased to be farmers or migrated to urban centres.[12]

Politically the post-1958 stability that land reform has achieved rests on something of a paradox.[13] In 1945 the deprived peasantry were an electoral majority so that attention to their needs— the land reform—made good political sense. Venezuelan society is now predominantly urban but the capricious nature of the urban voter since 1958 has permitted rural voting blocs to dominate elections. The two most popular political parties (Democratic Action and the Social Christians) enjoy a core of dependable rural support, even though the peasantry are a dwindling minority group (less than 30 per cent of the electorate as opposed to 65 per cent in 1945). Herein lies the Venezuelan peasantry's dilemma. The necessity of the agrarian reformers to find support for land reform from non-peasant groups means an inevitable compromise with the original aims of the reform. Land reform can, consequently, no longer be formulated just as a programme of peasant welfare; it must also include a policy of commercial development to gain support from other farm and business interests.

COLOMBIA

The Colombian agrarian reform law of December 1961 resembled Venezuela's in intent, but has proved rather less significant in execution. As the first reform of the Alliance for Progress era, Colombia's attracted a great deal of attention, especially from American writers; consequently, the reform spawned a tremendous literature, which belies its modest achievements. It was called a pattern at which other Latin American countries could aim in their own land reform programmes,[14] but this optimism for real democratic land reform was soon diluted by subsequent events. Much more than in Venezuela, the government has concentrated on granting titles to public land. In nine years the reform has settled 88 000 families, but only 1 194, with average holdings of 12 hectares, in *asentamientos* on land expropriated from private owners.

Colombia's tenure problems are clear-cut and closely related to its agricultural geography. The pattern, nevertheless, is partly irrational. Large, extensively-run cattle estates occupy the flat, fertile valleys (notably of the Cauca and Magdalena rivers) and the upland plateaux, while *minifundistas* intensively farm the steep mountainsides where erosion is a threat.[15] Coffee, the main export crop, occupies small or medium hillside holdings, one third of them sharecropped. By contrast, landless labourers are more characteristic of the humid coastal plains, where plantations grow cotton, bananas, rice and sugar. Overall, 3·5 per cent of the landowners, holding more than 100 hectares, controlled 66 per cent of the land in 1960; half the large estates were absentee-owned; and half the land under irrigation was in holdings of over 200 hectares. The basic spatial misallocation of land and labour resources is thus clear: excess land and deficient labour on the large farms, the reverse on the smallholdings.

INTELLECTUAL GOVERNMENT AND RURAL VIOLENCE

In Colombia, traditionalism still successfully opposes modernisation. The survival of the Spanish heritage—the social class divisions, feudal land tenures, the bureaucracy, the Church, the extended family, and the myth of an aristocratic class fit by education and inheritance only to rule—largely explains this situation. Colombia, it has been said, is a country where philosophers are kings, and intellectuals presidents. Co-opting the talented and the educated into the ruling class has tended to prevent the development of a frustrated elite which might otherwise become revolutionary. Frustration has, instead, settled on the peasantry. Reforms, apparently real, become token gestures when related to the country's broader socio-economy. Examples include free health treatment, while neither hospitals, nor equipment nor sufficient medicine are available; obligatory free education, when neither transport, nor sufficient schools nor trained teachers exist; and a 'land reform' legislated and administered largely by the landowning classes.

Colombian rural conflict began in the late 1920s and continued through '*la violencia*' of 1948–58 into the land invasions of the 1960s.[16] The locus of these conflicts has shifted from the coffee-producing departments of Tolima and Cundinamarca to the northern coastal areas. The land invasions of the 1960s in northern departments like Sucre, Bolívar, César and Córdoba were related to the above average degrees of land concentration (exacerbated by increasing population), lack of alternative outlets for peasant land hunger (e.g. public land available for colonisation or squatting), and the degree of tenure security (proportion of owner-operated farms to leases).[17] One-third of northern Colombia's rural population in the 1960s were landless labourers; 75 per cent of the land was under *latifundia*. When mechanised cotton cultivation in the early 1960s brought massive benefits for the landowners but only seasonal unemployment and low wages for the labourers, rural conflict worsened, and pressure for land reform intensified. Around 1960, too, the Colombian peasant movement received a fillip (if not financial support) from the success of the Cuban revolutionaries; young student activists went into the mountains to seek out peasant guerrilla leaders, and stimulated political consciousness in the rural movement.

THE 1961 AGRARIAN REFORM

Prodded by Cuba-inspired rural unrest and by the Alliance for Progress call for agrarian reform, the conservative-liberal National Front government felt that reform legislation was inevitable to appease the dissatisfied peasantry. Late in 1961 the 'Social Agrarian Reform Law' promised final enforcement of a 1936 law which had aimed at security for squatters and tenants and had authorised expropriation of land uncultivated for ten years or longer. Although the 1961 law was comprehensive legislatively, its approach to land reform was piecemeal, and, like Venezuela's reform, provided generous compensation for most land expropriated. The main task of the reform agency—INCORA—was to settle independent cultivators on family farms, although some communal assignments have been made recently. In order of priority, territory is acquired from public lands (for settlement), land farmed by tenants and sharecroppers (for tenancy regulation and ultimate conversion into freehold), and only lastly lands 'inadequately cultivated' by their owners (for 'real' redistribution).[18] Ceilings on private landholding were vague, with notional limits of 2000 hectares for uncultivated estates and 100 hectares for more intensively farmed *latifundia*. No time period is prescribed for any reform accomplishments. Significantly, the law does not mention *farms* on which land is unused or inadequately managed, only *land* inadequately used. So only the poorly used portions of an estate —generally the worst land—are available for the reform, and tracts of lands are expropriated or purchased without reference to the owner's total land holdings. Land reform in the traditional areas of good farming, where *minifundistas* desperately need access to the extensively used but fertile valley lands, is made virtually impossible.[19] Preference in distribution goes, in order of priority, to: (1) tenants, sharecroppers and labourers on the land being subdivided; (2) other local landless peasants; (3) owners of plots of under 3 hectares adjoining the subdivided land to raise their farms to 'family size'. Size of beneficiary plots varies according to land use. Where vegetables can be grown and marketed, lots may be only 5 hectares; for maize, rice, yuca and plantain main crops the units are 10–20 hectares; where only grassland is farmed farms may be 50 hectares or more. Finally, a 1968 supplementary law gives tenants and sharecroppers of less than 15 hectares (25 per cent of all farmers in 1960) the opportunity to purchase the land they lease. Little information is available on the progress of this last measure.[20]

PROGRESS AND PROBLEMS

INCORA has three main activities: land titling, irrigation and reclamation, and supervised credit. By 1970 INCORA had titled 100 000 parcels of land (3 million hectares), 91 per cent of them only confirming *de facto* squatter and settler claims on public land. The 100 000 'new land owners' represent a 14 per cent increase over the 694 000 small farmers (with under 50 hectares) recorded in the 1960 census, and 10 per cent of the estimated 1 million families who need land.

Titling of land acquired from private owners was to be central to the 1961 reform, but expropriation measures have been almost wholly unsuccessful. The legal procedures have been slow and cumbersome; landowners have been able to stall indefinitely or negotiate favourable purchase prices with INCORA. Landlords maintained that altering the tenure structure of western Colombia would reduce production, and cited the idle public lands in the east, where 'the government is the biggest *latifundista* of all'. By 1969 INCORA had acquired 124 000 hectares of private land by expropriation, purchase and gifts. Only 18,000 hectares of this was obtained by expropriation, and only 13 600 hectares of it actually assigned, to 1194 beneficiaries, little more than the estimated number of new families added to the rural population each week.[21] Only 4 per cent of INCORA's expenditure in the late 1960s went on land purchases and expropriations, 40 per cent on irrigation projects.[22] In practice, the only speedy way found to obtain sufficient extensions of land suitable for settlement is by establishing irrigation districts, which are exempted from many restrictions which impede progress elsewhere, and where the quota retainable by landowners is only 100 hectares. But irrigation projects involve costly investments and lengthy delays in settlement. They benefit only a selected few *campesinos*, yet large landowners may be awarded a substantial block of newly irrigated land. A reported 456 500 hectares are scheduled for irrigation by INCORA, including projects absorbed from other agencies. By 1970 about 40 000 hectares on 18 projects had been irrigated.

Supervised credit, the reform's third main feature, has been facilitated by loans of £8 million during the 1960s from the Agency for International Development. By 1970 37 000 families were benefiting under the programme, but with difficulties in supervising small loans to small farmers INCORA has shifted attention to larger borrowers. The agency is under increasing pressure to abandon true land redistribution and credit extension to small farmers and concentrate on technical developments and aid to larger farmers. American aid commitment seems to conform. In 1968 the US granted the Colombian livestock industry a loan of £5 million 'to allay fears engendered amongst ranchers by the agrarian reforms'. Despite increasing rural violence, in 1971 the conservative president Pastrana suspended all redistribution activities, arguing that the interests of national agricultural production required all help to be directed towards the existing beneficiaries.[23]

WHEN IS LAND REFORM A LAND REFORM?

This question is particularly poignant in Colombia.[24] Its land reform follows the Colombian tradition of issuing well-meaning and socially advanced laws which prove ineffective through lack of enforcement or clever obstruction. The law was a political compromise between the traditional vested landed interests and the moderate reformers. But conservative elements are not alone in slowing down land reform in Colombia. Duff writes of a strange autoconviction amongst INCORA personnel that the agency's programme is admirable, leading agrarian reform progress in Latin America.[25] While this attitude persists, the Colombian countryside will change little. Above all, the law is permissive, not mandatory: it gives INCORA certain broad powers for agrarian reform, but does not require it to accomplish such reforms by fixed deadlines. The problem of absentee landowners has not been solved. Striking discrepancies exist between land acquired and land distributed. The falsity of the official view that land in *latifundia* is unsufficient to provide holdings for the bulk of the needy rural population (hence the emphasis on public land) has been exposed.[26] In 1964 INCORA concluded that landownership concentration was not a problem and land redistribution was unnecessary. The institute even claimed that *latifundia* occupied only a small proportion of poor quality land. This is probably history's first instance of a land reform agency arguing away its own right to existence!

CHILE

Unlike Colombia, whose promising land reform rapidly petered out, Chile's land reform started weakly but steadily gained strength. It resulted from incremental changes in tenure and the growing strength of peasant movements spanning a

decade or more, rather than from a party or presidential programme. Thus although Allende and the *Unidad Popular* party
emphasised land reform in the early 1970s, their accomplishments built on legislation and institutions created during the
preceding Frei and Alessandri administrations.

BACKGROUND TO CHILEAN LAND REFORM

Geographical facts of shape and physique give Chilean life
and agriculture their character. Owing to Chile's elongation
(4160 km long, averaging 175 km wide), its component parts
vary from hot desert to the raw, windswept end of the inhabited
world. The best farmland forms the core of Chile, the Central
Valley region; here landownership has been the cornerstone of
Chilean social history. Although remote for early colonisation,
the Mediterranean climate, scenic beauty and fertile soils of central Chile gave the Spanish conquerors an environment most
like that of their homeland.

Uncharacteristically in Latin America, Chile has a long
history of industrialisation and democratic government. By mid-
twentieth century the country had attained high social modernisation and political development. Copper provides over 65 per
cent of export revenue. Farm population was only 35 per cent of
the total by 1940 and has declined proportionately ever since
(30 per cent in 1960, 25 per cent by 1975). Absolute numbers
are now also falling. Despite excellent agricultural potential,
Chile has gradually become a net food importer. The agricultural export surplus disappeared in 1940. By 1964 agricultural
imports were five times exports, and agriculture's contribution
to GNP was only 10 per cent.

The worsening economic situation of agriculture was the
chief factor behind land reform. Falling productivity was
blamed on the landholding structure, particularly in the Central Valley where in 1955 large estates kept 35 per cent of the
irrigated land in natural pasture. By the 1930s McBride, in a
fundamental study on rural Chile, had sensed the inevitability
of land reform. He concluded that the *hacienda* had outlived its
purpose and that its passing would bring fuller utilisation of
natural resources and higher standards of living for most
people.[27] The 1955 census showed that Chile ranked amongst
the world's countries with the highest degree of land concentra-

tion: 87 per cent of the farmed area was in holdings of over 200 hectares, 55 per cent in *latifundia* of over 5000 hectares numbering only 0·5 per cent of total landholdings. Smallholdings of under 20 hectares were 63 per cent of all holdings by number but covered under 2 per cent of the agricultural area.

The debate over land reform has focused mainly on the ten provinces of the Central Valley (Aconcagua to Ñuble). This region contains 39 per cent of the arable and 76 per cent of the irrigated land, produces 45 per cent of Chile's agricultural produce by value, including nearly all the grapes, and concentrates on supplying greater Santiago with fruits, vegetables and cereals. The typical form of tenure was owner-operated and manager-operated large farms, called *fundos*, which particularly predominated in Santiago and Valparaíso, the key provinces of Chile's core. Plot-holding resident workers (*inquilinos*), supplemented by daily wage labourers (*jornaleros*) and semi-nomadic migrant labourers (*afuerinos*), provided the estate labour. Sharecropping (*medieria*) was also widespread, accounting in 1955 for 30 per cent of the land in crops and 14 per cent of agricultural production by value. In the landscape the expansively laid out *fundos* with their headquarters approached through long avenues of trees and labourers' cottages contrasted with the tiny *minifundio* plots relegated to scraps of hillside or stony valley land. Despite *latifundistas'* privileged access to credit, urban markets, advanced technology and irrigation, they lacked social and economic compulsion to vitalise their enterprises; many reaped high profits only at the expense of their workers. Up to half the land on the large estates was idle; mechanisation further increased unemployment; 80 per cent of the farm population were landless.[28]

CHILEAN LAND REFORM: AN ACCELERATING PROCESS

Chilean agrarian reform can be divided into the following periods: (1) pre-reform (1925–64); (2) the evolutionary reform period of Eduardo Frei (1965–70); (3) the rapid reform period of Allende's government (1970–3); and (4) the period of retrenchment since the fall of Allende.

The pre-reform period was characterised by a policy of 'benign neglect' on the part of various governments. Under the 1925 constitution private property could only be appropriated

G

with an immediate cash payment by the government to the owner. In 1928 the *Caja de Colonización Agrícola* (Agricultural Colonisation Bank) was established to settle colonists on public land and on underutilised private land purchased from land-owners. During the ensuing 34 years (the *Caja* was absorbed by the new Chilean land reform institute CORA in 1962) only 4206 colonists were settled (averaging 124 per year) on 166 schemes. These assignments represented only 2·5 per cent of the agricultural enterprises in Chile, or 1 per cent of the Chilean families engaged in agriculture. Only 618 (15 per cent) of the colonists were settled in central Chile where the landholding structure was most inequitable. Only a fifth of the parcels were awarded to *inquilinos* and *medieros* (sharecroppers). Most assignments were to former administrative personnel from large farms and to others with professional training. German and Italian immigrants were also settled. After 1960 assignments to *inquilinos* and low status rural workers were garden plots of about one hectare, the supposition being that these people would spend most of their time as labourers on the larger plots assigned to professional agriculturalists—a re-creation in effect, of the social system traditional in Chilean agriculture.[29]

An important stage in Chile's growing commitment to land reform during the early 1960s was the land redistribution effected by the Catholic Church. Although insignificant in area terms, this redistribution of church land was considered useful in demonstrating a workable technique of 'gradualistic private land reform',[30] and instructive in its variety of experimentation in forms of colonisation and communal farming.[31] By 1966 INPROA (the church settlement body) had sponsored 200 colonists on 5 schemes covering 5625 hectares (50 per cent irrigated), about 11 per cent of the ecclesiastical land in the country (Fig. 3). Of the five schemes, Los Silos was transferred to a *campesino* co-operative in 1962; Las Pataguas concentrates on individual ownership; and Alto Las Cruces and San Dionisio were operated by a sharecropping-tenancy co-operative for some years before becoming individual tenure in the late 1960s. All four schemes were mainly to benefit local estate labourers. The fifth project, Alto Melipilla, benefited higher status *fundo* employees, who have since become independent farmers receiving little INPROA help. Some remarkable income increases

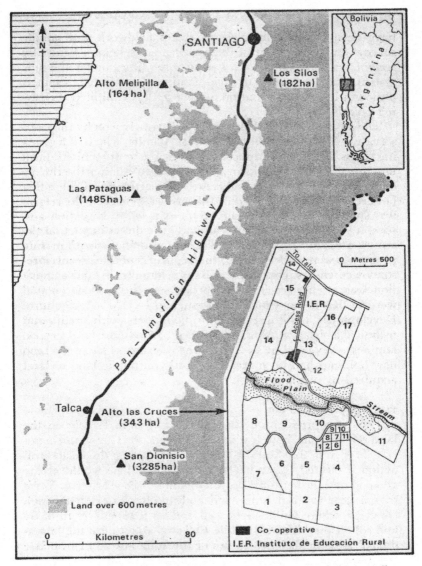

Fig. 3. Chile: location of Church land reform projects, and the parcelisation plan of Alto Las Cruces (each holding consists of a farmland plot of about 15 hectares, some have additional 1-hectare garden plots). *Source:* W. C. Thiesenhusen: *Chile's Experiments in Agrarian Reform* (Madison, University of Wisconsin Press, Land Economics Monographs 1, 1966), pp. 71, 146

have been revealed by Thiesenhusen's fieldwork and sample surveys on the first four of these settlement schemes.[32] Initially *campesino* incomes increased two to three times under the new system, and from 1964 to 1970 continued to rise consistently, although income distribution among settlers exhibited increasing polarisation.

The 1958 presidential election was narrowly won by the Conservative Alessandri over the Marxist Allende, who had a growing mass of voting support from newly enfranchised farm labourers in the central provinces. It was to counter the threatening strength of the left and centre-left parties that Chile's first land reform law was passed in 1962. Since, however, the reform was sponsored by the conservatives as a self-preservation gesture, it was limited in scope and had little direct impact on the tenure structure. Only 'abandoned' and 'inefficient' private properties were expropriable; the vagueness of these terms foreshadowed endless court proceedings if large scale land acquisition was attempted. Two important new institutions created were CORA to carry out the reform, and INDAP (Agricultural Development Institute) to aid smallholders with credit and technical assistance. Alessandri aimed to distribute land to 5000 families per year, but by 1964, when he lost office, only 1200 new holdings had been created, mostly on public land or land acquired by outright purchase.

THE 1967 FREI REFORM

The 1964 presidential campaign was fought largely on the land reform issue, both leading contenders, the Christian Democrat Frei and the Marxist Allende, promising drastic reform action if elected, After his victory. Frei said he would create 100 000 new agricultural proprietors in his six-year term. Yet it took a year to draft a new bill and another to get it through congress, where landowners used endless manoeuvres to delay and soften the bill. Meanwhile Frei was able to use the 'abandoned' and 'inefficient' clauses of the 1962 law to expropriate 480 *fundos* and assign land to over 8000 families during 1965–7.[33]

The 1967 law provided the legal framework for a comprehensive land reform. Any holding of over 80 irrigated hectares of Central Valley land or its equivalent elsewhere (detailed ratios were specified) qualified for expropriation. The law, however, was not mandatory on this: land over this limit *may* be expropriated. Escape clauses have been well used; for example, an owner presenting an investment plan to improve soils may have his land exempted. Abandoned or badly managed lands could be expropriated regardless of size, but vineyards and certain 'extraordinarily well-run' farms could be left intact up to 320 hectares.[34] To counter cases whereby *fundos* had been split into 80 hectare lots during the bill's passage, the size limit was made retroactive to 1964. Compensation was by a small cash payment, with the remainder in long-term low interest bonds partially adjusted for inflation. To avoid the possible economic chaos of an immediate transfer of estate land to peasants, the law stipulated a 2–5 year transitional phase, during which CORA supervises the co-operative administration of the transferred land in *asentamiento* settlements, before individual titles are granted. Ultimate communal assignments were also envisaged. Finally, important in a country with much irrigated farming, the 1967 law contained a framework for 'water reform', eventually embodied in the 1969 Water Code.

The transitional *asentamiento* phase recognised the belief that peasants needed to be taught how to farm properly, but was criticised for creating uncertainty in the land reform process for the peasants; Ernest Feder called it 'land reform on the instalment plan'.[35] During the year *asentados* are advanced lump sums per week or month. Day-to-day management of the *asentamiento* is by a five-member administrative committee elected from among the *asentados*. CORA provides supervision and technical assistance, and most agricultural inputs—seeds, machinery, fertilisers and credit. The assignees contribute their labour. Yearly accounts are made and after credit and various costs due to CORA are deducted, the balance is distributed among the *asentados*. Each year the *asentados* are graded by a committee of three of their members and one CORA official; only those who meet the required minimum points score are awarded full ownership titles. Beneficiaries pay for their land over 30 years at 2 per cent interest; instalments are adjusted to 70 per cent of the annual rise in the consumer price index, and no interest is charged on the first three instalments.[36]

CORA concentrated its limited funds on equipping the reform settlements with visible infrastructure provisions (houses, schools, roads, services and machinery) rather than technical assistance, livestock and other productive services. This emphasis may have been misplaced, but has magnified the observable changes in the landscape.[37] A significant new element in the Chilean rural scene since the late 1960s has been the appearance of new *villorios* of prefabricated and wooden houses for the *asentados*. These regularly arranged houses, located in open fields or in planned hamlets (Fig. 4), contrast markedly with the humble houses of labourers lining the old roads to the *fundos*. Land use changes on expropriated farms have also been marked, with arable crops colonising land often previously reserved for pasture. Stock farming, however, has declined on reform land.

The Frei reform was strongly criticised for slow implementation, for relative lack of *campesino* participation in decision-making, for giving reform beneficiaries privileged treatment over other peasants, and for virtually completely ignoring the *minifundistas'* problems. The law itself was difficult to understand, with 160 pages of small type containing 357 'excruciatingly detailed legalistic articles'.[38] The diverse interest groups within Frei's coalition—peasants and capitalist farmers, industrialists and workers, old politicians and young reformers—hindered the emergence of a coherent reform ideology and compromised the programme's execution.[39] Only one quarter of the 100 000 target families had received land by the 1970 election, when Frei was ousted by Allende. Achieving the stated aim would have meant expropriating half the total irrigated area; in fact about 18 per cent of the country's irrigated land was expropriated, rising to a third in the three most important and densely populated provinces of central Chile—Santiago, Valparaíso and Aconcagua (Fig. 5). Overall impact on tenure structure was slight. In 1965 13 478 farms of over 1000 hectares (5·3 per cent of total farms by number) held 87 per cent of farmland; in 1970, after CORA had expropriated 3·5 million hectares from 1410 large holdings, the largest 5 per cent of holdings still contained 77 per cent of total farm area. By 1970, too, 5668 families on 500 000 million hectares of *asentamiento* land had terminated their trial period and obtained full title.[40]

Economically, much discussion prevails on what Frei's *asentamientos* achieved. At £2500–£4000 per beneficiary family, the cost was high. Economic performance varies widely from one

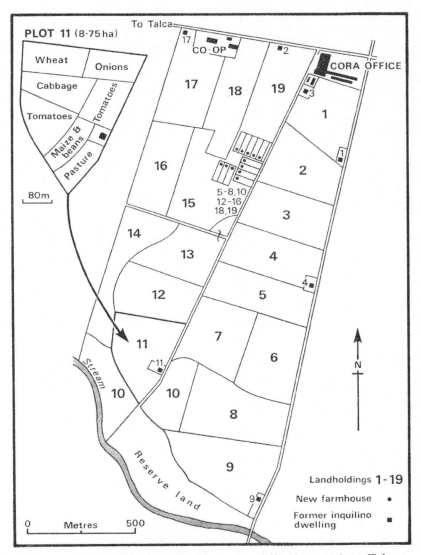

Fig. 4. Landholding and land use on San Miguel *asentamiento*, Talca, Chile. *Source:* K. Rother: 'Stand, Auswirkungen und Aufgaben der chilienischen Agrarreform', *Erdkunde*, 27 (4), 1973, p. 315

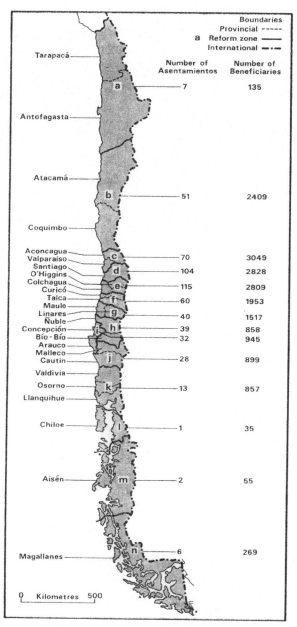

Fig. 5.   Zonal activities of CORA, 1969. *Source:* W. C.
Thiesenhusen: 'Land reform in Chile', in Agency for
International Development: *Spring Review of Land Reform*
(Washington, Department of State, 1970), Vol. 5, p. 10

settlement to another—hardly surprising considering the variety of soil, labour density and other resource endowments they inherited from the *fundos*. Goussault judged the *asentamiento* sector to be undercapitalised and incapable of competing with the large-farm private sector.[41] He calculated its disadvantage in terms of land per worker (7·3 hectares as against 14·4 hectares), capital per cultivated hectare (£80 as against £190) and capital per worker (£220 as against £550). Swift's study of 17 *asentamientos* in Coquimo and Ñuble provinces found little overall change in production since the reform; some settlements had increased output, others stagnated or even declined. Her conclusion was not that there had been no change, but that there was insufficient evidence to support CORA's claims of widespread production gains.[42] True economic evaluation is impossible over such a short period and is complicated by the 1968 drought (the worst for 100 years), which also affected the harvest the following year.

For many peasants CORA's paternalistic control merely replaced their former landlords' authoritarianism. On schemes which achieved individual ownership privileged closed systems tended to be created—and jealously guarded by their members against further entrants from outside. Generally the reform improved the situation of the *inquilinos* (the top stratum of the peasantry who before the reform enjoyed job security, housing and other service provisions from the landlord), but not of the *minifundistas* or *afuerinos*, who remained increasingly underemployed. Many former *inquilinos* hire labour in imitation of the old landlord system.

The Frei reform was, however, complemented by stricter enforcement of minimum agricultural wages, widespread unionisation of rural workers and effective programmes of credit, technical assistance and co-operation, producing more change in agrarian structure than the number of direct beneficiaries might indicate. About 140 000 rural workers joined unions. Largely through collective bargaining and strikes, real farm wages doubled between 1964 and 1970.[43] Few of the unionised peasants, however, were *afuerinos* (the most needy group), while the multiplication of peasant organisations fragmented rural class interests instead of promoting peasant unity.[44] With discontented peasants excluded from the reform, with *afuerinos* outside the unions, and with landowners smarting from expropriation, Lehmann concluded that the Frei land reform was more important in creating rural instability than in integrating rural workers into the national polity.[45]

ALLENDE AND RAPID REFORM[46]

Salvador Allende's *Unidad Popular* administration (a socialist-communist coalition) rapidly hastened the land reform process. This acceleration used the legislative tools developed under Frei, since Allende lacked the power over parliament to enact more drastic legislation. However, at least 1000, and possibly 2000 of the 8000 farms expropriated under Allende were taken over illegally and sometimes violently by peasant unions. The *Unidad Popular* land reform programme aimed at elimination of *latifundia* by the end of 1973, extending social and economic benefits of reform to the poorest strata of the peasantry, who were excluded from the Frei programme. The pre-emptive acts of the peasant unions in taking over many *latifundia* encouraged Allende to accelerate his reform programme and *latifundia* were virtually eliminated by mid-1972. Some 75 000 *campesino* families benefited directly from these expropriations and an estimated 50 000 additional workers indirectly, mainly from part-time employment on the expropriated farms. Marketing, credit and the supply of agricultural inputs were nationalised to prevent the gains from land reform being controlled by monopolists and middlemen.

Abolishing *latifundia* proved easier than reorganising the reformed sector. Initially the Allende government continued creating *asentamientos*, but realisation of the shortcomings of these units from the socialist point of view—particularly the emergence of peasant capitalism—led to the establishment on all *fundos* expropriated after 1970 of *centros de reforma agraria*. These were locally or regionally organised co-operatives, larger than *asentamientos*, with more peasant participation, and membership extended to the non-resident *afuerinos* and even to local *minifundistas*. *Centros* were intended to break down the local geographical boundaries, economic inequalities and social barriers dividing the peasantry, while facilitating regional planning and the rational allocation of labour and machinery. Work was organised in production teams, and improving social infrastructure in rural areas was emphasised, thus absorbing more workers and lessening rural unemployment. All workers got a minimum guaranteed wage, with bonus to high-productivity individuals. Payments were also made to funds for building and capital equipment and to a community development fund for the entire region. Each family was entitled to a house and garden plot, but the combined area of these was not to exceed one-fifth of the total farmed land. The *centros* co-exist with the *asentamientos* set up during 1965–70, but *asentamientos* were encouraged to join to form a *centro*. Some state farms (*centros de producción*) were also established in forest and livestock areas, and the government encouraged *minifundia* to merge into cooperatives.

Allende's land reform record was at first sight impressive. After less than two years he could announce the end of the *hacienda* system. By mid 1972 36 per cent of Chile's productive land was in the 'reformed' sector (Table 6). All this was achieved without the general violence, social dislocation and decline in production common in sweeping reforms elsewhere. The peasants, in their local councils and unions, had been closely involved in the reform process. Peasant union members increased from 140 300 in 1970 to 253 500 in 1972. Real agricultural wages increased; unemployment dropped.

Yet the rural revolution was not complete. Modern, mechanised farms of 40–80 hectares still constituted a citadel of Chilean rural capitalism, possessing much of the best land and employing most of the unattached wage labour. Peasant participation in and enthusiasm for the new *centros de reforma agraria* were limited. *Inquilinos* in particular, having become accustomed to their privileged position in the *asentamientos*, were opposed to the incorporation of *afuerinos* and *minifundistas* within the *centros*. The Christian Democrats fanned peasant suspicion into a wave of mistrust for the new, complex, bureaucratic organs, rumoured to be a step to the peasant becoming a 'slave to the state'. The government accordingly moved slowly in creating *centros*. In many cases a compromise unit, the *comité campesino*, was formed, with equal rights in running the farm and in fringe benefits, but with *afuerinos* and *minifundistas* excluded. Granting of individual titles on pre-existing *asentamientos* was recommenced in November 1971 to appease Christian Democrat propaganda.

TABLE 6

CHILE: LAND TENURE STRUCTURE, 1972

(all figures are percentages)

Sector	Land (irrigated hectares equiv.)	Workers	Value of gross product	Value of marketed product	Proportion of gross product marketed
Reform sector (*centros de reforma agraria, asentamientos* etc.)	36	18	29	29	80
Minifundia (below 20 irrigated hectares equivalent)	22	60	28	15	45
Intermediate sector (mostly holdings of 20–80 irrigated hectares equivalent)	42	22	43	56	95
Total	100	100	100	100	76

Source: S. Barraclough and A. Affonso: 'Diagnosis of agrarian reform in Chile, 1970–2', *Land Reform, Land Settlement and Co-operatives*, 1, 1973, p. 3.

Although Chilean peasants had demonstrated revolutionary fervour in multiple land seizures, Allende never succeeded in fully converting rural workers to a socialist mentality, for he had insufficient foresight and political power to eradicate remaining rural capitalism.[47] Stimulated by the development of a black market, peasants in the *centros* devoted increasing attention to their garden plots, so that collective output suffered. No effective system of economic incentives on the *centros* was devised: workers were paid irrespective of amount or quality of work. The real minimum rural wage was increased 75 per cent but production, having risen 6 per cent during 1970–72, fell 10 per cent in 1973 (partly through bad weather and a truck owners' strike), just when demand for food and clothing rose sharply. Food imports doubled, while the world price of copper, Chile's main revenue earner, slumped seriously. Allende could not move fully to meet the crisis because of the increasing right-wing opposition which eventually engendered the coup of late 1973.

THE FUTURE

Although the present government of General Pinochet imposes rigid military rule in an effort to extirpate Marxism, it does not contemplate, nor could it implement, a massive reversal of land reform. About 120 000 hectares have been returned to former owners, but the present mixed land tenure structure of communal, *minifundia* and medium-sized private holdings seems stable.[48] The government has attempted to institute a free market in land, but most beneficiaries, having mortgaged their new land, cannot sell it until the payments are complete. Pinochet's government has also concentrated on issuing titles to reform farms by breaking up *asentamientos* into smaller units. This, apparently, has been popular with *asentados*, but the withdrawal of credit and other aids enjoyed under Frei and Allende reduces rural standards of living. Inflation, rising imports, stagnating agricultural production and other economic problems bequeathed by Allende have, if anything, worsened, and the future is very unclear.

PERU

Peru is perhaps the continent's best illustration of the mix of geography and land tenure systems commonly known as the Latin American agrarian structure. Geographers have stressed how the three Peruvian regions of *costa*, *sierra* and *selva* (the coast, the mountain, and the jungle) are worlds apart. In some parts of the highland plateaux and Andean intermontane basins the *hacienda* system still exists, the poorer lands relegated to traditionally-organised communities. The arid coast, enriched by irrigation, has export-oriented plantations, notably of sugar, 65 per cent foreign owned. The vast tropical jungles, sloping down to the Amazon basin, are largely inaccessible and exploited by scattered groups of primitive gatherers and slash-and-burn cultivators.

In Peru agrarian reform is clearly a core issue, not a marginal one. A fundamental change in the landholding system is essential to the development and modernisation processes, despite some development through urbanisation and economic diversification in recent decades. Indeed this partial modernisation increasingly highlights the anachronistic nature of an outmoded agrarian system, while the perception of the possibility of change increases rapidly among the peasantry.[49] The 1964 reform was typical of the post-Alliance era of the early 1960s, a token effort quickly stifled by landlord opposition. But the 1969 law, introduced by the military government which seized power in 1968, seems to introduce something entirely new into Latin American land reform. With Cuban land reform subject still to the wrangles of dogmatism and with most other countries surveyed in this part of the book retreating from reform, Peru may well be the significant country in the 1970s.

LAND TENURE AND PEASANT ACTIVITY

Land distribution in Peru is very uneven.[50] In 1961 under 4000 farm holdings (only 0·4 per cent by number) occupied 76 per cent of the farmland. The 1000 largest (those over 2500 hectares) occupied 61 per cent of the total. On the other hand 700 000 smallholders (83 per cent of landholders) with under 5 hectares occupied barely 6 per cent of all farmland. One-fifth of all holdings had under half a hectare each. The lack of independent peasant proprietorship was striking. Farms estimated as 'family size' (averaging 8 hectares) were only 11 per cent by number (4 per cent by area) in the coastal region, and 12 per cent by number (5 per cent by area) in the *sierra*. Irrigated land was also very highly concentrated. In the coastal region 180 holdings over 500 hectares occupied half the irrigated land, while 36 000 smallholdings of under 5 hectares occupied only 6 per cent of the irrigated area. Some 700 000 families (3 million people, over a quarter of the total population) comprised landless agricultural workers and tenant labourers who, concentrated in the *sierra*, have the lowest levels of income in Peru. The tenant-workers are called *colonos* or *feudatarios* on the *sierra*, *arrendires* in the *selva* and *yanaconas* on the coast. *Comuneros*, finally, belong to indigenous communities, whose landholding patterns date to Inca times. These communities, estimated at 3 000–4 000 containing 2·5 million people, have had to fight constantly against *hacienda* encroachment on their land.

The common association of feudal landlord power with national government no longer operates in Peru.[51] Since the end of the nineteenth century the economic and political power of the highland *hacendados* has declined. Republican inheritance laws requiring the division of estate land amongst all heirs split feudal domains into smaller units. The development of the guano industry and of export markets for cotton and sugar encouraged the consolidation of large commercial plantations along the coast. The Casagrande estate, based in the Chicama Valley near Trujillo, comprised 19 000 hectares of irrigated sugar cane; owned by Gildermeisters (the largest sugar company in South America), it produced 30 per cent of Peruvian sugar, exported via the company's own Puerto Chicama. Throughout the twentieth century the ruling oligarchy has been allied with the coastal commercial landowners not the traditional *sierra* landlords. Geographical population shifts have reinforced this tendency. Between 1940 and 1961 *costa's* population increased from 25 to 40 per cent of the national total and by the latter date included 69 per cent of the electorate.[52]

During the 1950s and early 1960s evidence accumulated that agriculture's lagging performance stemmed, at least partly, from the landholding pattern. Food production (increasing at 2·5 per cent per year) was not matching population growth (3 per cent), and met just over half of expanding food demand (4·4 per cent). Agricultural exports were declining, and food imports increased from £6 million in 1960 to £50 million in 1967. Extensive land use on large estates was held partly responsible. Farms of over 500 hectares cultivated only 10 per cent of their area; farms under 10 hectares worked 66 per cent of theirs. It was estimated that 1 million hectares of estate land could be cultivated without significant infrastructural investment, and another 1·5 million hectares with moderate investment.[53]

Although economic and ideological considerations operated, land reform was really forced into the open by peasant rebellion and land invasions, beginning in the early 1950s and particularly important in the central and southern highlands.[54] The most active peasant organisation was the federation of rural unions, headed by Hugo Blanco, in the Convención Valley in the Cuzco area in the early 1960s. Here the conflict grew out of landlords' excessive demands on *arrendires* who had cleared plots of virgin estate land, planting them to coffee and dealing directly with outside merchants. The peasants refused to work on landlords' land and organised self-defence groups to resist attempts by the landlords and the police to dislodge them from their coffee-plots. Military units were sent to the area and numerous acts of violence occurred. Eventually, when the movement had driven many landowners from the area, the government instituted in 1963 a special local land reform decree to end the conflict. Politically, the land reform issue was prominent throughout 1962–3 when all parties except the extreme right-wing landowners' group included reform in their election propaganda. The peasant movement spread to include an estimated 300 000 members—among the largest in the continent's history—and only hatred when the agrarian reform law was approved in 1964 and some land distribution carried out.

THE 1964 REFORM AND ITS LIMITED EFFECTS[55]

Shortly after taking office in 1963, President Belaunde Terry introduced a new land reform bill, which was considered jointly with proposals forwarded by other parties. The outcome was a compromise bill, long, complicated and outwardly comprehensive, passed in May 1964. It was, however, permissive, not mandatory, and provided elaborate safeguards for large property holders. Public lands were to be allocated first, thereafter abandoned and absentee-owned properties. Three *sierra* regions (Cuzco, Puno and Pasco-Junín) were designated as reform priority areas; these were the prime areas of peasant agitation, although the law specifically excluded land invaders from benefiting. Coastal sugar plantations, efficiently farmed estates, corporately-owned land and agro-industrial operations were exempted. This regional impact of the reform reflected the fact that the Lima oligarchy drew its wealth from coastal agriculture and commerce and was indifferent to what happened to remote *haciendas* whose owners had only local, not national, political power, and whose expropriation provided an acceptable placebo for the ills of agrarian unrest. The land reform in fact was a mere continuation of the 'internal colonialism' by which the *costa* had exploited the *sierra* for a century or more.

Other aspects of the law were: (1) rental contracts extended to six years and rental fee limited to 20 per cent of farm's annual output; (2) opportunity for squatters to become legal owners of up to 15–30 hectares (depending on region) if they could prove *de facto* tenant status; (3) elimination of semi-feudal labour arrangements, including personal servitude. Compensation was partly in cash, partly in bonds. The bonds could be yielded as tax payments or, more interestingly, converted into industrial investments. Indemnity payments were calculated from the average of three figures: declared tax value; market value; imputed potential income under good management. Beneficiaries pay for their land in twenty annual instalments, with a grace period determined by ONRA (the National Bureau of Agrarian Reform) of up to five years.

It soon became clear that the political determination to apply the 1964 law rigorously was lacking and that the law itself was too weak to function effectively. Only a fifth of the budget promised ONRA materialised, and a third of that went on running colonisation schemes. So long-winded was the legal and administrative procedure for expropriation that the average property took eighteen months to process.[56]

Data on reform achievements are sparse and conflicting. Between 1964 and 1968 some 2·7 million hectares appears to have been acquired, including 1·4 million hectares of abandoned land and 615 500 hectares by expropriation from 61 properties, but actual distribution was only 300 000 hectares benefiting about 10 000 families. If land transfers and colonisation schemes are included, the totals become 835 000 hectares acquired, 385 000 hectares assigned, and 14 345 beneficiaries. Title provision for squatters also proved problematic. Some 128 000 of an estimated total of 160 000 squatter families applied for registration, and 55 000 were awarded provisional certificates of occupancy rights (very few got permanent titles). Most occupied plots, however, were small allocations (average size 6 hectares) of poor land, so that often more *minifundistas* were created. Worse still, many landlords evicted squatter-tenants to prevent them claiming more secure rights under the law.

THE 1969 REFORM: A PROMISE OF THINGS TO COME?

Although the military take-over of October 1968 was not directly concerned with the agrarian situation, the new government of General Juan Velasco Alvarado quickly moved towards more radical land reform, passing a new law within eight months. The June 1969 reform is largely a reiteration of the

1964 law, 'but with more muscle'.[57] Funding is increased, obstacles to rapid implementation removed and coastal, irrigated, corporately-owned and plantation estates are no longer exempted. In assignment emphasis is placed on group operation for plantations and some livestock ranches whose economies of scale would suffer from subdivision, and on co-operative organisation for all service activities. Landholding limits are 150 hectares for irrigated land in the *costa*, 300 hectares for non-irrigated coastal farms and 1 500 hectares for coastal grazing lands. The *sierra* and *selva* regions have much lower limits on arable land, 15–55 hectares irrigated (30–110 hectares un-irrigated), depending on province, and an area suitable for 5000 sheep, of grazing land. These ceilings are subject to few exemptions, in contrast to the 1964 law. Non-compliance with agrarian labour laws is an additional cause for expropriation, enabling the government to disregard upper size limits in zones of strong social unrest. The 150 hectare limit for coastal irrigated plantations is quite generous and reflects the government's desire to preserve the entrepreneurial character of commercial agriculture, but the great foreign-owned sugar estates of the northern *costa* were expropriated in their entirety. Valuation is now based entirely on self-declared tax assessments of 1968. Cash compensation is half the level of the 1964 law; the remainder comes in bonds maturing in 20, 25, or 30 years at 4, 5 or 6 per cent interest, depending on type of land and criteria for expropriation. Another important new provision enables squatter-tenants not only to gain possession of the land they are occupying but also to increase their plots up to family unit size (minimum 3 hectares) by taking more land from the same landowners. Finally a new Water Reform Law declares all surface and sub-surface water the property of the nation, to be allocated in the best public interest.

Contrasting with the Belaunde reform's plodding pace, the military junta's reform programme began dramatically. Within 48 hours of the President's announcement of the law, eight major sugar estates and their associated processing plants in the northern irrigated valleys were expropriated. A ninth was added soon after. Together these estates employed 15 000 workers and embraced 380 000 hectares, 65 per cent of the total Peruvian cane area and 50 per cent of the cultivated area in the important agricultural provinces of La Libertad and Lambayeque. The psychological impact of this move was enormous, for it underlined to the peasants the seriousness of the government's intentions in land reform. Peru became the second Latin American country, after Cuba, to expropriate highly intensive and profitable commercial plantations. This was interpreted as a move to undercut the power of foreign corporations and of the Peruvian commercial class (in contrast to previous governments, the junta's personnel represented mostly humble provincial origins), and at the same time reduce the power of the sugar workers' unions. The government wisely decided to maintain the sugar estates as large production units. Initially they functioned as semi-state farms, managed by government technocrats, with little sign of the production co-operative model promised by the reform law. Only after strikes over the suppression of trade unions and the lack of worker participation were workers' delegates appointed to the management teams of the estates. Both the plantations and the mills apparently continue functioning efficiently without any technical deterioration or lack of worker discipline.[58]

Reform progress in the uplands has been slower and less documented. The winds of change blow slowly over the *sierra*, and the severe earthquake of June 1970 undoubtedly set back the reform programme here.[59] The reform agency found co-operatives less easy to establish amongst traditional highland *campesinos* than among the literate coastal workers with their trade union experience. Lack of education is development's major deficiency in the *sierra*; the result is that peasants fail to grasp the significance of land reform.[60] The seemingly low priority for highlands land reform has met criticism. Of the 90 000 beneficiaries granted land up to 1971, only 20 000 were in the *sierra*. Peasant pressures for more attention to *sierra haciendas*, much of it organised by Hugo Blanco aided by radical students from the La Molina Agrarian University, brought further commitment to highland reform in the early 1970s, and probably most future effort will be there.[61] Many highland landowners, although entitled to a residual area, are voluntarily ceding their entire holdings on the grounds that the reserve plots are too small and remote to justify continued investment effort.[62]

The quantitative aims and achievements of the Velasco reform are difficult to interpret because of lack of reliable and non-conflicting data. The government's initial reform target was to grant land to half a million families by 1975. Just about enough land could be acquired from the 7000 large land-owners theoretically subject to expropriation to satisfy the half million target, but achievement of this by 1980 or 1985 is more realistic. According to Van der Wetering about 110 000 families had been allotted land up to early 1973.[63] The 3 million hectares expropriated (of which 2·2 million hectares have been assigned) represents only 10 per cent of Peruvian farm and pasture land and 17 per cent of the potential total available for distribution. The reform thus progresses steadily, though well below target rate. Although attempts have been made to help *comuneros* and *minifundistas*, in Peru as in other South American countries the permanent *hacienda* workers have benefited most from reform (in Peru this includes the 23 000 sugar-cane workers, who—as in Cuba—are the most privileged reform group of all). Nor has the reform reached the seasonal agricultural workers (15 per cent of total rural labour force), whose opportunities for work have diminished with the shrinking *latifundia*.

The reform's economic effects have been unremarkable so far. Van der Wetering calculated the total income redistribution effect as of mid-1972 to be more than £20 million, or 9·4 per cent of total value added in crop and livestock production, or 1·7 per cent of total national income: levels with a fairly minor impact on developmental prospects.[64] The reform policy tends to create a climate of uncertainty, and therefore disinvestment, in the non-reformed sector which still encompasses 70–80 per cent of total agricultural resources. Horton, in a detailed 'before-after' study of four expropriated estates, shows that the organisation of production and work changed very little with the creation of production co-operatives.[65] True, great social changes have resulted on ex-*haciendas*, with members' assemblies discussing the running of the estate in detail, but reform agency technicians take the important decisions often on exactly the same criteria as the former *patrón*. The estates, therefore, have become '*haciendas* without *hacendados*'.

The crucial condition for the long-run success of the Peruvian reform is thus the development of a working alliance between the government, represented by reform agency personnel, and the peasants. The future hinges less on the problem of land than on re-ordering human relationships. It needs both sensitive agency workers, willing to live in isolated rural areas, and also competent peasant leaders. These new links have yet to be forged. Peasants still distrust outsiders as part of their defence mechanisms and lethargy bred of centuries of oppression. Bureaucrats are too paternalistic; the *mestizo's* aspirations of a desk job in Lima leave him unwilling to be stranded among the Indians. Gitlitz[66] contends that 'throughout, the reform h been an exercise in rule from the top down, with no participation in decision-making by the concerned sector'. Whereas in Cuba the old *hacienda* mansions house schools as a symbolic and effective functional contribution to the new rural society, in Peru most are inhabited by reform agency functionaries and even army colonels. The dilemma is to give reform beneficiaries enough assistance to meet minimum technical and developmental needs, but not so much as to stifle initiative. This reform conundrum, along with the repercussions of Peru's experiments on neighbouring countries, will be interesting to watch.

REFERENCES

1. D. Warriner: *Land Reform in Principle and Practice* (Oxford, Clarendon, 1969), p. 349. Large oil revenues, small population and underused land are factors of economic geography common to both countries. The problem for both countries is to inject investment into agriculture via land reform in such a way as to increase production and living standards of the rural masses.

2. C. Furtado: *El Desarrollo Reciente de la Economia Venezolana* (Caracas, Ministerio de Fomento, 1957).

3. See J. D. Powell: *The Role of the Federación Campesina in the Venezuelan Agrarian Reform Process* (Madison, University of Wisconsin Land Tenure Center Research Paper 26, 1967), pp. 3–13.

4. G. Coutsoumaris: 'Policy objectives in Latin American land reform with special reference to Venezuela', *Inter-American Economic Affairs*, 16 (2), 1962, pp. 25–40.

5. H. E. Wing: 'Land Reform in Venezuela', in Agency for International Development: *Spring Review of Land Reform* (Washington, Department of State, 1970), Vol. 5, p. 27.

6. R. J. Penn & J. Schuster: 'La reforma agraria de Venezuela', *Revista Interamericana de Ciencias Sociales*, 2 (1), 1963, pp. 29–39.

7. R. C. Eidt: 'Agrarian reform and the growth of new rural settlements in Venezuela', *Erdkunde*, 29 (2), 1975, pp. 118–33.

8. International Bank for Reconstruction and Development: *The Econo-*

mic Development of Venezuela (Baltimore, Johns Hopkins Press, 1961), pp. 57, 148.

9. M. J. Eden: 'Irrigation systems and the development of peasant agriculture in Venezuela', *Tijdschrift voor Economische en Sociale Geografie*, 65 (1), 1974, pp. 48–54.

10. Warriner: *op. cit.*, pp. 357, 367.

11. *Ibid*: pp. 358–9, 368–9.

12. T. van der Pluijm: 'An analysis of the agrarian reform process in Venezuela', *Land Reform, Land Settlement and Co-operatives*, 2, 1972, pp. 1–21.

13. J. D. Powell: 'Venezuelan agrarian problems in comparative perspective', *Comparative Studies in Society and History*, 13 (3), 1971, pp. 282–300.

14. V. W. Johnson and B. H. Kristjanson: 'Programming for land reform in the developing agricultural countries of Latin America', *Land Economics*, 40 (4), 1964, pp. 353–60.

15. D. Adams: 'Colombia's land tenure system: antecedents and problems', *Land Economics*, 42 (1), 1966, pp. 43–52.

16. P. Gilhodès: 'Agrarian struggles in Colombia', in R. Stavenhagen (ed): *Agrarian Problems and Peasant Movements in Latin America* (New York, Doubleday Anchor, 1970), pp. 407–51.

17. R. E. Soles: *Rural Land Invasions in Colombia* (Madison, University of Wisconsin, Land Tenure Center Research Paper 59, 1974).

18. In fact, INCORA can acquire private land by four methods: (1) 'extinction of the rights of private ownership' (i.e. expropriation without indemnity); (2) expropriation with compensation; (3) negotiated purchase; (4) gratuitous transfer. See R. W. Findley: 'Problems faced by Colombia's Agrarian Reform Institute in acquiring and distributing land', in R. E. Scott (ed.): *Latin American Modernization Problems* (Urbana, University of Illinois Press, 1973), pp. 122–92.

19. E. Feder: *The Rape of the Peasantry: Latin America's Landholding System* (New York, Doubleday Anchor, 1971), pp. 197, 202.

20. INCORA claims to have given 'provisional security of tenure' to 45 000 renters and sharecroppers; these awards will become 'permanent titles when they reach certain performance requirements'. INCORA: 'Agrarian reform in Colombia', in Agency for International Development: *Spring Review of Land Reform, op. cit.*, Vol. 5, p. 26. The object is to convert all small tenants to owners by 1978, but the programme will need to be accelerated greatly to achieve this.

21. *Ibid*: p. 22.

22. *Ibid*: pp. 22–3.

23. Findley: *op. cit.*, pp. 144–5, 191–2.

24. E. Feder: 'When is a land reform a land reform? The Colombian case', *American Journal of Economics and Sociology*, 24 (2), 1965, pp. 118–34.

25. E. A. Duff: *Agrarian Reform in Colombia* (New York, Praeger, 1968), p. 214.

26. INCORA'S arguments are clearly based on faulty interpretation of

land holding data. See D. W. Adams: 'Landownership patterns in Colombia', *Inter-American Economic Affairs*, 18 (3), 1964, pp. 77–86, for an explanation of this extraordinary situation.

27. G. M. McBride: *Chile: Land and Society* (New York, American Geographical Society Research Publication 19, 1936), pp. 379, 385.

28. P. Dorner: *Issues in Land Reform: The Chilean Case* (Madison, University of Wisconsin, Land Tenure Center Discussion Paper 5, 1965).

29. W. C. Thiesenhusen: 'Agrarian reform and economic development in Chile: some cases of colonisation', *Land Economics*, 42 (3), 1966, pp. 282–92.

30. W. C. Thiesenhusen: 'Chilean agrarian reform: the possibility of gradualistic turnover of land', *Inter-American Economic Affairs*, 20 (1), 1966, pp. 3–22.

31. W. C. Thiesenhusen: *Chile's Experiments in Agrarian Reform* (Madison, University of Wisconsin Press for Land Economics Monographs 1, 1966).

32. W. C. Thiesenhusen: *Chile's Experiments in Agrarian Reform: Four Colonisation Projects Revisited* (Madison, University of Wisconsin, Land Tenure Center Paper 97, 1974).

33. R. R. Kaufmann: *The Politics of Land Reform in Chile 1950–1970* (Cambridge, Harvard University Press, 1972), p. 69.

34. For the exact criteria for these special cases and exemptions see J. Swift: *Agrarian Reform in Chile: An Economic Survey* (Lexington, Heath, 1971), pp. 37–9.

35. E. Feder: *The Rape of the Peasantry*, *op. cit.*, p. 231.

36. R. L. Meyer: *Financing Agrarian Reform through Beneficiary Repayments: the Chilean Case* (Ithaca, University of Cornell Press, 1972).

37. A. Jeffries: 'Agrarian reform in Chile', *Geography*, 56 (3), 1971, pp. 221–30.

38. J. R. Thome: 'Expropriation in Chile under the Frei agrarian reform', *American Journal of Comparative Law*, 19 (3), 1971, pp. 489–513.

39. Kaufmann: *op. cit.*, chs. 3–8.

40. W. C. Thiesenhusen: 'Agrarian reform in Chile', in Agency for International Development: *Spring Review of Land Reform, op. cit.*, Vol. 5, pp. 3, 22–3.

41. Y. Goussault: 'La réforme agraire chilienne: hesitations ou impasse?' *Tiers Monde*, 13 (51), 1972, pp. 541–58.

42. Swift: *op. cit.*, p. 107.

43. C. Barriga: 'Chile: peasants, politics and land reform', *Land Tenure Center Newsletter*, 36, 1972, pp. 11–14.

44. D. Lehmann: 'Peasant consciousness and agrarian reform in Chile', *Archives Européennes de Sociologie*, 13 (2), 1972, pp. 296–325.

45. D. Lehmann: 'Political incorporation versus political instability: the case of the Chilean agrarian reform', *Journal of Development Studies*, 7 (4), 1971, pp. 365–95.

46. Based on P. Winn and C. Kay: 'Agrarian reform and rural revolution in Allende's Chile', *Journal of Latin American Studies*, 6 (1), 1974, pp. 135–59, with some data from S. Barraclough and A. Affonso: 'Diag-

nosis of agrarian reform in Chile 1970–72', *Land Reform, Land Settlement and Co-operatives*, 1, 1973, pp. 1–7.

47. C. Kay: 'Agrarian reform and the transition to socialism in Chile, 1970–3', *Journal of Peasant Studies*, 2 (4), 1975, pp. 418–45.

48. J. C. Collarte: 'New agricultural policies in Chile', *Land Tenure Center Newsletter*, 46, 1974, pp. 1–5.

49. T. F. Carroll: 'Land reform in Peru', in Agency for International Development: *Spring Review of Land Reform, op. cit.*, Vol. 6, p. 2.

50. J. Brodsky and J. Oser: 'Land tenure in Peru', *American Journal of Economics and Sociology*, 27 (4), 1968, pp. 405–21.

51. F. Bourricaud: *Power and Society in Contemporary Peru* (London, Faber, 1970), pp. 38–40.

52. J. Cotler: 'The mechanics of internal domination and social change in Peru', in I. L. Horowitz (ed.): *Masses in Latin America* (New York, Oxford University Press, 1970), pp. 407–44.

53. Carroll: *op. cit.*, pp. 10–11.

54. There is a wide literature on the Peruvian peasant movement, much of it focusing on the charismatic Hugo Blanco. See, e.g. G. Huizer: *The Revolutionary Potential of Peasants in Latin America* (Lexington, Heath, 1972), pp. 114–24; W. W. Craig: 'Peru: the peasant movement of La Convención', in H. A. Landsberger (ed.): *Latin American Peasant Movements* (Ithaca, Cornell University Press, 1969), pp. 274–96; J. Cotler and F. Portocarrero: 'Peru: peasant organisations', in *Ibid*: pp. 297–322.

55. Based on Carroll: *op. cit.*, pp. 14–27.

56. R. Medina: *Agrarian Reform Legislation in Peru* (Madison, University of Wisconsin, Land Tenure Center Paper 73, 1970), p. 13.

57. Carroll: *op. cit.*, p. 30.

58. A. Saco: 'In Peru land is restored to the Indians', *Land Reform, Land Settlement and Co-operatives*, 1, 1970, pp. 26–39.

59. H. Handelman: *Struggle in the Andes: Peasant Political Mobilisation in Peru* (Austin, University of Texas Press, 1975), pp. 246, 248.

60. T. J. Peacock and P. J. Atkins: *The Progress of Agrarian Reform in the Peruvian Andes: Two Case Studies of a Society in Transition* (Cambridge, The Downing College Expedition to Peru Final Report, 1972), p. 40.

61. Handelman: *op. cit.*, pp. 248–56.

62. C. Mitchell: 'Peru's agrarian reform', *Land Reform, Land Settlement and Co-operatives*, 2, 1969, pp. 89–92.

63. H. Van der Wetering: 'The current state of land reform in Peru', *Land Tenure Center Newsletter*, 40, 1973, pp. 5–9. This apparently is a cumulative total and therefore includes the 14 000 assignees in existence before 1968.

64. *Ibid*: p. 8.

65. D. E. Horton: *Haciendas and Co-operatives: A Preliminary Study of Latifundist Agriculture and Agrarian Reform in Northern Peru* (Madison, University of Wisconsin, Land Tenure Center Research Paper 53, 1973), pp. 77–80.

66. J. Gitlitz: 'Impressions of Peruvian agrarian reform', *Journal of Inter-American Studies and World Affairs*, 13 (3), 1971, pp. 456–74.

PART 3

Land Reform in Asia

Introduction

Asia's problems, though very different from those of Latin America, are no less intractable, for here agrarian development in general and land policy in particular face the additional crucial factor of population pressure. Asia has a fifth of the world's land area but over half its population. Application of modern medical science to communities still largely pre-industrial has drastically reduced the death rate without as yet significantly affecting the birth rate, and the consequent progressive imbalance between man and land has worsened in the post-colonial period. The rate of population increase has itself been increasing: the annual rate averaged 1 per cent during 1920–50, 2 per cent during 1950–70 and now stands at around 2·3 per cent.[1] Asia's population, 1355 million in 1950, 2118 million in 1970, is projected to reach 2668 million in 1980 and perhaps 3600 million by 2000. Although a slight reduction in fertility seems likely within this century, the conclusion is inescapable: however successful birth control among the masses may prove, the labour force will continue to increase annually at between 2 and 3 per cent until the end of this century.[2] The farm population continues to increase dramatically; as Dovring[3] has shown, it does not decline until well after it has become a minority in the total population, and at present the farm population percentage of the total declines slowly, if at all. Only part of this rapidly increasing population can be absorbed outside agriculture, so intensifying pressure on land constitutes a major source of tension. Asian agricultural families (outside Russia and Middle East countries) average less than 2 hectares of arable land. In

Japan, Taiwan, South Korea, Indonesia and Nepal the proportion is nearer to half a hectare. The great alluvial valleys and
deltas of south-east Asia record rural population densities of 500
per sq. km. Traditionally, rice farmers react to population pressure by farming their continually subdivided holdings ever more
intensively. This has been well documented by Geertz in Java,
where, with maximum densities locally approaching 1500 persons per sq. km, the limit is being reached.[4]

With the landholding pattern highly skewed, this tension
brings pressure for expropriation and redistribution to ease the
situation. Indeed, according to some analyses radical reorganisation of the agrarian structure is the only way to provide employment for an increasing rural population.[5] Although accurate
data on landholding systems are scarce, partly because of the
complexity of tenures, it seems that in most countries an elite
group of large landowners controls some 20–40 per cent of the
farm area, besides having better access to resources such as
credit, capital and fertilisers. Restricted access to these important
complementary inputs has prevented the smaller farmers from
benefiting from the seeds and technology of the Green Revolution. In India, for example 70 per cent of the benefits of improved seeds have gone to the small group of affluent landowners,
and only 15 per cent of co-operative credit has gone to members
with less than 2 hectares.[6] Most Asian peasants are economically, socially and politically crushed by a small minority of
leading personalities who combine key functions as landowners,
money-lenders, traders, employers and local officials. This type
of landowner, exerting political power through control of land
and labour yet often concealing himself in censuses as a money-
lender, merchant or village official, was eliminated by the socialist revolutions of China, North Vietnam and North Korea.

A second major problem of rural Asia is tenancy. Many Asian
countries have half their land tenanted. Apart from Pakistan,
where tenanted farms are frequently as large as owner-operated,
tenants almost invariably cultivate smaller units than owners.
In India, for example, owner-farmed holdings average 3 hectares, tenanted farms only 1½ hectares. The facts that the tenant
usually pays half his gross output to his landlord and frequently
has little or no security of tenure emphasise his hopeless position.
Agreements are rarely written, and where significant profits can

be made by intensifying production (as with the new hybrid seeds) or when the threat of tenancy reform becomes imminent, tenants are evicted, to join the landless labourers, now the largest class in some Asian countries. The evils tenancy can promote, outlined in Chapter 1, are further discussed by Myrdal, who concludes that the prevailing systems of tenure are a strong deterrent to intensified agriculture and rural social development.[7]

These then are the twin evils barring Asian agricultural development: population pressure, aggravated by land consolidation, and high rates of tenancy. In North Vietnam before 1953, 61·5 per cent of peasants had no land at all; in Java 78 per cent of the peasants own less than ½ hectare; and in Luzon 60 per cent of the land is farmed under sharecropping. There is less population pressure in Burma, Thailand and Cambodia, but almost everywhere peasants labour under high rents and annual interest rates of 50–70 per cent.

Yet despite these handicaps, small farms generally have both greater input and greater output per unit area than the larger concerns. Indian Government studies in several states recorded output per hectare figures 10–30 per cent higher on smallholdings. These data support the conclusion that splitting up the larger farms and recombining resources would produce both more output and more employment, without the need for heavy injections of capital.

Reforms of landlord-tenant relationships are less dramatic than redistributive reforms but no less difficult to apply. Land redistribution can be compared to a major surgical operation, tenancy reform to a delicate internal cure. Effective tenancy reform requires close administrative control, which most underdeveloped countries of Asia cannot provide. The established power structure protects landlord-tenant relationships in favour of the former. Tenancy laws will work only when the tenant has achieved influence and bargaining power.[8]

Asia is instructively varied in typology of approaches to land reform. Whilst the endowments of human and natural resources (and the ratio between the two) are broadly similar, the spectrum of development from Nepal, with 94 per cent of labour force in agriculture and 80 per cent of the population illiterate, to highly industrialised Japan with 24 per cent of labour in agriculture and 2 per cent illiterate, is wide. Further contrasts appear between communist and non-communist countries. The former group consists of China, North Vietnam and Nortn Korea; the latter includes Japan, Taiwan and South Korea. Japan and Taiwan are widely considered as two of the most successful reforms ever undertaken anywhere, although they can also be viewed as American-guided strategies against possible communist insurgency.[9]

Land reform laws have, however, been drafted in nearly all Asian countries, particularly during the 1950s, the first decade of independence for most. Generally, these laws have either remained dead or have been too feeble to have any impact on land tenure patterns and agricultural development. Powerful vested interests have obstructed implementation and laws have emerged full of loopholes and escape clauses. Such emasculated laws sometimes have unintended results. Redistribution of plantation land in West Malaysia promoted land speculation and the emergence of a landlord class, actual cultivation being done by tenants rather than small owners.[10] In Indonesia the 1960 Land Reform Act imposed ceilings but collusion between officials and landowners sabotaged its early operation. In Burma only 13 per cent of the land earmarked under the 1953 Nationalisation Act had been dealt with before the policy was suspended in 1958. The application of the 1955 Philippine Land Reform Act was impeded by heavy compensation to landowners and by providing that estates could be acquired for transfer only when a tenant majority petitioned for it. The 1954 Tenancy Act and 1963 Reform Code, designed to regulate tenancy and turn sharetenants into leaseholders and owner-occupiers, fared little better; at best the trend towards land concentration was delayed somewhat. Recent events, in Indonesia especially, suggest that students and peasants will not tolerate this situation indefinitely. Even Thailand, never colonised and with the least acute land problems in Asia, is not free from tension created by disparities in rural areas.[11]

REFERENCES

1. R. Narain, D. Basu and G. Celestini: 'Population and food supply in Asia', *FAO Monthly Bulletin of Agricultural Economics and Statistics*, 22 (1), 1973, pp. 1–9.

2. G. Myrdal: *Asian Drama* (London, Allen Lane Penguin, 1968, 3 vols.), see especially Vol. 2, chas. 27 and 28.

3. F. Dovring: 'The state of agriculture in a growing population', *FAO Monthly Bulletin of Agricultural Economics and Statistics*, 8 (8–9), 1959, pp. 1–11.

4. C. L. Geertz: *Agricultural Involution: the Process of Ecological Change in Indonesia* (Berkeley, University of California Press, 1963).

5. Z. M. Ahmad and M. J. Sternberg: 'Agrarian reform and employment, with special reference to Asia', *International Labour Review*, 99 (2), 1969, pp. 159–83.

6. *Ibid*: pp. 164–5.

7. Myrdal: *op. cit.*, Vol. 2, ch. 22.

8. E. H. Jacoby: *Man and Land* (London, Deutsch, 1971), pp. 253, 256.

9. See A. McCoy: 'Land reform as counter-revolution: US foreign policy and the tenant', *Bulletin of Concerned Asian Scholars*, 3 (1), 1971, pp. 14–49.

10. U. A. Aziz: 'Land distribution and land policy in Malaya', *Malayan Economic Review*, 3 (2), 1958, pp. 22–9.

11. W. Klatt: 'Agrarian issues in Asia', *International Affairs*, 48, 1972, pp. 226–41, 395–413.

8

Japan

Land reform in Japan is generally acknowledged one of the most successful post-war schemes. It transferred the ownership of over a third of the farmed land and affected 70 per cent of the agricultural population; yet it was carried out smoothly and quickly. The old tenancy system was abolished at a stroke, and tenanted land is now virtually non-existent. The effects on the living standards of the former tenants, on agricultural productivity and on political and social life generally, have been far-reaching.

The 1947–50 reform, imposed by the Allied Occupation, was not the first in Japan's history. Land reform started in the seventh century and continues to the present day. Particularly important were the reforms of the Meiji Restoration (1868–1912); indeed this period was the first phase in a two-stage process of modern land reform, with each stage followed by ancillary measures. Japan provides a good case study of continuous land reform, always related in a two-way link process to development as a whole. Whether Japanese economic development and the role of land reform therein can serve as a model for other, especially Asian, countries, is doubtful. The specific conditions in which Japanese land reform was effected are unlikely to recur; there is, however, some evidence that the general sequence of events in Japanese economic history is not unique and is being followed in other developing Asian countries.[1]

GEOGRAPHICAL AND EARLY HISTORICAL BACKGROUND[2]

Japan is a mountainous country; three quarters of the land slopes at more than 15° and only 5 million hectares, 15 per cent of the total, is cultivated. In the late 1940s this land was worked by over 6 million farm families, comprising 38 million people, 46 per cent of the total population; 73 per cent of the farmers cultivated holdings of less than 1 hectare. The land is mostly under food crops, such as rice (55 per cent of the cultivated area), wheat, barley and potatoes. Pasture land and livestock husbandry are relatively unimportant—except in Hokkaido, which, colonised late, largely on 'European' lines, has mixed farming with an average holding size five times that of the rest of Japan. Elsewhere the main geographical contrasts are: (1) between flooded lowland rice fields and upland dry fields planted to cereals and vegetables; and (2) between the south (of about the 37° parallel), where two or even three crops are harvested per year, and the north, where winter cold permits only one crop per year.

Japanese agrarian history is long and varied. A radical land reform in the mid-seventh century, modelled on the system of T'ang China, ended the tribal stage of Japanese society and initiated the long period of feudalism. This reform declared all land government owned, individual holdings being granted to families according to their size. Whether this system was thoroughly established or not, by the end of the twelfth century it had been superseded by a decentralised feudal structure. By the mid-fourteenth century the right to collect taxes depended on the local lords' powers. The 16th century trend towards centralised, especially military, power permitted further modification of the feudal structure. By the late-seventeenth century the Tokugawa government owned about a quarter of the land, with the rest divided into some 300 fiefs. The division between the *daimyo* (feudal lord) living in his fortified castle town with his *samurai* retainers and foot-soldiers, and the peasants in the domain villages, was complete. The lord's wealth derived from the rice tax—up to 60 per cent of the crop—levied on the peasants. *Samurai* stipends paid in rice and Tokugawa regulations decreeing that lords spent half their time in the competitive extravagance of life in the capital explained the heavy tax. Increased indebtedness promoted a large increase in tenancy during 1800–68 as land was mortgaged to landlords, rich peasants and money-lenders.

H

THE MEIJI REFORM

The Meiji Restoration dismantled the old feudal régime, starting with an 1868 edict declaring all agricultural land the property of the peasants to use or dispose of as they liked. Some 80 per cent of all peasants became free owner-farmers, but half of them acquired plots too small for family subsistence and had to rent additional land from those who had more than they needed.[3] The landlord-warrior caste was compensated by pensions, later replaced by bonds. Most *daimyo* benefited financially from the land reforms since they received cash instead of rice and were freed from paying retainers' stipends and attending at the Tokugawa court. The *samurai*, however, the mass of the ruling class, suffered severely. Unlike the *daimyo* pensions, which matched former income, the *samurai* pensions amounted to 43 per cent of their Tokugawa stipends, and after the commutation to bonds to only 15 per cent.[4] Land redistribution and the removal of feudal obligations thus led to considerable redistribution of income and status, and, with conspicuous consumption lessened, to increased savings and investment.

In 1873 an important land tax reform law made taxes payable in cash and not in crops, based on the value not the yield of the land. Following a new cadastral survey, the first since 1586, the tax was fixed at 3 per cent of the land price (reduced to 2½ per cent in 1878), payable to the central government, plus 1 per cent to the local administration. Initially the new money tax (equivalent to 35 per cent of the value of the average crop) gave the peasant little improvement, and he lost the automatic lowering of the tax when the harvest was bad. Gradually, however, inflation and the progressive rise of crop prices diminished the real weight of the tax. Land tax contribution to government revenue fell from nearly 75 per cent in 1873 to 20 per cent in 1902 and to only 3 per cent in 1940.[5]

The Meiji reform aimed at destroying feudalism, at increasing total production and at creating a sound rural tax base in order to maintain the civil service and build up industry. All were achieved. Without the Meiji land reform modernisation of agriculture, indeed of the whole Japanese economy, would have been impossible. But one vital issue—tenancy—was overlooked. Renting of land had been illegal under the old feudal régime (although some tenancy had developed in the later feudal period), but tenancy increased markedly to comprise 41 per cent of the cultivated land by 1900. The 1898 Civil Code, legalising tenancy, heavily favoured the evolving landlord class. A maximum tenancy term of twenty years was set, but no minimum. Landlords could cancel contracts and evict tenants at will, but a tenant could withdraw from the agreement only if, for reasons beyond his control, his rent exceeded his earnings for two consecutive years.[6] By the time the scale and significance of the tenancy problem were fully apparent, landlord interests had consolidated control in the government and were able to present the vice as a virtue.[7] Tenant unions grew rapidly after the agrarian disputes of 1918–21 occasioned by a sharp fall in rice prices (the 'Rice Riots'), but these peasant organisations were later either dismantled or changed into government-controlled institutions. With emergent tenant power successfully contained by the landlords little change occurred in the percentage of cultivated land tenanted between 1900 (41 per cent) and 1941 (46 per cent).

The approach of war, however, brought considerable changes. For the first time, surplus population, instead of bidding up agricultural rents, was recruited to war industry and the forces. The overwhelming need to ensure maximum food output at last produced measures designed to benefit the tenants: rents pegged at 1939 levels and the system (Rice Autonomous Control Law, 1940) of a higher price for rice from cultivators than from landlords.

THE 1947 REFORM AND ITS IMMEDIATE EFFECTS

Japan surrendered in August 1945. The role of the Americans in pushing through land reform in Japan is important but difficult to evaluate precisely. Some kind of reform would probably have taken place anyway, but—particularly after General MacArthur's order to the Japanese Imperial Government to ensure that the situation of the peasants was improved—the occupying authorities certainly lent vigour to the process.

The 1947 Acts expropriated, with fixed indemnity based on rice prices and production costs, all farmland of absentee landlords and all resident owners' rented land exceeding 1 hectare (4 hectares in Hokkaido).[8] In 1952 a 3 hectare limit (12 hectares in Hokkaido) was set on farm sizes, all land thus acquired to be sold within two years to the occupying tenant farmers. 80–90 per cent of the tenanted land, nearly 2 million hectares, was covered by this provision (Table 7). Rampant inflation, however, made all indemnity and peasant repayments a farce, and hit the former landlords badly: by the time compensation was paid, money had depreciated to below 5 per cent its former value. The law also assisted the tenants on the remaining 10 per cent of tenanted land: rents were fixed at 25 per cent of the harvest on paddy fields and 15 per cent on upland fields; contracts had to be written, registered with the appropriate authorities, and rents paid in cash. Tenure security was, in fact, made complete. Overall, the reform changed the property rights of 6 million families (4 million favourably, 2 million adversely).

The land reform transfer was administered by local, prefectural and national land commissions. The local commission, composed of 5 tenants, 2 owner-farmers and 3 landlords, was the key organ of the reform since it operated at the village level. The prefectural commission, twice the size, but with the same percentage representation, channelled the policies of the Central Land Commission to the 11 000 villages of Japan. The fact that, despite landlord opposition, the whole process was complete by 1950, largely reflected the valiant work of the tenants on the local commissions.

Economically the reform came at a difficult, though crucial time. Communications were not yet working properly after the war, and funds were short. Technical difficulties chiefly reflected the law's inability to deal with the complexities of Japanese agriculture. Much supplementary legislation was necessary to deal with unforeseen problems which kept cropping up. The chief was landlord sabotage and repossession. Particularly where the local land commissions were weak or landlord-dominated, the landlords made sure of retaining their best land under the 3 hectare owner-farmer and 1 hectare rented land clauses, land was 'sold off' hastily to relatives to avoid expropriation, or tenants were evicted to enable the landowner to reconstitute the permitted 3 hectare holding. The 1949 census indicated 88 000 hectares, 4 per cent of the total tenanted land, as repossessed by landlords in such ways.[9]

The land reform's obvious impact was to reduce tenancy and

TABLE 7

LAND ACQUIRED BY THE JAPANESE GOVERNMENT FOR REDISTRIBUTION
AND RESALE, 1950

(all figures in '000 hectares)

	Paddy fields	Upland fields	Total	Per cent
Tenanted land purchased by government				
Land owned by absentee landlords	353	277	630	32·6
Land owned by resident landlords	490	300	790	40·9
Land owned by corporate bodies[1]	77	109	186	9·6
Land voluntarily submitted by landlords	56	42	98	5·1
Sub-total	976	728	1704	88·2
Other land sources				
Owner-farmed land[2] purchased by government	16	22	38	2·0
Land submitted in lieu of land tax	144	28	170	8·8
Other	3	18	21	1·0
Sub-total	163	68	229	11·8
Grand total	1139	796	1933	100·0

Notes: 1 Shrines, temples, churches, etc.

2 Badly-managed, uncultivated or voluntarily submitted.

Source: T. Ogura: 'The economic impact of postwar land reform in Japan', *Land Reform, Land Settlement and Co-operatives*, 2, 1968, p. 16.

increase owner-occupancy (Table 8). Tenanted land fell from 46 per cent of total farmed area in 1945 to 10 per cent in 1950; and tenants and part-tenants who previously constituted 69 per cent of all farm households, fell to 31 per cent. The fact, however, that land went to those tenants who happened to be cultivating it at the time produced uneven distribution of the benefits; it was generally 'unto him that hath it shall be given'. Moreover, the tenants of big landlords fared better than those of small. For example, a tenant renting all his land from three landlords, each of whom had 1 hectare or less, would get nothing if each landlord claimed his reserve allotment, whereas a tenant renting all his land from a landlord possessing 50 hectares would probably

TABLE 8

CHANGES IN JAPANESE LAND TENURE: 1945, 1950, 1965

(a) By cultivated area ('000 hectares)

		owner-farmed land		tenanted land		total
Pre land reform	1945	2787	(54)	2368	(46)	5156
Post land reform	1950	4685	(90)	515	(10)	5200
	1965	4819	(95)	272	(5)	5091

(Italic figures within brackets are percentages)

(b) By type of farm households ('000 households)

		owner-farmer[1]	predominantly owner-farmer[2]	predominantly tenant[3]	tenant[4]		total
Pre land reform	1945	1729 (31)	1114 (20)	1102 (20)	1574	(29)	5537
Post land reform	1950	4228 (70)	1310 (22)	286 (5)	240	(4)	6075
	1965	4538 (80)	857 (15)	157 (3)	100	(2)	5665

(Italic figures within brackets are percentages)

Notes: 1 Households owning over 90 per cent of their farmed land.
  2 Households owning 50–90 per cent.
  3 Households renting 50–90 per cent.
  4 Households renting more than 90 per cent.
Source: T. Ogura: 'The economic impact of postwar land reform in Japan', *Land Reform, Land Settlement and Co-operatives*, 2, 1968, p. 17.

get it all. Correcting this sort of inequality proved impracticable. Furthermore, to prevent land from going to inefficient farmers in too small units, minimum limits were fixed of 0·5 hectares in Hokkaido and 0·2 hectares elsewhere in Japan on landholdings transferred to tenants. Although these limits were not always strictly applied by the local commissions, many very small farmers were excluded from the benefits of the reform.[10]

SOCIO-POLITICAL EFFECTS

The first objective of the 1947 land reform was the elimination of the landlord class and the democratisation of Japanese rural society. Communist-inspired tenant unions and other farmers' movements were becoming increasingly threatening in the early post-war years. In emancipating, socially and politically, a large section of the rural population the reform undermined the communist arguments; with no major grievances or political issues left to fight for, farmers' unions collapsed and their strictly economic functions were undertaken by the co-operatives. The reform removed post Meiji Restoration neo-feudal power; this major social upheaval was accomplished rapidly and with virtually no violence. The land reform left Japanese rural society without the class hatred and the yearning for revenge that characterise violent revolutions, and by removing landlords, especially absentee landlords with outside interests, from the village scene it promoted local autonomy and peasant participation in village affairs.

In other respects the reform has been less than revolutionary. Traditional social distinctions have been blurred, not abolished. Dore has shown that the landlord group has not been destroyed; they have lost their domination, but 'ex-landlords . . . still have the cards stacked in their favour'.[11] Where the road to local power is open to all, wealth, education and experience replace heredity and landownership as the main criteria for individual status and progress; and landlords' families still have a major share of these assets. They have the experience of administration and decision-making and are still accorded traditional attitudes of respect and loyalty; their geographically wider social and political connections are advantages for local office; and with their retained 3 hectare farms (besides outside interests) they are better off than most villagers.

ECONOMIC EFFECTS

The need to boost Japan's agricultural production after the war was an important objective of the reform. Numerous figures and indices demonstrate the rapid increase in output since 1947, particularly in the non-rice sectors. Agricultural production has grown impressively by 3–4 per cent per year since the reform, though this is well below the 10 per cent rate of the industrial sector. Output of livestock products leaped by six times, and fruit by three times, during the period 1950–60, despite a drop in agricultural labour force from 16 to 12 millions. Labour productivity, static before the reform, averaged an annual 5 per cent increase from 1954 to 1968. Similarly, land productivity increase, under 1 per cent per year before the reform, was 4 per cent after.[12] Much of the output increase might reflect the fact that farmers could now invest the farm capital previously drained off by rent payments, but several studies reject such a direct cause-effect relationship. Kawano's analysis concluded that, at least in the 1951–4 period, the reform stimulated a marked rise in the propensity to consume; effects on productivity via increased agricultural investment were feeble.[13] Dore found no clear correlation between post-reform regional increases in the proportion of owner-farmers and spatial variations in agricultural productivity increases.[14] Finally Voelkner demonstrated that if trends from 1895 on are produced forward across the slump of the interwar and war years, the post-war productivity increase is only marginally superior to the previous trend. Only after about 1960 does the overall agricultural production index show a higher rate of increase than pre-reform trends, but this does not hold for rice, which levels off after 1960.[15] Arguably, therefore, the productivity rise would have been *possible* without land reform, with the rapid post-war industrialisation attracting rural labour and changing the tenure situation by natural structural evolution. 'Natural' adjustments to the tenure structure, however, would have been more difficult, and probably accompanied by social violence (as in 1918–21), which would, in turn, have injured production. Land reform undoubtedly forestalled such violence, but its direct contribution to increased production was probably subsidiary to factors such as the technological development of farming, industrial development and the general trend of governmental policy in favour of the farmer.

Farmers' income patterns reveal much the same situation. Farming families' average annual income in the early 1950s fluctuated at about 45 per cent above the pre-reform level, despite an increased agricultural population and consequent reduction in the average farm size. The distribution of national agricultural income changed radically: incomes from rents dropped from 35 per cent to 4 per cent of the total, while labour income rose from 60 per cent to 90 per cent. Villages had become manifestly more prosperous by the mid-1950s: bicycles, radios, small agricultural machines and modernised and extended houses were in evidence. Again, however, this reflected only in part the removal of the rent burden and an increase in unit area production. Far more important were increased employment of farm families in non-agricultural occupations and maintenance of agricultural prices above, and costs below, pre-war levels.[16]

Land reform had comparatively little effect on rural employment. The increase in the agricultural population from 14 million pre-war to over 16 million in 1946 (caused by urban unemployment, evacuations, repatriation and demobilisation) meant holding sizes kept small to absorb as much as possible of this considerable post-war influx. The reform indeed reduced somewhat the average farm size, farm units of under half a hectare increasing from 33 per cent to 42 per cent of the total between 1945 and 1950. From 1946 to 1953 the agricultural population remained static at around 16 million and the land reform structure of small owner-operated farms was generally in tune with this situation. After about 1955, however, with increasing industrialisation, the agricultural population declined rapidly, at about 4 per cent per year. Land distribution changed too, but far more gradually (Table 9). By the 1960s land reform was

TABLE 9

CHANGE IN DISTRIBUTION OF JAPANESE LAND AS BETWEEN FARM
SIZE CLASSES, 1945–70

(figures are percentage of total farm households)

		Under ½ hectare	½–1 hectare	1–2 hectares	Over 2 hectares
Pre land reform	1945	33	30	27	10
Post land reform	1950	42	33	22	3
	1960	39	33	24	4
	1970	38	31	25	6

Note: Hokkaido not included.
Sources: T. Ogura: 'The economic impact of postwar land reform in Japan', *Land Reform, Land Settlement and Co-operatives*, 2, 1968, p. 22; T. Misawa: 'Agrarian reform, employment and rural incomes in Japan', *International Labour Review*, 103 (4), 1971, p. 398.

seen to have a negative effect on rural employment by chaining much rural labour to sub-marginal holdings their owners could neither sell nor rent.[17]

Table 10 reveals some interesting anomalies. Whilst total agricultural population dropped by 40 per cent between 1955 and 1970, the total number of farms decreased by only 12 per cent. Full-time farms dropped by 60 per cent; part-time farms *increased* by 15 per cent—indeed part-time farms where off-farm income exceeds on-farm income increased by 63 per cent. In 1970 on average 1·3 persons per farm household had off-farm employment, and 84 per cent of all farms in Japan were part-time.[18] Those leaving agriculture are predominantly young males, but they leave alone, parents and other family members staying behind as farmers. Further, about half remain in the household and commute to their new place of work—hence the type of farming called *Sanchan Nogyo*, which means agriculture practised by a young wife and her parents-in-law. Another million agricultural workers work seasonally in the construction and other industries. Generally Japanese farmers are reluctant to sell their land because of its value as a hedge against redundancy and for retirement, and this is a serious obstacle to farmers who wish to enlarge their holdings and employ machines which need a larger area to be economic. The rigidity of this small-scale owner-farmer and part-time farmer structure stems largely from the land reform.

RECENT REPERCUSSIONS OF THE LAND REFORM

The 1947 land reform had little alternative to creating a large number of small-scale proprietors: economic and technological conditions did not favour enlargement of the individual holding. Unfortunately, from about 1955, the small farm structure proved insufficiently flexible to cope with rapid economic changes. An ageing rural population was tied to the land, and the gap between rural and urban growth rates and incomes widened appreciably. True, most of this gap results from the phenomenal rise of Japanese industry rather than from inherent weaknesses in the agricultural sector, and some of it is bridged by price supports to agricultural produce, but the polarisation between the rural and urban sectors in standards of living is clear. Agricultural production grew on average 4 per cent per year during 1950–60; from 1960 to 1970 the rate fell to 2 per

TABLE 10

CHANGES IN FARM STRUCTURE AND EMPLOYMENT IN JAPAN, 1955–70

(figures in '000 farm households)

	1955	1960	1965	1970	percentage change 1955–70
All farms	6043	6057	5665	5342	−12
All full-time farms	2106	2078	1219	832	−60
All part-time farms	3937	3978	4446	4510	+15
Category I, part-time[1]	2274	2036	2081	1802	−21
Category II, part-time[2]	1663	1942	2365	2709	+63

Notes: 1 Farms where the net farm income is more than total off-farm income of the farm household.
     2 Farms where the net farm income is less than total off-farm income of the farm household.

Source: T. Misawa: 'Agrarian reform, employment and rural incomes in Japan', *International Labour Review*, 103 (4), 1971, p. 405.

cent. In recent years agricultural productivity within the small farm structure has reached its peak. Once small-scale machinery, increased fertiliser and pesticide application have been disseminated, production is hard to raise much further.

The 'Basic Agricultural Law' of 1961 aimed at overcoming some of these new problems. Two principal avenues of approach are envisaged: enlargement of small farms to viable units (the upper limit of 3 hectares on farm size was removed to facilitate this), and the encouragement of co-operative farming. Table 9 shows that larger farm units are in fact increasing, and some 5000 co-operative farms, largely operated by the younger generation, have been established since 1961. Revolutionary geographical changes have already appeared, as farming changes from a peasant subsistence and local market pattern to cash cropping for a national market. Crop competition between regions is intensifying, especially near the great cities, and marked areal specialisation is emerging.[19] The dominance of rice is gradually receding: 55 per cent of total agricultural production by value in 1955 to 44 per cent in 1965.

CONCLUSION

The first phase of land reform freed the Japanese peasants from feudalism and removed the obstacles to social and economic progress; the second phase consolidated their position by reducing the economic influence of the new landlord class which had developed since 1868. Yet inequalities still remain. The division today is between those who own and cultivate a medium to large holding, say 2 hectares and above, and those who scrape a living out of less than 1 hectare. The categorical division between landlord and tenant was superseded by gradations, but economically the poles are not much closer together.[20]

The catalytic effect of the American occupation was crucial in the timing and execution of the Japanese reform but was probably not important in making it radical. Factors responsible included memories of peasant rebellions, the well-intentioned, though unsuccessful, pre-war reforms, the strong tenant unions, widespread disillusionment with the old oligarchy, and active pre-reform leadership in the Japanese Ministry of Agriculture, which drafted legislation. Moreover, Japan had a strong base of land-improving technology: Japanese farmers had centuries of experience in managing the intricate interrelations among land, water, plants, levels of fertilisation and density of population, experience which already gave them high rank among the world's husbandmen. The stage was ripe for further rapid intensification, given a motivation for higher rates of investment. The educational levels of the Japanese peasantry were also crucial. Strong parallels can be suggested with the Danish experience following the 1901 reforms, which argues against hasty extrapolation of the Japanese model to the rest of South-east Asia. Except for mainland China, Taiwan and Korea, post-war rice yields in south-east Asia have been more comparable to pre-Meiji Japanese yields. In other countries heavy investments in drainage, flood control and irrigation are still needed. Since the 1950s in Japan, uniquely among the countries east of the Khyber Pass, land is no longer a major factor in politics.[21] Herein lies perhaps the greatest tribute to the land reform.

REFERENCES

1. H. Voelkner: 'Land Reform in Japan', in Agency for International Development: *Spring Review of Land Reform* (Washington, Department of State, 1970), Vol. 3, pp. 77–8, Appendix A, figs. B and C.
2. Based on R. P. Dore: *Land Reform in Japan* (London, Oxford University Press, 1959), pp. 3–14.
3. Voelkner: *op. cit.*, p. 44.
4. J. I. Nakamura: 'Meiji land reform distribution of income, and savings from agriculture', *Economic Development and Cultural Change*, 14 (4), 1966, pp. 428–39.
5. Dore: *op. cit.*, p. 15.
6. Voelkner: *op. cit.*, p. 19.
7. Dore: *op. cit.*, pp. 18–20. The landlord class itself was not a uniform group. Dore recognises three main categories—absentee landlords, non-farm residence landlords and farmer landlords—and a number of sub-categories (elite families, merchants, moneylenders, traditional paternalistic, progressive paternalistic, etc.). Dore estimated that in 1947 18 per cent of the tenanted land was owned by absentee landlords, 24 per cent by local non-farmer groups, and 58 per cent by men who were farmers themselves. The very largest holdings exceeded 1 500 hectares. Of the 3 000 large landowners (with over 50 hectares each), a third were in Hokkaido.
8. The 1 hectare ceiling was an average figure for all Japan excluding Hokkaido. Actual limits varied according to prefecture, from a maximum of 1·5 hectares in Aomori to a minimum of 0·6 hectare in Hiroshima. For maps and other information relating to the regional (prefectural) distribution of tenancy and land affected by reform see G. Trewartha: 'Land reform and land reclamation in Japan', *Geographical Review*, 40 (3), 1950, pp. 376–96.
9. Dore: *op. cit.*, pp. 150–165.
10. *Ibid*: pp. 177–8.
11. *Ibid*: p. 329.
12. T. Ouchi: 'The Japanese land reform: its efficacy and limitations', *The Developing Economies*, 4 (2), 1966, pp. 129–50.
13. S. Kawano: 'Effects of land reform on consumption and investment of farmers', in K. Okhawa, B. F. Johnston and H. Kaneda (eds.): *Agriculture and Economic Growth: Japan's Experience* (Tokyo, University of Tokyo Press, 1970), pp. 374–97.
14. Dore: *op. cit.*, pp. 239–40.
15. Voelkner: *op. cit.*, p. 64; Appendix A, fig. 7.
16. Dore: *op. cit.*, pp. 226, 239–41; Ouchi: *op. cit.*, pp. 142–3. Agricultural prices increased 49 per cent during 1960–5; prices of industrial products only 6 per cent.
17. Voelkner: *op. cit.*, p. 67. This tying effect is seen by the fact that whereas male landless agricultural workers decreased by 14 per cent

per year during 1956–62, self-employed workers fell by only 2 per cent per year.

18. T. Misawa: 'Agrarian reform, employment and rural incomes in Japan', *International Labour Review*, 103 (4), 1971, pp. 393–413 (pp. 404–6).
19. F. Ueno: 'Areal specialisation in Japanese peasant farming and agricultural settlement', in W. A. D. Jackson (ed.): *Agrarian Policies and Problems in Communist and Non-Communist Countries* (Seattle, University of Washington Press, 1971), pp. 399–435.
20. Dore: *op. cit.*, p. 240.
21. W. Ladejinsky: 'Agrarian reform in Asia', *Foreign Affairs*, 42 (3), 1964, pp. 445–60.

9

Taiwan

The Taiwanese land reform, spanning the years 1958–43, is generally judged the most important in Asia after the Japanese. Partly because the two countries had similar pre-reform agrarian structures, and partly because of similar American involvement after the war, the two reforms share many similar features.

Taiwan shows two distinct phases of recent agricultural development. In the first (1895–1945) the Japanese Government introduced and extended modern technology to agriculture. In the second the post-war land reform provided the impetus to agricultural development. The reform itself had three stages: a programme of rent reduction in 1949, sale of public land in 1951, and a 'land-to-the-tiller' policy in 1953.

BACKGROUND TO LAND REFORM

From 1895 to the late 1930s Taiwan achieved impressive agricultural progress. Per capita income of the agricultural population doubled, despite increase of the farming population by 43 per cent. With little of indigenous mineral or energy resources, agricultural produce, especially rice and sugar which were in heavy demand in Japan, was emphasised. Japanese technical and professional personnel rapidly improved agricultural technology, in particular water management and new crop varieties. Ponlai rice, adapted to local conditions, quickly replaced the local Chailai variety. The sugar cane area increased from 16 000 hectares in 1902 to 170 000 hectares in 1939, and cane yield increased with a new heavy-stalked variety. The irrigated area was greatly increased in the 1930s by the huge Chianan irrigation development in the west-central part of the island.

These advances were important for the success of the post-war reform. Thorough extension services organised by the Japanese had made the farmers innovation and productivity minded, ready to respond to the improved incentive provided by the 1949 rent reduction measures. Even more important for the carrying out of the post-war reform was the complete cadastral survey of the densely settled western part of the island between 1898 and 1904. Ownership characteristics were fully noted and the cultivated land mapped at 1:1200. This survey enabled 'double landownership' to be abolished in 1905. Holders of so-called 'first titles', mostly large absentee landlords who were creditors of smaller resident landlords or holders of 'secondary' titles, had to give up their claims in return for compensatory bonds. Secondary title-holders consequently became sole owners of the land. A by-product of the survey, the uncovering of farms that had not been on the tax roll, increased the tax base and raised the revenue for development. Further surveys of 1910–14 (concentrating on forested upland) and 1915–25 (of the rugged eastern side of the island) completed coverage of the whole island.[1]

Tenancy conditions, however, had little attention during the Japanese period. Throughout the period some 40 per cent of farmers were tenants, and another 25 per cent were part-owner/part-tenants; around 56 per cent of the cultivated area was tenanted. Average farm size was below 2 hectares but half the holdings were below 1 hectare. In 1930 6 per cent of the land-lords owned half the cultivated land. Average farmland rental was around 50 per cent of the annual crop yield (payable in rice), running as high as 70 per cent in more fertile areas. A farmer who grew other crops had to sell part of them to buy rice to pay his rent. An arrangement known as 'iron-clad rent' bound a tenant to pay a fixed minimum sum irrespective of the harvest output. Rents were also levied on farm by-products. Very few contracts were written or were for fixed periods. Sub-letting of land, also common, encouraged cumulative exploita-tion and 82 per cent of farmers' credit needs were supplied by private moneylenders, most of them landlords. Most of the pro-ceeds of pre-reform rural economic growth went to the landlord

class. Between 1926 and 1940, per hectare yield of rice increased
1·4 per cent annually, land rents 1·2 per cent and the value of
paddy land 2·0 per cent.[2]

Although Taiwan was largely spared the commotion of the
Chinese civil wars and the Sino-Japanese conflict, it was heavily
bombarded by the Allies during the later stages of World War
Two. Damage from this and by several severe typhoons reduced
agricultural production by around 12 per cent annually during
the war. Population growth, however, was rapid during the
early post-war years. The collapse of the Japanese administration in 1945 initiated a migration from urban to rural areas;
and the resident population was further swollen by an influx of
1·5 million refugees from the mainland and the arrival of the
630 000 strong Nationalist army. The consequent extra pressure
on land enabled the landlords to raise rents even higher. The
flow of migrants from the mainland, however, created some
prerequisites for land reform. The refugee movement included
an intellectual elite able to fill the administrative void left by the
Japanese, and these officials largely were loyal supporters of the
Nationalist government. The existence of an army of 630 000
men on a relatively small island (35 960 sq.km.) rendered possible any reform accepted by the political and military leaders.
Through fear of a communist victory in Taiwan and of the
drastic reform that would then result the landlords offered little
resistance to the implementation of reform after 1949.[3]

FARMLAND RENT REDUCTION

The first stage of Taiwan's reform was rent reduction. Rent
regulations promulgated in 1949 were easily evaded by landlords, so they were embodied in a new law, the 'Farm Rent Reduction to 37·5 per cent Act' of 1951, whose most important
provision was the reduction of rent to a maximum of 37·5 per
cent of the 'standard annual yield of the main crop'. Instead,
therefore, of the rent being, as previously, a percentage of the
actual harvest, it became a fixed amount, determined by the
'expected' standard yield of the main crop—rice, sugar cane or
sweet potatoes—on each particular holding, in its local conditions. Here the Japanese agrarian cadaster, with its 26 categories
each of dry and irrigated land, was invaluable. Excess of crop
yield above the standard went wholly to the tenant; crop yields

below 70 per cent of the standard, through poor weather or
natural catastrophe, cancelled rent for that crop season. The
tenants' extra burdens, such as advance rent payments and
security deposits, were abolished; many of these impositions,
such as the landlords' habit of charging house and water rents,
had crept in after 1949 to compensate loss of land rent by the
1949 Act. Their abolition by the 1951 Act gave the Taiwanese
tenant security never known before. The minimum contract
length was six years (three years under the 1949 law). Even
when this expired the landlord could take the land back only
if: (1) he could prove he could work it himself, (2) his income
was insufficient to support his family, and (3) the tenant had
other proven means of support. Sub-letting was prohibited, and
written contracts were compulsory. As in Japan, a hierarchical
structure of committees, from national to village, applied reform
policy and adjudicated on thorny local matters: such local involvement undoubtedly improves the operation of a land reform over a centralised, bureaucratic approach. In a few
months virtually all contracts—377 000, affecting nearly
300 000 hectares—had been revised. The stringent checking
procedures of the 1951 Act disclosed that nearly 35 000 of the
1949 revised contracts had been violated, chiefly by landlords.
After 1951 many landlords chose to sell their land, feeling that
rent reduction cut too deeply into their incomes. Others, anti-
cipating future expropriation, sold portions of their land before
expropriation came. Generally these early sales by the landlords proved advantageous to the tenants, who got the land for
less than the price set by the 1953 Land-to-the-Tiller Act.[4]

This first phase of the Taiwanese land reform was probably
also the mildest; it sought improvement in the tenants' standard
of living without abolishing tenancy or changing the tenants'
relative status. Even so, economic changes took place. Land
values declined sharply, the value of farmland being closely connected with the rent the landlord can command. A Taiwanese
Research Institute of Land Economics survey revealed a 19 per
cent decrease in the average price of paddy fields between
December 1948 and December 1949; dry land values dropped
42 per cent in the same period.[5] The proportion of the net annual crop left to the tenants increased by 10–20 per cent. The
significance of this for a tenant habitually hard-pressed for rice

to feed his family cannot be overstressed. Besides improving the position of the tenants, the first phase of reform also created certain prerequisites for further reform measures, both organisationally, by revising the cadaster and setting up efficient local tenancy and rent committees, and psychologically, by awakening the self awareness of the tenants and by bringing down the price of land.

SALE OF PUBLIC LAND

As early as 1948 sale of land belonging to the expelled Japanese had begun, but most of this was transferred to public enterprises such as the Taiwan Sugar Corporation, and this transfer stopped when the rent reduction programme began in 1949. The project was revived in 1951. Of the six sales held between 1948 and 1958, the two chief ones involved the sale of national and provincial land in mid-1951, and of the expropriated Taiwan Sugar Corporation holdings in early 1952.

Before the sale, tenants on public land paid a rent of 25 per cent of the annual crop production. After the sale the financial burden was somewhat greater, for although the 20 semi-annual repayments to the government (totalling $2\frac{1}{2}$ times the mean annual crop yield) were equivalent to the previous rent of 25 per cent of the crop, taxes and other charges raised farmers' outgoings. Koo calculated the yearly instalments to be equivalent to 25·5–32·5 per cent of the standard annual crop yield: still a lower proportion than the tenants on the 37·5 per cent rule, and of course the new landholders could expect full ownership within ten years.[6]

In assigning public land, former tenants of the land and local farmers with insufficient land received preference. Altogether around 130 000 tenant families bought a total of 70 000 hectares, an average of just over $\frac{1}{2}$ hectare each.[7] The relatively slow and limited sale of public land reflects on the one hand the care exercised in selecting the purchasers and in deciding on repayment procedures, on the other the success of the public enterprises in obstructing the enactment of the law and the general unsuitability of much of the land for small-scale private farming. Only 40 per cent of the public land went into private ownership. The public land sale programme, by converting a small fraction of the tenants to owner-farmers, served as a pilot stage before the final phase of Taiwan's land reform, the Land-to-the-Tiller Act, effective in 1953.

LAND TO THE TILLER

The 1953 Act empowered the government to expropriate landlords possessing land above a certain limit, and to create owner-farmers out of the tenants. Private landowners could retain land up to 3 hectares of medium grade paddy or 6 hectares of average quality dry land. The ceilings varied with land quality but absolute maxima on the poorest land were 6 hectares paddy and 12 hectares dry land. Land above these limits was compulsorily purchased by the government for $2\frac{1}{2}$ times the standard annual crop yield; 70 per cent of the compensation was in land bonds tied to agricultural product prices, and 30 per cent in shares in four government industries (cement, mining, pulp and paper, and agricultural and forestry development) transferred for this purpose into private ownership. The tenant paid two and a half times the standard crop yield, plus 4 per cent interest, over ten years in twenty instalments, one after each crop yield. Payments, in rice or cash, were generally less than the 37·5 per cent rental rates payable for the previous four years. In addition purchasers were assisted by cheap credit for land improvement and by clauses preventing such landlords' malpractices as the re-acquisition of land on the open or black markets. Some 140 000 hectares of land were sold to 195 000 new owner-farmers. The reform increased the proportion of owner-farmed land from 56 per cent of total farmland in 1948 to 86 per cent in 1959 (Table 11). The wider distribution of farm ownership also brought a reduction in the average size of holdings. In 1952 25 per cent of land was in holdings of below 1 hectare in size, in 1955 35 per cent.

ECONOMIC EFFECTS OF THE LAND REFORM

Since 1953 the landlords' share in the country's total farm income has sharply declined. In 1936–40 25 per cent accrued directly to landlords and money-lenders. By 1950–55 it was 10 per cent, and during 1956–60 only 6 per cent. For these three periods the cultivators' share of aggregate income was 67 per cent, 77 per cent, 81 per cent.[8] The same trend is corroborated by other figures. In 1950 rent and interest payments drained 30 per cent of total farm income out of agriculture; in 1955 it was 18 per cent and by 1960 11 per cent.[9] Real income

TABLE II

TAIWAN: TENURE PATTERNS BEFORE AND AFTER LAND REFORM

		1948	*1953*	*1959*
(a)	Land			
	Area of owner-cultivated land (hectares)	456 640	695 507	728 801
	Owner-cultivated as percentage of total farmland	56	83	86
(b)	Population			
	Owner-farmer families	211 649	385 286	479 391
	As percentage of total farming families	33	52	59
	Part owner-farmers families	154 460	169 547	182 121
	As percentage of total farming families	24	23	22
	Tenant families	231 224	147 490	118 890
	As percentage of total farming families	36	20	14
	Farm labourers families	43 521	41 657	38 551
	As percentage of total farming families	7	5	5

Source: C. Chen: *Land Reform in Taiwan* (Taipei, China Publishing Company, 1961), p. 312.

of Taiwanese farm families went up by approximately 60 per cent from 1952 to 1962. Investment also increased, particularly in farm implements, and although the impact of massive American aid should not be discounted, the higher incomes and increased security generated by land reform seem to have been the main source.[10]

The reform beneficiaries had three sources of increased income: rent limitation, increased productivity, and non-farm income. Rent reduction was most significant in the first few years following land reform. Since rent became a fixed charge under the 1951 Act, it became a smaller fraction of total cost as over the years the scale of production increased. In 1949 85 per cent of the increased rice income was represented by reduced rent, by 1960 it was 24 per cent. In the late 1950s, too, non-farm income began to make a considerable contribution. In 1955 it contributed 14 per cent of family incomes, in 1960 30 per cent.[11] The fixed rent charge as a percentage of the 'standard' crop yield was highly advantageous to the tenant as productivity increased through time. For farmers covered by the Land-to-the-Tiller reform, however, immediate economic benefits were much smaller, repayment costs and taxes being only 5 per cent lower than the former average rental outgoings. Again, however, constant repayment costs permitted raised disposable income as productivity increased.[12]

With increased income, consumption of protein foods (pork, fish) and of luxuries such as cigarettes and radios increased markedly. House construction also increased. New houses built immediately after the reform were popularly called '375 houses', built with savings through the 37·5 per cent rent reduction law. Table 12 illustrates standard of living changes of various tenure groups following land reform.

Under the Land-to-the-Tiller law landlords were indemnified at two and a half times the annual yield, which reflected the 1953 market value of land, although before 1949 paddy farms brought three or four times the annual yield. So any capital loss by the landlords was from rent reduction, not from the Land-to-the-Tiller programme. Land reform markedly affected the economic behaviour of Taiwan landlords both in the village and nationally. After land reform wealthy Taiwanese ceased to buy land for investment and security: it was no longer a profitable, or even a safe, investment. Accordingly in addition to their forced participation in industry through payment in shares for expropriated land, ex-landlords shifted excess capital into urban industry and business activities, sometimes even selling portions of their retained 3 hectares to finance further industrial development. On the other hand, whilst the land bonds were tied to inflation by being redeemable in kind (rice for expropriated paddy land; sweet potatoes for dry), the 30 per cent of compensation paid in industrial shares was widely resented. Taiwan Cement Corporation stock fared fairly well, but shares in the other three industrial concerns became virtually worthless and most landlords sold their holdings.[13]

Productivity, as already noted, increased considerably after the reform. How much this was a direct outcome of the reform,

TABLE 12

RESULTS OF A SAMPLE SURVEY REPORTING CHANGES IN LIVING
CONDITIONS AFTER LAND REFORM IN TAIWAN

	No.	per cent
(a) Former Tenants:		
Improvement	748	60
No improvement	477	38
No answer	25	2
(b) Current Tenants:		
Improvement	105	42
Little change	92	37
Deterioration	52	21
(c) Former landlords:		
Improvement	44	7
Little change	199	35
Deterioration	330	58
(d) Original owners:		
Improvement	77	31
Little change	113	45
Deterioration	57	23
No answer	3	1
(e) Farm labourers:		
Improvement	20	8
Little change	49	20
Deterioration	181	72

Note: These figures refer to families reporting their own changed conditions.
Chinese people are usually modest about their own living conditions, but
less inhibited about neighbours—whereas only 60 per cent of former tenant
households reported improvement in their daily lives, the proportion of
households attributed improvement by their neighbours was 75 per cent.
Also, not all respondents reporting improved living conditions held land
reform responsible; 12 per cent of the 748 tenants, for example, registering
post-reform improvements cited non-reform factors.

Source: M. M. C. Yang: *Socio-Economic Results of Land Reform in Taiwan* (Honolulu,
East-West Center Press, 1970), pp. 263, 267–8.

however, cannot be specified—other factors, such as improved
rice varieties, greater application of fertiliser and pesticides,
more advanced technology, all strongly promoted by the Sino-
American Joint Commission on Rural Reconstruction, contributed importantly. One set of data shows inputs increased
11 per cent, outputs 23 per cent, from 1953 to 1960, a gross
productivity increase of 12 per cent.[14] Labour input for this

period increased by 10 per cent, through (a) an increase in rural workers from 1 427 000 to 1 486 000 and (b) an increase in the average number of days worked per year from 173 to 181 per worker. Some capital inputs, such as fertiliser, increased by up to 40 per cent; land remained constant. So intensity of land use has increased, with higher yields per crop and increased multi-cropping. Of the agents of output growth, capital increase contributed half, increased labour and technological change a quarter each.

SIGNIFICANCE OF TAIWANESE LAND REFORM

By any standard land reform in Taiwan was a fine achievement. Lease contracts revised under the tenancy law totalled 377 000; about 140 000 families bought public land; and land was transferred from 106 000 landlords to 195 000 new farm-owners. Administratively the three-stage process was by no means simple. Politically land reform, by bringing peaceful and progressive rural social changes and economic prosperity to Taiwan, was considered a powerful weapon against communist infiltration. Socially, reform gave self-esteem to great numbers who had lacked it: an essential precondition for the modernisation of rural life. Economically, the reform had both immediate and far-reaching effects. Income redistribution was considerable, yet the landlords' interests were protected. Post-reform economic progress has been rapid. Agricultural output has increased at 8 per cent per year, a rate maintained after US aid was terminated in 1965.

The rapid farm output increases since land reform are all the more remarkable for occurring in a country of high population growth—only just slowing down to below 3 per cent per annum —and scarce land resources.[15] The present population of 14 million is projected to stabilise at 20–25 million at the end of this century. Such, however, is the growth of the non-farm sector that already by 1960 absolute numbers in agriculture were declining and by 1970 the agricultural population had fallen to 40 per cent of the total. Taiwan is now achieving a more balanced agro-industrial economy. The present high degree of commercialisation of agriculture—over 75 per cent of produce is marketed—was reached via the small family farm, intensively cultivated and served by mostly labour-intensive technology.

Currently much effort is devoted to expanding the cultivated area, through multiple cropping and coastal swamp reclamation. Consolidation and co-operation, too, are important. Indeed these measures can be regarded as a fourth phase of land reform.[16]

Taiwan's model of a progressive, small-farm agriculture, in which land reform was a keystone, may be a good model for other Asian countries, more relevant than Japan's.[17] Taiwan's significance lies in maintaining the social values of the small family farm while compensating, through governmental and co-operative action, for its economic weaknesses. Although the particular combination of private and government initiative may be difficult to achieve in Taiwan's less fortunate Asian neighbours, 'in this small but densely peopled island, Asia's oldest and most burning issue has been peacefully solved for more than six million rural folk'.[18]

REFERENCES

1. C. and P. VanderMeer: 'Land property data in Taiwan', *Journal of Asian Studies*, 28 (1), 1968, pp. 144–150.
2. A. Y. C. Koo: 'Land reform in Taiwan', in Agency for International Development: *Spring Review of Land Reform* (Washington, Department of State, 1970), Vol. 3, pp. 12, 18.
3. M. Burisch: 'Legislative and administrative aspects of land reform in Taiwan', *Land Reform, Land Settlement and Co-operatives*, 1, 1969, pp. 16–28.
4. *Ibid*: p. 20.
5. A. Y. C. Koo: *Land Reform and Economic Development: A Case Study of Taiwan* (New York, Praeger, 1968), p. 33.
6. *Ibid*: p. 36.
7. But many of these $\frac{1}{2}$ hectare units were supplementary to land already possessed. In fact the mean total holding size of farmers buying land was 1·2 hectares, very close to the 1950–2 national average of 1·3 hectares. Actually there is considerable discrepancy over the figures pertaining to sale of public land. Koo (*Ibid*: p. 37) gives 72 000 hectares bought by 140 000 families, Burisch (*op. cit.*, p. 24) 54 000 hectares and 122 000 families.
8. Koo: 'Land reform in Taiwan', *op. cit.*, pp. 16–17.
9. Koo: *Land Reform and Economic Development*, *op. cit.*, p. 56.
10. Y.-T. Chang: *Land Reform and its Impact on Economic and Social Progress in Taiwan* (Taipei, National Taiwan University, 1965).
11. Koo: *Land Reform and Economic Development*, *op. cit.*, pp. 52, 58–60.
12. *Ibid*: pp. 48–56.

13. *Ibid*: p. 47.
14. *Ibid*: pp. 65–77.
15. A. Y. C. Koo: 'Agrarian reform, production and employment in Taiwan', *International Labour Review*, 104 (1), 1971, pp. 1–22.
16. According to Chen, 60 000 hectares of tidal lands are available for reclamation along the deltaic west coast, enough for 30 000 farming families. Consolidation is even more important. A 1952 JCRR report on 16 sample villages indicated that owner-farmed holdings were split into an average of 14 plots (tenanted farms, average of 9 plots). 'Redemarcation' has already had encouraging results: land area available for farming up 4 per cent, output by 20–35 per cent, plots directly accessible by road up from 22 to 92 per cent of the total. The consolidation of 760 000 hectares, 87 per cent of the cultivated area, is targeted for 1976. The co-operative movement dates from 1970 and entails merging of small farms with only a nominal retention of individual ownership; production increases of 25 per cent have reportedly been achieved. Chen: *op. cit.*, pp. 93–4, 100–2; Koo: 'Agrarian reform, production and employment in Taiwan', *op. cit.*, pp. 15–16.
17. S. C. Hseih: 'Taiwan's model of agricultural progress: potentials of small family farms and their implications for developing countries', in W. A. D. Jackson (ed.): *Agrarian Problems and Policies in Communist and Non-Communist Countries* (Seattle, University of Washington Press, 1971), pp. 381–95.
18. Chen: *op. cit.*, dust jacket preface.

10

North and South Korea

North and South Korea shared a common ethnic, cultural and historical experience until 1945 when the splitting of the country along the 38th parallel into Russian and American zones to facilitate Japanese withdrawal destroyed immediate hopes of maintaining a unified national identity. On the other hand, this division of the country into two nearly equal halves made possible a unique comparison between the socio-economic performances of the self-reliant socialist system in the North, and the neo-colonial capitalist economy in the South.[1] In both cases land reform was an integral part of the political and developmental processes. Starting with the 1946 land reform, North Korea has carried out the most comprehensive socialist reform programme yet seen in the Third World.[2] The South, with the US military initially holding the reins of power, followed the land reform path already trodden by Japan and Taiwan, a path of reformism as a counter to communism.

HISTORICAL AND GEOGRAPHICAL BACKGROUND
TO TWO LAND REFORMS

Korea's strategic location, a peninsula set amongst larger more powerful neighbours—Russia, China, Japan—has inflicted upon the country a turbulent history. Until the late nineteenth century Korea was in the Chinese sphere of influence, and already the gradual consolidation under a monarchy of pre-existing tribal groups had formed the beginnings of a landlord-tenant structure. From 1910, following Japan's 1904 defeat of Russia, Korea was a Japanese colony until 1945, during which period it had two virtually separate societies. The Japanese constituted the prosperous landowning, industrialist, commercial and administrative classes. The Koreans, apart from a few wealthy landlords who came to terms with the Japanese, lived in poverty. It was a system of *de facto* apartheid.[3] Oppressive tenancy conditions left most Korean peasants barely enough for subsistence. Labourers on large Japanese-owned farms worked 6 days a week for 10–13 hours a day. Landownership concentration accelerated during the Japanese occupation and rural living standards declined. Aspiring Japanese landowners took advantage of the ignorance of the Korean peasants by simply 'reporting' land as their own when the Japanese land surveys were being carried out. In 1945 60 per cent of the farmland was owned or managed by 5 per cent of the farm households, whereas poor peasants, 57 per cent of farm households, owned less than 6 per cent of total arable land. About 65 per cent of farmland was tenanted. A 50 per cent rental share, the tenant bearing all the input expenses, was common, but landlords' agents often inflicted higher rates to benefit their own pockets. Security of tenure was normally for one year only. The Korean peasants never managed to organise themselves into a coherent political unit. Land productivity was, however, quite high for the Japanese instituted effective systems of land survey, extension, credit and fertiliser distribution. The agricultural surplus was largely creamed off for the Japanese market, rough Manchurian rice being imported to satisfy home demand.

Regional economic dualism within Korea was also very marked. Under direct Japanese control North Korea experienced rapid development of heavy industry to serve military expansion into China and Manchuria; South Korea, on the other hand, was organised to provide food for Japan itself. The industrial North and the agricultural South, geographically separate, were economically complementary. The eventual split of the country shattered hopes of integration. North Korea thus inherited most mineral resources (notably coal), the lion's share of the industry (although, with the Japanese gone, expertise to run the factories was lacking), and 92 per cent of electricity generating capacity. With more rugged terrain and a harsher climate, however, agricultural conditions were less favourable. In South Korea 80 per cent of the population depended upon agriculture. Following partition, population pressure was aggravated by 2–3 million refugees from the North, and South Korea's population grew from 16 million in 1945 to 20 million in 1949.[4] With no land available for colonisation, equalisation of income meant that the country, both North and South, was virtually destined for land reform.

SOUTH KOREA

South Korea became the third east Asian country where American involvement after the war produced a moderately sweeping land reform. In contrast to Japan and Taiwan, however, it has in South Korea hardly been successful. The Korean War of 1950–53, coming immediately after the reform, probably made this inevitable and certainly makes realistic judgment on the effects of the reform difficult.

LAND REFORM ACTIVITIES

When the US occupied South Korea in 1945, an immediate measure was to vest all Japanese-owned land (280 000 hectares, 13·5 per cent of the total arable area) in the Military Government under the New Korea Company. Conveying this 'vested' land to its 588 000 tenants (35 per cent of all farm families) represented the first stage of Korean land reform. The procedure was simple, involving little financial burden as no compensation was paid to landlords. Tenants paid three times the standard production of the land, in instalments over fifteen years at nil interest. Rapid inflation virtually cancelled out these repayment obligations. New Korea Company staff, acting as extension personnel, filled the void left by the Japanese, a service which was discontinued just when it was most needed, with the outbreak of the Korean War.[5]

In 1945, too, the US Military Government limited rents to a maximum of one-third of crop production and prohibited unilateral cancellation of tenancy contracts. Many landowners, foreseeing more thorough-going reform, sold their farmland, so that tenancy dropped and owner-farmers increased between 1945 and 1949. These actions, however, did not remove all the abuses of the traditional tenant system, and more sweeping legislation was soon drafted. This law, the main element in the land reform, was not operative until 1950 because of delays in its passage through the National Assembly.

The 1950 legislation established a ceiling of 3 hectares on farm ownership, and declared most forms of tenancy illegal. By the time the reform was executed, however, much land in ownership tracts of over 3 hectares had been sold or divided into smaller units. The balance was purchased for land securities equal to 150 per cent of the standard output. The priority of distribution was: (1) farmers currently cultivating the land in question; (2) farmers cultivating very small areas in relation to their households' capabilities; (3) bereaved families; (4) agricultural labourers; (5) farmers returned from abroad.[6]

A major goal was to lay a firm foundation for a democratic rural society. Political instability characterised the immediate post-liberation period, and the newly-established government wanted to stem the increasing diffusion of communist ideology in rural areas. Socially the reform aimed at mitigating class conflicts engendered by the landlord-tenant relationship and the arrival of refugees from the North. It also aimed at increasing agricultural productivity and encouraging the formation of industrial capital.

Reform activity was disrupted by the invasion from the North. Land records were destroyed, soil damaged and cropping patterns adversely affected. Implementing the reform was postponed almost everywhere. The programme was resumed in late 1950, after the recovery of the capital, Seoul, despite the loss of land documents. The reform continued, even during the conflict, for three reasons: socio-politically emancipation of tenants had to be demonstrated; selling land securities provided much needed war finance; and rice payments from beneficiaries were needed to feed soldiers.[7]

The original aim had been to distribute (including the vested lands) 833 000 hectares, or 40 per cent of South Korean arable land. When the reform was halted, 577 000 hectares (69 per cent) of the tenanted area, just less than one-third of total farmland, had been transferred. Some 1 646 180 families, 66 per cent of total farm households, were affected. The remaining 31 per cent consisted of clan land, land sold before or during land reform, and land illegally withheld by landlords.

TENURE PATTERN CHANGES

Data on tenurial changes after reform are summaried in Table 13. The reforms largely succeeded in reducing, if not eliminating, tenancy. Around 10 per cent of the reduction had already occurred during 1945–50 by landlords selling land to avoid expropriation and uncertainty of levels of compensation. Of the tenancy remaining (17 per cent of the farm area in 1968), half is land legally exempt from re-assignments; the rest is held illegally.

TABLE 13

SOUTH KOREA: STATISTICS OF REFORM

Programme	Land area (hectares)	No. of beneficiary families	Average land per household
Vested land distribution (1945)	254 554	727 632	0·34
Main land reform (1950)	331 766	918 548	0·36
Total	577 320	1 646 180	0·35

Tenure patterns by households (percentage)	1945	1965
Full owner	14	70
Part owner	34	23
Tenant	49	7
Slash and burn farmers	3	0
Total farm households (percentage)	100	100
(no.)	2 065 000	2 507 000

Tenure patterns by land type (percentage)	Paddy	Upland	Total
Pre land reform (1945)			
Owner-operated	30	56	37
Tenanted	70	44	63
Post land reform (1965)			
Owner-operated	85	80	82
Tenanted	15	20	18

Source: R. B. Morrow and K. H. Sherper: 'Land Reform in South Korea', in Agency for International Development: Spring Review of Land Reform (Washington, Department of State, 1970), Vol. 3, pp. 38–41.

As in Japan and Taiwan, South Korean land reform accentuated the trend towards small farms, at least initially. In 1947 74·5 per cent of farmholdings were below 1 hectare in size, in

1953 78·1 per cent. Holdings over 3 hectares virtually disappeared. The increase in small farms was, however, only partially related to land reform. Apart from land sold just before the reform, the refugee influx caused pressure for further farm sub-division. To this extent the land policy of 1945–50 helped absorb excess population at a cost probably less than by other means. Subsequently, however, many of these small farms have been consolidated into larger units, so that, ironically, by 1968 the landownership distribution had returned almost to its pre-reform pattern, though absentee landlord holdings had been replaced by large owner-operated farms.[8]

ECONOMIC EFFECTS

Economically the reform flowed far from smoothly. Compensation to landlords was so low (one-third the 1936 market value of land), and further eroded by inflation, that their investment in industry practically ceased; indeed most dispossessed landlords promptly went bankrupt. The beneficiaries also experienced financial problems. Many assignees, forced into debt to local moneylenders by lack of adequate credit, mortgaged land and thereby illegally renewed tenancy. Whereas the North Korean regime cancelled all tenant debts to landlords in the 1946 reform, the South Korean reformists seemed to assume that such problems would solve themselves when landowner-ship and tenancy issues were solved. Extension services, discontinued during 1945–8 and again during the Korean War (1950–3), were spasmodic and ineffective until the organisation was reconstituted in 1958. According to a survey of 1954–5 no farmer in a 360 household sample had joined an agricultural co-operative organisation or been contacted by the extension service.[9]

This situation was exacerbated by war, with much land over-run and damaged, and by a serious drought in 1952. No available data indicate what proportion of the new owner-farmers failed through the above causes. 'Distress sales' are known to have taken place, and the general concensus is that they could have been reduced by an adequate credit programme. Even so, post-reform agricultural productivity levels were higher than pre-reform, especially on the distributed vested lands, which enjoyed three years of extension and supply services.

The fact that South Korean peasants owned their land was, however, significant, especially when thousands of disillusioned refugees from North Korean collectivisation were streaming in. The present South Korean tenure system, with its small owner-farmer capitalist holdings, seems to have contributed to a rational use of abundant labour, limited land and shortage of capital. Expansion of government and private supplies and services has also improved farmers' response to market forces, so that, after a decline during the Korean War, agricultural output increased at 5 per cent annually during 1960–70. High crop yields reflect high land productivity, but the fact that a farmer in effect feeds only his own and one other family reflects relatively low labour productivity, and he produces with relatively fixed amounts of capital. Marked crop diversification has occurred since about 1960. Labour intensive products such as fruits, vegetables, tobacco and livestock have increased their share of total agricultural value, whilst foodgrains have decreased from 69 per cent to 46 per cent.[10]

Work by Pak indicates some increase in rural welfare following reform.[11] Tenant farmers purchased their land at much below market values and the burdens of ownership (taxes, water fees etc.) have been normally exceeded by returns to entrepreneurship. Since 1962 increased credit availability has been breaking the strangle-hold of limited capital on farm expansion. Irrigation has been a major beneficiary. In 1969 42 per cent of all arable land (76 per cent of paddy land) was irrigated, against 27 per cent (47 per cent for paddy) in 1950.

EVALUATION OF LAND REFORM IN SOUTH KOREA

Although 31 per cent of the land originally identified for land reform was never transferred to tenants, and although tenancy has not disappeared, the reform succeeded in reducing political and social unrest and in increasing agricultural productivity. South Korea's early attack on its land tenure problems, even in the face of such considerable obstacles as the Korean War, lack of finance and breakdown of agricultural services, had several positive effects. Centuries-old landlordism was destroyed and for the first time farmers enjoyed the rights of democracy and ownership. Land reform has unquestionably reduced the feeling of personal subordination and has increased independence and

I

individualism. 'Land-to-the-tiller' was already established when the Korean War ended; thereafter the government could concentrate on other development aspects instead of vacillating between the two related issues of tenure and development, as has happened elsewhere. The War may indeed have contributed some help, in that landowners were unable to consolidate their opposition and the farmers who persevered strengthened their claim to the land.[12]

There are, however, other ways of interpreting South Korean land reform. As in Japan and Taiwan, the dominant small-farm orientation of reform was related to the American concept of democratisation of rural life as a policy against communism. But the rural sector is now very much a secondary consideration. Since the land reform South Korea has developed into an industrial neo-colony of Japan and America. Labour-intensive, foreign-controlled industries take advantage of a cheap labour pool continually fed by rural-urban migration. South Korea's land problems are now not those of tenure and inequitable rights in land but of adjustments in a semi-industrial society with urban incomes nearly twice those of rural. Lack of farm incentives has induced reliance on imported foodstuffs, exacerbated by flood and drought in 1967 and 1968. The 1976 rice plan (4·8 million tons) will meet only 1969 domestic requirements; in 1973 3·5 million tons of grain were imported. The problem is less the waiving of the 3 hectares ceiling—with the current labour surplus and small-scale technology the 3 hectares limit need not impede increase in efficiency (the optimum crop farm in South Korea is said to be 2–3 hectares)—than of consolidating the 35 per cent of farms that are below ½ hectare and incapable of really supporting a farm family let alone yield a marketable surplus.[13]

NORTH KOREA

After the partition, North Korea, under Russian and Chinese influence, followed a very different path from the South. A decree issued in March 1946 ordained that all land formerly possessed by 'Japanese imperialists', 'national traitors', Korean landlords with more than 5 *chongbo* (roughly 5 hectares), absentee landlords, religious bodies with more than 5 hectares, and all land held continuously in tenancy, be confiscated without compensation and be distributed free to peasants with little or no land. Further, all peasant debts to landlords were cancelled and all farm animals, machinery and houses formerly owned by landlords were to be confiscated for distribution among the peasants; the government retained the option of using any buildings thus acquired as schools, hospitals etc. Irrigation facilities, orchards and forests of expropriated landlords became state owned. Within a month the North Korean People's Committee confiscated 1 million hectares, 54 per cent of the arable area. Actual redistribution—to 724 522 households—was effected by local committees (Table 14).

TABLE 14

STATISTICS OF THE 1946 LAND REFORM IN NORTH KOREA

(a) Origin of confiscated land		*hectares*
Japanese nationals and organisations		100 797
National traitors		21 718
Landlords with over 5 hectares		285 692
Landlords who rented out all their land		577 717
Churches, monasteries and other religious groups		14 401
Total:		1 000 325

(b) Disposal of confiscated land	*No. of families*	*hectares*
Farm labourers	17 137	22 387
Tenants	442 973	603 407
Farmers with little land	260 501	345 974
Landlords wishing to farm small plots in new localities	3 911	9 622
Totals:	724 522	981 390

Source: C.-S. Lee: 'Land Reform, collectivisation and the peasants in North Korea', *China Quarterly*, 14, 1963, p. 68.

Little is known of the precise effects of this land redistribution, although there is some evidence of increased agricultural output between the reform and the outbreak of the Korean

War in 1950.[14] Newly instituted Farmer's Banks provided loans to beneficiaries to enable them to buy seeds, fertilisers and tools. 'Shock-brigades' of workers, students and clerks were sent into the countryside to help with rice transplanting and harvesting. Enthusiasm was high. The cultivated area was expanded and many formerly dry fields turned into paddy.[15] For those in power, however, the reform created immediate ideological problems. The elimination of the feudalistic and colonial components of rural society by no means created favourable conditions for the desired transition to socialism. In fact the land reform divided society into two distinct sectors: the socialised urban industrial sector and the capitalistic rural sector.

The second stage of land reform, the creation of a socialised agriculture, coincided with the Korean War. Just as the war had some beneficial spin-off effects on land reform in the South, so in the North it expedited socialist reform. Patriotism could be invoked to stimulate rehabilitation of war-devastated land by expanding collective farms, establishing tractor stations and launching irrigation projects. Labour shortage further facilitated, and necessitated, socialist control of agriculture: migration to the South and war casualties reduced population by an estimated 2·1 million and the peasant proportion of the population declined from 74 per cent in 1946 to 66 per cent in 1953.

SOCIALIST AGRICULTURE IN NORTH KOREA[16]

This was the background of the North Korean 'co-operativisation' campaign. After a brief experimental period in 1953–4, the entire farm population was inducted into 13 300 cooperatives in less than four years up to August 1958. Almost immediately, however, the Pyongyang regime, following the Chinese commune movement begun earlier in 1958, started merging co-operatives into larger collective units. By 1963 3732 collective farms held 1 847 000 hectares and 190 state farms had 130 000 hectares.

Farm workers are drafted into 'work brigades' and 'work teams'. Each member of a co-operative is assigned according to his ability and qualifications to one category of work. Work brigades are specialised (crops, livestock, tractors and other branches) and each, except the tractor brigade, comprises three work teams, 'specialised', 'mixed', and 'all-purpose'. The activities of the specialised teams are highly seasonal, covering a wide area and restricted to a single crop or livestock species. The mixed team works on two or more crop or livestock types, its regional boundary defined by a 'natural' village of about 20–60 households (as opposed to the much larger 'administrative' villages). The all-purpose team is assigned to non-specialised farming and often deals with both crops and livestock. Workers labour up to 12 hours a day under strict supervision and a self-criticism report system. Although individual farms no longer exist, workers can own a private plot of up to 1 hectare to produce vegetables, fruit and livestock for family consumption. The size of co-operatives was influenced by the Chinese pattern: 300 households in plains areas, 100 in mountainous country. Originally the natural village was the basic co-operative unit but several villages are now included in an administrative unit or *ri*, and much decision-making now takes place at the still larger *kun* or 'county' level. Identification of the co-operatives with the *ri* doubtless simplified administration, but certainly increased regimentation of farmers. For labour control, incentive, evaluation and payment, all farm jobs are classified into categories (light, heavy, simple, complex etc.) and assigned grades equivalent to 'evaluated labour days'. Grade 1 work—a simple, menial, unimportant task—is equivalent to 0·5 labour days; Grade 7, equivalent to 2·0 labour days, might concern some skilled aspect of livestock management. Thus a worker's grade and earnings can vary by season and by type of job assigned; his grade remains constant while he remains in the same job. But the regime also adopted a 'minimum work amount schedule' to punish lazy workers and stimulate initiative for harder workers. Payment is made by distributing the harvests after deducting production costs, taxes, welfare contributions, education costs etc. A bonus of 40 per cent is added if targets are exceeded. Thus an individual's earnings depend not only on his grading and the actual amount of work performed, but also on the performance of other members.

Farmers are being relocated from their scattered hamlets to newly-built agro-cities, ostensibly for sanitary reasons. Exact information on this programme is unavailable, but substantial progress appears to have been made in some areas. For instance, an agro-city under construction in the early 1960s in Chaeryong-gun, Hwanghae Namdo (the granary of North Korea) housed 5220 households from eight *ri* and provided clubs, theatres, schools, hospitals, parks, laundries, dining rooms, barns, storehouses, rice-cleaning plants and mills.

Judging the 'co-operativisation' movement in North Korea solely from stated goals and announced achievements forces the conclusion that the policy has been a success. Thousands of workers, students and troops have been mobilised; dissident farmers have been silenced or suppressed; rapid increases in agricultural output have occurred. Demands upon the farmers are, however, onerous; North Korea's top priority is further industrialisation, and peasant sacrifice is essential for that goal. Although largely derived from China, the North Korean collectives seem to have some advantage over their Chinese and North Vietnamese counterparts. Besides a higher level of industrialisation (partly inherited from the Japanese), North Korea has twice as much land per person as China and 56 per cent more agricultural output per head. There is nothing reminiscent of China's 'collective folly' during the Great Leap in 1958.[17] In both agriculture and industry North Korea leads the east Asian communist bloc. Food production doubled and the irrigated area increased sevenfold (to 40 per cent of the total area) during 1944–64—from low base points, however. Agricultural population in that period fell from 74 to 43 per cent of the total; industrial rose from 18 to 55 per cent. In fact during 1954–60 North Korea grew economically at an almost unparalleled rate. Agricultural progress has, however, slowed since 1961 and population growth has increased to 3 per cent a year.

NORTH AND SOUTH KOREA: A COMPARISON

The two halves of Korea present profound differences in rural institutional settings and in economic incentives to farmers. The North has the collective, with the State controlling all the factors of production, virtually inclusive of human beings themselves; family farm management in the South provides relatively free choice of enterprise, but has problems of small scale and of economic fragmentation of production. Strict comparison is difficult because of diametrically different ideologies and because data are scanty for North Korea. In the 1960s the

North had higher growth rates in the use of land, labour and fertiliser. The North uses more tractors and fertiliser on almost the same area of cultivated land as the South, where animals still provide most of the farm power. Post-reform labour absorption has been greater in the South, due to lower mechanisation and the need to accommodate refugees.

Comparative data assembled by Pak on agricultural productivities shows little significant difference between North and South.[18] The South has a rather higher land productivity record. This reflects expansion of cultivated land in the North too aggressive to sustain continued land productivity improvement and the easier relief and climate in the South, permitting greater intensification and double-cropping (40 per cent of farmed land double-cropped in 1964; 20 per cent in the North). Labour productivity, at first sight, shows the reverse: productivity per capita is somewhat higher in the North. The entire labour force in the North is compulsorily active; in the South large numbers of rural workers are underemployed. The Northern worker averages about 320 days of work per year, the Southern only 200; this suggests that productivity *per hour worked* is higher in the South. Figures for gross agricultural output favour the North: a 10 per cent annual increase during 1954–60 and an average 6·3 per cent during 1961–70 compared to corresponding Southern figures of 2·7 per cent and 4·4 per cent. It appears that the North's agricultural expansion (grain production grew steadily from 3·4 million tons in 1959 to 5·7 million tons in 1972) has been more uniform than the South's, where average rates are composed of relatively high rates in alternation with negative years, reflecting lack of modernisation and dependence on weather conditions.[19]

REFERENCES

1. G. Breidenstein and W. Rosenberg: 'Economic comparison of North and South Korea', *Journal of Contemporary Asia*, 5 (2), 1975, pp. 165–204.
2. E. Brun and J. Hersch: 'Aspects of Korean socialism', *Journal of Contemporary Asia*, 5 (2), 1975, pp. 138–52.
3. G. Henderson: *Korea—The Politics of the Vortex* (Cambridge, Harvard University Press, 1968), p. 76.
4. G. Trewartha and W. Zelinsky: 'Population distribution and change in Korea 1925–49', *Geographical Review*, 45 (1), 1955, pp. 1–26.

5. R. B. Morrow and K. H. Sherper: 'Land Reform in South Korea', in Agency for International Development: *Spring Review of Land Reform* (Washington, Department of State, 1970), Vol. 3, pp. 13, 19–22.

6. *Ibid*: pp. 23, 27.

7. K. H. Pak, W. B. Han, K. H. Lee, J. H. Park and K. C. Han: *A Study of Land Tenure System in Korea* (Seoul, Land Economics Research Center, 1966), p. 83.

8. Morrow and Sherper: *op. cit.*, pp. 40–1.

9. K. H. Pak: 'Outcome of land reform in the Republic of Korea', *Journal of Farm Economics*, 38 (4), 1956, pp. 1015–23.

10. Morrow and Sherper: *op. cit.*, pp. 47–8.

11. K. H. Pak: 'Economic effects of land reform in the Republic of Korea', *Land Reform, Land Settlement and Co-operatives*, 1, 1968, pp. 13–27.

12. Morrow and Sherper: *op. cit.*, pp. 62–3.

13. Y.-K. Oh: 'Agrarian reform and economic development: a case study of Korean agriculture', *Koreana Quarterly*, 9 (2), 1967, pp. 91–137.

14. Y. T. Kuark: 'North Korea's agricultural development during the post-war period', *China Quarterly*, 14, 1963, pp. 89–93.

15. Brun and Hersch: *op. cit.*, pp. 142–3.

16. C.-S. Lee: 'The "socialist revolution" in the North Korean country-side', *Asian Survey*, 2 (8), 1962, pp. 9–22; J. S. Chung: 'A pattern of agricultural development: size, organisation and work incentives of the North Korean collective and state farms', in J. S. Chung (ed.): *Patterns of Economic Development: Korea* (Kalamazoo, Korea Research and Publications, 1966), pp. 55–79; C.-S. Lee and N.-S. Kim: 'Control and administrative mechanisms in the North Korean countryside,' *Journal of Asian Studies*, 29 (2), 1970, pp. 309–26.

17. The *Chollima* or 'Flying Horse' movement, an echo of China's Great Leap, was launched in September 1958. Although this coincided with the period of rapid collectivisation of North Korean agriculture, it was implemented with more caution than the Great Leap, and had its most profound successes in industry. Kuark: *op. cit.*, pp. 90–2.

18. K. H. Pak: 'A comparative study of the agrarian systems of North and South Korea', in W. A. D. Jackson (ed.): *Agrarian Problems and Policies in Communist and Non-Communist Countries* (Seattle, University of Washington Press, 1971), pp. 436–58.

19. Breidenstein and Rosenberg: *op. cit.*, p. 171.

11

North and South Vietnam

It may appear surprising to expect land reform in war-torn Vietnam, but the land tenure issue underlies the whole story of war, the Viet Cong and American involvement. Opposing land reform ideologies go far towards explaining the cause and nature of the conflict, and a mass of legislation has accumulated over the past 20 years. In the South this ranges from the token declarations of Emperor Bao Dai in 1951 through the Diem laws of 1955–8 regulating tenancy and expropriating large landowners, to the 1970 land-to-the-tiller reform. North Vietnam has generally followed the Chinese model in a two-stage process. The first reform (1953–6) was a sweeping land redistribution. Despite clumsy execution, partially corrected in the 'rectification of errors' campaign of 1956–7, the government considers this reform successful in giving the working peasants the land and eliminating landlordism. The second stage began in 1958: the government, to prevent re-emergence of rural class stratification and to cope with land shortage, initiated co-operative ownership and working of land.

TRADITIONAL TENURE AND THE FRENCH COLONISATION
The traditional Vietnamese village was a rather well-organised community, with certain communal principles, notably reciprocal assistance in rice transplanting, prominent, yet with religious concerns dominating much daily behaviour.[1] Individually owned land (*tu dien*) could be used and divided as the family wished (except that no land others were willing to farm could be left uncropped); *cong dien*, communally owned

rice land whose usufruct rights were periodically reallocated by village officials amongst villagers, provided a tax base for the emperor. This system was more egalitarian than the South Asian villages, where caste dominated social relations. The level of living, too, was well above subsistence, even though abundance was lacking. Both state and village economy and society were developing dynamically when the French arrived on the scene in the 1860s.

French tax and tenure policies cut across traditional land codes and greatly altered wealth, power and social relations. Land wealth came rapidly into the hands of absentee landlords, especially in the south, and the customary claims of individuals and communes to land and produce were annulled. Village life was disrupted through the imposition of monopolies on products like salt and sugar, and the introduction of basically monocultural farming choked the diversified subsistence agriculture. Associated with this was the *cai* labour recruitment system for the working of plantations and mines. The French were primarily interested in developing underutilised land resources. Vietnamese colonisation of the Mekong Delta, in progress when the French arrived, still left vast areas to be exploited. Large land grants for rice, rubber, tea and coffee cultivation went to Frenchmen, Chinese and favoured Vietnamese on condition of clearing the land, building canals and making other improvements. Between 1880 and 1930 the Mekong Delta rice area quadrupled to over 2 million hectares. But the amassing of vast landholdings by the colonists also worsened the peasants' condition. Rice they could have consumed was extracted through land rents and exported. In 1937 French landowners possessed 250 000 hectares in Cochinchina and 57 per cent of the population was landless. Virtually all large landholdings were cultivated by tenants on small 2–3 hectare plots. French companies held the few really big rice holdings, of which the largest covered 20 000 hectares.[2]

Unlike the more recently colonised Mekong Delta, traditionally a rice-surplus region, Tonkin and northern Annam (the area which became North Vietnam) were the most densely-peopled parts of French Indochina, and rice exports from the Tonkin Delta had already ceased by 1932. As in the South, the conditions of the Tonkinese peasantry worsened under the French: concentration of land ownership, especially of communal land acquired by speculators and village chiefs, increased taxes, monetisation of the economy and French reliance on frequently corrupt Vietnamese officials were factors. From field surveys in the 1930s Gourou noted the grave social dangers in a very large rural proletariat of very small landowners, renters, sharecroppers and landless agricultural labourers.[3] In Tonkin 91 per cent of the landowners (with under 1·8 hectare each) held 37 per cent of the land area; the other 9 per cent monopolised 43 per cent (the remaining 20 per cent being communal). And these figures exclude the landless 61·5 per cent of the peasantry! Most Tonkin land was rented. Rent, generally a third to a half of a normal harvest, in cash or in kind, was fixed in advance (and paid in advance, if cash). Landlords in regions subject to natural disaster such as flood or drought and absentee landlords, who could not supervise the harvest, preferred cash rent. Sharecropping was prominent in Annam, the commonest sharing being half each to landlord and peasant. Interest rates on loans averaged 3–5 per cent per month, but could be up to 10 per cent. A French attempt to eliminate usury by setting up the *Credit Populaire Agricole* in 1928 failed—the small peasant had insufficient collateral to borrow—and the landlords and rich peasants used the funds to make usurious loans to the poorer farmers. Rice yields were low at the time (1928–30): 13 quintals per hectare, against 15 in Java, 18 in Thailand and 34 in Japan. Irregular rainfall caused considerable year to year fluctuations in yield. The French did, however, extend irrigation into the rice fields (although the landlords derived most of the benefit) and carried out a comprehensive programme of dyke building and strengthening after the flood of 1927 in the Tonkin Delta.

NORTH VIETNAM

As with the partition of Korea, the division of Vietnam in 1954 split two economically complementary regions: the industrial resources, chiefly coal, to the North, the agricultural resources to the South. Yet rural overpopulation was the chief problem in the North, where two-thirds are mountainous, and contain only 5 per cent of the cultivated land. Four-fifths of the population live in the crowded rice-growing deltas, the most important, the Red River, the 'heartland' of the Vietnamese, containing 74 per cent of the arable land and 75 per cent of the population. Under the French, the Delta's population grew from 6·8 million in 1928 to 8·7 million in 1936; Gourou calculated that only 125 days of work were available per farmworker per year.[4] By 1960 rural population density in the Delta was 700 per square kilometre, among the highest in the world. For the whole country, only about 0·1 hectare of cultivated land is available per inhabitant.

The seeds of peasant insurgency appeared quite early. In 1930 a communist-led uprising occurred in northern Annam. For a year landlords and French officials were driven from large rural areas. Government buildings were destroyed, tax and cadastral records burnt and mandarins and notables killed. In some areas land was confiscated and redistributed before the French regained control.[5]

In 1941 the Viet Minh was established as an anti-French united front organisation led primarily by the Indochinese Communist Party but including other nationalist groups, and in 1945 Ho Chi Minh declared independence and appointed a Viet Minh government. A protracted war followed lack of international recognition and the French determination to regain control and the Viet Minh became masters of most of the country.

Viet Minh agrarian policy during 1945–53 confiscated land of French colonials and pro-French Vietnamese landlords. The right of other, 'patriotic' landlords to collect rent was recognised, though rents were reduced by 25 per cent; since most rents had been about 50 per cent of the annual crop value, the payment came down to about 37·5 per cent of the crop, the same as the Kuomintang rent ceiling in China and the 1951 ceiling in Taiwan. The main agrarian priority in the late 1940s, especially after the disastrous famine of 1944–5 in which up to 2 million people died, was to raise production. A May 1950 decree expropriated outright all land which had been idle over the previous five years or which was still uncultivated at the end of 1950. Another May 1950 decree abolished debts contracted before 1945 and reduced interest rates on loans to 13 per cent per year for cash and 20 per cent for loans in kind. These reforms changed slightly the landholding system before its radical modification in 1953. Land reform up to 1953 affected 310 200 hectares, 15 per cent of the total cultivated area, of which 91 000 hectares were actually redistributed.[6]

THE 1953 LAND REFORM

The Agrarian Reform Law of December 1953 constitutes the basic legislation governing the first phase of North Vietnamese land reform. The law mainly concerned land redistribution in the rice-growing deltas. Mechanised estates, orchards and plantations of coffee, rubber, etc. were left alone; many of these later became state farms. The basis of the law was the expropriation of land from landlords without compensation (the law provided for some indemnity to 'progressive' as opposed to 'traitorous' landlords, but none seems to have been paid) and its distribution, free, to landless and semi-landless peasants. As in China, five rural classes were recognised: landless workers, poor peasants, middle peasants, rich peasants, and landlords. Land was distributed within the village, according to need (mouths to feed rather than workers available per family) and previous occupancy of land (priority to incumbent tenants). Special land reform committees administered the law. Top government and party leaders assumed responsibility in the land reform campaign, indicating the importance attached to it; Ho Chi Minh himself presided over the national committee.

In the villages three separate organs, the Executive Committee of the Peasants' Association, the Special Land Reform Tribunals and the land reform cadres, carried through the reform.[7] The 'mass mobilisation of the peasantry' proceeded in four stages: (1) land reform cadres arrived in the village, gained the peasants' confidence, explained how landlords had oppressed them and prepared them for the reform; (2) the population was classified, based on the judgments of the cadres and the most influential of the poorer peasants in the Peasants' Association; (3) the landlords were dispossessed by the Tribunals; (4) distribution took place. Cadres were specially trained because of the ideological importance of the reform, which the Party could not entrust to normal administrative channels. The redistribution was carried out entirely within the village framework: only if a village had surplus land and few potential beneficiaries were outsiders considered.

The most troublesome aspect of the law was which land was to be redistributed.[8] Landlords were to lose their land but not rich peasants, but the distinction between the two was difficult to make. A 1955 attempt at clarification, by which a landlord worked 120 days on his land, renting most of it out, probably aggravated the confusion, for who should say whether a land-owning farmer worked 120 days on his land, thereby qualifying as 'rich peasant' entitled to keep his land, or worked 110 days, thereby becoming subject to expropriation? The Party's class line—'rely on poor peasants and agricultural labourers'—hinged classifications mainly on the judgment of the very people who were to receive expropriated land, and, given the extreme population pressure, the land-hungry peasants naturally tried to find as many landlords as possible to dispossess, to secure enough land to go around. Consequently intimidation of land-lords and 'would-be' landlords, and even execution, undoubt-edly took place, although accusations of a 'bloodbath' are probably exaggerated.[9]

In 1956 grave errors in the execution of the reform were offici-ally acknowledged. The major cause of these errors was that the cadres were under pressure, both from above (ideologically, to eliminate the landlord class) and from below (to find as much land as possible), to bring before tribunals as many landlords as possible. By this stage, however, many landlords had fled south, and some of the land anyway had been already distributed as a temporary measure by the Viet Minh. Many rich peasants were therefore unjustly labelled landlords and expropriated, and much ancestral cult and religious minorities' land, legally ex-empt from expropriation, was usurped. The Catholics were particularly severely treated and in fact comprised most of the migration to the south. The reform was judged socially and economically successful—landlords were eliminated and agri-cultural production increased 52 per cent in value during 1955–9—but politically it failed; in correcting the colonial right-wing society leftist excesses caused serious unrest in both the Party and the population.[10]

The 'rectification of errors' campaign of 1956–7 comprised three stages.[11] The first was release from prison of wrongly classified persons; the régime admitted that 30 per cent of persons convicted as landlords were wrongly condemned. The second included reclassification of peasants and landlords and compensation for wrongly expropriated property. The third was 'review, inventory and re-indocrination', and the campaign ended with 'recapitulation conferences'. Both in its form and in the preoccupation of the press and the Party with mistakes, the campaign is unique. Nevertheless this back-tracking delayed the socialisation of agriculture more than just the year of the campaign.

Data on the impact of the 1953 reform vary according to source, but it seems that about half of North Vietnam's 1·5 million hectares of cultivated land changed hands; 144 000 hectares of this land abandoned by emigrants to South Vietnam. Official statistics give 2·2 million families (9 million people), or 72 per cent of the total rural population, affected by reform; Gittinger[12] estimates 1·6 million households (8 million total) or 67 per cent of the population. Both sets of figures are large enough to include all peasants classed as landless in 1953 (6·8 million persons, 61·5 per cent of the rural population). The régime also reported the distribution of 100 000 head of cattle and an unspecified quantity of farm equipment and buildings. Table 15 reveals the differential class impact of the reform: all three 'lower' classes improved their positions; the rich peasants

TABLE 15

NORTH VIETNAM: AVERAGE PER CAPITA LAND ENDOWMENT
FOR RURAL CLASSES BEFORE AND AFTER LAND REFORM

(figures in square metres)

Rural class	Before	After
Landlord	6779	825
Rich peasant	2116	2159
Middle peasant	999	1565
Poor peasant	343	1372
Landless worker		1421

Source: North Vietnamese government statistics cited in C. P. White: 'Land Reform in North Vietnam', in Agency for International Development: *Spring Review of Land Reform* (Washington, Department of State, 1970), Vol. 4, p. 41.

remained relatively unaffected; the landlords lost much land, to become the poorest group. Considerable, but by no means complete, equalisation of landholding was achieved. The landlords' low status (some were imprisoned or even killed) was officially justified by the debt they owed the people for their exploitation of the other classes.

THE CO-OPERATIVES

Conforming to standard communist land policy, land redistribution was intended to be only a step *en route* to socialism. Exemption of large non-rice estates from expropriation in 1950 indicated thoughts of their eventual transformation into state or collective farms. By 1955 pilot co-operatives were being established. As in China, co-operativisation showed successive phases. Small scale mutual aid teams accustomed the peasants to working together. During this stage ownership of land and equipment was retained; the peasants worked together in seasonal or permanent exchanges, much like the traditional pattern. In the second stage of semi-socialist or lower-rank co-operatives the peasant rented his land and other production equipment to the co-operative, which payed him rent, managed his land and organised labour. In the full socialist co-operatives all means of production belong to the collective. Rent to the former owner is eliminated. All co-operative revenue, after deduction of expenses, goes to members, 'to each according to his work'. North Vietnam has not yet created communes. Co-operatives generally remain the size of a village.

The basic legislation governing semi-socialist co-operatives, enshrining three guiding principles, voluntariness, mutual benefit and democratic management, was issued in 1959. Landlords and rich peasants were initially excluded from co-operatives, but were later given probationary membership. Each family has a private plot for the 'supplementary family economy', but the size of plot is restricted to 5 per cent of the per capita share of the co-operative land. Much social and political pressure was exerted on the peasants to join, but there was no coercion, as there had been in the confiscation tribunals of 1953–6 or the Soviet collectivisation of 1928–30. The first year (1959) brought few volunteers (8 per cent of the total peasantry), but by 1960 co-operative production equalled that of individual peasant farming and soon exceeded it, thanks to irrigation and other state-provided benefits. By 1961 86 per cent of the peasants were in co-operatives. The transition to higher level co-operatives occurred during the 1960s with the gradual withdrawal of rent payments by the co-operatives. In 1960 only 12 per cent of peasants were in higher-level co-operatives, by 1968 95 per cent, when the 22 360 co-operatives controlled 93 per cent of all cultivated land. The average Red River Delta co-operative counts 270 families, 405 labourers and 128 hectares of land. In the northern, hillier part of the country the averages are lower: 136 families, 276 workers and 77 hectares. Large co-operatives characterise the hinterlands of large cities, for example the Yen-duyen co-operative in the suburbs of Hanoi, comprising 545 families, 1127 workers, 253 hectares of land and 54 hectares of ponds.[13]

Starting in 1963, to facilitate drainage, irrigation and labour application, fields and plots were enlarged and given a more regular layout. New dykes follow the contours of the ground and the new rectilinear plot boundaries rather than the intricate borders of the old properties.[14] Full labour utilisation and provision of small scale or 'intermediate technology' have been emphasised; much new machinery has apparently been designed to promote fuller use of female labour.[15] From 1960 regional industries were established to produce agricultural implements and consumer goods; the aim here is partly to restore the town-country balance, which the French had disturbed when Hanoi and Haiphong were expanded as colonial enclaves.

The output record of post-reform agriculture is not clear. Official sources claim an increase of 5 per cent per year, even in conditions of heavy bombing. Gittinger gives figures indicating stagnation of rice production at around 4 million tons throughout the late 1950s.[16] Dumont in the mid 1960s estimated an annual agricultural growth rate of 3 per cent, barely equalling population growth, and described the country's agriculture as a classic case of diminishing returns.[17] The rationing of basic foodstuffs since 1957 indicates that agriculture produces barely enough to cover the needs of the population, let alone provide capital for industrial development. By the late 1960s, however, the new high-yielding rice varieties were making themselves felt, and 1972, with a quarter of the paddy area planted to new hybrids, produced a record crop of 5·3 million tons.[18] The impetus, however, has not been maintained and output remained below 5 million tons during 1973-5, due partly to the war and bad weather. Per capita production of rice (192 kg in 1975, when the harvest was 4·7 million tons) is still below the 1965 figure of 233 kg (when the harvest was 4·3 million tons). Even if the 1976 target of 5·5 million tons is achieved, per capita production would still be below that of 1965, although reliance on Chinese imports would be erased. Since 1975 there has been a policy of amalgamating co-operatives into larger 500–800 hectare units with a view to increasing mechanisation, irrigation and, therefore, production.[19]

For the peasant the most significant achievement of the post-1959 policy is the provision of security. Without the co-operative the 'race for rice' would have left him unable to cultivate his vegetable garden, raise pigs and poultry, or enjoy certain health, social and educational services. Both the traditional and the French systems took from the agricultural sector without providing more in return than the hydraulic works essential for production. Today, with 85–90 per cent of peasants in higher-level co-operatives (the remainder mainly northern mountain folk), the standard of living is still low but significantly improved. Inequality of wealth has been minimised and everyone has at least social and economic security. One cannot conclude that the individual farm system would have fared better.

SOUTH VIETNAM

Recent (pre-1975) South Vietnamese government land reform efforts followed three paths: distribution of the remaining lands acquired from large landowners and the French in the 1950s; the 1970 land-to-the-tiller reform, intended to transfer all privately tenanted and communally owned rice land free to the farmer actually cultivating it; and a montagnard project designed to clarify titles of tribally farmed land in the highlands. Little information is available on land reform activity since the 1975 American withdrawal.

1945 found rural South Vietnam with both landlessness and abundant land. In the Mekong Delta landownership concentration was amongst the highest in South-east Asia. 2·5 per cent of the landowners, with over 50 hectares each, owned half the cultivated land; peasant proprietorships of under 5 hectares, numbering 70 per cent of the landholdings, totalled only 12 per cent of the land. Two-thirds of the farming population was landless. In central Vietnam, by contrast, peasant-owned farms covered three-quarters of the cultivated land. Of 650 000 landowners in this long-settled central lowland region, only about 50 owned over 50 hectares each, and barely a dozen over 100 hectares. Landlords fell almost entirely into the 5–10 hectare category, resembling the former petit bourgeois landlordism of Japan, Taiwan and Korea. Here, too, communal land tenure persisted—up to 70 per cent of the land in some villages. The third major physiographic region, the highland Chaîne Annamatique, was almost exclusively royal family domain until 1955. This area had not been extensively exploited, but establishment of rubber, coffee and tea plantations by the French caused resentment amongst the swidden-farming montagnards.

During the troubles from 1945 to 1954, when the Geneva Agreement, ending the Indochina War, partitioned Vietnam along the 17th parallel, the Viet Minh insurgents, combining anti-colonial nationalism with promised land reform, found ready support amongst the southern rural population, especially in the Mekong Delta. By 1954 they controlled 60–90 per cent of what became South Vietnam. The land reform they were carrying out there was pragmatic rather than centrally-conceived. Strict limitations on rents and interest rates were enforced. Lands held by the French, communal land and the land of 'traitorous' Vietnamese landlords were confiscated and given to the poorer peasants. Quasi-military religious sects, such as the Hoa Hao and the Cao Dai, controlled substantial areas of the Mekong Delta along the Cambodian border; citing traditional concepts of land usage, they, too, encouraged the peasants to occupy abandoned land without considering legal title. So a virtual, if confused, land reform had been widespread before independence.

Continual guerilla warfare seriously damaged the rural economy, however. Markets were interrupted, water control activities stopped and crop production fell. Thousands of confused, isolated peasants left their holdings for the relative security of larger villages and towns. By 1954 about 700 000 hectares of rice land in South Vietnam had been abandoned. Faced by this abandonment and the need for rural repatriation the Diem government, which assumed office in 1954, agreed, with American aid, to institute an 'official' land reform.

THE 1955–8 REFORMS AND THEIR EFFECTS

President Diem's programme had three objectives: (1) to restore abandoned land to cultivation; (2) to regularise landlord-tenant relationships with particular reference to rent reduction and tenure security; and (3) to effect some land redistribution.

Ordinance 7, 1955, required landowners to declare their uncultivated land and intentions regarding it. Those unable or unwilling to cultivate such land had to lease it to farmers who would; tenant farmers who restored land to use got a written guarantee of tenure with reduced rent for three years. By 1960 60 per cent of the abandoned land was producing again. Much such uncultivated land was used for settling 500 000 refugees from North Vietnam. The largest refugee resettlement scheme was the Cai San project in the Mekong Delta; some 50 000 refugee families, each assigned a 3 hectare plot at a nominal price, reclaimed the land, cleared the canals and grew rice. With growing insecurity in the 1960s, however, the project declined and fewer than 70 of the 210 original village centres were occupied in 1970.[20]

Besides refugee settlement, the government tackled land reclamation in the Central Highlands. Some 100 000 people were moved from the crowded Central Lowlands to the sparsely populated Highlands, exchanging their tiny tenant holdings for a gift plot of 2–3 hectares. The scheme included resettling approximately 25 000 montagnards, independent and considered vulnerable to communist subversion, in new locations in the area. By 1965, however, most of the lowlanders had returned to their native villages and their presence in the Highlands had only exacerbated the ill-feeling of the montagnards toward the Vietnamese.

Ordinance 2 of 1955, initiating tenancy control, enforced a rent ceiling of 25 per cent of the annual harvest, gave the tenant security of tenure for five years under a written contract and first right to purchase should the landlord decide to sell his land.

By 1959 800 000 tenancy contracts, 80 per cent of the total theoretically possible, were registered. Only in non-Viet Minh controlled areas, however, did the reform bring a significant erosion of landlords' status, power and wealth. To the hundreds of thousands who had acquired land from the Viet Minh and had not paid rent for years, the reform seemed an imposition, a return to the *status quo ante*. The tenancy contract became the means whereby landlords forced their former tenants to pay back rent at 25 per cent for the previous ten years. Land reform ironically became the tool for destroying the free peasant economy it had been designed to create, a tactical blunder which restored, rather than controlled, the landlord-tenant relationship, thus favouring, rather than averting, revolution.[21]

Diem's most important reform was Ordinance 57, 1956, which forbade the owning of more than 100 hectares of rice land (other crops were exempt), plus an additional 15 hectares of *huong hoa*, ancestral worship land. The government expropriated land above this ceiling and distributed it to peasants in lots of up to 5 hectares. The reform was clearly meant for the deltaic south, where most large single properties were and where it was estimated that one third of the tenants would benefit from redistribution, but various sub-clauses of the ordinance gave landlords considerable protection. The ceiling itself was high, thirty times those adopted in Japan and Taiwan for example. Landowners could, moreover, choose which 100 hectares they retained, and convert rice land into other crops to avoid expropriation. Loop-hole regulations ultimately gave landlords eight years to 'prove' that 'pre-ordinance' sales of land had taken place; inevitably spurious sales to relatives and strawmen were common. Generous compensation—10 per cent in cash and 90 per cent in 12-year, 3 per cent bonds convertible into government industrial enterprise shares—represented 50–100 per cent of the market value of the land, depending on its quality. Priority of land purchase went to incumbent tenants, followed in turn by relatives of deceased soldiers, refugees, the unemployed, owner-farmers with under 3 hectares and more than five children, and the landless. The price of the land, roughly equalling the landlord's indemnity, was payable in six annual instalments, each approximately equivalent to a year's rent, the government withholding permanent title until payments were complete. Again, however, most peasants considered the official reform unfavourably in the light of the Viet Minh programme which it ostensibly ousted. Expropriation proceeded moderately rapidly, but the distribution process involved a whole bureaucratic chain from village to the ministry in Saigon back to the village again. Staffing was inadequate at every stage and nearly everywhere the programme did not begin until 1957 or 1958. In 1960 sale of land and assignment of provisional titles began in earnest, but by then rural security had deteriorated and progress ceased in 1962. By then the government had distributed only 210 000 hectares of the 453 000 hectares expropriated from 2000 Vietnamese landlords, and none of the 230 000 hectares formerly owned by the French (assignment of this started in 1966). Less than one-tenth of South Vietnamese tenants had benefited from the reform; the government had become, in fact, the largest landowner in South Vietnam.[22]

The Diem reforms brought few significant changes in land tenure patterns.[23] Since most recipients owned no land before, and most of them received little land, the number of landowners was increased (by about 30 per cent), but with little equalising of overall landholdings. Very large landowners were removed, but, since the land distribution, based on amounts previously rented, had its own pattern of inequality, very many landowners held tiny amounts of land. The reform did virtually nothing for the landless, because they had the very lowest assignment priority.

THE TROUBLED YEARS OF THE 1960s

As, with rising terrorism, the village authorities began abandoning rural areas in 1960 and subsequent years, the Viet Cong, successors to the Viet Minh, moved in and instituted their own land reform, the third within 10–15 years. The Viet Cong acquired much rural support by promising to maintain and extend the Viet Minh land reforms. Diem's reform was heavily attacked from Hanoi and the Viet Cong worked tirelessly to disrupt the official programmes. The Viet Cong rice land policy established a ceiling of about 5 hectares, approximately what a 'middle peasant' could hold. The Delta peasant came to regard this as a norm reflecting social justice. The dramatic disparity between the Viet Cong ceiling of 5 hectares and the Ordinance 57

ceiling of 100–115 hectares inevitably gave the Viet Cong a political advantage over the government, even though peasants receiving land from the Viet Cong did not know how long they would
be able to keep it.[24] The Viet Cong gave the landless first call on
the available land, followed by peasants who had contributed to
driving out the government, and then by those with some land
but still in need. The first two categories always received some
land, the best going to those who had most actively supported
the Viet Cong. The reform was implemented on a village or
hamlet basis, and was usually completed within three months.
Another important aspect was that landlords were encouraged
to remain and work with the revolution. The ceiling of 5 hectares is quite generous in this respect, and even renting land is
not forbidden, though rents are firmly fixed at a maximum of
15 per cent of the crop.

While the Viet Cong programme gained momentum in the
1960s, Diem abandoned land reform. From 1961 to 1966 the US
ceased supporting basic agrarian reforms and adopted military
measures against communism, culminating in the 1965 landing
at Danang. The deteriorating political situation in the countryside stimulated an 'agroville' programme to resettle peasants in
rural agglomerations linked by strategic route systems.[25] In
1961 this policy was modified into the 'strategic hamlet' programme, a major campaign, supported by American finance, to
relocate the rural population in a series of armed stockades. This
approach appealed to Diem because it reincarnated the procedure the Vietnamese had used for centuries in their migration
south into the Mekong Delta. Under the direction of British
officials, responsible for a similar programme in Malaya, 5753
hamlets were established by the end of 1962, and another 6000
for two million evacuees were planned. In fact this policy, interrupted by the upheaval of Diem's assassination, only heightened
rural alienation. Peasants were unwilling to leave their established villages to build the strategic hamlets by forced labour.
Herded behind walls and deprived of their household plots,
their dependence on landlords and government officials was increased. The organisational effort also absorbed substantial resources needed elsewhere. The programme, the last effort of the
Diem government to develop a viable political and economic
policy for rural Vietnam, proved an unqualified failure.

Some support for land reform returned during the mid 1960s but with little result. In 1964 illegal squatters on government land received ownership rights up to 10 hectares if they had already cleared the land. Also in 1964 the beneficiary repayment period for land acquired under Ordinance 57 was extended from six to twelve years. In 1965 Prime Minister Ky's programme for the reform and distribution of communal lands, like other government reforms, made little progress because of lack of qualified personnel. After 1966 more of the Ordinance 57 and former French land temporarily held by the government was distributed, but by 1970 21 per cent of the original acquired total was still undistributed, mostly because, lacking investment since its abandonment, it had become uncultivable.

THE 1970 REFORM

The 1968 Tet Offensive having portended unacceptably high American combat losses, the idea of a major land reform revived. President Thieu convened a national congress on land reform to demonstrate publicly his determination to tackle this fundamental issue. Land reform now was a precondition for ending the war, not, as the Americans had hitherto assumed, something to follow the establishment of security. On 26 March 1970 the new Land-to-the-Tiller bill, aimed at undercutting the Viet Cong's position as social reformer, creating revolutionary economic progress and instant rural security, passed into law. The reform was exalted as 'a programme more far-reaching than any other similar . . . undertaken by any democracy in any other part of the world'.[26] Had the law been implemented in 1945 it would indeed have been revolutionary. By 1970, however, it was hardly so and in fact was 'little more than Saigon's approval stamp for the land redistribution already carried out by the Viet Cong'.[27]

The spirit of the Land-to-the-Tiller law continued that of the 1956 law, but with ownership limited to 15 hectares of rice land (and then only if the owner himself, with his family, cultivated the land), plus another 5 hectares (which could, however, be rented out) of worship land. Assignment of land was limited to plots not exceeding 3 hectares in Mekong Delta and 1 hectare elsewhere. Land was granted free (outstanding beneficiary repayments from the earlier reforms were cancelled), the government compensating the landowner at two and a half times the average crop value of the previous quinquennium, payable 20 per cent in cash and 80 per cent in 8-year bonds bearing 10 per cent interest (but annual inflation was 30 per cent!). Communal land was also subject to redistribution to tenants cultivating it. Priority for assignment, like the 1956 law, put the landless last of all.[28]

With the power of large landowners largely erased in 1956, the 1970 law took land mostly from the 'medium landlord' category. However, the 15 hectare limit was still much higher than the 5 hectare the Viet Cong and many peasants considered 'just'. Official claims were that 90 per cent of South Vietnam's farmers would become owner-operators and that up to 1 300 000 hectares would eventually be distributed. In fact, with over a million potential beneficiaries requesting land, most of them eligible for 3 hectares, a shortage of land would still remain. Moreover much of the land theoretically available was in insecure areas, which had often already experienced Viet Cong land reform. But perhaps the greatest misconception was that this reform could by itself transform agrarian society.

THE FUTURE

The fall of South Vietnam to the communists in April 1975 was perhaps the most important event of recent world history. The reintegration of Vietnam is nigh. The South will probably now play a role of food-provider for the whole country. It has been estimated that the South's war-damaged rice paddies (fallow land in the Mekong Delta alone amounted to half a million hectares) could immediately absorb a million people, many of whom will come from the planned deflation of Saigon (now Ho Chi Minh City) from a population of 3 million to 1 million.[29] The accent, still, is on private means; unlike the fundamentalist revolutionaries in neighbouring Cambodia, the Provisional Revolutionary Government of South Vietnam is proceeding to restructure the economy gradually. Already, however, land taken from rich officials and supporters of the Thieu régime has been redistributed to landless peasants and families of dead National Liberation Front soldiers and cadres. Other landlords have had to lower their rental share of the crop. Collective farms are being set up in newly developed zones, and in traditional farming areas 'labour exchange teams' have been formed. The future process of socialisation of agriculture will be interesting to watch.

REFERENCES

1. J. Adams and N. Hancock: 'Land and economy in traditional Vietnam', *Journal of South East Asian Studies* 1 (2), 1970, pp. 90–8.
2. C. Robequain: *The Economic Development of French Indochina* (London, Oxford University Press, 1944), pp. 192, 220.
3. P. Gourou: *The Peasants of the Tonkin Delta* (New York, Human Relations Area Files, 1955).
4. *Ibid*: p. 658.
5. C. P. White: 'Land Reform in North Vietnam', in Agency for International Development: *Spring Review of Land Reform* (Washington, Department of State, 1970), Vol. 4, pp. 8, 12.
6. *Ibid*: pp. 9, 24.
7. *Ibid*: pp. 31–3, 37.
8. *Ibid*: pp. 28–9.
9. On this point see D. G. Porter: 'The myth of the bloodbath: North Vietnam's land reform reconsidered', *Bulletin of Concerned Asian Scholars*, 5 (2), 1973, pp. 2–15.
10. White: *op. cit.*, pp. 32, 34, 36, 38–9.
11. J. P. Gittinger: 'Communist land policy in North Vietnam', *Far Eastern Survey*, 28 (8), 1959, pp. 113–26.
12. *Ibid*: p. 119.
13. A. Woodside: 'Decolonisation and agricultural reform in Northern Vietnam', *Asian Survey*, 10 (8), 1970, pp. 705–23.
14. White: *op. cit.*, p. 54.
15. Woodside: *op. cit.*, pp. 710–12.
16. J. P. Gittinger: 'A note on the economic impact of totalitarian land tenure change: the Vietnamese experience', *Malayan Economic Review*, 5 (2), 1960, pp. 81–4.
17. See R. Dumont: 'Problèmes agricoles au Nord-Vietnam', *France-Asie*, 20 (1), 1965, pp. 41–60. Shortly afterwards a widespread birth-control campaign was initiated and in 1970 the population growth rate was down to 2 per cent.
18. A. Gordon: 'The "Green Revolution" in North Vietnam', *Journal of Contemporary Asia*, 4 (1), 1974, pp. 128–33.
19. N. Chanda: 'Rebuilding shattered Vietnam', *Far Eastern Economic Review*, 91 (7), 1976, pp. 92–6.
20. M. Salter: 'Land reform in South Vietnam', in Agency for International Development: *Spring Review of Land Reform, op. cit.*, Vol 4, pp. 69–70.
21. J. Race: 'South Vietnam: the battle over land', *Far Eastern Economic Review*, 69 (34), 1970, pp. 19–22.
22. R. L. Prosterman: 'Land Reform in South Vietnam', *Current History*, 57 (340), 1969, pp. 327–32.

23. J. B. Hendry: 'Land tenure in South Vietnam', *Economic Development and Cultural Change*, 9 (1), 1960, pp. 27–44.
24. Nor were they informed about the ultimate communist goal of collectivisation. For the landless peasant who for generations had been worrying about where the next bowl of rice was coming from, rumours about what the communists would do with the land in 5 or 10 years time were not important; the short run benefit of acquiring the land was paramount. W. Bredo: 'Agrarian reform in Vietnam: Viet Cong and Government strategies in conflict', *Asian Survey*, 10 (8), 1970, pp. 738–50.
25. J. Zasloff: 'Rural resettlement in South Vietnam; the agroville programme', *Pacific Affairs*, 35 (3), 1963, pp. 327–40.
26. Salter: *op. cit.*, p. 8.
27. Race: *op. cit.*, p. 20.
28. More details of the 1970 law can be found in R. L. Prosterman: 'Land-to-the-Tiller in South Vietnam: the tables turn', *Asian Survey*, 10 (8), 1970, pp. 751–64.
29. Chanda: *op. cit.*, p. 94.

12

China

The account of North Korea and North Vietnam has already foreshadowed the Chinese land reform model, which we shall now examine. China presents more difficulty than any other country in this book. Not least is the problem of sheer demographic and geographic scale, for this country, stretching latitudinally as far as from Copenhagen to Senegal, houses a quarter of the world's peasants. Yet physical obstacles to agriculture are great. Over two-thirds of the country lies above 1000 metres in altitude; only 15 per cent lies below 500 metres and only 15 per cent is regarded as cultivable.[1] Chinese land reform is complex in its evolution, traversing linked stages over a period of fifty years, quite apart from the land reforms of ancient China. The whole subject of China is charged with political emotion and source material, both Chinese and Western, is often biased, misleading and inaccurate. Perhaps most difficult of all is the cultural problem, the need to sense, if not completely understand, the significance of what the Chinese are doing. 'The Chinese way' differs from both Western and Soviet models of development. Basically, it is less concerned with production for its own sake than with using economic development to create a 'new socialist man'. Unless this is remembered, most of what has happened in the last twenty-five years makes little sense. Chinese land reform, like the Great Leap Forward, the Cultural Revolution and other great stages in the Chinese saga, must be evaluated not in strictly economic terms, but in terms of the type of society the Chinese seek to create. Most important is the potential significance of China for the Third World. As René Dumont emphasises, China is not only the premier agricultural nation of the world, it has also seen the greatest rural transformation of our times—'the attempt to convert some 700 million people from an individualistic and clannish outlook to a national and international outlook in which the greatest good is held to be the good of the people.'[2] Transference of 'the Chinese way' unadulterated to other countries may not be feasible, but many attitudes and techniques—such as investment largely in 'human capital' rather than costly foreign technology, 'walking on two legs' (harmonising advanced industry with local crafts), decentralisation of decision-making, and perhaps especially the psychological drive to convince the peasants that they can initiate development themselves, not relying on the 'twin crutches of outside expertise and outside aid'—could be applied in the Third World.[3]

LAND IN CHINESE HISTORY

China is an agricultural country of long history. As Keith Buchanan says in his classic work on Chinese geography: 'The history of China is the history of the Chinese peasant, of a people whose association with their cradle area was so intimate, so ancient, that they have been termed the Children of the Yellow Earth.'[4] Already by 2500 BC the cradle area of the Yellow River in north China supported a dense village-dwelling population with a varied agriculture and complex culture; and from the basins of the Hwang Ho and the Wei Ho, regions of fertile, easily-worked loess, the Chinese gradually pushed southward, so that by the time of the Han Dynasties (202 BC–AD 220) virtually the whole of 'China Proper' was conquered. Early rural society was partly slave-based but the Chou Dynasty (1030–221 BC) ushered in a new era. During this 'golden age' the estate was ideally divided into nine fields; the central field was the lord's, the other eight belonging to peasants, who also cultivated the lord's land. The Chou Dynasty was overthrown by Ch'in Shih Hwang Ti, who broke the power of the lords and unified their domains under central rule. Peasants were no longer bound to the soil, but lost security with the development of a landowning class. Formation of large estates ultimately reduced the peasants to serfdom, with recurrent peasant revolts, right up to the twentieth century. Some of these peasant revolts managed to overthrow dynasties (e.g. the Ming Dynasty of 1368–1644) but not to establish a new organised government. Indeed the pattern and structure of Chinese rural society remained basically unchanged from Han times right down to the twentieth century.[5] The great peasant mass, living at subsistence standard, holding small plots either in ownership or leased from large landowners, formed the broad base. Merchants and handicraftsmen formed a small middle class, above which an even smaller but all-powerful oligarchy of land-owning scholar-officials, through their control of education—the only channel of admission to their ranks—governed nearly all walks of life. The Confucian respect for tradition, order and humility was another obstacle to change. Laws restricting landholdings size were passed at various times but were largely ineffective.

Conditions of tenure, throughout Chinese agricultural history up to the Second World War, exhibited great regional variation.[6] The north had larger farms (average about 3 hectares) and owner cultivators predominated; in the rice-growing south the smaller farms (around 1 hectare) were mostly tenanted, with rents of about 50 per cent, occasionally up to 80 per cent, of the crop. Absentee landlordism increased markedly during the early twentieth century. Co-operatives were rare: most peasants borrowed from their landlords, from moneylenders, merchants and pawnbrokers. The recognised interest rate was 2–3 per cent per month, but it could be up to four times as high. The village of Sseu Tsien, just one of nearly a million, was typical of land concentration in the 'pre-Liberation' period.[7] The village, at the frontier between the 'wheat and cattle north' and the 'rice and buffalo south' counted 471 cultivated hectares, 913 families and 3936 persons (density, 837 per square kilometre). Twelve landlord families owned 441 hectares (93 per cent of the total), and 56 rich and middle peasants the remaining 30 hectares. Global figures for the country—beyond those estimates in Table 16—are lacking.

The hazards of peasant life greatly increased in the political conditions of the early twentieth century. Japan defeated China in 1894; then followed the Boxer Riots. The Manchu Dynasty fell in 1911, but for sixteen years the Chinese Republic suffered the disunity of contending warlords. The 1927 revolution, which promised relief to the peasants, introduced a further 22 years of civil war and war with Japan. The peasants bore the brunt of this chaos: ravaged alike by warlord, bandit, landlord, government troops and the Japanese, their plight was desperate. Keith Buchanan paints starkly the misery of the peasants, who reached 'the level of mere survival, a subhuman level far below anything ever experienced in the West.' It is against the conditions of this 'zero degree of life' that we should attempt to measure the achievements of the present government.[8] The outstanding elements of rural life in pre-reform China were, first, the isolation and helplessness of the individual peasant family—the marginal, precarious quality of a life balanced perpetually on

TABLE 16

LAND DISTRIBUTION AMONGST RURAL CLASSES IN VARIOUS
REGIONS OF CHINA, 1937

	No. of families (million)	per cent	Area possessed (million (hectares)	per cent	Mean holding per household (hectares)
Landlords	2·4	4	44·0	50	18·2
Rich peasants	3·6	6	15·5	18	4·3
Middle peasants	12·0	20	13·0	15	1·1
Poor peasants and agricultural labourers	42·0	70	14·4	17	0·3

Source: H. Marchisio: 'Réforme agraire et organisations coopératives en Chine de 1927 à 1952', *Archives Internationales de Sociologie de la Coopération et du Développement,* 22, 1967, p. 148.

the knife-edge of starvation; and second, the monopolisation of land and other production forces by a corrupt landlord class. These features formed part of the prism through which the influence of the environment impinged on the peasant community. They intensified natural calamities, in which millions perished, for each flood or drought brought the individual family problems insuperable in the old society, and if the family survived at all it was only by finding itself deeper in debt to the landlord group.[9]

EARLY LAND REFORM AND THE RISE OF COMMUNISM[10]

Before 1949 the feudal backwardness of the Chinese economy was accentuated by the presence of foreign colonial powers in 'concessions' in the ports, their manufactured imports destroying Chinese artisan industries. In one of these towns—Shanghai—the Chinese Communist Party (CCP) was founded in 1921. At Canton a Peasants' Department (Mao Tse-Tung was a lecturer) trained cadres to spread communist propaganda in the villages. Peasant unions, centred in Hai-pheng, rapidly developed in the mid 1920s and locally exterminated the landlord class. The combined forces of the Kuomintang (Sun Yat Sen's Nationalist Party) and the CCP, combined in 1924 to eliminate warlordism, swept northward into central China on the Northern Expedition. By that autumn the whole Yangtze valley below the gorges was held by the combined forces, with Chiang Kai-Shek at Nanking and the CCP and their Russian advisers at Wuhan. As the combined armies pushed northward Mao Tse-Tung encouraged many rural districts, especially in Hunan, to form peasant unions. In early 1927, in the provinces of Hunan and Hopei alone, peasant unions counted 4·5 million members representing over 20 million people.

Land-to-the-tiller had been an early ideal of Sun Yat-Sen and of the Kuomintang, but with the right wing opposing drastic land reform, a split with the CCP was inevitable. It came in 1927, and Chiang Kai-Shek made the eradication of communism his major objective, pursued relentlessly until the Sino-Japanese war began in 1937. Repression following 1927 forced the CCP from the towns into the countryside. Here the party became more firmly identified with the peasants' struggle, thus furthering the difference from Russian communism based on the industrial proletariat.

From 1928 to 1934 land reform policies were more moderate. They included: (1) confiscation of landlords' property and conciliation, until 1931, of the rich peasants; (2) nullification of contracts bearing a high interest rate; (3) abolition of 'feudal' taxes; and (4) egalitarian land redistribution. Actual practice in the scattered but considerable areas in south-east China (Hunan, Kiangsi) controlled by the CCP varied considerably, both 'leftist' and 'rightist' deviations occurring. These deviations were partially corrected in 1938 following the issue of more precise administrative documents on land reform, including Mao's celebrated analysis of rural classes.

In 1934 the Red Army, dislodged from its bases in south-central China, withdrew, in the famous Long March, to the north-west frontier province of Yenan. During this trek of thousands of miles, which only a third of the 90 000 strong Red Army completed, Mao Tse-Tung established his leadership. Important, too, was the amount of indoctrination and education in communism the retreating army undertook in the districts it traversed. The strict discipline and moral fibre of the Red Army, so different from the Kuomintang and warlords' bands, and the immediate application of land reform in favour of the poor peasants, ensured considerable rural support when the CCP finally came to power.

Once securely established in Yenan, the CCP underwent a period of consolidation, developing theories of land reform and experimenting with redistribution, rent control, co-operation and socialisation. The aim was to combine class struggle with economic pragmatism.[11] Almost immediately after completing the Long March it promulgated a Land Law to: (1) allow all persons to keep as much land as they could farm with their own labour—all surplus was confiscated and redistributed to the landless; (2) abolish usury; and (3) levy a low but progressive land tax. After 1937, with a CCP-Kuomintang alliance reconstituted to fight the Japanese, communist land reform influence, moderated by the nationalists, spread widely. By 1945 the party counted 1·2 million members, had an army of 900 000, and controlled 19 organised bases with a population of 90 million. After 1946 landowners who had co-operated with the Japanese were expropriated. Defeat of the common enemy, however, re-opened the bitter conflict between the CCP and the Kuomintang, with three more years of civil war.

THE 1950 LAND REFORM

The CCP swept to power in 1949 in a China of economic chaos caused by the long period of warfare. It faced an enormous task of re-establishing peace and order, restoring production and repairing the disrupted trade and communications networks so vital to a country of 8·4 million square kilometres

K

and 536 million people. Profiting from a study of Russian mistakes, the communist government of 1949 initially preserved bourgeois elements (rich peasants, traders, artisans) to avoid the further collapse of the economy. Only the non-working landlords were not tolerated. This class was completely dispossessed by the 1950 land reform, whose working philosophy was 'to rely on the farm labourers and poor peasants, to unite with the middle peasants, to neutralise the rich peasants, and to liquidate the landlords'.

Landlord dispossession and land redistribution amongst the tillers was the deliberate first step towards communal ownership of land. This intention was made clear, although in the early stages probably only a small minority of peasants grasped that. The 1950 land reform programme was launched from the top. Although rapid, it was essentially piecemeal, moving generally from north to south during two to three years, varying considerably in detail. The reform's administrative unit was the *hsien* (county), the *hsiang* (rural district) normally being the operational unit. To each village the party sent specially trained cadres, who stimulated 'land reform committees' and 'peasant associations' to foment class struggle and implement the land redistribution. Peasant hatred of landlords indeed was sometimes fanned to a pitch difficult to control. Bitterness and vindictiveness characterised the redistribution meetings and the land reform was perpetrated with not a little loss of life. The crucial significance of the cadres stemmed from their strategic position between the official Party organs and the local peasant associations. Wong considered them, not the peasants, the sinew of the land reform movement, although as the peasants became awakened the cadres gradually withdrew, leaving activist peasants in charge.[12] A model cadre was readily accessible to the peasants, holding no special privilege. He won their confidence by a combination of manipulation and friendly understanding. Comradely friendship with the peasants was achieved via the *santung* ('three togethers') system—working with the peasants (without payment), eating with them (the cadres paying their own share), and sleeping under the same roof with them. But a good cadre was also conscious of his leadership and Party policy roles in bringing government directives to remote villages. In short, he integrated personal relationships with Party policy.

Most cadres came from peasant activist, army and Party backgrounds. Always short in supply, they were given three-week crash training programmes on land reform methods. Many land reform cadres were inadequate to the job. In Kiangsi province, for example, 6 per cent of the 9200 cadres, classified 'politically impure', were subjected to disciplinary action.

Land reform, achieved thus in a rough and ready fashion, consisted of confiscating the above-average quantity of land, draught animals, buildings and implements of the landlords, and also of some rich peasants (village peasant associations progressively treated rich peasants as landlords), and assigning it free to the poorest of the rural classes. By the end of 1952 46·7 million hectares (half the country's agricultural area) had been redistributed to some 300 million peasants and landless labourers, about 65 per cent of the rural population. The lands of 10 million landlords were expropriated after their nightmarish confrontation with the peasants at the 'mass struggle meetings'. The result was the largest land reform in the world.

The reform did not affect the Border Regions, which contain most of the national minorities of some 20 million people in predominantly pastoral economies. Nor did it proceed uniformly wherever it was applied. Aside from the north-west, largely reformed before 1950, progress was fastest in eastern China. Elsewhere, regionalism and localism presented problems which were inherent in the diversity and sheer size of China and had been sharpened by decades of self-sufficient guerilla life. The Kwantung area, for instance, had always exercised the central government because of its physical and social remoteness from Peking. It also had most Overseas Chinese (owning one-fifth of the land and posing considerable problems for local cadres), and a highly commercialised rice agriculture, the economics of which demanded stability, not revolutionary upheaval. Reflecting this regional cleavage, Kwantung land reform made slower progress than almost any other, not being completed until 1953.[13]

The 1950 reform did not, however, produce egalitarianism. Redistribution created millions of tiny farms. The average amount of land received was 0·13 hectares, varying from a mean of 0·5 hectares in North Manchuria to less than 0·1 hectares in southern China. Few Chinese landlords possessed large estates on the pre-revolution Russian model. The modal area owned by Chinese landlords was 10–20 hectares; few held over 30 hectares. No figure is available for the average farm unit after land reform, but it must have been below the pre-war averages of 2·3 hectares for wheat farms and 1·2 hectares for rice. The rich and middle peasants, however, preserved above average holdings; indeed elimination of the landlord class enhanced their relative social and economic importance.

Nor did redistribution solve the problem of production. True, 1952 farm production was 43 per cent up on 1949, but this reflected three years of good weather following a year of civil war and the worst flood since 1931. Chao showed that in the post-1951 peasant economy gross factor productivity had actually declined as the peasant sector regressed into a subsistence situation, squeezing food supplies on urban markets.[14] Many land redistribution holdings were too small to be viable, especially as the redistribution of draft animals and farming implements was not as complete as the redistribution of land (most animals and farm tools belonged to rich and middle peasants). The poor classes remained short of animals and equipment, and removal of the landlords, the main source of loan capital, made credit short. Some peasants did improve their lot; others, unable to manage, sold land and animals to those able to take advantage of the situation. Opportunities for employment as hired labour dwindled as the more prosperous peasants avoided employing farm labour for fear of political ostracism and possible higher reclassification in the social scale.

The communist authorities, aware of the production dilemma from the beginning, had decided on the aim of ultimate collectivisation well before completion of redistribution, which they regarded as an essential first step to facilitate later moves. Overthrowing the landlords gave the government effective control of over 86 per cent of the population. Argument centred on how long to allow between land redistribution and the beginning of socialisation of agriculture, and on how fast to press the socialisation process. To Mao, land redistribution was necessary only on political grounds; when it had served this purpose, it should be replaced by collectives; agriculture should be transformed in the shortest time possible. He believed that Chinese farmers had a strong inherent inclination towards socialism, but that capitalist economic forces might override this feeling. Therefore, collectivisation became increasingly difficult the longer it was delayed. Already by 1953 there was a trend to land reconcentration and village money lenders were re-appearing. On the other hand, Liu Shao ch'i (the reform's original architect), appreciating the strong initiative of peasants under private ownership, urged the maintenance of a private sector in farming as a useful middle-term goal. Liu postulated that only after 70–80 per cent of the peasants had attained the income levels of 'rich farmers' and only after industry had provided enough suitable machines to mechanise agriculture, would the time be ripe for collectivisation. The problem was that 70–80 per cent was unlikely ever to be reached under a partial free enterprise system. By 1954 some 60 per cent of peasants had reached the 'middle peasant' income standard, but polarisation between rich and poor was already breaking down this trend.

MUTUAL AID TEAMS, CO-OPERATIVES AND COLLECTIVES

As early as December 1951 an internal Party document listed four kinds of co-operative arrangements for Chinese farming: (1) the temporary mutual aid team, (2) the permanent mutual aid team, (3) the elementary, semi-socialist co-operative, and (4) the advanced producers' co-operative, or collective. Drawing on early experience in north-west China, mutual aid teams were widely established immediately after land redistribution. In the temporary mutual aid team about three to six households combined to work on common tasks on each other's lands during the busy seasons. This merely reinstated the co-operation traditional in Chinese agriculture. Its advantages were obvious and, since it acknowledged the newly acquired ownership title, it was quickly adopted fairly universally. By 1952 the teams were converted to permanent organisations for the whole year, including more households (6–10). Some animals and tools were also owned jointly, and any reclaimed land was owned and farmed in common. So the embryo of socialisation was introduced into the womb of China's mother earth.

In 1953, while mutual aid teams were still being formed, experiments were already being made with elementary or semi-socialist producers' co-operatives, units of 20–40 households in which members contributed their land, animals and tools for joint cultivation by the co-operative, receiving rewards according with the respective input contributions as well as the actual amount and quality of work done (in 7–10 member 'production teams'). The intention was to change gradually the proportion of remuneration from land contributed and from work done, starting with 60 per cent from land and 40 per cent from labour, moving in successive years to 50:50, then 30:70 and in the fourth year 0:100. Peasant entry was voluntary and exit free; retention of private smallholdings (average size 0·02 hectares—but not to exceed 5 per cent of the local average of farm land per caput) was allowed. The mutual benefits of co-operation were emphasised; the rich and middle peasants were assured that their incomes would not be reduced; the poorer groups could expect substantial rises. Managing individual co-operatives was theoretically by the members, who elected annually a management committee, but in practice Party cadres often took control. Voluntariness of entry and exit also had limits. Once a major part of a village had become a co-operative, it was very difficult for peasants to refrain, owing to mutual dependence in irrigation and other matters, and to state inducements to co-operative members in credit, marketing etc. Although free withdrawals from co-operatives occurred, requests for 'opting out' were often labelled 'agitation' and those making them denounced as 'landlords, rich peasants, counter-revolutionaries and bad elements'.

In 1953 the clash between the two strategies for socialisation —'all-out drive' and 'gradualist' approach—became overt. Spurred by Mao Tse-tung, elementary producers' co-operatives multiplied faster than had been anticipated, nearly doubling their numbers between April and August of 1954 from 58 000 to 100 000, and having 1·7 million member families. The 'gradualist' group, well represented in the office responsible for agrarian policy, considered this increase too rapid and some co-operatives were dissolved. Late 1954 brought a compromise between the two factions, but subsequent events reflected Mao's undoubted ascendancy. By May 1956 about 110 million families, 91 per cent of the rural population, formed about a million producers' co-operatives (Table 17).

Before 1954 collectivisation (as opposed to co-operativisation) was considered dependent upon prior mechanisation, but thereafter collectivisation was judged the prerequisite of mechanisation and of other technical developments. Mao was impatient for collectivisation and for rapid increase in agricultural production to provide the surplus for capital for industrial development. So, early in 1956 elementary producers' co-operatives began to be converted into advanced or socialist producers' co-operatives, which were, effectively, collective farms. Individual ownership of land, draught animals and implements was forfeited. The individual farmer got some compensation in lieu, but his income thenceforth depended entirely on labour performed, except for the small plots and pigs and chickens he was allowed to retain. These higher level co-operatives were considerably larger than the elementary type—100–200 families (up to 300 eventually), organised into production brigades and teams.

Progress in converting co-operatives to collectives was quickest in the north and north-east and slowest in the south-west, nor did all units necessarily experience all the steps to collectivisation. Essentially, the process involved superimposing larger planning units over those already existing. Thus the co-operative of 30–40 households replaced the mutual aid teams of 6–10 households, but the co-operative itself was actually worked by production teams corresponding to the former mutual aid teams. Similarly the collective, with its 100–300 households, had three tiers: collective, production brigade and production team. The brigade was the same size as the entire co-operative, now abolished. Using the existing structure in this way maintained considerable flexibility in rural planning; it was, unintentionally or otherwise, an ingenious institutional structure.[15]

Initial opposition to losing ownership rights diminished surprisingly quickly. This was the so-called 'high tide of socialism' in the Chinese countryside; 63 per cent of all peasant households joined collectives between June 1955 and June 1956. By then 75 million rural households out of 120 million belonged to collectives and by December 1956 the households numbered 110 million. The degree to which Mao had pre-empted the 1953–57 Five Year Plan for complete collectivisation by 1970 was obvious.[16] Sharp criticism emerged in 1957 largely reflecting increased bureaucracy consequent upon the increased size of units, but before government could place greater responsibility with the peasants, an even greater opposite movement became manifest—the establishment of 'people's communes'.

Economically the policy from 1950 to 1957 had mediocre to good, rather than outstanding results. They were better than in the USSR between 1917 and 1925, but did not provide the full increase demanded by industrial capital formation and by the rapid population growth following widespread health measures. Threatening food shortages stimulated birth control propaganda in 1956, soon, however, abandoned in the euphoria of the Great Leap Forward of 1958–60. The effect of land reform and the formation of co-operatives on production is difficult to disentangle from the operation of other factors, including weather fluctuations, rehabilitation of transport, and repair of irrigation channels and dykes (the irrigated area apparently increased from 23·3 million hectares to 37·3 million hectares during the Five Year Plan period). Farm production undoubtedly rose, but not to the high levels rashly promised by the régime during the recruitment campaigns. Grain output, according to official sources, rose 20 per cent during 1953–7 (population growth over the same period was 11 per cent), but livestock numbers fell; loss of draught cattle in the North China Plain forced people to pull the ploughs, and manure resources dropped. Peasant hostility, co-operative slackness and the loss of the rich peasants' skills all contributed to this mediocre performance.[17]

STATE FARMS[18]

Before discussing the Chinese people's communes, we may briefly consider state farms, a small, stable subsector of post-reform Chinese agriculture which, strikingly, has escaped the frequent institutional changes elsewhere. Defined as a 'true socialist agricultural enterprise', and the equivalent of the Soviet *sovkhoz*, it has a certain ideological superiority over other forms of agricultural organisation. All state farm assets, including land, belong to the government: in Chinese communist terminology, 'ownership by all the people'. Management staff, often ex-military personnel, are government-appointed and the workers are hired labourers, with wages fixed in advance. Whereas in a co-operative or collective the members share the risks and the profits, in a state farm the government takes the profits and stands the losses.

TABLE 17

The Development of Forms of Organised Farming in China, 1950–60

	1950	1951	1952	1953	1954	1955	1956	1957	1958	1959	1960
Mutual aid teams:											
No.	2·71 m	4·23 m	8·03 m	7·45 m	9·93 m	7·15 m	*	—	—	—	—
Households ('000)	11 510	19 161	45 364	45 637	68 478	60 389	*	—	—	—	—
Co-operatives:											
No.	—	129	3 634	15 053	114 165	633 213	685 231	*	—	—	—
Households ('000)	—	2	57	273	2 285	16 881	15 109	*	—	—	—
Collectives:											
No.	—	—	10	15	201	529	311 935	700 000	740 000	—	—
Households ('000)	—	—	2	3	12	41	97 422	115 000	123 000	—	—
People's communes:											
No.	—	—	—	—	—	—	—	—	26 000	24 000	24 000
Total peasant Households ('000)	105 536	*	113 683	116 325	117 331	119 201	120 000	121 500	123 250	*	*

Notes: — nil or negligible
* data unavailable

'Co-operatives' are here taken to mean 'elementary producers' co-operatives'.
'Collectives' are taken to mean 'advanced producers' co-operatives'.

Sources: L. Lichnowsky: 'Agricultural policy in mainland China since 1949,' *FAO Monthly Bulletin of Agricultural Economics and Statistics*, 11 (10), 1962, p. 5; H. Marchisio: 'Communes populaires et organisations coopératives dans les campagnes chinoises', *Archives Internationales de la Sociologie de la Coopération et du Développement*, 20, 1966, pp. 130–131.

State farms are primarily organs of reclamation. A linked function is settling Han Chinese (the majority race) in minority-dominated frontier zones. State farms are, consequently, relatively concentrated in peripheral regions—Manchuria, the north-west and the south—where most reclaimable virgin land is located. Originally state farms were established by different government authorities—local or regional administrations, the central Ministry of Agriculture, or military authorities either to settle demobilised servicemen or to provide food for garrison troops. Their number and extent are therefore difficult to document, but they seem to have grown rapidly, at least until 1960. By 1957 710 large central government state farms (Fig. 6) covered over 1 million hectares, employing 500 000 workers and 10 000 tractors. Some 1890 smaller local state farms (also cultivating 1 million hectares) brought the total up to 2600. In 1956 all central government state farms were put under the newly-

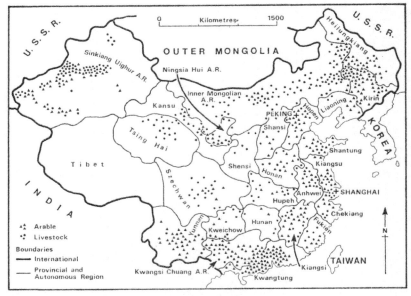

Fig. 6.   State farms in China, 1957. *Source:* T. R. Tregear: *An Economic Geography of China* (London, Butterworths, 1970), p. 44

formed Ministry of State Farms and Reclamation, but few data have since been published.

The other major official objectives of the state farms are to increase production and to provide examples to surrounding collectives and communes, giving them assistance when required. Experimental, demonstration and seed farms are essential for the national agriculture as a whole. Suburban state farms near big cities, supplying fresh vegetables, fruits and industrial crops, reflect the policy of encouraging local and regional self-sufficiency. State farms also link industrial and rural ways of life by introducing peasants to the wage system and to working with machinery. Most agricultural machinery goes to the state farms which, with their huge fields, can use machines more effectively than collectives or communes. In 1964 state farms (4 per cent of the country's farmed area) had 32 per cent of total tractor power, 50 per cent of mechanical farm tools and 82 per cent of combine harvesters in Chinese agriculture. Partly because of this state farms come into production rapidly and can produce supplies of grain almost immediately. Mostly located on relatively poor soils or in climatically difficult areas—all good land having been long since occupied in China—they have lower per hectare yields than other forms of agricultural enterprise. Yields on newly cultivated virgin soil often fall off rapidly after the first couple of years. Perhaps a third operate at a loss. Labour productivity, however, is generally higher on state farms: up to ten times higher for wheat. These government enterprises recognise marginal productivity criteria—workers are not hired if their marginal yield falls below their marginal cost in wages; collectives and communes on the other hand, with little freedom to reduce membership, may become overburdened with excess labour, whose productivity drops concomitantly. So state farms cannot be a realistic substitute for collectives in China, and cover only 4 per cent of the cultivated area (cf. the Soviet Union with over 25 per cent). Only in sparsely populated border areas and in regions of difficult environment are state farms viable undertakings.

PEOPLE'S COMMUNES

The exact origin of the people's communes is obscure, but in April 1958 27 collectives in Honan merged into a single unit to solve labour organisation problems. The result was the Weih-sing (Sputnik) People's Commune, the first of its kind. Other local mergers followed. Press coverage of these communes was intense, but government attitudes towards the innovation appeared uncertain. In August 1958 Mao Tse-tung visited the Honan communes and gave them his approval. This initiated a massive rush to amalgamate the 740 000 collectives into communes as part of the Great Leap Forward. In just four months, the entire face of Chinese agriculture was transformed virtually beyond recognition. By the end of 1958 99 per cent of the rural population were organised into some 26 000 communes averaging just under 5000 households apiece (regional averages varied considerably: for Kweichow 1400, Kwantung 9800 and country districts within the big municipalities of Peking, Shanghai etc. 11 000). Generally the communes were coterminous with local government areas, corresponding to one or more *hsiang* (districts) or even a whole *hsien* (province), but size of commune also correlated with level of development, for the larger communes needed adequate transport and communications systems to function effectively. Average commune size soon grew even larger for in 1959 their number fell to 24 000. A typical commune was about thirty times as large as a collective and some twenty times as big as an average Soviet *kolkhoz* (245 families in 1957). Unlike the *kolkhoz*, an almost purely agricultural association, the commune discharged industrial, trading, taxation, education, welfare, military and security responsibilities and functions, blending the worker, the peasant, the trader, the student and the soldier into one. Communal living under the 'five-together' slogan—working, eating, sleeping, studying and drilling together—was established. All private plots and farm animals were taken into communal ownership. Communal refectories, nurseries, tailor teams and laundries were established to free female labour from family chores. Everyone who could was expected to work on the commune, and to be paid partly in kind (free food, clothing and welfare services). Communes of this early period were typically subdivided into large production brigades, representing roughly the former collectives.

Conflicts of opinion, or at least interpretation, exist about the early CCP policy towards communes. On the one hand they seem a logical extension of the mutual aid team-co-operative-collective trend of increasing scale. Hélène Marchisio showed that contradictions had been appearing under the co-operative-collective system: contradictions between co-operatives in implementing major schemes of afforestation or reclamation or water management, contradictions between economic units and administrative units and contradictions within co-operatives regarding production and accounting units.[19] In one sense, therefore, communes became a more geographical expression in that they accorded more closely with drainage basin and administrative regions in solving some of these conflicts. It is doubtful, however, if Mao had visualised communes in concrete terms before 1958; indeed in 1957 an official suggestion was made that collectives should be reduced to around 100 households (equivalent to the traditional village) and stabilised for ten years.

Whatever the relative weightings of spontaneity and central direction in their origins, communes were soon encouraged as a means of mobilising the enormous latent productivity of the underemployed masses of rural China. In the context of the Great Leap Forward, communist thinking regarded this population excess not as a burden, but as an enormous asset and source of capital accumulation. The Great Leap Forward unleashed fanatical enthusiasm and energy, with economic planning jettisoned in favour of boundless optimism and the need to break all production records. The people's commune was likened to 'a fine horse which, having shaken off its bridle, is galloping courageously along the highway to communism'. With such slogans the communes blazed into existence, pooling all labour, abolishing private plots, distributing free food—the first practical applications of 'from each according to his ability, to each according to his needs'. Birth control, introduced tentatively in the mid 1950s, was abandoned as official policy in the prevailing euphoria. Over-enthusiasm, over-centralisation, over-industrialisation, over-investment and a premature announcement of bumper harvests all ended in the rude awakening of a year or so later: the country was on the verge of famine.

The 'three bitter years', 1959–61, experienced unusually adverse weather conditions, and the food situation remained serious until 1962. How far production was reduced by mismanagement and unsound agricultural policy, and how far by the weather is debatable, but malnutrition was endemic and it was estimated that per capita food consumption fell from 2200 to 1850 calories per day between 1959 and 1961.[20] Yet, in contrast to pre-1949 China or India today, the welfaristic structure of the communes at least provided all peasants with the necessary minimum to tide them over.

The commune organisation, probably the most drastic change in Chinese rural history, achieved its primary goal of easy mobilisation of labour for increased production, but whether effectively remains problematical. The attempt to make communes self-sufficient 'states within a state' often disregarded the basic facts of local economic geography and resource availability. There was apparently much shifting of labour within communes and their constituent units as production became more diversified and specialised. Brigades, organised like military units, assembled at bugle call and marched to the fields with banners flying. Many tasks were enormous, beyond even the ant-like armies of workers. They were often tackled with genuine patriotic zeal but some proved too exhausting, even for the tough Chinese peasants. Somewhat less patriotically, there was evidence of shoddy work too, possibly for lack of incentives. In places, careless autumn reaping and threshing in 1958 necessitated a large-scale gleaning campaign to recover grain left in the fields and on the threshing floors. Widespread weed calamities threatened in 1960. Deep ploughing broke up the clay floors of paddy fields in the south. Reckless irrigation caused alkalisation of soils in the north. Near-impossible production targets were never reached and returns were falsified.[21]

Disillusionment accompanied the bad harvests, both as cause and effect. With personal incentives drastically reduced, labour productivity, crop yields and agricultural production all fell. Communes learnt the lesson that there are limits on organisational and psychological inputs beyond which only material and technological inputs can significantly increase productivity.[22] So the policy of the Big Leap was restated as one of readjustment, stabilisation and uniform progress. Agriculture was accorded priority in national planning instead of being impossibly squeezed to service industry.

Three significant changes represented a retreat from the original ideal. Firstly, the size of many communes was reduced, and their number increased to 74 000 in 1961 (78 000 by 1966).

In 1971 most communes were 2000–5000 hectares in size, with an average of 1900 households.[23] Skinner's detailed work suggests that frequently the size reduction of communes reharmonised them with the scale of natural marketing systems which they had unwisely usurped: an illuminating example of Cristaller-type principles.[24] The trend towards smaller units was most marked in upland regions where environmental factors isolate farmland and settlements and hinder communications. In lowlands bordering big cities communes remained large in population, with intensive market gardening supplying nearby urban markets (Fig. 7).

Secondly, private plots, whose loss had caused great resentment, were restored, to a limit of 5 per cent of the commune's farmed area. Private plot income, 10–30 per cent of total peasant income, was assured by re-opening free markets in rural areas. Thirdly, within the commune organisation and responsibility were decentralised and the production team reinstated as the basic operational unit. Brigades and teams resumed ownership of means of production—land, animals, tools— under their jurisdiction, and are responsible for profit and loss accounting, setting production targets and distributing income to members.

Restoring these 'small freedoms' seems to have revitalised the communes. Communal feeding—probably never widespread— reverted to the normal family pattern. Labour payment also reverted to the work points system previously used by the co-operatives, although the size and complexity of the communes, with hundreds of different jobs to be evaluated and measured, make the work point calculations extremely complicated and a source of continued discussion.

Contrary to the expectations of many outside observers ideologically opposed to communism, the changes of the early 1960s gave the communes the incentives and the flexibility they needed to evolve and develop. Peking repeatedly emphasised that the 'small freedoms' were not a 'tail of capitalism' but necessary and logical in Marxist-Leninist terms. Politically the retreat, forced by the crisis years 1959–61, from the original commune ideal represented another temporary decline of Mao and the rise of Liu Shao ch'i and the moderates who, in fact, wanted to push private farming much further. Mao countered

Fig. 7. Zhonga People's Commune, 20 km east of Peking. Zhonga, also called the China–Albania Friendship Commune, was formed in 1958 by merging 3 collectives. Its 11 000 workers are organised into 6 brigades, 27 general production teams and a number of specialised teams for tending livestock and other sidelines, including 300 workers in small factories. *Source:* A. B. Tschudi: 'People's Communes in China', *Norsk Geografisk Tidsskrift*, 27 (1), 1973, p. 7.

that commune farming had failed not from its inherent short-comings but from the peasants' lack of adequate political preparation: therefore instead of abandoning the commune system, China should intensify socialist rural education. Because Liu's proposals for individual farming went too far Mao regained the initiative in 1962, and his policy of rural socialist education formed a lead-in to the purgative Great Proletarian Cultural Revolution.

Little can, however, be said unequivocally about the commune; over a country of China's vast size and regional diversity there is much variation in both policy and results. Western academics' interpretations differ according to ideological sympathy. Donnithorne, for example, is critical, maintaining that the communes have in most respects not succeeded, and that agricultural organisation has largely returned to where it was under the earlier, lower stage co-operatives.[25] Buchanan, *per contra*, considers the changes of the early 1960s an excellent example of the realism and capacity for honest re-appraisal which are outstanding features of Chinese economic planning.[26] Clearly, however, as the Norwegian geographer, Aadel Brun Tschudi says, the people's communes are the most extensive land tenure system in the world: they constitute the boldest and perhaps the most promising experiments in rural development of this century.[27]

In the early 1970s, the people's communes seemed not greatly different in situation from ten years earlier. They still numbered about 70 000, containing some 750 000 production brigades. Communes approximate to former *hsiang* and to the size of marketing communities (traditionally a town surrounded by about 20 villages). The production teams (generally of 20–30 households each) comprising a brigade are usually coterminous with villages or hamlets; in south China some still correspond with lineage units. The production team remains the basic accounting unit, and private plots still exist, having been affected little by the Cultural Revolution, which was primarily urban. In 1971 communally worked land accounted for 90 per cent of the country's arable area. About 5 per cent was privately operated, the balance being state farms. Considerable differences in prosperity and income levels do, however, exist between communes and between brigades and teams on the same commune, due to differences in soil quality, water availability and management skills. Such differences are being tackled, and better-off brigades are urged to make contributions to the incomes of the poorer ones, but the struggle against threatening polarisation will be long.[28]

CONCLUSION

The Chinese land reform represents probably the most massive, far-reaching and flexible reorganisation of agriculture ever attempted. It started with a primitive but practical redistribution of land, animals, implements and housing confiscated from landlords and rich peasants who did not labour on the land themselves. This stage culminated in the Land Reform Law of 1950 and saw 50 per cent of China's farmed area transferred to 65 per cent of the rural population comprising landless labourers and poor peasants. Considering the obstacles it encountered, this giant land reform was implemented relatively smoothly, for seldom has a country been so ready for radical reform as China was when the CCP came to power.

The Chinese land reform was also original. It was not borrowed from other countries' experience (although there were ideological links with Russia and Eastern Europe) but evolved through trial, error and experimentation carried out by the CCP during its long struggle for power; indeed few developing countries have experienced such a thorough learning process before actually launching a reform programme. Pragmatism was another striking feature. Legal niceties, theoretical issues and policy polemics were subordinate: the end was always more important than the means. The stress on an informal, personalised approach and the antipathy towards elaborately codified regulations reflected partly the quality of the cadres who implemented land reform—dedicated politically but frequently poorly trained technically—but partly the danger of overemphasis on administrative legalistic details, which has stifled land reform progress in many other countries. The Chinese land reform, in contrast, stimulated further institutional changes that stabilised only when the communes were formed. China is one of the very few countries where most, if not all, reforms of an underdeveloped agricultural system have been implemented successfully as a strategy, completely outgrowing initial land redistribution—a step after which (even before which) most countries have hesitated and come to a halt.

Despite problems, the commune seems to have been a viable institution for solving China's rural problems, and offers valuable suggestions for developing and even developed countries.

Communes are structured to implement state planning yet facilitate local self-sufficiency and maximum popular participation. They have been remarkably successful in getting innovations and all available knowledge into use at the farm level; the provision that all officials do some manual labour increases administrative competence. Communes' abilities to mobilise resources in such labour intensive investments as terracing, afforestation and irrigation will raise long run productivity; the fact that many communes coincide with natural regions such as drainage basins increases the effectiveness of these projects complementary to cultivation. The new Chinese social system achieves maximum feasible social justice while allowing some scope for increased consumption and economic incentive. Chinese rural life is better than before 1949; abject poverty has disappeared, and peasants are better protected from famine, flood and disease than in most underdeveloped countries. Illiteracy has, it is claimed, dropped from 90 per cent in 1949 to 5 per cent in 1971, thanks largely to the schools set up by the communes. Teaching centres on work, not 'academic' subjects, and teachers and pupils spend part of each year working in fields and factories. Keith Buchanan considers China's schools and technical institutes 'are making possible that marriage of modern science and traditional peasant wisdom, of theory and practical work, which is China's most original and important contribution to the elimination of rural underdevelopment'.[29] The commune also provides health and social services. For a small annual subscription, every commune member is entitled to free medical care, provided mainly by part-time 'barefoot doctors', who receive a six-month town hospital training and work in farming outside surgery hours.

Towards the end of the 1950s the institutional transformation gave way to technological transformation. Ideological development had reached an apex with the people's communes but economic problems remained. The Great Leap Forward was the catalyst. Agricultural development became technologically oriented, with innovations in chemical fertilisers, machinery, seed choice and other inputs.[30] China's rural equality may enable her to avoid the intra-village class polarisation engendered in capitalist Asian countries by the green revolution. By 1970 20 per cent of China's cultivated area was under the new seed technologies, the increased yields from which accounted for an estimated 42 per cent of the increase in food grain output between 1956 and 1971.[31] Unfortunately the statistical vacuum in China over the past fifteen years precludes firm conclusions on the long term economic results of Chinese land policy. The 1971 grain harvest, 246 million tons, was the first official announcement of its kind for ten years. It represents a 60 per cent increase over 1952, or a compound annual growth of 2·4 per cent. Other estimates of Chinese agricultural performance are so varied that no safe general conclusions can be drawn.[32] Even so, the likely decrease of population growth to 2 per cent per annum in the late 1970s and 1·5 per cent in the 1980s allows some optimism for increased food output per capita and improved dietary standards.[33] And even if Chinese land reform does not yield spectacular results in terms of standard economic theory, the experiment will not necessarily have failed: proper assessment requires consideration of the special economic system and of the political-ideological reality of China, precisely those aspects difficult for an outsider to judge.

The Cultural Revolution promised a 'new leap forward' in agricultural production; 1969 was to be the year of increased output. New rural reforms again increased agriculture's share of national resources in order to boost farm production. Communes were made more self-reliant, and production of tools and fertilisers in small local plants, financed largely by the brigades, has been encouraged. At the same time, educational reforms and the transfer of skilled labour back to the countryside aim at reducing the gap between urban and rural society. But the dust generated by the ideological wind of the Cultural Revolution has yet to settle, and is unlikely to settle soon, for, as Mao forecast at the end of 1967, the Cultural Revolution is the first of many, 'one step in a thousand-league march'. The Chinese experiment, it seems, is only just beginning.[34]

REFERENCES

1. See G. Cressey: *China: Land of the 500 Million* (New York, McGraw Hill, 1955), p. 30.
2. R. Dumont: *Révolution dans les Campagnes Chinoises* (Paris, Editions du Seuil, 1957), pp. 8–9.

3. K. Buchanan: *The Transformation of the Chinese Earth* (London, Bell, 1970), pp. 112–13.

4. *Ibid*: pp. 5–6.

5. T. R. Tregear: *An Economic Geography of China* (London, Butterworths, 1970), pp. 4–5.

6. The classic study of land tenure and agriculture before the communist take-over is J. L. Buck: *Land Utilization in China* (Nanking, University of Nanking, 1937; reprinted New York, Paragon, 1968).

7. Dumont: *op. cit.*, p. 30.

8. Buchanan: *op. cit.*, pp. 96, 98, 115.

9. *Ibid*: p. 117.

10. S. Klein: 'The land reform policies of the Chinese Communist Party 1928–1948, a brief economic analysis', *Agricultural History*, 35 (2), 1961, pp. 59–64; H. Marchisio: 'Réforme agraire et organisations coopératives en Chine de 1927 à 1952', *Archives Internationales de Sociologie de la Coopération et du Développement*, 22, 1967, pp. 138–93.

11. G. Agostini: 'Agrarian reform in China: objectives, approach and achievements', *Land Reform, Land Settlement and Co-operatives*, 1–2, 1974, pp. 26–42.

12. J. L. Wong: *Land Reform in the People's Republic of China* (New York, Praeger, 1973), pp. 99–101, 109.

13. See E. Vogel: 'Land reform in Kwantung 1951–1953: central control and localism', *China Quarterly*, 38, 1969, pp. 27–62.

14. K.-C. Chao: *Agricultural Production in Communist China 1949–1965* (Madison, University of Wisconsin Press, 1970).

15. K. R. Walker: *Planning in Chinese Agriculture* (London, Cass, 1965), pp. 18–19.

16. K. R. Walker: 'Collectivisation in retrospect: the "Socialist High Tide" of Autumn 1955–Spring 1956', *China Quarterly*, 26, 1966, pp. 1–43.

17. Y.-L. Wu: 'Some economic effects of land reform, agricultural collectivisation and the commune system', in W. Froelich (ed.): *Land Tenure, Industrialisation and Social Stability: Experience and Prospects in Asia* (Milwaukee, Marquette University Press, 1961), pp. 17–37.

18. A. Donnithorne: *China's Economic System* (London, Allen & Unwin, 1967), pp. 92–111.

19. H. Marchisio: 'Communes populaires et organisations coopératives dans les campagnes chinoises', *Archives Internationales de Sociologie de la Coopération et du Développement*, 20, 1966, pp. 76–129.

20. R. Dumont and B. Rosier: *The Hungry Future* (London, Methuen, 1970), pp. 132–3.

21. Chao: *op. cit.*, pp. 62–3, 257–8.

22. B.-J. Ayn: 'The political economy of the people's commune in China: change and continuities', *Journal of Asian Studies*, 34 (3), 1975, pp. 631–58.

23. Agostini: *op. cit.*, p. 38.

24. G. W. Skinner: 'Marketing and social structure in rural China', *Journal of Asian Studies*, 24 (1), 1964, pp. 3–44.

25. Donnithorne: *op. cit.*, p. 88.
26. Buchanan: *op. cit.*, pp. 131–2.
27. A. B. Tschudi: 'People's Communes in China', *Norsk Geografisk Tidsskrift*, 27 (1), 1973, pp. 5–37.
28. W. F. Wertheim: 'Polarity and equality in the Chinese people's communes', *Journal of Contemporary Asia*, 4 (1), 1974, pp. 24–35.
29. Buchanan: *op. cit.*, p. 128.
30. L. F. Kuo: 'Technical transformation of agriculture in Communist China', in W. A. D. Jackson (ed.): *Agrarian Problems and Policies in Communist and Non-Communist Countries* (Seattle, University of Washington Press, 1971), pp. 250–79.
31. B. Stavis: *Making Green Revolution: The Politics of Agricultural Development in China* (Ithaca, Cornell University Rural Development Committee, 1974).
32. R. P. Sinha: 'Chinese agriculture: a quantitative look', *Journal of Development Studies*, 11 (3), 1975, pp. 202–23.
33. R. P. Sinha: 'Chinese agriculture: past performance and future outlook', *Journal of Agricultural Economics*, 25 (1), 1974, pp. 37–52.
34. Buchanan: *op. cit.*, p. 308.

13

India

In the 1971 election the largest democracy in the world returned a government committed to bringing socialism to the most conservative, hierarchical, heterogeneous and poverty-stricken society on earth. India is full of such contradictions and conflicts. The avowedly socialist government is sustained by a pampered private capitalism. India's backcloth of poverty is studded with the riches of millionaires. Egalitarianism co-exists with the intransigent bonds of caste. Agricultural land is scarce, but is concentrated in few hands. Yields are low, but rents high. Farmers are poor, yet farms are expensive. India wants, and needs, progress, yet it reaches forward against the tremendous gravitational pull of the past. Conflicts characterise the post-1947 delicate and often impracticable division of power between central and states' authority. Land reform was an early testing ground for the federal constitution system. The states differ bewilderingly in economic growth and social constraints. Tenurial conditions vary widely both between and within states. To emphasise the complexity, state boundaries have shifted since Independence from the political boundaries of the British era more toward cultural and linguistic expressions. New states have been created and others have new names. These problems and antitheses are central to the Indian land reform issue.

Land reform in India varies in date because land law is state law and progress varies between states. The central government issues general pronouncements on tenure policy, but local legislatures have to pass and implement land reform laws. India probably has more land reform laws than any other country, but the laws were conferred upon, rather than stemming from, the peasantry. Insistence on democratic methods in such a huge and complex country inevitably slows progress.

GENESIS OF INDIAN LAND TENURE PROBLEMS

Pre-British land tenure rights rested on tradition rather than on law.[1] The communal solidarity of villages was strong but joint ownership and control of land covered only pasture and waste. Because of the close link between land rights and caste, 'family tenure' rather than individual or communal tenure prevailed, the head of the family acting for his kinsmen. The Moslem conquerors did not dispossess the local inhabitants; they simply, like the Hindu kings, demanded a share of the produce, but a much bigger share, often to the limit of what the cultivators could bear.

The dominance of Indian land tenure patterns by revenue extraction was intensified under the British. Just when feudalism was being exterminated in Great Britain and Europe, it was re-inforced in India, without its assuaging customs and courtesies. India's present land reform problems originate in the so-called 'permanent settlement', superimposed on the traditional peasant ownership system by the East India Company in 1793. Revenue collection was farmed out to the highest bidder and his proprietary rights were confirmed. The settlement thus created a new class of landlords, the 'zamindars', who were placed over the small owners and actual tillers of the soil to collect rents for the state. Allocated a share of one-eleventh of the rent, the zamindars raised the rents to enlarge their own share, thus increasing the farmers' burden. As the margin between the fixed land revenue and the economic rent increased, new intermediary interests proliferated. Exceptionally, up to 50 intermediaries were identifiable. By 1946 the state was realising only 39 per cent of the total land revenue exacted by the zamindars, instead of the original 91 per cent.

The permanent settlement system is not synonymous with *zamindari* tenure, but the two are generally associated with the same geographical area—Bengal, Bihar, Orissa and the United Provinces (Uttar Pradesh). Difficulties were, however, encountered in introducing permanent settlements to the Punjab and Madras. Accordingly the policy was replaced in 1833, initially in Agra and Oudh, and later in the Punjab, by the *mahalwari* system (called *gramawari* in south India), in which settlement was made directly and communally with villages, the state usually demanding 40–70 per cent of the rentals. Another system, *ryotwari* tenure, first introduced in Madras in 1792 and gradually extended to other provinces, recognised the *ryot* or peasant landholder as holding the land directly from the government, with no intermediaries; the land revenue was fixed for thirty-year periods and collected by village headmen.

Despite their apparent dissimilarities 'all three types of tenure led to the disintegration of the village economy, permitted the parasitic class of absentee-owners to appropriate a large portion of returns to the soil, reduced all cultivation to subsistence farming and impoverished the actual tiller.'[2] Rural economic deterioration is clearly evidenced by increasing rural indebtedness. Already in 1875 Bombay province suffered riots against the money-lending rentier class, and collective acts of violence and non-violent resistance were common throughout later British rule. Basically these revolts stemmed from the increasing exactions of the colonial economy. Among the largest revolts were the Muslim rebellions of Malabar district in North Kerala; between 1836 and 1898 Muslim tenants rebelled twenty-five times, killing many Hindu landlords, British officials and soldiers. Before about 1920 such peasant actions often focused on local leaders and were caste-based. After 1920 they reflected regional, national and urban-based political movements, notably the Communist Party. The first politically-sponsored movement of its kind, the Congress-Khilifat movement of 1920–1 in Kerala, encouraged labourers, peasants and mill workers to stage strikes and boycott British goods. The British replied violently, and some 10 000 rebels died in the fighting before the revolt was quelled.[3]

Data on the pre-land reform land problem in India (i.e. before 1951) are abundant.[4] In 1931 in British India nearly 70 per cent of the 100 million persons employed in agriculture owned no land: 35 per cent were tenants and 33 per cent were landless labourers. About 4 per cent were non-cultivating landowners and the balance, 28 per cent, were cultivating owners. Even amongst this last group, 50–80 per cent (according to region) possessed under 2 hectares and were thus only nominal owners, spending much of their time working as labourers on others' land. Moreover, both the number and the percentage of landless were increasing: 7 million in 1882, 34 million in 1931, 100 million today.[5] Agriculture has had to absorb, not only an increasing number of persons, but also an increasing proportion of the total population—63 per cent in 1900, 70 per cent in 1950. The agricultural population has grown by 150 million over the past twenty years, and the 1970 total population of 540 million may double by the year 2000. Pressure on land is a perennial problem, with a mean area now of about 1 hectare per rural family. Between 1931 and 1951 cultivated land per family fell by 20 per cent, while yields hardly varied.

To regard Indian rural society as comprising solely landowners, peasants and labourers is, however, gross oversimplification. Innumerable strata and interrelationships characterise the spectrum of tenure and social structure. All roles are interdependent in an architectonic whole. Each group has its privileges over, and duties towards, others. A person could be landlord to one individual and tenant of another. This blurring of distinctions in the relationships of one man to another and of both to the land remains a major confusing aspect of agrarian India.[6]

The German geographer, Bronger,[7] from information collected and mapped in two Andhra Pradesh villages, has emphasised the importance of caste in India's cultural landscape, especially in settlement, land use and land tenure patterns.[8] Since the castes still largely perform their traditional functions, the division of a settlement into caste-quarters indicates a functional pattern. Landlords are generally members of the highest castes, here the Brahmins and the Kshatriyas. Caste rules forbid them to cultivate the land themselves. *Ryots*—peasants cultivating their own land—are from the upper Sudra castes. Tenants range from the upper to the lower Sudra castes, whereas the agricultural labourers come from the lower Sudra castes, notably the 'untouchable' Parias. Caste and tenure systems obstruct agricultural improvement on both upper and lower caste land. Since caste rules forbid field labour by Brahmins and Kshatriyas, their fields are worked by tenants and labourers. Labourer cultivation especially is commonly sub-standard, which means considerable slack in potential productivity. Much fallow land, called by Bronger 'social fallow', occurs, particularly in the unirrigated areas with precarious yields. Whereas the upper castes do not cultivate their land efficiently because of wealth and status, the lower Sudras and Parias cannot improve their enterprises because of plot fragmentation, lack of finance and the need to fulfil caste-dictated jobs.

INDIAN LAND REFORM LEGISLATION

Land reform legislation, mostly mild and local, extends back into Indian history. Under the British tenancy problems were the main issue. Examples were the Oudh and Punjab Tenant Acts (both 1868) which fixed rents, occupancy rights and compensation for improvements. After the 1936 elections provincial governments introduced further legislation to protect tenants. The Bombay Tenancy Act, 1939, created a class of protected tenants who could only be evicted for certain specific reasons such as non-payment of rent. Uttar Pradesh declared a moratorium on rent arrears and debts and prohibited evictions. The U.P. Tenancy Act of 1939 conferred permanent and heritable occupancy rights on 7 million tenants farming 65 million hectares.

From its base in the post-1936 provincial governments the national Congress Party began to formulate more general land reform policy. Thanks largely to Gandhi, the peasants were integrated into the national independence movement. Commitment to land reform, however, varied enormously among the disparate groups comprising the Congress Party. The proponents of radical land reform were largely of urban origin, exposed to Western liberal thought. Others sympathised with the Chinese experiment. Conservative elements represented the traditional elites, generally rural in origin, created or maintained by the British system, with values rooted in sacred texts and in inherited rural mores. Even Gandhi, whose influence bridged the gap between the radicals and the conservatives, was ambivalent on land reform. These are complex issues, but it has been maintained that these ideological conflicts and ambiguities amongst the original land reform theoreticians are at least as responsible for subsequent relative non-fulfilment of Indian agrarian reform as the more commonly cited environmental, administrative and social-caste problems.[7]

Definite progress in land reform awaited Independence in 1947. The Agrarian Reforms Committee, appointed by the Congress president, unequivocally declared that land must belong to the actual tiller of the soil. It recommended placing an upper limit on individual holdings and co-operative farming of all palpably uneconomic holdings of markedly sub-family size. The first two Five Year Plans (1951-6, 1956-61) contain the guidelines for the host of measures designed and implemented during the early post-independence years by state legislatures. However, individual states' administrators, although familiar with land administration and tax collection, were unfamiliar with, and sometimes hostile to, any policy of redistribution of wealth. Accordingly a wide gap separated the progressive Planning Commission in New Delhi and the states' administrations, where landed interests, caste and class divisions were firmly entrenched. Individual states' land reform progress varied widely. Uttar Pradesh approximates most closely the reform model contemplated by the ruling Congress Party. In contrast Bihar, Madhya Pradesh and Rajasthan reflect the views of regional elites formed partly of traditional landowners.

The history of post-independence Indian land reform broadly shows three phases. Legislation to abolish intermediaries marked 1948-54. Then, starting in 1953, tenancy reform measures were implemented in many states. Finally, legislation for imposing ceilings on holdings began in 1956. More recently, measures facilitating consolidation and various kinds of cooperation have been important, while the Gandhi-inspired Bhoodan land gift movement has, in a sense, transcended government policy.

BHOODAN YAGNA: THE LAND GIFT MOVEMENT

This humanitarian movement sought to achieve land redistribution through moral persuasion. Organised in 1951 by Vinobha Bhave, a disciple of Gandhi, it was a pious man's simple plan to solve a complex problem—landlessness. Travelling on foot from village to village, 'India's walking saint' appealed to landowners to donate one-sixth of their holdings to the poor. The aim was to collect 50 million acres (21 million hectares) to distribute to 10 million landless families by 1957.

Less than 10 per cent of that amount was acquired. Progress

was encouraging for five years but thereafter slowed dramatically, and in the 1960s some land actually reverted to the donors.
By 1956 (peak year of Bhoodan activity), Bhoodan workers had
collected pledges of land totalling 1 709 893 hectares of which
208 843 hectares had actually been distributed. In 1961 the
corresponding figures were 1 813 694 hectares and 347 277 hectares. In themselves, these figures represent a remarkable achievement, made possible largely because Bhave persistently invoked
the image of Gandhi, a very powerful image in the countryside.

Nevertheless, the benefits of Bhoodan Yagna were less impressive. The amount distributed represented only 0·3 per cent of
India's farmland. Much donated land was uncultivable waste
or land in legal contention. Partly because of the idealistic-re-
ligious appeal, some of the land came from poor rather than rich
farmers. Tomasson Jannuzi, who investigated the Bhoodan in
Bihar, the state most affected by the movement, concluded that
it failed to provide a significant proportion of the landless with
land.[9] Awareness of the movement was not spreading spontaneously from villages visited by Bhoodan workers (of whom
there were only a hundred in Bihar) to others. In some villages
the landless who had not received land resented those who had.
The formerly landless beneficiaries had no bullocks or implements to till their new holdings, and could not acquire the necessary capital to get started. Bhoodan, as an instrument for
collecting and distributing land gifts, was eventually considered
obsolete. By 1970 Bhave had retired from active fieldwork and
gone into spiritual retreat.

Since 1957 the Bhoodan movement has been carried on in the
somewhat different form of Gramdan (village donations), a
wider movement, emphasising a new pattern of community life
rather than mere redistribution of land. Farmers are requested
to renounce the larger part of their lands in favour of their villages so that communal cultivation can be set up. Ideally the
village would receive title to all land, but subsequent relaxations
of requirements (e.g. only 5 per cent of the land donated to the
landless) have considerably diluted the significance of the movement. Not surprisingly, the earliest successes were in India's
tribal regions. In the Koraput district of Orissa, 1226 gramdans
already existed by 1956, and Bhave's 1957 endorsement of this
early trend lent the movement momentum. The movement also

scored some notable successes in Kerala. By 1966 India claimed over 18 000 gramdan communities, but, given the dilution of gramdan ideology, many of these are probably only 'paper successes'.[10]

ZAMINDARI ABOLITION

The first—some would say the only—land reform in India was the abolition of *zamindari* and other (e.g. *jagirdari* and *inamdari*) intermediary tenures, which covered 40 per cent of India's farmed area and subjected 20 million tenants to iniquitous rental relationships. The *zamindari* system being localised in central and northern India, the legislation had most impact in Uttar Pradesh, Bihar, West Bengal and Andhra Pradesh (in rough order of importance). Basically the legislation enables state governments to acquire all intermediaries' rights, on payment of compensation and subject to certain exceptions—chiefly land personally cultivated by the intermediaries. In all 72 million hectares were acquired; 2·6 million intermediaries had their interests abolished. Acquisition of rights over these lands brought the statutory tenant (but not necessarily the sub-tenants) into direct relationship with the states' governments. Some tenants acquired full ownership without payment; others had to make some payments to the state for full occupancy rights, and remained tenants of the state until these charges were paid.

In view of the 65 acts and the welter of research literature on *zamindari* abolition, the summary following concentrates on the results in Uttar Pradesh, by far the most important state for this reform and the first one to consider *zamindari* abolition. Here, as elsewhere, zamindars fought the passing of the abolition bills, mainly on the grounds that expropriation was contrary to the constitution, in progressively higher courts until finally they were defeated by an amendment to the constitution itself.

The peasants of Uttar Pradesh, now no longer paying their taxes to the zamindars, were given a choice of what their relationship with their land should be. With a lump sum payment to the government of ten times their annual land rent (or twelve times their annual rent paid over four years) they could become *bhumidars*, with full rights to use or dispose of the land how they wished. In addition they enjoyed a 50 per cent reduction in their annual land tax. Tenants unable to make these payments became *sirdars*, with a permanent, heritable interest in the land while they and their descendants continued to use it agriculturally and to pay the annual rent, but with no sale or house-building rights and no reduction in their annual land tax. The act also included two other small categories of peasants: *asamis* (permanently recognised, but not hereditary, tenants) and *adhivasis* (a temporary transitory class, largely to give five-year security to sub-tenants, abolished in 1954). The zamindars automatically got *bhumidari* tenure of their *khudkasht* or *khas* ('home farm'), *sir* ('personally supervised') and grove lands, and compensation of eight times their net rentals, paid over forty years in 2·5 per cent bonds.[11] Extra rehabilitation grants were also awarded, graded to benefit most the smaller zamindars. To prevent a new class of *de facto* zamindars from emerging the act, although not affecting existing estates, limited future property acquisition to 12 hectares per nuclear family (reduced to 5 hectares in 1958). The act also placed a 'floor' of 1·3 hectares below which a farmer could not in future subdivide or sell his land, but this limit remains largely inoperative.

Apart from ridding society of the parasitic zamindars, *zamindari* abolition had few positive spin-offs. There was no noticeable increase in agricultural productivity, at least that could be attributed to *zamindari* abolition, and no change in the peasants-to-land ratio. For all but the *bhumidars* the annual land tax remained what it had been under the zamindars; the government had merely replaced the zamindar as the tax collector, although the zamindars' illegal exactions were eliminated. The state, therefore, appears the main beneficiary, but most of its new capital inflow goes in compensation payments to the ex-intermediaries. According to 1957 figures, of the total area affected by *zamindari* abolition in Uttar Pradesh, 18 per cent was held by ex-zamindars as *bhumidars*, 13 per cent by peasants who purchased *bhumidari* tenure, 67 per cent by *sirdars*, and the remaining 2 per cent by the minor categories.[12] Two-thirds of the land were thus held in *sirdari* tenure—which meant 'no change' from the preabolition situation. *Sirdars'* rents remained unaltered; both before and after reform *sir* land was heritable, not transferable, and had to be used for farming. The *asamis* benefited most of all, for they moved from tenants-at-will to recognised holders of land, but they occupy a tiny portion of the total land area involved.

That *zamindari* abolition produced no broader effects is widely acknowledged. Warriner says: 'the effects on development have been negligible; on income distribution at best neutral, at worst disastrous'.[13] Neale concluded that 'the abolition of zamindars will not end poverty in Uttar Pradesh or even contribute much to the solution of that problem'.[14] Thorner lists Uttar Pradesh among those areas where 'some perceptible change' followed intermediary abolition, but in which the agrarian structure remains basically the same.[15] If the situation is faintly positive in Uttar Pradesh, and also perhaps in Andhra Pradesh,[16] it is resoundingly negative in Bihar, to judge by available accounts.[17]

The great absentee zamindars have gone, but the resident zamindars and the big tenants, reinforced in their *bhumidari* holdings, have taken their place.[18] In Bihar, where no ceiling was imposed, zamindars twisted the 'personal possession' clauses ruthlessly, enlarging *khas* and homestead lands by evicting tenants so that some ex-zamindars retained all their pre-abolition land.[19] In *jagir* and *inam* areas provision was even made for allotting additional land, including tenanted land, to bring the *khas* land to a prescribed limit: such limits were as high as 100 hectares in former Vindhya Pradesh (the northern part of Madhya Pradesh bordering on Uttar Pradesh). These provisions have strengthened, not reduced or abolished, the rights of intermediaries. Many ex-zamindars have become forward-looking 'gentleman farmers' on their remaining estates; others have compensated for their loss of rural rent by increasing their town business activities.[20]

TENANCY REFORM

Having settled, at least on paper, the intermediary problem, attention was focused on the primarily *ryotwari* 60 per cent of India where land was cultivated mostly by tenants and sharecroppers, burdened by high rent and insecure tenure. Legislation aimed primarily at (1) rent regulation, (2) security of tenure, (3) tenant purchase of land, and (4) preventing resumption of land by landlords for direct cultivation. Minor regulations concerned prevention of sub-letting, compensation for improvements and rights over common lands. In general the mid-1950s tenancy laws seem not to have achieved their purpose. More owner-cultivation has been created, but much of it by resumption of cultivation by former landlords following eviction of tenants. Absentee landlords' power has been weakened, but not resident landlords'. Evasion is widespread.

Table 18 details differences of rent regulations amongst the states. Generally the maximum rent is expressed either as a share of gross produce, commonly a fifth or a quarter, or as a multiple of the revenue assessment, commonly two to five times the assessment. The maximum rent for irrigated land often differs from that for dry land. Jammu and Kashmir and West Bengal permit rents of up to 50 per cent of gross produce in certain circumstances. In contrast, rents are fixed as low as one-sixth of gross produce in Gujarat and Maharashtra, even lower in the communist state of Kerala. But practice differs between different land types even within one state, and frequently plural criteria involve calculating several rent maxima and selecting the appropriate one; so some figures in Table 18 are simplifications of quite complex alternative situations.

The security of tenure provisions assure tenants of continuing on their land if they meet certain requirements—usually a history of 6–12 years on the same land. Hence tenants are classified as 'protected' (those having the necessary continuous possession) or 'ordinary'. At first the tenancy regulations actually decreased security of tenure in some areas because landowners wished to minimise the occupancy history of tenants. The applications for permanent rights in most states have generally been few, probably because of the initiative required of tenants. In Madras, for example, tenants had to apply for their possession right within thirty days of the poorly publicised Cultivating Tenants Protection Act, 1955.

The other main branch of tenancy legislation aims at converting tenants into owners. Progress has been uncertain and uneven: apparently by the fourth Five Year Plan (1966–71) some 3 million tenants had acquired ownership of about 3 million hectares, chiefly in Gujarat, Maharastra, Madhya Pradesh and Uttar Pradesh.[21] An interesting tenancy enactment, however, occurred in 1957 as a radical amendment to the largely ineffective 1939 and 1948 Bombay Tenancy Acts. Under the so-called Tillers' Day Law (now effective in the 'Bombay' parts of Gujarat and Maharastra) tenants of more than one year's standing were declared owners as from April 18, 1957, and obliged to

L

TABLE 18

INDIAN RENT REGULATION LAWS: SUMMARY FEATURES

State or Union Territory	Rent Limit (*percentage of gross produce unless otherwise stated*)
Andhra Pradesh	
(a) Andhra area	up to 50 per cent on dry land; 28 per cent on irrigated
(b) Hyderabad area	20 per cent on dry land; 25 per cent on irrigated
Assam	25 per cent if landlord supplies bullocks; 20 per cent if tenant does
Bihar	25 per cent
Gujarat	17 per cent
Kerala	12½–25 per cent for paddy; 10–33 per cent for gardens; 12½ per cent for unirrigated land
Madhya Pradesh	2–4 times the revenue assessment
Madras	40 per cent of normal gross produce for irrigated land; 33 per cent of n.g.p. for dry land (for crop yields below 75 per cent normal rent may be reduced)
Maharastra	17 per cent
Mysore	20–25 per cent depending on land class
Orissa	25 per cent
Punjab	33 per cent
Rajasthan	17 per cent
Uttar Pradesh	No official leasing allowed; 50 per cent where the *batai* sharecropping system is practised
West Bengal	No regulation except for *bargadars* (sharecroppers) where limit is 40–50 per cent according to who supplies seed, manure and plough
Jammu and Kashmir	25 per cent of irrigated; 33 per cent on dry land (but up to 50 per cent if landlord holds less than 5 hectares)
Delhi	20 per cent
Himachal Pradesh	25 per cent

Source: G. Wunderlich: 'Land Reform in India', in Agency for International Development: *Spring Review of Land Reform* (Washington, Department of State, 1970), Vol. 1, pp. 40–2.

pay, in a lump sum or by instalments, an officially decreed price for their land. The tenant could avoid this reform only by appearing before a tribunal and declaring his opposition. Purchases were limited to holdings above 6 hectares (1·5 hectares if irrigated). Progress has, however, been slow: the usual Indian story. The act has succeeded on absentee-owned land, but resident landowners have pressurised tenants to declare their opposition.[22]

Generally, tenancy legislation has been unsystematic, uncoordinated and contradictory. Sometimes it has done more social harm than good. Lessons from the past have been ignored. The main problem has been to combine security of tenure and rent control in the same legislation. Fixation of rents is useless without tenure security, and vice versa. Landlords can either simply raise rents extortionately and eject tenants for non-payment, or they can threaten to evict tenants who attempt to invoke rent fixation and right of purchase. Another landlord ploy is to rotate tenants around their land to prevent them getting occupancy rights (a similar defect in the 1859 Bengal Rent Act was corrected in the 1885 Bengal Tenancy Act, which assured a peasant an occupancy right if he occupied for twelve years *any* of the landlord's land). An early field study documenting the ineffectiveness of tenancy legislation was Khusro's study of Hyderabad.[23] Of the protected tenants created in 1951, only 45 per cent enjoyed their protected status in 1957; 12 per cent had purchased their lands and become owner-cultivators, 3 per cent had been legally evicted, 22 per cent had been illegally evicted and 17 per cent had 'voluntarily' surrendered (but few of these surrenders were genuinely voluntary). Thus the diminution of the Indian tenanted area from 36 per cent (1950) to 11 per cent (1961) of total land, which *a priori* one might regard as desirable, was largely achieved 'through illegal and objectionable methods of naked or subtle eviction of tenants'. Studies in Andhra Pradesh reveal similar results.[24] Finally, an intensive study of two Punjab villages found tenant families reduced from 10 per cent of the total in 1950 to 2 per cent in 1966, whilst the landless labourers increased from 9 to 29 per cent; 76 per cent of the tenanted area (24 per cent in 1950) is now under yearly lease, to prevent tenants establishing occupancy rights; and rents are around 50 per cent of gross produce, notwithstanding the 33 per cent legal maximum. Tenants removed from the land by 'voluntary surrender' become landless labourers on increased-size farms owned by the landlords and larger farmers.[25]

Ceiling legislation was the third prong of the triple reform movement of the 1950s. Proponents used two main rationales.[26] In one, social justice requires redistribution of existing land-holdings both to satisfy land hunger and to reduce inequalities in control and use of land resources. Ex-Gandhian intellectuals believed, like the Bhoodan followers, that economic considerations were subsidiary to the social need for land redistribution. Unfortunately they glossed over questions of scale and man-land ratios; in stressing the need to satisfy land hunger the amount of 'surplus land' available was not investigated. The second rationale focused more on economic arguments: because of increased incentives and of the apparently statistically-proven relationship between smallness of holding and land productivity, ceilings should be implemented to increase agricultural production. Neither set of arguments was watertight. Few states had enough land to go around, and ceilings on holdings might lead to reduced production of commercial food-stuffs and industrial crops by fragmenting economic holdings (from which marketable surpluses were common) down to uneconomic subsistence holdings.

Official documents usually suggested for ceilings a multiple of what was variously called the 'family holding' or the 'economic holding'. The size of these units obviously had to be determined regionally and it was suggested that such a holding should afford 'a reasonable standard of living' and provide 'full employment for a normal sized family and at least a pair of bullocks'. Unfortunately, although the Congress Agrarian Reforms Committee recommended a ceiling of three times the economic holding, 'reasonable standard of living', 'full employment', and 'normal sized family' were never exactly defined. To prevent ceilings from restricting production, however, the Second Five Year Plan recommended exemption of plantations, orchards and specialised livestock enterprises (see notes to Table 19).

Initially the Indian Planning Commission estimated that 12 hectare ceilings would leave 14 per cent of the area owned available as surplus. This would be 90 per cent of the area required to give every landless family a minimum basic holding; or 42 per cent of the area required to increase sub-basic holdings

TABLE 19

CEILING LEGISLATION IN INDIAN STATES AND UNION TERRITORIES

State and date of act	Ceiling* acres	hectares	Family or Individual†	Types of land exempted§
Andhra Pradesh, 1961	27–324	11–135	I‡	1–4, 7–10, 25, 26, 28
Assam, 1959	50	21	F	1, 2, 4, 5, 26, 28
Bihar, 1961	20–60	8–25	I‡	1, 2, 21, 23, 25, 30
Gujarat, 1960	19–132	8–55	F	6, 23–6, 28
Jammu and Kashmir, 1950	23	10	I	4, 14, 15, 26
Kerala, 1960	15–38	6–16	F‡	2, 3, 7, 16, 17, 25, 26, 30
Madhya Pradesh, 1960	25–75	10–31	I‡	1–4, 8, 23–8
Madras, 1961	24–120	10–50	F‡	1–4, 7, 9, 10, 14, 17, 19, 24–6, 29–31
Maharashtra, 1961	18–126	7–52	F‡	11, 23–6, 31
Mysore, 1961	27–216	11–90	F‡	1–4, 7, 9, 10, 13, 17, 28
Orissa, 1960	25–100	10–42	I‡	1, 2, 4, 7–9, 16, 18, 22, 26–8
Punjab, 1955	30–100	12–42	I	1, 2, 4, 8, 9, 25, 26, 28, 31
Rajasthan, 1960	22–336	9–140	F‡	1, 8–12, 26, 28
Uttar Pradesh, 1960	40–80	17–33	I‡	2, 3, 7, 9, 10, 12, 20, 23, 25, 32
West Bengal, 1955	25	10	I	2, 4, 9, 10, 24–6
Union Territories:				
Delhi, 1960	25–60	10–25	F‡	4, 8–10, 26–8
Himachal Pradesh, 1953	30	12	I	4, 28
Manipur, 1960	25	10	F‡	1–4, 7–10, 26, 28
Tripura, 1960	25–75	10–31	F‡	1–4, 7–10, 26, 28

Notes: * Most states and territories prescribe several ceilings according to quality of land and nearness to water. Only the lowest and highest ceilings are given in this column. In many acts, ceilings are given in 'standard acres', which may be converted to ordinary acres by pre-established formulae. All figures here are in ordinary acres. All the ceilings reported here are for existing holdings. Ceilings on future acquisitions are the same except for Andhra Pradesh (18–216 acres, 7–52 hectares), Mysore (18–144 acres, 7–60 hectares), Uttar Pradesh (12¼ acres, 5 hectares).

† Some laws applied to ceilings on family ownership, others to ceilings on registered individual holders.

‡ Extra allowance for large families; allowances vary but for most states are up to twice the ceiling area.

§ Key to types of land exempted: 1—sugar cane; 2—tea; 3—coffee; 4—orchard; 5—citrus; 6—fruit trees; 7—rubber; 8—cattle raising; 9—dairy farming; 10—livestock; 11—stud farm; 12—groves; 13—pepper; 14—fuel trees; 15—grass; 16—cashew nuts; 17—cardamon; 18—casuarine; 19—chinchona; 20—pharmacological products; 21—lac-brood farms; 22—sisal; 23—specially approved lease farms; 24—commercial or industrial undertakings; 25—religious, charitable, educational or medical institutions' land; 26—co-operative society land; 27—government approved exempted area; 28—'efficiently managed farms in compact blocks whose break-up might result in fall in production'; 29—hill land; 30—Bhoodan and gramdan land; 31—land awarded for gallantry; 32—miscellaneous/other.

Source: India Planning Commission: *Progress of Land Reforms* (Delhi, Government Press, 1963).

to basic holdings; or 29 per cent of the area for both of these purposes. The basic holding was taken as 1 hectare for Kerala, 2 hectares for seven other states and 4 hectares for the rest of India. Realising, however, that these estimates reflected considerable over-reporting in censuses of personally cultivated land, the Planning Commission admitted that only a small proportion of the landless could be given ceiling surplus land.

Ceiling land reform's most important feature is its limited impact. Although all states have some legislation, ceiling levels vary arbitrarily, with little reference to the surplus potentially available or the extent of requirement for land. Compensation varies, but is generally expressed as a multiple of net annual income—partly recouped by beneficiary repayments, to make the reform self-financing. In states dominated by landlord influence loopholes were actually written into the laws. The Bihar legislation, for example, actually decreed the land transfers which would avoid expropriation; Article 5 of the Act of 1961 decrees that any landowner who has not transferred excess land before the law's enactment to his heirs shall do so within six months. Ceiling surplus land for redistribution was only 10 000 hectares in this large state.[27] In Mysore ceiling provisions were to come into force only 'on such date as the government may, by notification, appoint'. Since four years elapsed before this date was fixed, landowners had ample time to make the necessary arrangements for evasion. In Punjab land above the prescribed ceilings actually remains the property of the landowners; the state can settle peasants on the excess land but these tenants pay rent of one-third gross produce to the landowner, so there is no ownership redistribution at all. In West Bengal cultivators on ceiling-surplus land are insecure sharecroppers paying rent to the government. In Andhra Pradesh legal transfers raised the ceiling for a five person family to 135–1620 acres (56–575 hectares); in addition *mala fide* transfers have been substantial. Here, too, landlords formed spurious co-operative societies to escape ceiling expropriation. Because orchards were exempt there was a scramble to convert arable to orchard land; banana cultivation was the most common method of 'adapting' to the legislation. Only 23 000 hectares in Andhra became surplus: 'the difference between the estimated surplus (375 000 hectares) and that actually obtained is clear evidence of the phenomenal failure of ceiling legislation'.[28]

If the laws are fully implemented, the national potential is 1·1 million hectares, equivalent to 0·8 per cent of total cultivated area. At the average holding size of 2·7 hectares for India, only about 400 000 peasants could therefore be given land. But as delays in implementation allow large landowners to transfer their lands to relatives and others, this potential surplus will shrink: a realistic maximum might be only 200 000 cultivators.[29] Progress is slow apart from Jammu and Kashmir (187 500 hectares distributed—over a quarter of the sown area), West Bengal (76 391 hectares distributed), Uttar Pradesh (50 245 hectares) and Maharashtra (48 442 hectares): all figures are up to 1970.

CONSOLIDATION

Consolidation of fragmented holdings has long been a component part of Indian agricultural development planning. Land consolidation is the particular pride of Punjab and Haryana, where it has been associated, officially at least, with rural development success stories. Since the central government now subsidises states implementing consolidation schemes (up to 50 per cent of costs), other states, notably Uttar Pradesh, Madhya Pradesh and Maharashtra (Table 20), have made progress. The total area consolidated by 1969, 30 million hectares, was one quarter of the net sown area. Most states now have legislation for consolidation and also for preventing re-fragmentation; exceptions are Kerala and Orissa, where the fragmentation problem is not severe. Rapid implementation requires much trained manpower and adequate land records. Where neither is sufficient in quantity or quality, as in Bihar, progress is very slow.

The 1953 Uttar Pradesh Consolidation of Holdings Act, one of the most important, had the following features: (1) consolidation was compulsory in any area the government selected as appropriate; (2) for quick judgment a government arbitrator

TABLE 20

PROGRESS OF CONSOLIDATION OF HOLDINGS IN VARIOUS INDIAN STATES

State	Area consolidated 1969 'ooo hectares	Area anticipated 1974 'ooo hectares
Andhra Pradesh	346·9	346·9
Assam	2·0	44·3
Bihar	73·1	243·0
Gujarat	873·1	1 295·2
Haryana*	124·6	124·6
Jammu and Kashmir	24·7	66·9
Madhya Pradesh	3 108·3	4 374·6
Maharashtra	3 842·3	7 286·3
Mysore	1 361·1	1 361·1
Punjab*	9 475·1	9 475·1
Rajasthan	1 795·6	1 795·6
Uttar Pradesh	9 143·6	12 644·1
West Bengal		731·0
Delhi	85·1	85·1
Himachal Pradesh	190·5	274·9
Total	30 446·0	40 148·7

Notes: * work completed by 1969.
Source: G. Wunderlich: 'Land Reform in India', in Agency for International Development: Spring Review of Land Reform (Washington, Department of State, 1970), Vol. 1, p. 45.

heard all legal disputes involving land, and all land transfers and building activity were frozen; (3) in each village an official assistant consolidation officer, working with the existing village authorities, administered the consolidation procedure; (4) the exchange and allotment of plots were determined by rental value not size, except that new holdings must not vary by more than 20 per cent in size from old ones; and (5) dissatisfied farmers could appeal to the district consolidation officer, or, if necessary, to the settlement officer, whose decision was final. Besides amalgamating parcels by exchanges, UP consolidation undertook 'rectangularisation' of odd-shaped plots to provide a more efficient lay-out for farming operations. Roads, paths and canals were replanned to a rectilinear pattern. Consequently many 'consolidated' villages have a very different appearance from those not affected by the programme (Fig. 8).

A detailed study by Agrawal,[30] based on 165 cultivators randomised from consolidated villages around Lucknow, showed plots per holding reduced from 5 to 3, mean plot size increased from 0·25 hectares to 0·43 hectares and sub-letting reduced from 6·5 per cent of land to 2·9 per cent. Economically consolidation caused an immediate 7 per cent saving in costs (chiefly in travel time, particularly where bullocks were involved). More efficient farming and some increase in land area with removal of plot boundaries raised yields by about 10 per cent, but with the initial savings in human and bullock time reinvested in manuring, fertilising and irrigating, production and income increases were about 20 per cent. The consolidated villages showed a higher cropping intensity (35 per cent of the area double-cropped; 9 per cent in a control group of unconsolidated villages), more irrigated land (52 per cent as against 42 per cent), and less debt (mean of 167 rupees per household as against 228).

Economic gains are not, however, universal. Increased output on consolidated holdings is largely restricted to the richer farmers, who have the capital to intensify and mechanise their new compact holdings. A study of 342 consolidated villages in Mysore revealed that in most less than one third (and in some only 10 per cent) of the farmers benefited directly from consideration.[31] Administrators may be enthusiastic about the technical benefits of consolidation, but villagers view plot exchange with suspicion and allege bribery and corruption.[32] In Uttar Pradesh, where consolidation was nearly complete by 1970, the reform was judged 'on balance beneficial, but not particularly important, and not particularly popular'.[33]

INDIAN LAND REFORM: FACT OR FALLACY?

Observers agree that India's land reform efforts show a wide gap between goals and achievements. *Zamindari* abolition, tenancy regulation, consolidation of holdings, community development, co-operative credit and land ceilings have offered disproportionately little to the marginal farmer, tenant or labourer. The importance of land reform in the rhetoric of Indian politics raises peasants' expectations, but piecemeal and half-hearted implementation causes disappointment, disrupts

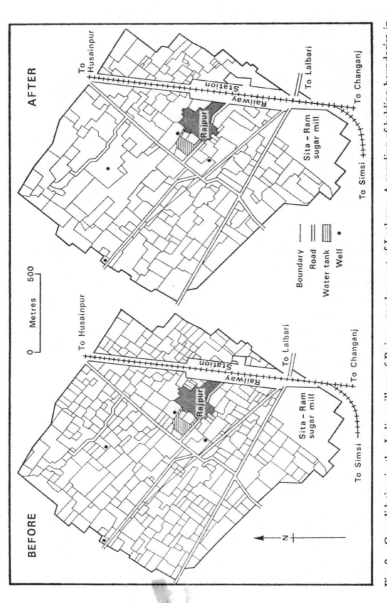

Fig. 8. Consolidation in the Indian village of Rajpur, 300 km west of Lucknow. A reording of holding boundaries in 1957–8 reduced 305 parcels to 158. *Source:* J. W. Elder: 'A case study of the Consolidation of Holdings Act in Uttar Pradesh', *Economic Development and Cultural Change*, 11 (1), 1962, pp. 28–9

rural life and spoils landlord-tenant relations. India illustrates democratic land reforms actually helping to polarise land property relations. The upgrading of superior tenures and guaranteed tenure security enable the relatively few middle and rich peasants to improve their position at the expense of the large absentee landlords and the zamindars. The lowest classes on the land, servants, hired labour, sharecroppers, have not been significantly affected, except adversely. The Indian agrarian problem remains serious, basic and deep-rooted.

Modest increases in production have followed land reforms but, outside of a few spatially limited cases, demonstrating that land reform played any causal role is virtually impossible. Available information suggests that effects, if any, were at least not negative: no long-term falls in production were reported in areas where reform measures were implemented. Otherwise, national or even regional correlations between reforms and production are likely to be invalid.[34] Uttar Pradesh, which has had the most thorough-going land reform of any Indian state, has had a particularly slow rate of agricultural growth. In many states, landlords, fearing land reform on the one hand and foreseeing greater profits from the green revolution on the other, have evicted peasants cultivating land under traditional forms of tenure. The evidence in the mushrooming green revolution literature confirms the trend to increasing inequality. The green revolution seems to be forcing a choice which is unlikely to be a short-term dilemma: whether to have an egalitarian land reform or to accept that the green revolution will increase unrest amongst the rural proletariat.

One policy which could theoretically bridge the land reform —green revolution dichotomy is co-operation. In the 1959 Nagpur Resolution on the agrarian structure, the Congress Party, surprisingly, stated 'the future agrarian pattern should be that of co-operative joint farming in which land will be pooled for joint cultivation'. The implication, though hardly attainable in the short term, was that co-operative farming would be the only mode of cultivation, embracing the entire land of the village irrespective of size of holding or tenure. The response of the state governments to the Nagpur Resolution was only faintly positive. By 1965 about 2400 co-operative societies were operating in pilot areas covering 100 000 hectares. Unfortunately many were badly organised and their consequent unsatisfactory achievements have strengthened the current disrepute of co-operative farming. Many co-operatives took over inferior land, such as government-donated waste land, with inexperienced landless people who, depressed by years of unemployment, could not overcome initial difficulties. The successful societies were often older ones dating from the 1920s or 1930s. Some large landowners evaded land holding ceilings by pretending to pool their land for joint farming. Indeed a recent investigation in Punjab and western Uttar Pradesh concluded that most of the 140 societies studied were bogus: they were either disguised family enterprises or associations of people largely engaged in occupations other than agriculture.[35] In general, the co-operative farm has not been successful in India. It may yet, however, provide a solution.

THE FUTURE

Indian agriculture has undergone dramatic developments since the peak of land reform under Nehru in the late 1950s. From near-famine in 1966, the green revolution brought projections of food self-sufficiency by the early or mid 1970s. Particularly in the north Indian wheat regions the new high-yield crops have boosted agricultural production to record levels and rural private capital has been mobilised at unprecedented rates. But the euphoria was short-lived and spatially confined. While bumper harvests overwhelm storage facilities in the Punjab there has been little effect in regions without irrigation or the other required inputs. Famine still threatens parts of India in the mid 1970s, and the threat of rural revolution looms large over India's complex agrarian scene.

The prospect for future Indian land reform is impossible to predict, but certain features are clearly important.[36] Political conflicts are mounting. Uncontrolled explosions of rural discontent may produce either repression or more radical land reform. After a decade of obscurity, land reform is re-emerging as a central issue. The 1969 Land Reforms Act in the communist-controlled south-western state of Kerala represents the most far-reaching legislation yet enacted in India; landlords' rights are taken over by the government and some 400 000 tenants may become owners.[37] Mrs. Gandhi's 1971 election victory largely reflected recognition of growing rural discontent and an aggressive agrarian policy involving both new reform activities and stricter enforcement of old laws. With *kulak* opposition growing, achievement of new reforms will be difficult, but essential for the viability of India's political system.

REFERENCES

1. P. T. George: 'The evolution of land tenure in India', *Artha Vijnana*, 12 (1–2), 1970, pp. 1–15.
2. M. L. Dantwala: 'Land reforms in India', *International Labour Review*, 66 (4), 1952, pp. 419–43.
3. K. Gough: 'Peasant resistance and revolt in South India', *Pacific Affairs*, 41 (4), 1968–9, pp. 526–44.
4. M. L. Dantwala: 'Problems in countries with heavy pressure of population on land: the case of India', in K. H. Parsons, R. J. Penn and P. M. Raup (eds.): *Land Tenure* (Madison, University of Wisconsin Press, 1956), pp. 134–46.
5. K. Ghose: *Agricultural Labourers In India* (Calcutta, Indian Publications, 1969), p. 95.
6. R. E. Frykenberg (ed): *Land Control and Social Structure in Indian History* (Madison, University of Wisconsin Press, 1969), p. XV.
7. D. Bronger: 'Der sozialgeographische Einfluss des Kastenwesens auf Siedlung und Agrarstruktur im südlichen Indien', *Erdkunde*, 24, 1970, pp. 89–106, 194–206.
8. C. Bell: 'Ideology and economic interests in Indian land reform', in D. Lehmann (ed): *Agrarian Reform and Agrarian Reformism* (London, Faber and Faber, 1974), pp. 190–220.
9. See F. Tomasson Jannuzi: *Agrarian Crisis in India: The Case of Bihar* (Austin, University of Texas Press, 1974), ch. 7.
10. T. E. Oommen: 'Myth and reality in India's communitarian villages', *Journal of Commonwealth Political Studies*, 4 (2), 1966, pp. 94–116.
11. The compensation period was 15 or 20 years in most other states. The compensation provisions on the face of it were generous, but inflation has eroded the bonds' value, and by 1968 only 40 per cent of the compensation had in fact been paid out. This was, no doubt, partly due to the enormity of the bill—£500 million, an amount equal to the entire expenditure on agriculture under the Second Five-Year Plan. D. Warriner: *Land Reform in Principle and Practice* (Oxford, Clarendon, 1969), p. 161.
12. W. C. Neale: *Economic Change in Rural India: Land Tenure and Reform in Uttar Pradesh, 1800–1955* (New Haven, Yale University Press, 1962), pp. 241–4.
13. Warriner: *op. cit.*, p. 159.
14. Neale: *op. cit.*, p. 288.
15. D. Thorner: *The Agrarian Prospect for India* (Delhi, University of Delhi Press, 1956), pp. 47–50.

16. B. Sarveswara Rao: *Economic and Social Effects of Zamindari Abolition in Andhra* (Delhi, Government of India Press, 1963), p. 100.
17. Tomasson Jannuzi: *op. cit.*, pp. 48–67.
18. G. Wood: 'From raiyat to rich peasant', *South Asian Review*, 7 (1), 1973, pp. 1–16.
19. Tomasson Jannuzi: *op. cit.*, pp. 32–44.
20. T. R. Metcalf: 'Landlords without land: the U.P. zamindars today', *Pacific Affairs*, 40 (1–2), 1967, pp. 5–18.
21. G. Wunderlich: 'Land reforms in India', in Agency for International Development: *Spring Review of Land Reform* (Washington, Department of State, 1970), Vol. 1, p. 62.
22. M. B. Desai and R. S. Mehta: 'Abolition of tenancy cultivation', *Indian Journal of Agricultural Economics*, 17 (1), 1962, pp. 127–34.
23. A. M. Khusro: *Economic and Social Effects of Jagirdari Abolition and Land Reforms in Hyderabad* (Hyderabad, Osmania University Press, 1958), esp. pp. 41–4.
24. G. Parthasarathy and B. Prasada Rao: *Implementation of Land Reforms in Andhra Pradesh* (Calcutta, Scientific Book Agency, 1969); L. Krishnamurty: 'Land legislation in Andhra Pradesh', *Indian Journal of Agricultural Economics*, 17 (1), 1962, pp. 161–74; P. T. George: 'Land reforms in Andhra Pradesh—some problems of implementation of tenancy reforms', *Artha Vijnana*, 12 (4), 1970, pp. 467–506.
25. J. S. Uppal: 'Implementation of land reform legislation in India—a study of two villages in the Punjab', *Asian Survey*, 9 (5), 1969, pp. 359–72.
26. R. Krishna: 'Agrarian reform in India: the debate on ceilings', *Economic Development and Cultural Change*, 7 (3), 1959, pp. 302–17; S. C. Jha: 'Land redistribution as a measure of agrarian reform in India; the issues of debate', *Asian Economic Review*, 10 (4), 1968, pp. 465–70.
27. Tomasson-Jannuzi: *op. cit.*, pp. 81–5.
28. Parthasarathy and Prasada Rao: *op. cit.*, pp. 175–7.
29. Wunderlich: *op. cit.*, p. 35.
30. S. K. Agrawal: *Economics of Land Consolidation in India* (New Delhi, Chand, 1971), chs. 2–6.
31. V. V. Shetty: 'Consolidation of holdings in Mysore state', *Indian Journal of Agricultural Economics*, 18 (2), 1963, pp. 46–54.
32. J. W. Elder: 'Land consolidation in an Indian village: a case study of the Consolidation of Holdings Act in Uttar Pradesh', *Economic Development and Cultural Change*, 11 (1), 1962, pp. 16–40.
33. W. C. Neale: 'Land reform in Uttar Pradesh', in Agency for International Development: *Spring Review of Land Reform, op. cit.*, Vol. 1, p. 44.
34. Wunderlich: *op. cit.*, pp. 65, 68, 79.
35. H. Laxminarayan and K. Kanungo: *Glimpses of Cooperative Farming in India* (London, Asia Publishing House, 1967), pp. 119, 126.
36. Bell: *op. cit.*, pp. 216–17.
37. W. Klatt: 'Caste, class and communism in Kerala', *Asian Affairs*, 59 (3), 1972, pp. 275–87.

14

Other Countries

PAKISTAN

Pakistan's rural problems, at least initially, were if anything worse than India's. Pakistan in 1947 inherited a country split into two parts with 1500 km of India in between: a geographical anomaly destined to last only twenty years. The differences were far more than geographical. The tall, light-skinned Punjabis and Pathans of the West were as ethnically different from the small, dark Bengalis of the East as are the Swedes from the Sicilians. Different languages, occupations, traditions, economies and farming systems separated the two halves of Pakistan. The West identifies strongly with the Islamic world; the easterners are part of the Bengal culture-region. The new country had few educated or technically trained people. Its peasantry was traditional, subsistence oriented, 80 per cent illiterate and had suffered centuries of exploitation. Nine million refugees intensified the pressure on land. For the first decade of independence, agricultural production fell seriously short of population growth. Although the 75 million easterners outnumbered the 60 million of the West and their jute produced most of the country's export earnings, the West had the capital city, 70 per cent of the foreign aid, 80 per cent of the country's budget expenditure, 85 per cent of civil service jobs and 90 per cent of army commissions. These figures, although only approximate, indicate the explosive imbalance inherent in old Pakistan, and it was not surprising that, in the December 1970 elections, the easterners gave Sheikh Mujibur Rahman's Awami League 167 out of 169 seats in the

East and an overall majority in the national 313-seat Assembly. From this electoral situation and the war that followed, Bangladesh emerged in December 1971 as the eighth largest, but probably the poorest, nation on earth. Meanwhile Bhutto swept to power in the West. While corruption and inflation persistently depress the economy of the independent East, the West is now a leader in Asian agricultural development, through the impact of the new high-yielding crops. Paradoxically, this high agricultural productivity has been achieved probably just because there has been no thorough-going land reform. Only in 1972, twenty-five years after independence, was a significant land reform in sight in West Pakistan; it took half that time, till 1959, to enact any reform whatsoever, though West Pakistan had one of the most skewed landownership structures in Asia.

BACKGROUND TO THE LAND TENURE SITUATION

Situated, then, as the two provinces were, in different historical and ecological conditions, their tenure systems developed differently. We shall therefore discuss each wing in turn.

At partition, Pakistani land tenures were almost as complicated as Indian. Geographical factors were largely responsible. West Pakistan is often referred to as a desert; East Pakistan as a swamp. In the West 80–90 per cent of the land farmed receives some irrigation water; tubewell irrigation in recent years has dramatically increased the cropped area. Currently about one fifth of the 80 million hectares is cultivated. East Pakistan is dominated by the Ganges-Brahmaputra delta system. Rainfall is 80 inches per year (cf. 7 inches at Karachi) and nearly two-thirds of the 14 million hectares are cropped. Every two or three years, however, the waters rise too far and too fast, and 5–10 per cent of the rice crop is destroyed. Expansion of the eastern cultivated area is very limited; new areas brought into cultivation by embankments and reclamation only offset annual losses of land to industry and expansion of settlement.

East Pakistan (East Bengal) had three-quarters of its cultivated land under the Permanent Settlement, and so resembled *zamindari* tenure in Indian West Bengal. In the Punjab government tenants farming sizeable holdings were prominent in parts, but elsewhere *zamindari* tenure was strong. Sind was officially a *ryotwari* area but *jagirdar* intermediaries had so developed that

most cultivators were *haris*, tenants without occupancy rights
and working on the *batai* sharecropping system which gave them
a nominal half, but often an actual third, of the crop. These tenants-at-will cultivated 80 per cent of the farmed area in Sind,
50 per cent in Punjab, 47 per cent in North-West Frontier and
50 per cent in Bahawalpur.[1] Partition saw a great exodus of non-
Muslim landowners but a greater influx of landless refugees.

Landownership distribution was extremely lop-sided, especially in the West, where only 0·1 per cent of the landowners, the
6061 with over 200 hectares each, owned 15 per cent of the land
area. In contrast, 65 per cent of owners owned 15 per cent of the
land in units of less than 2 hectares. In 1962 West Pakistan had
an estimated 200 000–250 000 landlords, 500 000 family owner-
cultivators (each with 3–8 hectares irrigated or equivalent dry
land), 1 600 000 marginal owner-cultivators (less than 3 hectares), 750 000 tenants with at least 5 hectares, 1 800 000 tenants-
at-will and 550 000 landless labourers.[2] Mean holding sizes
were 4 hectares in the West, 1·5 hectares in the East.

LAND REFORM IN WEST PAKISTAN: 1959 AND 1972

Before Ayub Khan's 1958 *coup d'état* each major province of
West Pakistan—Sind, Punjab and North-West Frontier—made
half-hearted attacks on land tenure problems. But with most of
the chief ministers of these provinces being large landlords,
little resulted. Rather, these attempts, instead of providing tenurial security, created an atmosphere of uncertainty among the
tenants and intensified animosity between them and the landlords.

Central to Ayub Khan's 1959 land reform was the limiting of
individual land ownership to 500 irrigated acres (208 hectares)
or 1000 acres (416 hectares) dry-farmed. Several exemptions
existed, including orchards, livestock farms and land of religious, charitable and educational institutions. Land could also
be transferred to female dependants. Ceiling-surplus land was
expropriated (with compensation in the form of 4 per cent bonds
redeemable in twenty-five years) and sold to tenants (with preference to those already cultivating the land) with 'reasonable
terms of payment' extending over twenty-five years. Intermediary interests were also abolished. Tenants, including the
haris of Sind, got security from the provision that no tenant could

be ejected unless he had not paid the rent, had not cultivated the land, had used the land abusively or had sublet it.

Not surprisingly, the effects of such mild legislation were modest. 5064 landowners declared excess land, but the government took land from only 763 of them and only 55 per cent of their declared surplus; the remaining 45 per cent left the 763 owners with an average of 520 hectares, plus compensation. One third of the 1 million hectares acquired by the government was unassignable, being waste, hill country and forests; in all less than 5 per cent of the country's farmland was affected by the reform. 200 000 families received land—only 8 per cent of the country's tenants.[3]

The Ayub Khan régime's commitment to land reform was only token. The really wealthy landlords had their influence reduced somewhat, but the reform could not risk adversely affecting the property interests of the military officers and bureaucrats, who mostly had middle-sized landlord backgrounds. A mild land reform was a means of achieving political legitimacy rather than an expression of fundamental concern with the peasants' conditions.

The strategy in the 1960s was rapid mechanisation to achieve productivity improvements on precisely those middle-to-large farms spared by the high ceiling. The Second Five Year Plan (1960–5) instituted numerous incentives to use modern inputs. Tubewells and agricultural chemicals were subsidised, cotton export duties reduced, tractors freed from import duty and wheat prices supported. These measures created an excellent infrastructure for the green revolution of the late 1960s, from which the profits provided for further such investments in the larger holdings. Tubewells, for instance, increased from 9000 (1960) to 34 000 (1965) to 79 000 (1970). By 1970 over half the irrigated area was growing the new high-yielding Mexi-Pak wheat, while fertiliser consumption similarly increased from 125 000 tons in 1965 to 296 000 tons in 1970 to 419 000 tons in 1972.[4]

Initially at least, only the larger farms could undertake these investments—and reap the profits; 70 per cent of the tubewells, for example, were installed on holdings above 10 hectares, and only 4 per cent on holdings of under 5 hectares. Policies between 1960 and 1970 aimed at growth, not equity. Rapid growth was indeed achieved—3·9 per cent during 1959–68 compared with 1·8 per cent during 1950–8—but income disparities widened. West Pakistan quickly moved from a food grain deficit to a surplus, but not without internal economic stress. Tubewell development threw up 'waterlords' who sold water to those without wells of their own, charging a quarter to a third of the crop as 'water rent'.[5] Frequently tenants and smallholders were worse off not only relatively, but absolutely, through difficulties in obtaining inputs, displacement of workers and tenants by 'tractor technology', bidding up of rents on tenanted land and the growing unwillingness of landlords, spurred by the profit motive, to meet traditional obligations.

By 1970 the improved farming practices of the green revolution were spreading from the large farms to neighbouring farmers with smaller holdings.[6] How rapidly this process will proceed is difficult to assess, but the return of Bhutto's Pakistan People's Party (the only party committed to land reform) in the 1970 elections indicated widespread discontent amongst the rural poor, the party's electoral strength lying in precisely those areas most affected by the green revolution.

The 1972 reform went further than the 1959, yet was hardly radical. Most important, it reduced the land ceiling to 150 irrigated acres (60 hectares) or 300 unirrigated acres (120 hectares), or any equivalent combination, with no exemptions and no compensation. For land owned by civil servants the ceiling was 40 hectares. Redistribution in subsistence sized plots (mostly around 5 hectares) was free. The regulation of tenancy followed the lines of the 1959 reform, except that land revenue payments and other taxes, including the water rate, were shifted to the landlord. The 1972 reform programme also envisioned the setting up of 'social co-operative farms' for the control of labour, irrigation water and machinery; the building of 'agro-villes', small rural service towns; development of large cattle farms to provide more protein for the diet; and afforestation to maintain the ecological balance. Little has been done on these last four points.

It seems that the impact of the 1972 reform will be minimal. Much cultivated land escapes the still too high ceiling. Moreover landlords may choose which portions of their land they yield to expropriation. Many dispersed their holdings when they saw Bhutto's victory; making the reform retroactive to early 1971 would have countered this and made much more land available for distribution. Precise estimation of the land area open to expropriation is difficult. Herring and Chaudhry indicate 1·2 million hectares as potentially available, but government estimates of 480 000 hectares (1972) and 355 000 hectares (1974) are much lower.[7] The landowners eventually expropriated may be as few as 600; probably under 5 per cent of the tenantry will get any benefit.[8]

LAND REFORM IN ERSTWHILE EAST PAKISTAN

At independence in 1947, most of the east wing was under Permanent Settlement, the government's revenue from this land being fixed in perpetuity. Hindu landowners, mostly from Bihar, held much land. This may explain why land reform was possible in East Pakistan so soon after partition: it enabled the Muslim majority to free itself from the economic control of the Hindu minority.[9]

The 1950 East Bengal State Acquisition and Tenancy Act provided for direct payment of peasant taxes to the state. A 1957 amendment abolished all rent-receiving intermediary interests from 14 April 1956; the land now belonged to the government. Occupancy rights and right of transfer to other cultivators were assured, but sub-letting was forbidden to prevent the re-emergence of rent-receiving intermediaries. Self-cultivated *khas* land was limited to 100 *bighas* (14 hectares) per family or 10 *bighas* (1·4 hectares) per family member (whichever was the greater), plus a further 1·4 hectares for the homestead. Tea and sugar plantations and dairy farms were exempted. In 1961 Ayub Khan raised the 14 hectare ceiling to 42 hectares. All land beyond these limits was to be distributed amongst small landowners and landless peasants. Compensation to outgoing rent receivers was in non-negotiable 3 per cent bonds payable in forty years; it varied from 2 to 10 times the annual rent according to area expropriated, the higher rate affecting the smaller holdings.

The main effects of this reform were the elimination of the zamindar as a force in rural society and an increase in the government's land revenue. For the peasants, only the destination of their taxes changed. The tenants liberated from the zamindars found themselves imprisoned in the straitjacket of compensation. Furthermore, the acts provided little protection for *bargadars* (sharecroppers) who cultivated 15 per cent of the farmland. Fragmentation, too, remains serious. The 1960 Agricultural Census listed 52 per cent of holdings fragmented into six or more parcels (29 per cent had 10 or more parcels). Although the 1950 Act provided for consolidation of holdings, very little has so far been done. Only 120 000 hectares materialised from the 1962 ceiling law. Legal and administrative difficulties initially slowed progress, but most of the land transfers were completed by 1970.[10] Overall, land reforms in East Pakistan had a negligible impact on agricultural productivity and rural living standards.[11]

Born late in 1971, Bangladesh inherited enormous agricultural, economic and demographic problems.[12] For 20 years food output growth has failed to match a population increasing at 3 per cent a year, reaching an estimated 80 million in 1975. Per capita food consumption fell 23 per cent 1963–72. Illiteracy is 82 per cent. Agriculture employs 76 per cent of the active population, supports 85 per cent of the total population, represents 57 per cent of gross domestic product and contributes 90 per cent of exports: due to decline of non-agricultural activities, these proportions are tending to increase. Food has to be imported in increasing quantities; famine has become endemic. A major factor has been the failure of tenure reform to create favourable institutional conditions for increased output.[13] Pressure on land becomes progressively acute. Mean farm size dropped from 1·46 hectares in 1960 to 1·16 hectares in 1974. Only 10 per cent of the rural population are totally landless, but another 25 per cent have under ½ hectare. 22 million hectares, one third of the cultivated land, is tenanted. The green revolution has scarcely started (affecting only 11 per cent of the rice area by 1973), although there are hopes for a new rice variety, IR20, tailored especially for the region's summer season.[14]

The government's espousal of land reform, vigorously preached in the revolutionary struggle, has produced only token policies: a notable parallel to the post-1971 situation in West Pakistan. Land reform measures issued in 1972 lower the ceiling to its 1950 level of 14 hectares (though the area beyond this amount is negligible) and abolish land tax on holdings below 25 *bighas* (3·5 hectares). The government has said that the 14 hectare ceiling is not final, hinting at a further halving to 7 hectares. Left-wing groups, meanwhile, press for 2–5 hectares. Since the inverse relationship between farm size and productivity seems to hold for Bangladesh (a recent study demonstrated that the 1–2 hectare class scored highest on all measures of productivity —land, labour and total factor), it follows that any agricultural policy which increases the area of land under small farms will increase productivity, incomes and employment.[15] Khan has estimated that a 3 hectare ceiling would potentially take 1 million hectares from 8 per cent of farm families.[16] Together with 580 000 hectares of government land, and assuming allocation in 1¼ hectare family subsistence plots, this would be more than sufficient for the 700 000 landless tenant and sharecropping families, but not for landless labourers and families with insufficient land for subsistence.[17] Lowering the ceiling to 2 hectares would yield more land (though still not enough for all needing it) but would provoke serious political troubles since 20 per cent of the existing landholders would be affected.

SRI LANKA

Ceylon gained independence in 1948, tagging along, like Pakistan, in the great slipstream of Indian emancipation. In contrast to India and Pakistan, Sri Lanka is lush and verdant, with a kindly climate not liable to natural disasters. However, a dense rural population—25 000 villages in as many square miles—and a demographic growth rate which has only now come down to 2 per cent per annum, have produced extreme land shortage in a deteriorating economic situation.

Agriculture has a pronounced dual structure, with plantations and peasant farms. Two-thirds of peasant smallholdings, mostly growing rice, are below one acre (0·4 hectares). Two-thirds of the cultivated area is occupied by tea, rubber and coconut plantations, the main export crops, earning 90 per cent of foreign exchange (tea alone 60 per cent). Sri Lanka is locked into a plantation economy with prices determined externally. Plantation prosperity has given little spill-over into the countryside; rather, as the plantations grew, peasant landlessness increased. The estates carry an estimated population of 1·3 million, many of them Tamil labourers, who have become over the years exploited 'second-class citizens'. In fact, with both industry and agriculture stagnant, employment opportunities do not match the rising expectations created in the young by years of improved and free education. Sri Lanka's 'proletariat of the educated unemployed' are increasingly a factor in the country's politics.

The 1946 Agricultural Census recorded 61 per cent of paddy holdings by number, and 55 per cent by area, as owner-farmed. The average paddy holding was 0·5 hectares; only 1 per cent of holdings exceeded 4 hectares. The major tenure problem on paddy lands was the *ande* sharecropping tenure, which covered 24 per cent of the total rice area (26 per cent of holdings), but nearly half the area and holdings in up-country 'Wet Zone' districts, like Kandy, Matala and Ratnapura. Being oral, the *ande* agreement gave little security to the sharecroppers, who generally consigned 50 per cent of their output to the landlord, plus a return at harvest time of seed paddy at some multiple of the seed borrowed at sowing time. In areas of high population pressure traditional token gifts (*madaran*) made to the landlord as proof of sharecroppers' loyalty had become a compulsory demand for cash.

THE 1958 PADDY LANDS ACT[18]

The Paddy Lands Act and its amendments did not seek to abolish tenancy or to expropriate landowners. The main objectives were: (1) to regulate the authority landlords exercised over tenants; (2) to control rents; (3) to confer permanent and heritable security of tenure; (4) to prevent further fragmentation and encourage consolidation of paddy land; (5) to establish farmers' committees for the local organisation of paddy cultivation; (6) to regulate interest rates and hire charges for implements and draught animals and to fix wage rates for farm labour.

The act took five years to achieve country-wide application, although tenancy rights provisions were made retroactive from 1956. The Commissioner of Agrarian Services had to stipulate rent regulations for each district. The maximum possible rent was fixed at either 15 bushels of rice per acre, or one-quarter of the produce, whichever was less, but in some areas rent ceilings were fixed as low as 2 bushels or one-eighth the crop. This regulation brought the important incentive that increased production beyond a certain level accrued entirely to the tenant, whilst in bad years the rent burden was proportionately lowered.

Although these controls seemed very favourable to the tenant, many continued to pay their old inflated shares of 50 per cent, chiefly for fear of eviction. The act provided for restoring evicted tenants but the cumbersome procedure deterred tenants from risking eviction by trying to hold their landlords to the letter of the 1958 law. Ironically, the Act, ostensibly aimed at protecting tenants' security, unleashed a wave of evictions by annoyed landlords.

Other factors, too, hindered the rent provisions' implementation. The limited availability of institutional credit for peasants seriously restricted the ability of tenants dependent on loans from landlords (in 1957 54 per cent of rural families were in debt to landlords) to enforce their tenancy rights under the law. A bill to provide co-operative credit was dropped because of opposing political and landlord interests. Finally, the 1958 Act ignored the serious fragmentation problem in the paddy regions except for stipulating that tenancy rights should evolve without subdivision. It preferred voluntary consolidation programmes, which have had little result, to an administratively less flexible directive, which might only aggravate local situations.[19]

SRI LANKA'S NEW LAND REFORM, 1972[20]

During the 1960s land reform was virtually forgotten. An insurrection in 1971 prompted Mrs. Bandaranaike to promise new land reforms. The 1972 act is more radical than previous legislation. It established a Land Reform Commission empowered to expropriate agricultural land above 10 hectares of paddy or 20 hectares of other farmland per individual. Discretionary clauses lessen somewhat the impact of the ceilings. Up to 0·2 hectares each is allowed for the owner's residence and the family burial ground. Where there are staff quarters, 0·05 hectares is permitted for each resident family. For land held by a private company or a co-operative society, shareholders are deemed to own land in proportion to their paid-up shares of the company or society. Public companies' land is exempt, although lessees of government land, on settlement schemes for example, are subject to the ceiling. Compensation, in 7 per cent land reform bonds maturing in twenty-five years, is a multiple of the land's income as declared to the Inland Revenue.

The crux of the legislation lies in what will happen to the expropriated land. There are no specific provisions for transferring land to tenants or labourers, although such transfers are not precluded. Proposals to give priority to persons already resident or employed on the land foundered on fears of landownership by Indian estate labourers. For the time being, land expropriated is vested in the Land Reform Commission. It is estimated that about 200 000 hectares (12 per cent of total agricultural land) will be expropriated, including only 7000 hectares of paddy. The 10 hectares individual ceiling, applied to an average family of four adults, becomes a 40 hectare holding ceiling. Only 1 per cent of the rice area is under such large holdings. Most holdings above the ceiling are company estates, which are exempt, largely for productivity reasons. The likely effects on the agrarian structure, especially in the rice areas, will be marginal.

INDONESIA

Indonesia provides yet another example of a passing rather than a firm interest in land reform. The fifth largest nation in the world, with 120 million people, Indonesia's population geography is dominated by the contrast between Java (plus the adjacent small islands of Madura, Bali and Lombok), which, on 10 per cent of the area carries 67 per cent of the population, and the sparsely peopled 'Outer Islands' of Sumatra, Kalimantan, Sulawesi and West Irian. Linked to this population contrast, and to the impact of Dutch colonial policy, are profound differences in land tenure and agricultural geography. Wet rice or *sawah* agriculture dominates Java and its small islands; shifting cultivation still covers large areas of the Outer Islands. Average population density for Java is 570 persons per square kilometre but in the rural, rice-growing central region it exceeds 1000. Over 92 per cent of smallholders in central Java possess units of under 1 hectare. This island's population increased from 6 million in 1830 to 63 million in 1960, the date of the land reform. The population employed in agriculture increased from 68 per cent in 1930 to 73 per cent in 1960. Estimates of current population growth vary from 2·3 to 3·0 per cent per year.

LAND REFORM[21]

Sukarno saw land reform as 'an indispensible part of the Indonesian revolution' and proposed 'the abolition of the class of landowners who have their land tilled by hired labourers' and 'a decrease in the number of landless peasants by granting real property only to those who till the soil themselves'. This enunciation in his 1959 *Manifesto Politik* was intended to fashion sweeping land reform, but opponents of the land-to-the-tiller ideal, mostly religious representatives who argued that proprietary rights in land were inalienable under Islamic law, forced recognition of the sanctity of property ownership even where the landowner organised the land with hired labour and sharecroppers.

The 1960 legislation aimed at providing every peasant family with a minimum of 2 hectares of arable land—an unrealistic objective. The maximum permitted holding depended on population density and land use. Ceilings on *sawah* land ranged from 5 hectares where population density exceeded 400 persons per square kilometre to 15 hectares where it was below 50 per square kilometre. Dry land ceilings were 20 per cent higher. For families containing over seven persons, the ceilings were increased 10 per cent per family member, up to a maximum of 50 per cent. Ceilings applied not only to land owned but also to land held or leased from others. Compensation was promised, but little paid. Excess land was to be distributed 'in the best possible way' to landless peasants—exactly how was not specified, and this vagueness presented the land reform committees with considerable difficulties.

In 1960 the government estimated that 966 000 hectares would become available for assignment to landless peasants. The 1963 Agricultural Census indicated a smaller potential— 720 000 hectares. The reform specified two stages. Some 337 445 hectares were to be redistributed in the high priority 'stage I' islands of Java, Madura, Bali and Lombok by late 1963 or early 1964. Stage II, following later, covered the rest of Indonesia. Difficulties of implementation made progress slow. Two years of preparatory work and land registration were necessary and the first assignments did not occur until 1963. Landowners liable to expropriation avoided the law by transferring land to relatives. In Java surplus land belonging to *hadjis* (pilgrims to Mecca) was transferred to religious institutions to hold for them while they continued to profit from it.

The laws were not strict enough, in concept or enforcement, to satisfy more than a proportion of the 3 million landless peasants. Lack of government zeal and landowners' subversive attitudes stimulated many peasants, often in peasant organisations affiliated with the Indonesian Communist Party, to direct action. By mid 1964 the government could no longer ignore the rural ferment. Reform action was speeded up so that by the end of 1964 all stage I surplus land had been acquired, although only 296 566 hectares had been distributed.

The attempted coup of 1965 entailed a severe setback for land reform. Many communist party members, including peasant activists, were murdered. Land reform, stigmatised as a communist product, virtually ceased. Known communist beneficiaries dared not work their newly acquired land and many fled to the city. All this facilitated landlords' resumption of their expropriated land, thus nullifying the results of the land reform. During 1966–7 about 150 000 hectares are thought to have reverted to former landowners. New redistribution was drastically curtailed; of the 200 000 hectares to have been assigned during 1967 only 33 640 hectares (17 per cent) were actually redistributed.

Positive progress recommenced in 1968 and by 1970 682 698 hectares had been distributed to 866 983 beneficiary families. Table 21 shows that 28 per cent of land remains undistributed and only 17 per cent came from ceiling-surplus and absentee-owned land (25 per cent in stage I areas, 11 per cent in stage II). The average assigned unit was 0·8 hectares (0·5 hectares in Java, 1·4 hectares elsewhere). The original objective of 2 hectares to every landless peasant is far from realisation, and at least 2 million peasant families are still without land.

LAND REFORM ABANDONED

Since the mid 1960s land reform has been replaced by other agricultural development strategies. Transmigration from overcrowded Java to land settlement schemes in Sumatra and else-

TABLE 21

INDONESIA: LAND ACQUIRED AND DISTRIBUTED 1960–70

	Land acquired hectares	Number of former owners	Area redistributed hectares	Number of beneficiary families
Stage I area				
Ceiling surplus	112 524	8 967	63 132	100 477
Absentee-owned	22 084	18 421	8 610	29 324
Provincial authorities	73 566		73 566	79 856
State demesne	147 344		147 192	383 301
Total Stage I	355 517	27 388	294 500	592 958
Stage II area				
Ceiling-surplus	49 001	unknown	34 548	25 981
Absentee-owned	8 132	unknown	8 026	9 239
Provincial authorities	52 712		37 850	53 244
State demesne	473 538		307 774	185 561
Total Stage II	583 384		388 198	274 025
Total Stage I and II	938 901		682 698	866 983

Source: E. Utrecht: 'Land reform and *Bimas* in Indonesia', *Journal of Contemporary Asia*, 3 (2), 1973, p. 155.

where seemed one way of reducing population distribution inequalities and improving the man-land ratio.[22] Problems of implementing this policy have, however, been legion. With roads and irrigation works lagging up to 13 years behind the establishment of the settlements, settlers have had to depend on rain-fed rice, with dry farming (especially cassava) the rest of the year. Soil deterioration makes many plots inadequate to support a family. Very few Javanese are willing to leave their home villages and extended families to pioneer in another island, and training prior to migration has been minimal. The difficulties and expenses involved have kept annual numbers below 50 000 since 1960.

The present Indonesian government under Suharto has not

the commitment to land reform of its predecessor: the aim is to raise food production, especially rice, to match swelling internal demand. In the mid 1960s *Bimas* (mass guidance) and *Inmas* (mass intensification) policies were directed towards achieving rice self-sufficiency inside three years, but the unsettled years of 1965–7, the low rice prices to the farmers (kept low to curb inflation), the high prices peasants encountered for fertilisers and other inputs, the lack of attention to irrigation works (70 per cent were in disrepair), and corrupt government personnel ensured overall failure.[23] Rice yields were below expectation and peasants largely deserted the scheme. Lacking a fundamental land reform, the sharecroppers, for example, already paying half their produce to the landlord, could hardly afford the additional one-sixth to the government for participation in *Bimas*. An amended *Bimas* programme, launched in late 1970, makes credit more freely available via village and mobile banks, subsidises fertilisers and insecticides and improves extension personnel. Farmers seem more willing to co-operate with this policy.

The latest development is to open up large rice estates in Sumatra. These 'neo-colonial plantations' work mostly with foreign oil company capital and apply green revolution technology. Predicted yields are up to ten times those of traditional tenant farmers. These estates continue the transmigration policy, since they mostly employ Javanese labour. Although they achieve impressive production, their efficacy in helping the vast majority of the Indonesian rural population is questionable. The estates currently being developed will provide, with relatively little labour input, 600 000 tons of rice per year, an amount which would require peasant households comprising 3·5 million people, including nearly 1 million workers, on average holdings of 1 hectare, to produce. The peasants naturally view these new estates, the main beneficiaries of which are foreign capitalists and the Indonesian ruling elite, as a threat to their already precarious livelihood. Only when further land reforms bring social justice to the countryside will current agricultural policies begin to benefit the majority of peasants at the 'rice-roots' level.

THE PHILIPPINES

The final country in this survey of Asian land reform, the Philippines, demonstrates perhaps best of all how land reform is convoluted with politics. From a small local issue in early Spanish times land problems have steadily increased in seriousness, number and regional scope. Yet despite almost a century of serious agrarian unrest the peasants' claims for security of tenure and for redistribution of estate land remain unrealised. Successive governments have faced the problem but a decisive assault is still awaited. The two major land reform measures of modern times—Magsaysay's 1955 legislation and Macapagal's of 1963—were crippled by lack of finance and feeble implementation due to the countervailing power of landlord vested interests.

BACKGROUND TO LAND REFORM

The two major problems, overpopulation and tenancy, appeared with the Spaniards in the late sixteenth century. Spanish rule in the Philippines, like Dutch rule in Indonesia, promoted both population growth and economic development, but the former accrued to the Philippines, the latter to Spain. From 1·5 million in 1800, the population increased to 20 million in the early 1950s. Spain made almost all cultivated land into private property and created large landholdings for the wealthy, the privileged and the Catholic Church. For faithful service to the crown, *encomenderos* were granted land, from which they collected peasant tributes. In the seventeenth century, after the *encomienda* system was abandoned because of its abuses, powerful religious corporations gained ownership of vast landed estates. From the late eighteenth century, many monastic orders and some private *hacendados* leased portions of their estates to intermediaries who in turn rented out small parcels to peasants. This system led to the *kasamá* or share-tenancy situation of the modern Philippines.

The American occupation in 1898 hastened the shift from the feudal system to a money economy, especially with the post-1909 sugar expansion into the Luzon rice lands. Gradually, favoured Filipinos also acquired large holdings. Many tenant farmers' sons accumulated sufficient capital to become land-owners themselves, a *nouveau riche* class disdaining the traditional obligations of helping tenants, which the old semi-feudal *cacique* families had observed.

During the first half of this century agricultural production struggled to keep up with population growth by expanding the cultivated area. Colonisation of underpopulated islands like Mindanao was pursued to reduce the need for land reform on existing farmland, but few transmigration projects succeeded, and only about 5 per cent of the colonists came from the over-crowded high tenancy areas of central Luzon, where agriculture and tenure systems were not changed to accommodate popula-tion increase and more exacting land use. In 1954 it was esti-mated that 75 per cent of Philippine farmland showed serious soil erosion.[24]

Tenancy increased from 3 per cent of the farmed area in 1903 to 35 per cent in 1948, reaching 88 per cent in Pampagna pro-vince (central Luzon). It dominates among rice farmers (48 per cent of the farms), who are concentrated in central Luzon. Here tenanted farms outnumbered owner farms by four to one, and in 1960 50 000 hectares, 8 per cent of the cultivated area, was con-trolled by 328 landowners. Yet out of over a million rice hold-ings in the Philippines in 1960 only 1042 exceeded 200 hectares, and only 4688 50 hectares. One-third of rice farms were between one and two hectares. Outside central Luzon the landlord-ten-ant relationship was close—indeed one-third of Philippine ten-ants are related to their landlords—but in the central rice core absentee landlordism prevailed, and still does. In the early 1950s underemployment was widespread. The average rice farmer worked 5·3 months per year on his farm, spent 2·1 months in off-farm employment, and was idle for 4·6 months. Only 6 per cent of his rice harvest was sold: 39 per cent went on rental payments, 20 per cent on loan repayments, another 12 per cent on harvest and threshing payments, 19 per cent was used by the household and 3 per cent kept for seed.[25]

Soon after American administration began, the 1902 Philip-pine Bill entrusted public domain to the government with a view to replacing tenancy by small farm ownership. Corpora-tions could not own more than 1042 hectares. Immediately thereafter 160 000 hectares of church land belonging to the Spanish Friars was purchased and distributed to 60 000 beneficiaries in the rice tenanted areas. Illiteracy and inadequate credit and marketing facilities forced new owners into indebtedness and within a few years most lost their land to large landowners, traders and even back to the Church.[26] Generally, American political dependence upon landlords prevented active reform beyond token colonisation efforts.

Wartime resistance to the Japanese in central Luzon saw tenant farmers organised into the communist-led Huk movement. After liberation, eight Huk sympathisers elected to Congress were denied their seats on the grounds of electoral terrorism. The Huks then tried armed revolt, which reached the outskirts of Manila in the early 1950s. The Huks began as a nationalist group but inevitably are strongest where poverty and tenancy are most prevalent.[27] For thirty years they have continually mobilised villagers against landlord-oriented governments, which pass much agrarian legislation, but fail to implement it effectively. Huk activity waned in the late 1950s but increased markedly after 1965, when central Luzon was labelled a 'zone of violence and terror'.[28] American aid missions identified land reform as the key to quelling this insurgency. Rice ceilings of 3–8 hectares were recommended.

MAGSAYSAY'S REFORM OF 1955

Of the three parties contesting the 1953 election, Magsaysay's was successful because he showed the greater sense of urgency towards land reform. His overwhelmingly rural vote reflected his energetic electoral campaign, in which he visited three-quarters of the country's municipalities and half the villages and hamlets, professing an obsession with the problem of the landless.

Magsaysay's 1955 Reform Act aimed to 'create a peaceful, prosperous and stable agrarian structure by distributing family plots to landless labourers through the opening up of public land and the division of private land either by agreement with the landowners or by expropriation'.[29] Despite Magsaysay's sincerity, the programme was under-financed, poorly administered and eventually corrupt. The president's appeal to rich landowners in central Luzon to trade their haciendas for public lands in Mindanao found few respondents. Landlords held up the bill for two years and inserted various provisions which blunted and even crippled its effectiveness. Magsaysay proposed a ceiling of 144 hectares, but landlords' amendments empowered the government to acquire land only upon petition of a majority of the tenants on a landholding and only for areas exceeding 300 hectares of 'contiguous land' owned by 'natural persons' (i.e. with no specification of individual or family membership, thus allowing estates to be subdivided to avoid expropriation), or exceeding 600 hectares of land owned by corporations. Even if these limits had been vigorously enforced only about 1·5 per cent of Philippine farmland could have been transferred. Compensation for expropriated land was to be in cash; land acquired was to be sold to tenants 'at cost', in lots not exceeding 6 hectares, for repayment in 25 annual instalments at 6 per cent interest. The Act's key provisions were weak and difficult to enforce, and Magsaysay's death in 1957 removed any chance the reform had of achieving significant progress.

No detailed information on the achievements of the 1955 reform is available, but they were clearly negligible. In central Luzon the position of tenants and smallholders worsened over the period of the 'reform'. Between 1948 and 1960 tenanted farms increased from 35 per cent to 40 per cent of the total. Population in the seven central Luzon provinces grew by 40 per cent while the number of farms below 1 hectare increased by 9 per cent, but the area they covered diminished by 22 per cent. Farms over 20 hectares decreased by 8 per cent but the area increased by 114 per cent. So a considerable concentration of land ownership—a 'reverse land reform'—was occuring *in spite of* the 1955 reform, with increasing unemployment, social polarisation, economic stagnation and political unrest.

THE 1963 LAND REFORM CODE

Renewed rural unrest in 1962 prompted President Macapagal to try a firmer approach to land reform. Again, however, landlord opposition within the government diluted the new Land Reform Code (1963) so that it was effective only as a political compromise. Land redistribution would be the end of a long and involved prgoramme of transition from tenancy to ownership. Expropriation was deferred to the unforeseeable

M

future. The Code (applying only to rice land) specified three stages in agrarian reform. During the first sharecropping would be converted into leasehold, consigning a 25 per cent rental share (of average net production over the previous three years) to the landowner. In the second the leasehold is converted, over twenty-five years, to ownership through amortisation, while the third stage, registration of ownership title, could not be reached until the tenant had paid off the costs of land acquisition. Purchase of private estates, by negotiation or expropriation, continued as before, with the ceiling set at 75 hectares (but estates of over 1024 hectares were to be tackled first). Financially, the Code favours the landlord; the constitution apparently allows expropriation only against payment of 'just compensation', interpreted by landowners as full market value. One tenth of the compensation is paid in cash, the rest in 25-year, 6 per cent bonds, exchangeable at par for various purposes. These compensation costs are eventually born by the beneficiaries, who pay in twenty-five annual instalments plus 6 per cent interest—possibly the most burdensome beneficiary repayments of any reform anywhere.

No quantified estimates were made in 1963 of what the reform would achieve, but Marcos, who became president in 1966, announced he would convert 350 750 share-tenants into lessees by 1970. In fact only 28 616, just 8 per cent of the target, had leasehold contracts by then. Only in 1970 was all central Luzon proclaimed land reform territory; although this implies that share tenancy officially ceases, on at least 20 per cent of the farms it continues.[30] Despite the law, landlords are still able to oppress attempts at emancipation by share-tenants.[31] Acquisition of estate land for redistribution has been similarly limited. Large landowners are reported to have subdivided holdings into 75 hectare parcels amongst family members, or converted rice land to surgarcane to avoid expropriation. Only 6100 hectares were redistributed during 1963–8, insignificant against the 7 million hectares of agricultural land.

The whole structure of the 1963 law favoured bureaucratic delays. Only when all the necessary services are installed for efficient land utilisation can a region be declared a reform zone. Only 31 per cent of the reform budget for 1966–70 was released. In the absence of yield records, the basing of leasehold rent on three years' average yield added another three years before this provision could operate, and produced conflict of interests between landlord and tenant. For the landlords, the longer the delay the better their chances of increasing the yield and therefore the eventual lease rent. The tenants refused to plant high-yielding varieties and use improved cultivation methods unless and until they held leasehold contracts. The 25 per cent level looks fair to the tenant at first sight but this stipulation applies only to the land. For seed, fertiliser, irrigation, etc., usually provided by landlords, additional rent could still be charged.[23]

The 1963 reform has brought few perceptible changes in land tenure patterns, rural living standards or agricultural productivity. Rice yields increased by 40 per cent between 1964 and 1970, reflecting essentially not land reform but new high-yielding varieties, greater inputs of fertiliser, irrigation and credit, and government encouragement of rice production (including a price increase of 35 per cent),[33]

THE FUTURE

In 1971 a new Amendment Act to the 1963 Code made some progress towards a thorough land reform. A new cabinet-level Department of Agrarian Reform replaced the various existing unco-ordinated departments and promises greater effectiveness. It will work closely with an Agrarian Reform Institute set up in the University of the Philippines for research, evaluation and training of personnel. Much needed emphasis is placed on co-operative development. The 1971 Act also abolishes all share tenancy in favour of leases, and empowers courts to decide lease rentals summarily.

The declaration of martial law and the promulgation of the government's 'New Society' programme in late 1972 again altered the prospect of agrarian reform radically. The whole country was made a land reform area and all tenants of privately owned rice and maize land will be owners of the land they till. The high priority accorded agrarian reform as a cornerstone of the New Society policy is further reflected in the national Four-Year Development Plan for 1974–7.

REFERENCES

1. S. M. Akhtar: 'The land tenure situation in Pakistan', in K. H. Parsons, R. J. Penn and P. M. Raup (eds.): *Land Tenure* (Madison, University of Wisconsin Press, 1956), pp. 125–33.
2. A. S. Haider and F. Kuhnen: 'Land tenure and rural development in Pakistan', *Land Reform, Land Settlement and Co-operatives*, 1–2, 1974, pp. 52–67.
3. W. Bredo: 'Land reform and development in Pakistan', in W. Froehlich (ed.): *Land Tenure, Industrialisation and Social Stability: Experience and Prospects in Asia* (Milwaukee, Marquette University Press, 1961), pp. 260–72.
4. See L. Nulty: *The Green Revolution in West Pakistan* (New York, Praeger, 1972).
5. G. Mohammad: 'Private tubewell development and cropping patterns in West Pakistan', *Pakistan Development Review*, 5 (1), 1965, pp. 1–53.
6. M. G. Chaudhry: 'Rural income distribution in Pakistan in the green revolution perspective', *Pakistan Development Review*, 12 (3), 1973, pp. 247–58.
7. R. Herring and M. G. Chaudhry: 'The 1972 land reforms in Pakistan and their economic implications', *Pakistan Development Review*, 13 (3), 1974, pp. 245–79.
8. B. J. Esposito: 'The politics of agrarian reform in Pakistan', *Asian Survey*, 14 (5), 1974, pp. 429–38.
9. Bredo: *op. cit.*, p. 263.
10. C. M. Elkington: 'Land reform in Pakistan', in Agency for International Development: *Spring Review of Land Reform* (Washington, Department of State, 1970), Vol. 2, p. 23.
11. I. Ahmed and J. F. Timmons: 'Current land reforms in East Pakistan', *Land Economics*, 47 (1), 1971, pp. 55–64.
12. See A. R. Khan: *The Economy of Bangladesh* (London, Macmillan, 1972).
13. M. A. Zaman: 'Bangladesh: the case for further land reform', *South Asian Review*, 8 (2), 1975, pp. 97–115.
14. M. Alamgir: 'Some aspects of Bangladesh agriculture', *Bangladesh Development Studies*, 3 (3), 1975, pp. 261–300.
15. M. Hossain: 'Farm size and productivity in Bangladesh agriculture', *Bangladesh Economic Review*, 2 (1), 1974, pp. 469–500.
16. Khan: *op. cit.*, p. 138.
17. Zaman: *op. cit.*
18. N. Sanderatne: 'Tenancy in Ceylon's paddy lands: the 1958 reform', *South Asian Review*, 5 (2), 1972, pp. 117–36.
19. B. H. Farmer: 'On not controlling subdivision in paddy lands', *Transactions, Institute of British Geographers*, 28, 1960, pp. 225–35.
20. N. Sanderatne: 'Sri Lanka's new land reform', *South Asian Review*, 6 (1), 1972, pp. 7–19.

21. This account is from E. Utrecht: 'Land reform in Indonesia', *Bulletin of Indonesian Economic Studies*, 5 (3), 1969, pp. 71–88.

22. S. M. P. Tjondronegoro: *Land Reform or Land Settlement: Shifts in Indonesia's Land Policy 1960–70* (Madison, University of Wisconsin, Land Tenure Center Paper 81, 1972), pp. 4–5, 9–13.

23. E. Utrecht: 'Land reform and *Bimas* in Indonesia', *Journal of Contemporary Asia*, 3 (2), 1974, pp. 149–64; G. Hansen: 'Rural administration and agricultural development in Indonesia', *Pacific Affairs*, 43 (3), 1971, pp. 390–400.

24. J. E. Spencer: *Land and People in the Philippines: Geographic Problems in Rural Economy* (Berkeley, University of California Press, 1954), p. 49.

25. See G. F. Rivera and R. T. McMillan: *An Economic and Social Survey of Rural Households in Central Luzon* (Manila, Philippine Council for US Aid, 1954).

26. E. H. Jacoby: *Man and Land* (London, Deutsch, 1971), p. 344.

27. E. J. Mitchell: 'Some econometrics of the Huk Rebellion', *American Political Science Review*, 63 (4), 1969, pp. 1159–71.

28. O. D. van den Muijzenberg: 'Political mobilisation and violence in central Luzon', *Modern Asian Studies*, 7 (4), 1973, pp. 691–705.

29. H. D. Koone and L. E. Gleeck: 'Land Reform in the Philippines', in Agency for International Development: *Spring Review of Land Reform*, *op. cit.*, Vol. 4, p. 39.

30. P. R. Sandoval and B. V. Gaon: 'Some effects of land reform in selected areas of the Philippines', *Journal of Agricultural Economics and Development*, 2 (1), 1972, pp. 235–42.

31. See A. Takahashi: *Land and Peasant in Central Luzon* (Honolulu, East-West Center Press, 1970).

32. See F. J. Murray: 'Land reform in the Philippines: an overview', *Philippine Sociological Review*, 20 (1–2), 1972, pp. 151–68.

33. Koone and Gleeck: *op. cit.*, pp. 78–81. A survey of 376 farmers in the Bulacan land reform district of central Luzon revealed that 60 per cent of those affected by the reform expressed disenchantment with the results and 44 per cent actually preferred the traditional share-tenancy or *kasam* to new leasehold contracts. A study of Nueva Ecija (the region that the 1963 reform had had most impact by 1970) reports that many lessees had no objection to the *kasam* system under a good landlord. See G. D. Feliciano: 'Sociological considerations in communicating change to Filipino farmers in five barrios of the land reform pilot area in Bulacan province', *Philippine Sociological Review*, 14 (4), 1966, pp. 257–65; R. Pahilanga-de los Reyes and F. Lynch: 'Reluctant rebels: leasehold converts in Nueva Ecija', *Philippine Sociological Review*, 20 (1–2), 1972, pp. 7–78.

PART 4

Land Reform in Africa

Introduction

The land reform problem in Africa south of the Sahara (see Part 5 for North Africa) differs from agrarian problems in other continents. In Tropical Africa tribal or communal ownership is dominant. With few exceptions, such as the *mailo* system of Buganda, which originated in colonial mismanagement of traditional land tenure, land ownership is widely diffused rather than confined to a small landowning aristocracy and tenancy is not widespread. Land redistribution *sensu strictu* is therefore limited to one or two countries, Kenya being outstanding. The problem has been to define rights to land and determine the relative emphasis on individual as against communal rights in changing technological and socio-economic conditions.

The exuberant growth of natural vegetation and the rapid regeneration of second growth following clearing disguise the fact that natural conditions in Tropical Africa are not very favourable for agriculture. Over much of sub-Saharan Africa rainfall is so marginal or erratic that farming is hazardous, or so intense that it leaches the soil, producing deterioration and erosion. Under half of Africa between latitutdes 30° north and south has adequate rainfall—about 800 mm per year—for intensive agriculture. By contrast, in the great rain forests of the equatorial and Guinean belts excessive rainfall becomes damaging as soon as monthly precipitation exceeds about 200 mm. Perhaps two-thirds of the land in Central and East Africa is not usable for agriculture. There is, nevertheless, no 'environmental curse' on Black Africa. Natural conditions may be rather more difficult than elsewhere in the world, but they can be overcome, particularly given the reserves of energy and minerals, the lack of pressure on land and the advances possible with modern agricultural techniques. René Dumont writes that men alone are responsible for Africa's economic backwardness.[1] The question is which ones, Africans or Europeans. Many Europeans, quick to call the Africans primitive and lazy, blame the natives, forgetting that white men exploited the African for centuries through slavery, colonisation and economic exploitation. This may be so, but nobody can say where Africa would be today had it developed without colonialism.

Over 80 per cent of Africans south of the Sahara live from agriculture. African agriculture is overwhelmingly that of peasant farmers, and mostly subsistence or semi-subsistence. This holds despite some European settlement, which anyway is being reduced with decolonisation and the division of European holdings amongst African smallholders. Subsistence production generally provides over two-thirds of the value of agricultural output, and is far less productive for land and labour than is commercial farming. It is undertaken within the customary tenure system by individual or extended family units, commonly part of a tribe or similar social structure, and is mostly non-monetised.

Initially, and still true in places, abundant land permitted extensive exploitation and ready access for the whole community to utilisation of land. In fact initial settlement and clearing of virgin land were major means of securing title; many groups and individuals still hold land solely by virtue of initial occupancy. With ample land available, society displayed little interest in how the land was utilised or in protecting people's rights of cultivation, and shifting cultivation was accepted without question. The problem originates when population growth, the increasing need to raise productivity and to husband natural resources leads to conflicting interests and rights between individuals and groups.

Since the First World War the productivity of African peasant labour has dropped by about 20 per cent. Since 1959 food output has risen on average 1·7 per cent per year, population 2·5 per cent. In West Africa particularly rates well above 3 per cent will, if sustained, cause an eighteenfold increase of population in a century. Areas or 'islands' of overpopulation are expanding outwards. Nevertheless, most of Tropical Africa remains thinly peopled. An average density of under one person per square kilometre gives a crude man–land ratio twelve times as favourable as that of India. Unlike the great riverine plains and deltas of the Far East, Africa does not yet have its back to the wall.

The African peasant cultivator has been characterised as a smallholder planting an area of around 1–4 hectares, frequently in small and scattered plots.[2] Although it is often assumed that limitations of technique keep holdings small, in fact few peasants cultivate as much as their labour and limited techniques would allow. Rather they generally cultivate enough for basic food needs and sell any surplus they can. Indeed underemployment is characteristic of African agriculture; one estimate gives around 100 days per year as an average peasant's workload.[3] A vital limitation is lack of market demand for surplus produce; the market system is still widely distrusted and non-economic activity, leisure is highly preferred to higher income. Beyond these general descriptive statements, the African peasant remains subject to widely divergent interpretations; objective studies of him and of the many African tenure systems are few. African peasant cultivation is criticised as primitive, wasteful of resources, even destructive of soil and vegetation; it has also been defended as a remarkable adaptation to the environmental conditions, and a low-cost form of production essential at that stage of economic development.[4]

European colonisation in Tropical Africa disturbed the equilibrium between Africans and the land, especially in East Africa. In West Africa, Europeans were interested primarily in trade and left production of tropical products to indigenous farmers; the threat of tropical disease and the later British policy of protecting African land rights overrode any desire to acquire and settle land. East Africa had substantial upland areas with environment favourable to European colonisation and farming, and in South Africa, too, Europeans were more interested in land than in trade. The effects of colonial rule and the extent of colonial exploitation of land have been conditioned by local geographical and socio-economic factors; they also reflect the degree of the natives' resistance and the different European powers involved—Britain, France, Germany, Belgium and Portugal.[5]

In Africa Europeans encountered land systems so different

from their own that they often misinterpreted them. They regarded the tribal chief as owning the land, whereas generally he was only the trustee of his tribe's lands. Sometimes tribal wanderings were spatially restricted by the establishment of native reserves; sometimes characteristics of tribal identity were suppressed. In nineteenth-century French colonial administration the theory of 'eminent domain' presumed that native chiefs had surrendered their domains to the state. Even when, at the end of the century, this view was abandoned, colonial legislators could still exploit the vagueness of customary tenures. The celebrated *Arrêté Faidherbe* of 1895 maintained that the *'terrains vagues'* in French West Africa belonged to the state and were available for colonial concessions. It also authorised natives possessing land to apply for full title to it. Consequently only possession of titled land so granted was recognised and legally protected, and others occupied land on sufferance. Despite this virtually no customary landholders applied for official title, preferring 'the gift of their ancestors' to what they considered a spurious title.[6] A 1955 law enabled chiefs legally to cede tribal rights over uninhabited forest land so that it could be occupied by large plantations worked by migrant labour. In the Ivory Coast and the Camerouns this law, allowing chiefs to draw large incomes by overriding communal ownership, impeded native development considerably.

Experience in British Africa was pretty similar.[7] Slavery disrupted the indigenous development of African society. Colonialism brought the economic life of Africans under the control of European governments and companies. Table 22 indicates the European penetration into the landownership pattern of various British African territories. In Southern Rhodesia, for example, the British South Africa Company purchased large areas and also established Native Reserves. After the 1925 Morris Carter Commission 'possessory segregation', officially endorsed, aimed at reducing contact between African and European landholders to a minimum. Finally, the right of Africans to own land in the colony was withdrawn.[8]

'African agricultural development' writes Dumont boldly, 'must go beyond its colonial framework'.[9] This is easier to prescribe than to perform. Even in the post-colonial era of aid and investment the pattern remains basically unchanged. Capital is attracted mainly to mining—to South Africa, Rhodesia and the Congo (Zaire)—while the expanded infrastructure is largely to

TABLE 22

EUROPEAN LAND AND POPULATION IN SOUTH AND EAST AFRICA, 1958–60

	Percentage of land alienated or reserved by Europeans	Percentage of population who are Europeans
South Africa	89·0	19·4
Basutoland	0·0	0·3
Bechuanaland	6·0	1·0
Swaziland	49·0	2·8
Southern Rhodesia	49·0	7·1
Northern Rhodesia	3·0	3·0
Nyasaland	5·0	0·3
Kenya	7·0	1·0
Uganda	0·5	0·2
Tanganyika	0·9	0·2

Source: M. Yudelman: Africans on the Land (Cambridge, Harvard University Press, 1964), Table 2, p. 19.

facilitate trade with Britain. With independence Africans inherited a situation which makes continuation of the colonial powers' economic policies almost unavoidable. The more modern sector of their agriculture remains geared to export crops, whose production does not necessarily meet the rural masses' needs. The luxury demands of the governmental elites, imitating expatriates' social habits, absorb much foreign exchange earning.[10] Urban prestige projects swallow money needed by rural areas: this 'South-Americanisation', the progressive separation of rich capital towns from poor countryside, is particularly notable in Abidjan.[11]

The colonial powers have left an indelible imprint on the economic structure, tenure institutions and land use patterns of their former dependencies. This maintains dualism in many forms: in the co-existence of customary and statute law, of subsistence and monetised sectors of the economy, of tribal majority and westernised elite. Only in Kenya has individual tenure penetrated far enough to generate land reform; other countries remain uncomfortably poised between customary tribalism and confused post-colonial tenure situations. Agrarian reforms have so far yielded only modest results, both in scope and quantity—they are in fact still in their initial stages.

REFERENCES

1. R. Dumont: *False Start in Africa* (London, Deutsch, 1969), p. 32.
2. W. B. Morgan: 'Peasant agriculture in Tropical Africa', in M. F. Thomas and G. W. Whittington (eds.): *Environment and Land Use in Africa* (London, Methuen, 1969), ch. 9.
3. M. Yudelman: *Africans on the Land* (Cambridge, Harvard University Press, 1964), p. 17.
4. Morgan: *op. cit.*, pp. 241, 243.
5. J. Hellen: 'Colonial administration policies and agricultural patterns in Tropical Africa,' in Thomas and Whittington: *op. cit.*, ch. 12.
6. F. M. Mifsud: *Customary Land Tenure in Africa* (Rome, FAO Legislative Series 7, 1967), p. 4.
7. J. Hatch: 'A note on English-speaking Africa', in Dumont: *op. cit.*, ch. 20.
8. B. Floyd: 'Land apportionment in Southern Rhodesia', in R. M. Prothero (ed.): *People and Land in Africa South of the Sahara* (London, Oxford University Press, 1972), pp. 225–38.
9. Dumont: *op. cit.*, p. 123.
10. D. Owen: 'The ecology of underdevelopment in Tropical Africa', *International Journal of Environmental Studies*, 4 (1), 1972, pp. 27–32.
11. Dumont: *op. cit.*, p. 239.

15

Kenya

As the one country in sub-Saharan Africa to carry out a large-scale land reform, including both consolidation and redistribution, Kenya merits special attention. Land has always conditioned Kenya's social, economic and political life. Largely through the lack of minerals and their industries, economic development signifies rural development. Yet two-thirds of the country, largely in the north and north-east, is unsuited to agriculture: these semi-arid lands are largely left to nomadic pastoralists like the Masai and the Turkana. Kenya is the first Black African country to opt decisively for individualised land tenure. Although individual tenure originated in colonialism, its diffusion over the settled parts of the country has been since independence in 1964. Good source material on Kenya's land reform, apart from some dearth of very recent studies, permits a fairly comprehensive picture. The picture must be detailed to be accurate, for different schemes, involving redistribution, consolidation, settlement and irrigation, operated at different places at different times, and the situation remains somewhat complex. We must, however, distinguish straight away two broad programmes: land tenure reform, chiefly land registration and consolidation of fragmented holdings, launched by British colonial officials in 1954 in 'African' areas, largely stimulated by the Mau-Mau rising, and continued by the independent African government; secondly, schemes for settling African farmers on former European land, particularly in the 'White Highlands'. Both reforms are continuing, the government simultaneously seeking to maximise economic productivity in the settlements, and extending land consolidation and title registration to the thousands of farmers not yet affected.

EUROPEAN COLONISATION OF THE WHITE HIGHLANDS

Apart from the climatic suitability for European settlement of equatorial land above about 1500 metres, two factors facilitated white colonisation in the Kenya Highlands.[1] Firstly, settlement was expedited by the construction (1896–1902) of the Uganda railway from Mombasa to Lake Victoria, and was necessary to make the railway pay. To the early settlers only land adjacent to the railway had any commercial value. Early settlement thus followed the alignment of the railway, and the boundaries of the Highlands were long determined with reference to two railway stations, Kiu and Fort Ternan, located at the points where the line crossed the 1500 metre contour. Secondly, the spread of European settlement away from the railway axis reflected the native population distribution at the time. Separating areas of dense African settlement and intensive farming (the high rainfall areas of Nyanza bordering Lake Victoria, the slopes of Mt Kenya and the Aberdares), extensive high plains with lower and more uncertain rainfall saw only occasional grazing, or were uninhabited no-man's-land between tribes. Large areas were controlled by the warlike Masai of southern Kenya. The Uasin Gishu plateau had remained unused since the mid-nineteenth century, when Masai tribesmen had evicted the original occupants. Another deserted tribal battleground, separating the territories of the Kisii and the Kipsigis, was occupied by the European farmers of Sotik, a colonial policy bid to separate warring tribes. Of the 4700 square kilometres of European settled land, 2800 consisted of former Masai grazing territory, evacuated under agreements between 1904 and 1910, most of the remainder being almost completely uninhabited. Under native methods of cultivation these areas could have supported only a sparse population. With the ox-drawn plough, however, Europeans could farm these areas effectively, and could set the profits of good years against the inevitable drought which would reduce an African subsistence farmer to starvation.

Implementing a racially-based European settlement policy, with landownership in the Highlands denied to Africans— though not to Indians, who having come as traders and railway navvies, were permitted to settle the lower Highlands towards Kisumu—was officially sanctioned in 1906, but not until 1939 were the boundaries of the 'Scheduled Areas' (the term 'White Highlands' has always been avoided officially) gazetted (Fig. 9). The Highlands was not a continuous region but comprised blocks of land between the great extinct volcanoes of Mt Kenya (5194 metres) and Mt Elgon (4321 metres), straddling, in a rough horseshoe, the Great Rift Valley, here at its highest eleva-

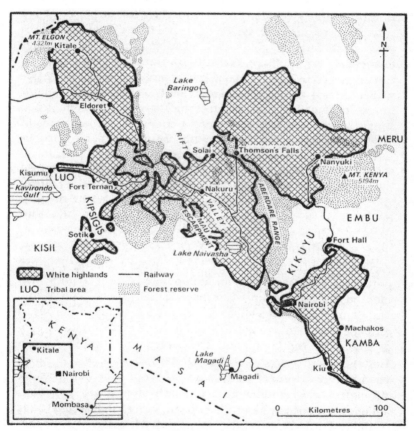

Fig. 9.   The White Highlands of Kenya. *Source:* W. T. W. Morgan: 'The White Highlands of Kenya', *Geographical Journal*, 129 (2), 1963, p. 143

tion. On either side lie the Aberdare and the Mau Highlands, elongated ridges reaching 4000 and 3000 metres respectively. The White Highlands blocks were separated by African-occupied territories, notably Kikuyuland, and Forest Reserves, the latter included within the Highlands for convenience but not available for settlement.

The European colonisation of the Kenya Highlands spanned the first sixty years of this century, during which the enclave group received much governmental assistance. The introduction of a money economy and of markets for surpluses above subsistence requirements were incidental to the main line of progress in the Highlands, where land use and other agricultural changes were impressive. Natural grassland and bush savanna were replaced by fields of maize, wheat and sisal, and the disease-ridden Masai cattle by imported high quality beef or dairy herds. In 1959–60 the farm land of the Highlands covered 30 000 square kilometres, and from this 5 per cent of the land area of Kenya came the vast majority of the country's exports, particularly of coffee, tea, sisal and pyrethrum.

The White Highlands thus initiated Kenya's agricultural export economy, but land alienation and settlement also created the current land problem. Although the land settled by Europeans was sparsely populated, most of it came under the geopolitical sphere of influence of tribal groups. Kikuyu claims were particularly strong and necessitated official enquiries as early as 1910. Expansion of Kikuyu territory and agriculture, particularly westward into underpopulated Masai country, was blocked by surrounding European-settled areas. The White Highlands' boundaries effectively created an island of European settlement surrounded by African lands, forming a natural pool of labour for the Highlands. Deliberate limitation of African Reserves increased pressure on Africans to work on the European holdings. Moreover, because of European settler pressure, Africans were forbidden to grow cash crops, such as coffee, which were successful on European farms and would have stimulated African rural development more directly. Also crucial to the 1960 decision to open the Highlands to farming by all races was the population pressure contrast between the 'empty' Highlands and the peripheral African territories, except Masailand. Within the Highlands, except for the Nairobi region,

densities were mostly well below 20 per square kilometre; elsewhere they averaged 25, and in problem areas (Kikuyu, Kisii
and Luo territories) exceeded 75.

DECOLONISATION AND LAND REFORM IN THE WHITE HIGHLANDS

The year 1960 was a turning-point. The Mau-Mau Emergency, which ended then, had produced considerable disruption, including the enforced 'villagisation' of over a million
Kikuyu. In 1960, too, an Order-in-Council ended the limitation of the White Highlands to exclusive European land ownership and occupation. Africans were assisted to buy land from
European farmers, many of whom wished to liquidate their
farming assets before independence occurred in December,
1963. Thefts, trespass and lawlessness emphasised the running
down of the colonial farms by their owners before their departure. Nationalist leaders urged redress of the 'unjust acquisition'
of the Highlands by Europeans as an essential element in giving
Africans justice. The economic desirability of land reform was
not questioned, because of its political inevitability; nevertheless the only likely alternative to an ordered resettlement programme was the collapse of commercial farming and reversion
to subsistence agriculture and random grazing. Out of the complex politics of this immediate pre-independence period (1960–
63) came the important programme of settling some 40 000 African families on about 500 000 hectares of former 'white' territory.[2]

Four main objectives governed the settlement programme.[3]
The first was to further diminish the European farmers' waning
influence in the Scheduled Areas by giving Africans land. The
second was social—to settle landless natives and help to relieve
pressure on the increasingly overcrowded African areas. The
third was economic-technical—to introduce, under supervision,
a significant number of African farmers to advanced agricultural
methods to raise per hectare production from £10·80 to £20·40.
From this increased production the settler could pay off loans
for land purchase and technical assistance, and eventually become much more prosperous. Fourthly, the programme had
long-term national objectives: to improve the country's social
and political climate by creating a stable landowning rural
society, with the African farmer possessing a secure position
and a respected socio-economic status.

With finance from the British and West German Governments, the Commonwealth Development Corporation and the
International Bank for Reconstruction and Development, three
types of scheme were initiated (Fig. 10):

(1) Most important in area covered (400 000 hectares, the
famous 'Million-acre Scheme', running from 1962–1967) and
numbers settled (35 000 smallholder families) are the 122 High-
density Schemes. Each settlement has 3000–4000 settlers on

Fig. 10. African settlement schemes in the former White Highlands of
Kenya. *Source:* H. Hecklau: 'Die agrarlandschaftlichen Auswirkungen der
Bodenbesitzreform in den ehemaligen White Highlands von Kenya', *Erde*,
99 (3), 1968, pp. 250–1

about 4000 hectares, averaging 10–13 hectares per family. Target net annual family income, originally £25, was subsequently raised to £40 then to £70 in parts of the Highlands. High-density schemes were for Africans with limited capital and agricultural knowledge; settlers were mostly selected on criteria of poverty and unemployment.

(2) Low density schemes are for farmers with some working capital and experience of advanced agriculture and farmers were recruited on their likelihood of proving competent settlers. They had to contribute £50 (later £100) of their own capital, and the holdings assigned them were designed to produce annual net cash incomes of £100–200. Some forty schemes embrace over 5000 families on 90 000 hectares. On average, each scheme has 100 settlers on 2000 hectares.

(3) Yeoman (or 'Assisted Owner') Schemes were for experienced farmers with substantial capital resources (at least £500). This foresaw European estates divided into rather large holdings capable of yielding African purchasers a net income of £250 per year, but after 129 transactions in 1961–2, it was discontinued.

In addition, European farms have been transferred to Africans by other means. Two important 'offshoots' of the main Highlands colonisation policy are the Nandi and Ol Kalou Salients, the former on 7000 hectares of land thought to have been wrongly alienated to Europeans, the latter on 60 000 hectares of land occupied by African squatters in 1965. Loan co-operatives also enabled groups of African farmers to buy European farms with help from the Kenya Agricultural Bank. Often the co-operative form continues to operate the farm; this form of organisation may have an important future in the Kenya Highlands.

From the beginning, tribal considerations seriously circumscribed the reform's freedom to relieve population pressure,[4] which was particularly high in Kikuyuland, the Kamba District of Machakos and in the Luo District of Central Nyanza. Tribal 'spheres of influence' in the Highlands remain strong; to have disregarded them would have produced tribal warfare. Generally the aim was to allocate each tribe both a High and a Low-density Scheme. The Masai, however, who originally had held much of the alienated land, provided almost no settlers for the land reform programme.

Controversy about the success of the land reform in the White Highlands centres chiefly on the economic merit of replacing large-scale European-run farms with African smallholdings. Many of the settlement schemes have not been conspicuously successful. One detailed survey found only 17 per cent of the farms reaching target incomes by 1967.[5] Another indicated average annual farm profits of 14–20 per cent, apparently impressive but frequently inadequate to cover loan repayments.[6] At the end of 1965, 62 per cent of repayments were overdue, mostly from High-density Scheme settlers who had had to borrow a higher percentage (up to 90 per cent) of their farming capital than farmers on Low-density Schemes. Defaulting on repayments is also related to settlers' views of the colonial land question. Kikuyu previously employed on European farms, therefore generally above-average farmers, have the worst repayment records, because they consider the land their natural right.[7] Equally, though, output and income have dropped where adequate management of the new holdings has been beyond the less educated beneficiaries.

Generally, despite local failures, the productivity of the land has been maintained, if not substantially increased. The disappointing early figures were partly explicable by the difficulties of the take-over and by a severe drought in 1964–5, which particularly affected the maize and livestock areas; output increases have since been impressive, even on High-density Schemes (Table 23). Indeed much recent evidence suggests that the High-density plots have become more successful than the Low-density holdings.[8] From recent sales by co-operatives, Odingo[9] concludes that crop production has been greatly intensified, pyrethrum suffering from occasional overproduction. Other cash crops include coffee, tea, sugar, sisal, wheat and vegetables. With active encouragement of livestock on the new farms, dairying is particularly strong, while many large co-operative settlements specialise on beef ranching. Labour productivity must, however, have fallen drastically compared with the European estates (figures are not available). Increased per hectare output must, therefore, reflect a greatly swollen population—4000 Europeans (plus their African labourers) being replaced by nearly 200 000 African settlers on the reform areas of the Highlands—rather than improved efficiency.

TABLE 23
FARM OUTPUT AND NET PROFITS ON THE KENYAN MILLION ACRE
SCHEME

Year	Value of output K shs. per hectare	Net farm profit K shs. per hectare
Pre land reform	161	n.a.
1964-5	160	13
1965-6	247	80
1966-7	299	122

Source: Official sample survey quoted in E. S. Clayton: 'Agrarian reform, agricultural planning and employment in Kenya', *International Labour Review*, 102 (5), 1970, p. 441.

The process of resettlement and racial *volta-face* in the former White Highlands constitutes, according to one observer, 'the most rapid change in the economic and human geography of an area of this size ever experienced in East Africa'.[10] About 40 000 smallholdings have replaced some 800 European estates covering nearly half a million hectares. The new farms with their fenced paddocks, stalls, Jersey cattle and crops display the new pattern of farming; and new roads, schools, shops and dairies show new communities being created. Buying, planning and allocating the land within the allotted time was a considerable administrative achievement. The change from large to small-scale agriculture may well have been economically too abrupt, but maximising output was considered less important than accommodating Africans on land previously owned by Europeans. True, against the total of needy agricultural folk in Kenya, the beneficiaries are few—about 3 per cent—but the programme has been socially and politically valuable. The White Highlands were a symbol of colonialism; their settlement by Africans was an accomplishment of nationhood.

LAND REFORM IN KIKUYULAND: REGISTRATION AND
CONSOLIDATION

Since 1965 the Kenya government has increasingly doubted the economic justifiability of settlement schemes like the massive White Highlands project and the smaller-scale, more rudimentary African Land Development ('ALDEV') schemes of the 1950s for resettlement in African areas, and this kind of policy has been drastically curtailed. A government policy statement in April 1965 indicated a radical shift from European to African areas and from settlement to consolidation. Few major new settlement schemes have been initiated, agricultural development funds being now channelled mainly toward land demarcation, registration and consolidation; these measures, basically aimed at individual, compact holdings, are the vehicle for rural improvement and peasant capitalist entrepreneurship throughout the country. It is claimed in Kenya that consolidation and individual tenure have made possible a rural revolution,[11] with cash crops like coffee and tea, formerly grown principally by non-Africans, increasingly produced at high quality standards on African smallholdings supplied with credit, quality control and other measures. Consolidation, however, pre-dates the White Highlands resettlement, and, like so much in Kenya, had its beginnings in Kikuyuland.

Kikuyuland roughly covers the districts of Nyeri, Fort Hall and Kiambu, the south-west of Central Province. Physically it is a dissected volcanic plateau, inhabited between 1200 and 2000 metres. Relief and clan organisation are closely linked, with clan boundaries along the ridge-tops between the many parallel east-west valleys running down from the Aberdare Mountains. Although shifting agriculture had once predominated, when the Europeans arrived Kikuyu land tenure had already achieved some individuality in the *githaka* system. Each *githaka* constituted the land or estate belonging to a sub-clan or extended family (*mbari*), in which each member had a plot for individual cropping use, grazing land remaining communal. Tenant relationships also existed: a *muhoi* (plural *ahoi*) enjoyed temporary cultivation rights based on friendship paying only an annual tribute of beer and produce; a *muthami* could additionally erect buildings on land he was working. There were no villages; each individual built his hut on his land, usually near the ridge tops.

This land tenure system provided no problems while population density remained low. It was possibly already quite high at the turn of the century, but changes introduced by the Europeans upset whatever traditional equilibrium remained. Although little Kikuyu land was alienated, elimination of tribal warfare and medical control of diseases, such as smallpox and plague, produced rapid population increase. Allan[12] put the critical population density for preserving a non-deteriorating agricultural ecology at about 65 persons per square kilometre; by 1940 Kikuyuland population density exceeded this by 50 per cent. Pressure for full individual ownership of increasingly scarce land was great, and communal grazings were enclosed. Fragmentation became excessive, land continually being divided up amongst farmers' sons. Cropping of land of over 30° slope caused soil erosion. In these circumstances the Kikuyu system broke down rapidly in a chaos of subdivision and fragmentation and degenerated into virtually continuous cultivation of a mixture of basic food crops. An obvious landless class emerged. Many were *ahoi* working fragmented parcels too remote for their owners to use, but the landless mostly migrated to work on European estates, or to Nairobi and other urban centres. In 1912 12 000 Kikuyu lived outside the Reserve, by 1940 200 000, a quarter of the Kikuyu population. Meanwhile, within the Reserve, land accumulation by chiefs, tribal elders and the educated minority fostered class antagonism amongst the Africans themselves.

Organised Kikuyu action against the British started in the 1920s. The Young Kikuyu Association and the Kikuyu Central Association, formed respectively in 1921 and 1924, campaigned for the return of the 'stolen lands'. The young men behind these movements, like Harry Thuku and Jomo Kenyatta, were mission-educated migrants to Nairobi; they could prosecute political activities characteristic of the country's capital, but they retained strong family and friendship links with the Reserve.[13] Disappointment with the 1934 Kenya Land Commission—it recommended the addition of just 78 square kilometres of land to the Reserve in compensation for Kikuyu 'losses'—spurred the growth of Kikuyu 'independence' action groups in the 1930s; whether this would have become a true African nationalist movement, or whether it would have degenerated into tribal chauvinism was still uncertain when the Second World War broke out. With early post-war colonial policy still short-sightedly favouring European settlers against Africans, the 'Mau Mau' storm exploded in the early 1950s. Mau Mau was largely inspired by deep-seated Kikuyu land hunger, but besides hatred of the Europeans antagonism erupted between those Kikuyu who had benefited from colonialism and those who had not.

The outstanding geographical aspect of the Mau Mau Emergency stemmed from the decision in 1954 to 'villagise' the Kikuyu. Within a year over a million Africans were herded into 854 villages, sited usually on or near the ridge-tops in easily defensible locations. Individual settlements were banned. The villages were laid out with geometric precision, each householder being allowed about ·05 hectares. Although 'villagisation' was essentially a punitive measure, to detach the guerillas in the forests from their supporters in the Reserve, it produced a marked change of heart of the population. Many Kikuyu came to like village life: it offered possibilities of employment in handicrafts; services could be provided in nucleated settlements, and in each village sites were allotted for schools, churches and community buildings. Punitive action was replaced by efforts to civilise the Kikuyu and complete their conversion from Mau Mau barbarism. Most important, however, 'villagisation' facilitated consolidation of Kikuyu land. With all the people removed from the land, consolidation of fragmented parcels proceeded unhindered by established homesteads, argumentative farmers and political interference. Consolidation and a vigorous programme of farm development, it was hoped, would deflate Kikuyu political agitation by creating prosperous farmers, who could employ most of the landless Kikuyu.

Consolidation was the cutting edge of the far-sighted Swynnerton Plan, which, on a budget of £8·5 million, aimed at increasing African farmers' incomes tenfold where agricultural potential was high, as in Kikuyuland. Many Kikuyu already realised that consolidation was necessary for agricultural improvement—indeed there had been instances of spontaneous consolidation in the 1940s—so the programme was not being forced upon unwilling recipients. Consolidation, within a *githaka* framework, was based on the common wish, ascertained at open meetings; if consolidation was desired, an adjudication area was designated for the programme. Generally areas which were 'loyalist' during the emergency were treated first.

The reform had two main ingredients. Firstly, consolidation ended fragmented holdings. Secondly, prevailing land tenure rules were replaced by freehold property. Transition to the new order entailed measuring and recording the fragments to which holders could establish a claim, calculating the entitlement of individual farmers, demarcating and assigning the new holdings, and, finally, registering these newly assigned units and issuing titles to their owners.

Each claimant received a consolidated holding roughly equal to the sum of his previous fragments, with a small percentage cut, usually 10 per cent, for land for roads, schools, community centres etc. Although the agrarian landscape was radically recast, no redistribution of rights occurred, the new holding sizes being governed by traditional claims on land rights. Wherever possible, the new holding was demarcated around the largest fragment or the parcel containing permanent improvements, such as buildings or tree crops. Where such investments were unavoidably lost through consolidation, compensation was paid. In siting the consolidated holdings the demarcation committees tried to give each plot access to road and water and to include the various types of land previously possessed. Consequently most holdings were laid out as long narrow strips running from ridge-top to valley bottom. Ridge-top land, flat with deep soils, is suitable for new huts and homesteads and for communications, and the deep soils favour garden crops. The well drained valley-side land is the chief cropping zone, especially for cash crops, like coffee and tea, and the valley-bottom land, with heavy black alluvial soils subject to seasonal flooding, is prized for sugar-cane, used for beer-making.

Four geographical patterns thus emerge in the evolution of Kikuyuland tenure and settlement.[14] First, the old clan-based system of dispersed settlement was associated with traditional, semi-shifting cultivation. Second, population pressure led to individual ownership of land, followed by fragmentation. Third came the strongly nucleated settlement pattern of the Emergency, and finally the more mixed pattern after post-1954 consolidation. This last, the present landscape of Kikuyuland, comprises well-defined parallel strip holdings, regular settlement dispersion and ribbon development along the ridge-top roads, with the old Emergency villages shrinking, but surviving, as people move out on to the land (Fig. 11).

The Swynnerton Plan also prescribed careful land use planning, to be implemented following consolidation, aimed at providing on each holding enough food for subsistence plus a cash

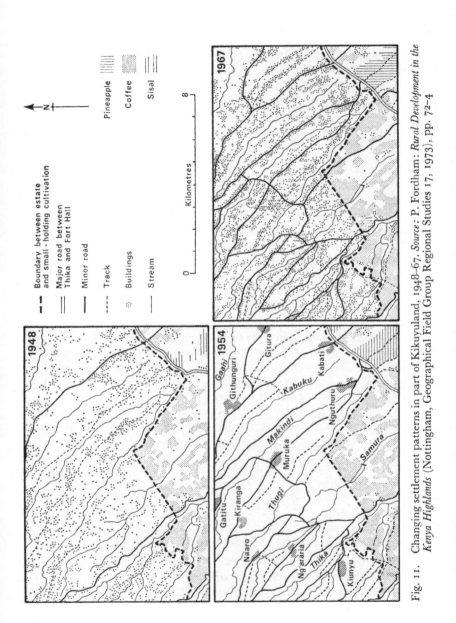

Fig. 11. Changing settlement patterns in part of Kikuyuland, 1948–67. *Source*: P. Fordham: *Rural Development in the Kenya Highlands* (Nottingham, Geographical Field Group Regional Studies 17, 1973), pp. 72–4

income of £100 per year. Although consolidation is now virtually complete, land use planning has lagged, essentially because of shortage of trained extension workers. Since 1963 the preparation of farm plans has ceased. Cash cropping, however, started immediately; *arabica* coffee is now the most important cash crop. From 1954 to 1965 Fort Hall District coffee growers increased from 109 to 12 920, the value of their product from virtually nil to £750 000. African smallholders, in co-operative societies, are actually producing better quality coffee than the European estates.

Consolidation in Kikuyuland quickly gained momentum. By 1958 it was complete in Kiambu District and by 1959 in Nyeri, but in Fort Hall, the third Kikuyu district, not until the late 1960s; here the difficult terrain, strong vested interests, the high percentage of absentee landowners and the necessity of some resurveying after 1960 combined to impede progress. Consolidation was truly a stupendous task. In Kiambu, for example, about 420 000 fragments were measured and consolidated into some 50 000 holdings, a job executed by 98 committees with 2 750 members, with a staff of 14 senior officers, 500 surveyors and measurers and 1000 labourers, at a cost of £2 per hectare.[15]

Balanced appraisal is, however, difficult because appropriate data are lacking and because consolidation is accompanied by other changes such as soil conservation, transport improvement and agricultural extension work. Any changes that have taken place—the doubling of incomes Taylor records[16] or the massively increased cash crop revenues reported by Barber[17]—therefore reflect all these factors rather than just consolidation. Other observers have noted the increase in number of schools and schoolchildren, and the increased funds of local people and local bodies.[18] Consolidation and registration, by ending traditional litigation over land, released for production resources previously wasted on court fees and bribery. Registration enabled many farmers, previously unable to obtain agricultural credit, to offer their land as security for loans from government credit agencies and commercial banks.

Other rural economic changes have also emerged. With the increased wealth, villages acquire additional functions. Specialised shops replace the former general stores and some villages approach the status of small towns, with branch banks and small post offices. With rural overpopulation still afflicting Kikuyuland, these incipient urban centres can provide some job opportunities for unemployed. Others become agricultural labourers on the new consolidated holdings. A 3-hectare Kikuyu farm under intensive cash crops has work for five adults. Although only 15 per cent of holdings are 3 hectares or larger (the average is just below 2 hectares), even smaller farms tend to devote much of their income increase to employing hired labour. De Wilde's detailed data on consolidation effects in Nyeri District revealed that most types of farm hired about half their total labour.[19] Although expenditure on hired labour could be reduced by more efficient use of family labour, this tendency does distribute more widely the economic benefits of consolidation and commercial farming. Male labour has also been working the land more actively than formerly. Originally, Kikuyu men considered themselves herders and warriors, leaving agriculture to the womenfolk. Consolidation and extension, by introducing high-grade cattle and high-value cash crops, coffee especially, have absorbed much underutilised male labour.[20]

Consolidation in Kikuyuland found its most intractable problem in the conflict between the political necessity to base holding sizes on land previously claimed and the Swynnerton Plan objective of economically rational farming. Most consolidated holdings were below the critical limit for 'rational farming', 2–3 hectares. For social reasons the government had to allow much subdivision down to subsistence level. The landless are still 10 per cent of the population, many of them *ahoi* moved off the land by consolidation.[21] In this respect consolidation reform actually intensified the problem of landlessness. Legislation forbids refragmentation, but with pressure on the land market traditional boundary marks have appeared within larger holdings, indicating that parts are being rented or sold off.[22] Within Kikuyuland progress varies between farmers and between districts. Only landholders with 3 hectares or more can get credit to improve their holdings. Kiambu, near Nairobi and the most progressive district, contains some of the most advanced, market-oriented farms in Tropical Africa; critical factors here have been the proximity of the largest urban market in Kenya and stimuli from close contact with the European urban and farming communities. Fort Hall, *per contra*, lags behind the other two districts; the Kikuyu 'heartland' has the most conservative elements, the most difficult topography, with much land too steep for cultivation, and the most serious migration and absenteeism.

Whilst there were, and still are, protests about the way consolidation took place, the Kikuyu have generally endorsed the new system by their subsequent actions. Allan wrote 'Nowhere else in Africa has there been any general programme of agricultural improvement so complete, and initially so successful, as the rehabilitation of the Kikuyu territory following the Mau-Mau Emergency'.[23] Consolidation brought peace to the region politically, and a near-revolution economically. The tenure innovations, indeed, might not have been so successful without the cultural shock injected by general land hunger, the loss of faith in the traditional land pattern and the Mau Mau movement.

PROGRESS ELSEWHERE

Consolidation has become an article of faith of post-independence agricultural policy. Although already by independence in 1963 over 500 000 hectares of land had been registered, mostly in Central Province, the new government extended and accelerated the reform. By 1971 2 235 000 hectares were registered, representing, with land consolidated but not yet registered, nearly a third of the agricultural land outside the former scheduled areas. Estimates for 1975 are 4 million hectares of agricultural land and 5 million hectares of range land.[24] Despite charging fees for surveying and titling, the government has been unable to match the demand for consolidation and registration.

In some regions, progress has been particularly slow. In Meru District, clan opposition is strong. The Meru were never 'villagised', and coffee growers with considerable investment in mature trees cling to their fragmented holdings. Where the Meru and the Embu have accepted the reform, the motive has been primarily to prevent landless Kikuyu from encroaching on their land. Nevertheless, only the Kamba of the Machakos District and the non-Bantu Luo of central Nyanza have registered outright rejection of consolidation, and even here there has recently been progress. The Kamba have been reproached for their lack of interest in agriculture and for their unresponsiveness to government efforts to improve farming, but the daunting ecology of the drought-stricken Machakos District is perhaps the principal obstacle to progress.[25] The Nilotic Luo, too, live in dry country, near Lake Victoria. They are predominantly pastoral, with few crops; 90 per cent of their output is subsistence production. Tea and pyrethrum cannot be produced at all, coffee in only limited zones. Population pressure and fragmentation are serious. The Luo, as the second largest tribe in Kenya and the main political rivals of the Kikuyu, regarded land reform as a punitive measure for the Kikuyu. Luo politicians preached that their people would be forced into villages like the Kikuyu during the Emergency, and that consolidation portended alienation of land to Europeans. Luo elders and large cattle owners opposed reform because it would diminish their powers and restrict their grazing areas. By 1960 fewer than 2000 holdings had been consolidated. With reform staff withdrawn in 1963 through financial stringency, post-independence progress remains extremely modest.

Irrigated settlement schemes form the final kind of Kenyan land policy considered here. Among government-organised projects the Mwea rice scheme, located 100 kilometres north-east of Nairobi on the dry plains south of Mount Kenya (Fig. 10), is largest and clearly most successful.[26] The scheme, commenced in 1952, accommodated landless Kikuyu detained during the Mau Mau revolt. Despite an unpromising start, with unwilling and unskilled labour, by 1960 the building and irrigation works were largely complete and considerable productive gains were being manifested. The scheme now supports about 1700 tenants and their families on holdings of four plots of one acre (0·4 hectares) each. On an area formerly made inhospitable by low rainfall, tsetse fly, wild animals and Masai raiding parties, irrigation and the efforts of new communities now produce 12 000–15 000 tons of rice, worth some £300 000, per year. By 1958 average annual income per tenant at £109 surpassed the £100 per farm family of the Swynnerton Plan. Irrigation is expanding from the first phase of 800 hectares to 4000 hectares. Rice yields on the 'black clay' soils reach 5·8 tons per hectare, among the highest in the world. Over 80 per cent of the rice consumed in Kenya comes from Mwea. Increased cash incomes have banished any recalcitrance there was immediately after Mau Mau. The economic success of the Mwea scheme reflects very tight official control over its running. The tenants do the weeding, transplanting, reaping and threshing. The management provides mechanical cultivation, thus controlling timing of operations, collects the bagged paddy and prepares it for transport to the mills. Mwea has succeeded after a very unpromising start —a rare achievement in Tropical Africa—and has pioneered irrigation and rice cultivation in Kenya.

CONCLUSION

Kenya's pioneering experience in land reform and land settlement is of undoubted interest to other African nations. It has ended the uncertainty of customary tenure and provided for improved incomes based on cash cropping. Its least publicised objective—the creation a stable middle class built around Kikuyu loyalists to forestall further subversion—has also largely been achieved. President Kenyatta's residence at a prosperous coffee farm outside Nairobi symbolises the new 'squirearchy' already apparent in parts of the country.[27] *Redistribution* effects of the reforms, however, were minimal: compensation to the Europeans displaced from the White Highlands was financed largely by the British taxpayer and African settler repayments; and what consolidation really did was to consolidate the position of existing landowners. 2·7 million hectares of land remains in large farms, including 800 000 hectares (over half) of the former White Highlands, while 50 per cent of smallholdings, covering 4 per cent of agricultural land, are less than 2 hectares in size. In Central Province 86 per cent of smallholdings have been unaffected by the development of commercial agriculture and remain at a subsistence level. The scope for further land reform is considerable.

Population growth—over 3 per cent per year—severely strains the country's resources. Local high man-land ratios and rural immobility aggravate the problem. Nevertheless agriculture must absorb the bulk not only of the existing population but also of its increase. The employment-creating aspects of Kenya's agrarian reforms are thus very important. Clayton's comparison of Kenya's three major reforms is therefore interesting. Irrigated settlements, such as Mwea, absorb far more labour, but at a far higher cost, than the other two policies. Subdividing large farms into smallholdings (land reform in the

N

White Highlands) contributes more modestly to additional employment at fairly high cost. Most effective, judged by cost-employment, is consolidation and intensification of existing smallholdings.

Nevertheless, over the last twenty years the gap has widened between the small minority of progressive farmers and most of the rural population. Again one must question whether reform can be truly successful unless the rural population share widely in its benefits. Even in Nyeri District, a major consolidation zone, only 15 per cent of the farm area and 10 per cent of the farmers were involved.[29] Reform policy is still implemented within a tribal framework; it is thus caught in the cross-fire between those who wish to push it to its logical, economic, non-tribal extreme, and those who fear that their own people could not compete in a non-tribal society based on individual landownership.

REFERENCES

1. W. T. W. Morgan: 'The "White Highlands" of Kenya', *Geographical Journal*, 129 (3), 1963, pp. 140–55.
2. For details see J. W. Herbeson: 'Land reforms and politics in Kenya 1954–70', *Journal of Modern African Studies*, 9 (2), 1971, pp. 165–87.
3. J. W. Maina and J. D. MacArthur: 'Land settlement in Kenya', in A. H. Bunting (ed.): *Change in Agriculture* (London, Duckworth, 1970), pp. 427–35.
4. N. S. Carey-Jones: 'The decolonisation of the White Highlands of Kenya', *Geographical Journal*, 131 (2), 1965, pp. 186–201.
5. H.-W. von Haugwitz and H. Thorwalt: *Some Experiences with Small-holder Settlements in Kenya* (Munich, Weltforum for IFO-Institut, Afrika-Studien 72, 1972), p. 43.
6. J. C. de Wilde: *Experiences with Agricultural Development in Tropical Africa* (Baltimore, Johns Hopkins for I.B.R.D., 1967), Vol. 2, p. 213.
7. *Ibid*: Vol. 2, pp. 196–7.
8. For example G. Gwyer: *Trends in Kenya's Agriculture in Relation to Employment* (Nairobi, University of Nairobi Institute of Development Studies Discussion Paper, 153, 1972), p. 12.
9. R. S. Odingo: 'Settlement and rural development in Kenya', in S. H. Ominde (ed.): *Studies in East African Geography and Development* (London, Heinemann, 1971), ch. 14, pp. 174–5. This may not be such a significant result as here implied because much European farming was not particularly intensive, partly because of localised poor land quality; indeed much of it is very marginal for African smallholder farming. Further, there are considerable regional variations in the agricultural regime and economic success of the small holdings. These

are detailed in von Haugwitz and Thorwalt: *op. cit.*, pp. 32–62; and H. Hecklau: 'Die agrarlandschaftlichen Auswirkungen der Bodenbesitzreform in den ehemaligen White Highlands von Kenya', *Erde*, 99 (3), 1968, pp. 236–64.

10. D. G. R. Belshaw: 'Agricultural settlement schemes on the Kenya Highlands', *East African Geographical Review*, 2, 1964, pp. 30–6.
11. But outside observers do not concur with this claim; for example de Wilde: *op. cit.*, Vol. 1, p. 82.
12. W. Allan: *The African Husbandman* (Edinburgh, Oliver and Boyd, 1965), p. 178.
13. M. P. K. Sorrenson: *Land Reform in Kikuyu Country* (Nairobi, Oxford University Press, 1967), pp. 21, 37.
14. D. R. F. Taylor: 'Changing land tenure and settlement patterns in the Fort Hall District of Kenya', *Land Economics*, 40 (2), 1964, pp. 234–7.
15. Sorrenson: *op. cit.*, ch. 9.
16. D. R. F. Taylor: 'Agricultural change in Kikuyuland', in M. F. Thomas and G. W. Whittington (eds.): *Environment and Land Use in Africa* (London, Methuen, 1969), ch. 17, pp. 479, 483.
17. W. J. Barber: 'Land reform and economic change among African farmers in Kenya', *Economic Development and Cultural Change*, 19 (1), 1971, pp. 6–24, especially the table on p. 17.
18. P. Fordham: *Rural Development in the Kenya Highlands* (Nottingham, Geographical Field Group Regional Studies 17, 1973).
19. de Wilde: *op. cit.*, Vol. 2, pp. 44–5, 55.
20. Barber: *op. cit.*, p. 19.
21. Taylor: 'Agricultural change in Kikuyuland', *op. cit.*, p. 480.
22. *Ibid.*
23. Allan: *op. cit.*, p. 392.
24. B. K. Herz: 'Land reform in Kenya', in Agency for International Development: *Spring Review of Land Reform* (Washington, Department of State, 1970), Vol. 9, p. 52.
25. de Wilde: *op. cit.*, Vol. 2, pp. 84–120.
26. *Ibid*: Vol. 2, pp. 221–41; also J. Nderitu: 'The Mwea-Tebere Irrigation Scheme in central Kenya', *East African Geographical Review*, 5, 1967, pp. 55–7.
27. Sorrenson: *op. cit.*, pp. 201, 233.
28. E. S. Clayton: 'Agrarian reform, agricultural planning and employment in Kenya', *International Labour Review*, 102 (5), 1970, pp. 431–56.
29. de Wilde: *op. cit.*, Vol. 2, p. 82.

16

The Problem of
Customary Tenures

The cardinal feature of African customary tenure, before its gradual breakdown under the impact of population pressure and colonial policies, was its consonance with traditional land use systems, which in turn were well adapted to ecological limitations. The extended family, the basic unit for land occupance, was both the production and the consumption unit. Agricultural production and social security were intertwined in a low-level equilibrium system evolved over centuries of trial and error.

The term is very generic distinguishing this type of land law from western or imported types, yet covering innumerable land tenure situations, with diversity as significant as common features.[1] Diverse customary tenures reflect diverse economic activity, settlement patterns, social and political organisation. Clear contrasts appear between, say, shifting cultivators and such settled farmers as the Kikuyu of Kenya or the Ibo and Yoruba of West Africa; or between pastoral nomads herding camels (e.g. the Somali) or cattle (the Masai) and settled pastoralists, such as the Zulu of South Africa and the Hima of East Africa. Nevertheless, certain features shared by different African customary tenures lend them a family likeness.

Most important is the communal aspect of tenure. At least theoretically, all members of a community have right of access to land for cultivation, pastoralism, hunting, gleaning, fishing and residence; there are no landless people since everyone has the right to live on the land and work it. Generally usage rights stop short of ownership, but continued usage itself guarantees some security of tenure. These communal land-operating groups are either social or political. Social or family organisation is intimately linked with the exploitation of land, with clan, lineage or household control over the individual's use of land. Bohannan[2] has demonstrated the spatial expression of customary tenure groupings among the Tiv of central Nigeria. The Tiv see geography in terms of social organisation; their names for settlements and for natural features are based on the names of the lineages customarily occupying the area. They see their land as a genealogical map, which moves about the surface of the earth, responding to the demands of the farmers.

Political groups may be merely the territorial expression of social groups, but in all larger societies the territorial limits, both central and local (the tribe, the district, the village), and the political authorities in these units (e.g. the chief, the village headman, the council of elders) have special powers connected with land rights. In many Central African tribes chiefs give land not directly to users but allocate it via sub-chiefs and village headmen, the number of steps depending on the depth of the socio-political structure.[3] Land, then, is the dominant element in rural Africa's social and political groups, not just because it provides subsistence but also because on it rests the maintenance of sovereignty; and the common African view of land as a sacred heritage whose integrity must be preserved reinforces this attitude.[4]

Secondly, customary tenure is closely associated with shifting cultivation and with subsistence agriculture. Shifting cultivation implies impermanence of titles to land, but even without shifting agriculture titles of individual ownership of farm plots may be impermanent, subject to control by tribal authorities. With impermanence of titles goes indeterminacy of plot or farm boundaries. Tenure boundaries often follow natural features; sometimes only a baseline and the direction of expansion of farming into virgin forest are indicated.

A third characteristic is absence of commercial transactions in land. Ancient customary law did not forbid alienation of land; rather, it did not provide for alienation since it was not needed. With plentiful land no one needed to buy or rent a plot, and with land matters controlled by a chief the individual occupier could not transfer what was not his. To many Africans, land is not a commodity but 'nature, which is not produced by man'. Economically, land under customary tenure may be para- doxically viewed as a free but rationed good: rationed because supply is not unlimited, the rationing process being the tribal allocative procedure; and a 'free good' because it has no price or market value, fertile land in a good location having the same zero price as poor land.[5] Any value it has is an intrinsic or psy- chic value, and this emotional value often surpasses the money value it would have as a factor of production. For Africans land has a mystical quality. It embodies the spirit of the Earth God- dess, 'a revered mother who blesses the land with her bountiful gifts'. Land is also the burial place of ancestors, and in West Africa it has been said to belong more to them than to the living occupiers; it comprises the patrimony of a vast family, many dead, some living, and countless numbers as yet unborn. So important can the land's religious or supernatural significance be that sometimes it is controlled by 'landpriests', such as the *tendanas* of northern Ghana, who are quite distinct from the political chiefs.[6]

The strengths and weaknesses of customary tenure should be recognised. Some writers consider customary tenures unequivo- cably bad, doomed to disappear sooner or later. This over- simplification ignores their advantages and also the considerable possibilities, at least in the short and medium terms, for develop- ing agriculture within the customary framework. Archaic features are not the rule everywhere. The customary system has proved sufficiently flexible to have accommodated the rapid recent increases in cash cropping in many African countries— examples are cocoa in Ghana and groundnuts in Senegal. A second advantage of customary tenures is that the absence of a land market has prevented significant native land speculation and land grabbing. Absentee landlordism has not yet appeared; nor, with security of occupation, if not of tenure, built into the system, has the problem of landless peasantry. Lastly, and above all, customary tenures condition and consolidate the cohesion of the group, whether a simple kinship group or the whole village community.

Customary tenure has the following major disadvantages: it is uncertain; it provides only limited security of tenure; it discourages conservation and improvement of natural resources; it does not encourage the credit and investment necessary for development; it perpetuates clan rivalries and tribal divisions.[7] In short it impedes individual efforts to improve farming methods. Giving the economic power to the heads of extended families confines the levers of progress to the oldest people, often the least receptive to new ideas. With most chiefs over sixty years of age, chiefdom seems a formidable brake on development.

THE DILEMMA OF INDIVIDUALISATION

Land policy in Africa is torn between the desire to preserve traditional tenure and the impulse to modernisation—which usually means westernisation and individualisation of tenure. Underlying this controversy are differences in the emphasis on security on the one hand and on maximising output on the other. Modern changes, such as cash cropping and technical innovations, have simplified tenure arrangements, with reduction in the number of right-holders; this relationship is supported by Uchendu's Tropical African case studies.[8] Some African countries have taken steps to create a system of individual private property like the western European, notably Kenya, Uganda, Malawi, Niger and Ethiopia, although not yet over the whole of any of them.

Several factors strengthen the individual's position in the political and family groups.[9] Titles are becoming more certain, often recorded in written form, and cultivation more settled as cash crops and tree crops are developed. Governments have encouraged individualisation with laws forbidding land use and land tenure arrangements which promote soil deterioration, or by prescribing new systems of land holding (e.g. the 1951 Native Land Husbandry Act in Southern Rhodesia). Population pressure is also important. The happy times when land was sufficient for all tribe or group members are passing in certain regions. Population growth, through health improvements and the cessation of slave raiding and inter-tribal warfare, has drastically affected regions like Kikuyuland in Kenya and Iboland in Nigeria. Whether to continue encouraging individual tenures is a difficult question for many African countries. A free land market, with unrestricted right to buy and sell, may well be dangerous. Land being bought up by the highest bidder could lead to land concentration of the Latin American or Asian type. In areas near big towns, where widespread individualisation of tenure has taken place, the tendency is to subletting at high rents to small and needy farmers. It would be an historical irony if, just when land reform action tries to change outdated tenures in Asia and Latin America, precisely the same agrarian systems were being established in African countries still in their early years of independence.

Generally, it seems that the introduction of individual tenures should be related to the stage of evolution of a country's farm sector. Gerschenberg[10] advises African governments to leave customary land laws well alone or to harmonise land reform legislation with local customary tenures. A revolutionary land redistribution reform is not a necessity in much of Africa. Where land reform legislation is enacted prematurely, entrenched local opposition prevents effective changes; Senegal and Cameroon exemplify reform legislation which has had little impact on the ground.[11] Mifsud describes the 1963 Cameroon reform legislation, which is linked to redistribution of population to the underdeveloped east, as 'one of the most comprehensive undertaken in Africa in recent years', adding almost as an afterthought that 'the programme of land redistribution in eastern Cameroon has still to be implemented'.[12]

ALTERNATIVES

Few countries have opted wholeheartedly for individual tenure in land reform policy. Realising the dangers in private land ownership, many have experimented with alternative tenure structures. The nucleus plantation, the *paysannat*, the Gezira type of settlement organisation, state farms, group and co-operative farming have all been tried. No single model is universally applicable because of the regional variety within the African continent.

Some countries, notably Nigeria, have introduced nucleus plantation schemes. A central plantation with a processing factory is surrounded by smallholdings growing the same crop as the plantation and using its processing services. The plantation is usually established and run by a foreign firm which offers technical assistance to the smallholders. Eventually the farmers may take over and run the scheme as a co-operative or with government management. Nucleus plantations are perhaps the best solution to the problem of existing plantations rather than a model for diffusion elsewhere, largely because of the difficulty of attracting foreign capital to start plantation farming.

The state farm, too, seems of limited value in Africa. Virtually all the state farms launched in Guinea appear to have failed. Much better documented is the Ghana state farm fiasco.[13] State farms were created in Ghana in the early 1960s to reduce food imports, diversify agricultural production and demonstrate the advantages of large-scale mechanised 'socialist' farming over small-scale peasant farming. They were also intended to break down the traditional life and social cohesion of the villages, which were felt to threaten Nkrumah's rule. Village land was taken with no compensation, many peasants being turned into landless labourers. In February 1966, when Nkrumah was ousted, 135 state farms had 20 800 labourers on their books. Nearly half these workers were, however, former Ministry of Agriculture employees declared redundant in a sweeping official reorganisation in November 1962. Under half the 100 000 hectares of state farm land was actually cropped; state farms never exceeded 1 per cent of the country's cropped area. Management was poor and over-centralisation of decision-making in Accra produced interminable administrative delays. Financial wastage was enormous; 'perhaps nowhere else in the tropics (could) so many tractors be seen lying . . . abandoned in the bush.'[14] After 1966 many state farms, including nearly all the arable ones, were disbanded. Labour strength on the rest, estimated at twice the real requirement, was substantially reduced. Pig keeping and cattle ranching had also proved unprofitable and livestock numbers decreased. Only with rubber, oil-palm, rice and poultry keeping was any success achieved.

At the opposite end of the spectrum the *paysannat* form has been developed, especially in the former Belgian Congo.[15] The Belgian approach to modernising traditional agriculture in the Congo was aimed at rationalising, rather than fundamentally altering, the indigenous systems. It recognised the lack of European experience in farming Tropical Africa, and appreciated the essential ecological and cultural soundness of traditional procedures. The first *paysannat* was established in 1936 by the *Institut National pour l'Étude Agronomique du Congo Belge* at its

Gandajika experimental farm in the low savannah; others followed, both locally and around the great Yangambi research station in the equatorial forest in 1940-2. The *couloir* system, which organises shifting agriculture into strip or corridor cultivation, became standard layout, particularly in high forest country. Long, east-west, parallel strips about 100 metres wide are demarcated and cropped for short periods and then revert to natural vegetation for a longer period (e.g. 3 years of crop rotation followed by 15 years fallow). Width and orientation of the 'corridors' are important: strips too wide make regrowth slow in the middle; strips too narrow reduce crops by shading and bordering effects of the forest. The east-west orientation ensures sufficient sunlight at this optimum width. In the high savannah, where long corridors are not required, a different form of *paysannat* put blocks of land (*fermettes*) under semi-individual family ownership. The *paysannat* system permits the introduction of cash crops (bananas, rubber, cotton), and of mechanisation, seed control, central processing and extension services without disturbing the basic traditional, customary framework. *Paysannats* were not, however, an end in themselves but a stage on the road to modernising and intensifying indigenous agriculture. What proportion survived the disruption of Congo's independence and the withdrawal of expert supervision is unclear.

Tanzania is implementing a more forward-looking communal land policy, with neighbouring Zambia following more cautiously. Nyerere's 1967 Arusha Declaration—judged by some as the high spot so far of African economic development policy—introduced an agrarian development strategy that aims at social and economic transformation of rural life by creating *Ujamaa Vijijni* or multi-tribal, communal, socialist villages. These are intended to retain the good of the traditional agrarian system, particularly the principles of co-operation, sharing and self-help, whilst incorporating the good of new agricultural technology. They avoid the inequalities modernisation and increased production bring when achieved solely by market forces. To Nyerere the Ujamaa village is a way of life, a political unit and an economic entity: 'while some nations are aiming at the moon, we are aiming at the village.'

In 1967 Georgulas estimated that 8·8 million Tanzanians lived in traditional scattered settlements, only 455 000 in nucleated rural villages.[16] The *Ujamaa* policy is to concentrate or 'villagise' the population, both to achieve the communal ideal and to provide social and economic services. By mid-1973 5630 *Ujamaa* villages, containing 2 million villagers, 15 per cent of the national population, were functioning. Most are in the more backward areas, especially in the south, bordering Mozambique, although Dodoma registered outstanding growth in 1971, when 80 villages were established in three months. Size varies greatly. Some *Ujamaa* settlements have fewer than ten families, yet Chamwino in Dodoma Region had 6000 inhabitants in 1971.[17] Some villages were established by the relevant government authorities, some voluntarily by the farmers themselves, while others were simply a move towards communal activities by some of the 500 or so traditional nucleated villages in Tanzania. So the *Ujamaa* village is not stereotyped. Within the basic *Ujamaa* philosophy (equality of all, dignity in communal work, no exploitation etc.) each peasant group is encouraged to find the form of socialist village which suits it best. This flexibility, recognising regionally varying conditions, is probably the best guarantee of success.[18]

Ujamaa works best where land is plentiful and peasants wishing to remain outside the new villages can find land to work on their own. With land scarce, as on Kilimanjaro, in the coastal plain and around Lake Victoria, problems are greater. Areas with profitable smallholdings or well-developed capitalist agriculture have few *Ujamaa* villages. Generally large farmers are unwilling to join, since their production, and hence their income, would decline, at least in the short term; very poor farmers are conservative for other reasons. The keenest candidates are younger men with little or no land.

Tanzania seems well started towards becoming a nation of Swahili-speaking co-operative farmers dwelling in multi-tribal, government-controlled villages. The President himself spends his vacations living and working in *Ujamaa* villages, an example followed by Tanzanian MPs. Criticisms concern poor organisation of labour, insufficient technical knowledge, undue importance attached to the individual plots, and the characteristic extremely high birth rate. Education and local leadership are crucial for the villages' progress. But the chief unknown concerns tenure. Although existing legislation could be used to expropriate land for *Ujamaa* villages, extinguish outdated tenure systems and institute new arrangements, the tenure position of the villages remains undefined, varying according to traditional custom.[19] When the landholding situation is cleared, Tanzania could well be 'a new recipe for rural Africa'.

Land settlement, the other main prong of African land policy, transforms agrarian landscapes and benefits small farmers and landless labourers, but as land is rarely redistributed from large landowners, it is not considered here in detail. Land settlement anyway is a much larger topic than land reform in Africa.[20] Settlement schemes are extraordinarily varied in motivation, organisation, administration, land use, size, cost and results. Gezira in Sudan and the *Office du Niger* project in Mali are two of the largest and oldest. In Ghana the huge Volta dam lake displaced a population which the government evacuated and re-settled, and examples and types could be multiplied. Motives have shifted somewhat from the need to redistribute population from overcrowded regions to the desire for agricultural moder-nisation and the establishment of a market economy. Gezira proved that settlement and agricultural co-operation could suc-ceed given intelligent, devoted leadership, but most government-sponsored settlements have faced severe difficulties and many have failed to meet their objectives and cost the governments large sums to little effect.[21]

ETHIOPIA: LAND REFORM IN EMBRYO

Finally we consider Ethiopia, a special case with unique ten-ure characteristics, where land reform has recently become a live issue. Ethiopia is one of the very poor countries of the world. The economy, with coffee forming 60 per cent of exports, is stagnating, with annual income only £30 per capita and nearly 95 per cent of the population illiterate. Ethnic and reli-gious diversity—Christian Amhara dominant in the Central Highlands, Moslems in the east and negroes in the south—threatens continual conflict.

The complexity of Ethiopian land tenure defies brief outline. Many features are archaic and untraceable in origin, and ten-ures display great regional variation. Landholding and social stratification patterns, at least of traditional Christian Ethiopia, are not typical of the more classless societies of sub-Saharan

Africa. Individual holding of land (or similar forms of tenure), tenancy and absentee landlordism lend a feudal flavour to the agrarian structure. Recent official sample surveys show two-thirds of the holdings in the north reduced to one hectare or less. In southern Ethiopia, more recently incorporated into the Empire, acquisition by northern noblemen of expropriated native land has rendered numerous peasants landless. Share-cropping agreements, generally unwritten, give the landlord 40 to 50 per cent of the produce. Tenants have little legal security but most remain on the same piece of land for some time. Absentee landlordism covers 20 to 30 per cent of the holdings in most provinces, over 40 per cent in some. Recent famines have forced many peasants to sell their land and livestock for a pittance to buy food.

Two basic tenure concepts in Ethiopia are *rist* and *gult*.[22] *Gult* rights rewarded members of the ruling elite for loyal service, and endowed religious establishments. *Gult*-holders collect taxes from those who farm their land, and exercise juridical and ad-ministrative authority over those who live on it; *gult* rights are, therefore, more than just a type of tenure. Virtually all culti-vated and settled land in Amhara is held by someone or some institution as *gult*. One *Ras* (feudal lord) or monastery may hold many such estates. To the peasants, however, each *gult* estate is a distinct unit, akin to a parish. *Rist* rights are basically land use rights, and have no exact parallel elsewhere in Africa. *Rist* hold-ings are assembled partly through heredity (both from immedi-ate ancestors and on supposed descent from a 'chief father' of the parish), and partly through status, power and need. *Rist* rights, too, carry eligibility for certain local administrative and minor ecclesiastical offices. The system admits, therefore, some social mobility: *rist*-holders are potential *gult*-holders, though few become so. *Rist* and *gult* are complementary types of land rights, which normally cover the same estate. A *gult* estate, com-prising perhaps a thousand hectares or more, would include scores or even hundreds of strips belonging to *rist*-holders. A locally-born *gult*-holder would have some areas of *rist* within his own *gult* estate, and the peasants living on his estate might be required to give the 'governor of the *gult*' several days of labour per year to help him cultivate his *rist* fields.

There is, however, considerable regional deviation from the

rist-gult system. In Eritrea the rough analogue of the Amhara *rist* is *resti*, rights based on membership of an Eritrean descent group. Another major form of Eritrean tenure is village ownership, *diesa* or *shehena*; here residence in a village rather than membership of a descent group justifies an individual's claim to usufructory rights over a portion of land. In southern Ethiopia the high rate of tenancy (about 45 per cent of holdings) reflects its nineteenth-century conquest by the Amhara. By the *sismo* system two-thirds of the conquered land was assigned to northern notables, the remainder to indigenous elites (*balabbats*), who thus prospered under Ethiopian rule. Finally, the Ethiopian Orthodox Church holds much land under various tenures in various areas.

Ethiopian history records many land reforms, all highly political, designed to reward one group, punish another or further the ruler's power.[23] Attempts at modern land reform date only from 1961 when the late Emperor appointed a Land Reform Committee, and in 1966 a Ministry of Land Reform. This ministry surveyed land tenure in the fourteen Ethiopian provinces (though with little information about size distribution), and drafted reform proposals, including tenancy reform, land tax reform and registration of titles. Expropriation and redistribution were only acknowledged as long term possibilities. Despite their mildness, these proposals received little legislative backing. Only two tax reform measures, enacted in 1966–7, carried implications for land reform. One required *gult* landowners to pay direct to the government treasury the land tax they had previously shifted to the peasants, making a profit on the transaction. The second extended income tax to agricultural activities, which were previously exempt. Yet these tax changes encountered armed resistance from the very peasants they sought to help. Proposals for tenancy regulation, repeatedly brought before the Council of Ministers in the early 1970s, were bitterly opposed by landowning interests in the government. Ethiopia's third Five Year Development Plan (1968–73) viewed short-term agricultural progress as attainable only by rapid expansion of large scale export-oriented commercial farms. Of the 1968–73 allocation to agriculture (which was only 12 per cent of the Plan budget), 61 per cent went on the relatively few commercial farms and only 10 per cent on the millions of peasant farms. At least 80 per cent of new land grants went to non-farming civil servants and military officers who simply leased the land to peasants.[24]

The 'Long Revolution' of 1974 finally overthrew the corrupt and feudal Selassie régime; a 3000 year old dynasty was broken. Land reform is the key issue for the new socialist ruling military council, the Dergue. Army-prompted student and worker demonstrations called for communal farming and the creation of collectives and state farms, but disagreement over how this was to be achieved produced delays. The new land reform law finally enacted in 1975 declared all rural land to be 'the collective property of the Ethiopian people'. All landlord-tenant relationships ceased to exist, the peasants being declared possessors of land currently occupied, pending more formal allocation of family-size plots of up to 10 hectares. Large-scale farms may be organised as state farms. Land distribution and most other agricultural services (including the constitution of various types of co-operative) are placed in the hands of newly created peasant associations based on existing villages or blocks of land up to 800 hectares. By April 1975 1300 peasant associations had been formed.[25]

At this early stage prognosis of Ethiopian land reform is difficult. While the south is largely held by absentee landlords in great estates, ripe for reform, *rist* smallholders in the north bitterly oppose co-operative farming and have demonstrated a tenacious desire to hang on to their plots which they see as the guarantee of their cherished values. Another problem is the Orthodox Church, owner of perhaps one-third of Ethiopian land. Nationalisation of ecclesiastical land could mean disestablishing a cornerstone of society on the Ethiopian plateau. In a country of such vast size and poor communications, provincialism is extremely strong. For most rural people traditional land rights, the church and local administration are the effective reference points; authority from Addis Ababa is only faintly perceived. Although land reform is being implemented rapidly by the army supported by 60 000 students directed into the field, it will probably fail unless carefully tailored to local requirements.

REFERENCES

1. F. M. Mifsud: *Customary Land Tenure in Africa* (Rome, FAO Legislative Series 7, 1967), p. 1.
2. P. Bohannan: 'Land, tenure, and land-tenure', in D. Biebuyck (ed.): *African Agrarian Systems* (London, Oxford University Press, 1963), pp. 101–11.
3. W. Allan: *The African Husbandman* (Edinburgh, Oliver and Boyd, 1965), p. 361.
4. D. Biebuyck: 'Land holdings and social organisation', in M. J. Herskovits and M. Marwitz (eds.): *Economic Transition in Africa* (London, Routledge and Kegan Paul, 1964), pp. 99–112.
5. M. Yudelman: *Africans on the Land* (Cambridge, Harvard University Press, 1964), p. 112.
6. V. C. Uchendu: 'Some issues in African land tenure', *Tropical Agriculture*, 44 (2), 1967, pp. 91–101.
7. Mifsud: *op. cit.*, p. 2.
8. V. C. Uchendu: 'The impact of changing agricultural technology in African land tenure', *Journal of Developing Areas*, 4 (4), 1970, pp. 477–86.
9. A. N. Allott: 'Modern change in African land tenure', in E. Cotran and N. N. Rubin (eds.): *Readings in African Law* (London, Cass, 1970), Vol. 1, pp. 236–42.
10. I. Gerschenberg: 'Customary tenure as a constraint on agricultural development: a re-evaluation', *East African Journal of Rural Development*, 4 (1), 1971, pp. 51–62.
11. R. Verdier: 'Evolution et réformes foncières de l'Afrique Noire francophone', *Journal of African Law*, 15 (1), 1971, pp. 85–101.
12. Mifsud: *op. cit.*, pp. 72–4.
13. M. P. Miracle and A. Seidman: *State Farms in Ghana* (Madison, University of Wisconsin, Land Tenure Center Paper 43, 1968); J. Gordon: 'State farms in Ghana (the political deformation of agricultural development)', in A. H. Bunting (ed.): *Change in Agriculture* (London, Duckworth, 1970), pp. 577–83; J. M. Due: 'What has happened to the Ghanaian state farms?', *Illinois Agricultural Economics*, 9 (2), 1969, pp. 25–35.
14. Gordon: *op. cit.*, p. 581.
15. Allan: *op. cit.*, pp. 437–45.
16. N. Georgulas: 'Settlement patterns and rural development in Tanzania', *Ekistics*, 24 (121), 1967, pp. 180–92.
17. J. Connell: *The Evolution of Tanzanian Rural Development* (Brighton, University of Sussex, Institute of Development Studies Communication 110, 1973), pp. 5–6.
18. F. Moderne: 'Villages communautaires et socialisme tanzanien', *Développement et Civilisations*, 39–40, 1970, pp. 147–66.
19. J. R. Pitblado: *A Review of Agricultural Land Use and Land Tenure in*

Tanzania (Dar es Salaam, University College, Bureau of Resource Assessment and Land Use Planning Research Notes 7, 1970), pp. 19, 35.

20. See R. Chambers: *Settlement Schemes in Tropical Africa* (London, Routledge and Kegan Paul, 1969).

21. O. A. Sabry: 'Starting settlements in Africa', *Land Reform, Land Settlement and Co-operatives*, 1, 1970, pp. 52–61.

22. A. Hoben: 'Social anthropology and development planning: a case-study in Ethiopian land reform policy', *Journal of Modern African Studies*, 10 (4), 1972, pp. 561–82.

23. See R. Pankhurst: *State and Land in Ethiopian History* (Addis Ababa, Oxford University Press for Institute of Ethiopian Studies, Monographs in Ethiopian Land Tenure 3, 1966).

24. H. C. Dunning: 'Land reform in Ethiopia: a case-study in non-development', *U.C.L.A. Law Review*, 18 (2), 1970, pp. 271–307; A. K. S. Lambton: 'Ethiopia: an approach to land reform', *Bulletin S.O.A.S.*, 34 (2), 1971, pp. 221–40; S. Pausewang: 'Peasant society and development in Ethiopia', *Sociologia Ruralis*, 13 (2), 1973, pp. 172–93.

25. J. Markie: 'Some recent developments affecting agricultural co-operatives, marketing and credit in Ethiopia', *Land Reform, Land Settlement and Co-operatives*, 1, 1975, pp. 54–61.

PART 5

Land Reform in the Middle East

Introduction

The final part of this book concerns the countries stretching from Morocco to Afghanistan. While this is a purely arbitrary, and unusually wide, definition of the Middle East, these countries have certain common characteristics which are important in agricultural geography and land tenure conditions. The area combines many of the land reform experiences of the other continents already surveyed. There are large estates resembling the *latifundia* of Latin America; tenancy is widespread, as in Asia; and African communal tenures have their equivalents in the ancient *hema* or communal grazings of the Arabian bedouin tribes and in the modern Israeli *kibbutzim*. This is not surprising, since here are both the crossroads of the Old World, with three continents radiating outwards, and an original and most productive culture hearth. The land reform record of the Middle East is extremely important; yet, partly because of its recency, it has received relatively scant attention. In only twenty years the region has seen at least half a dozen major land reforms, only two of which (Egypt and Iran) have received full documentary recognition. But notwithstanding the Middle East's notable parallels with other world regions in its land tenure structures and its unrecorded lessons for other countries in the reforming of these structures, it also has unique characteristics which go far towards defining it as a distinct geographical region.

First of all the region is an arid land dominated by vast deserts and rugged mountain ranges. Ecological conditions are unfavourable to agriculture except in certain high rainfall zones and in the great Nile and Tigris-Euphrates riverine basins. Only about 7 per cent of the region is cultivable. Large areas, including much of North Africa and nearly all the Arabian Peninsula, receive less than 100 millimetres of average annual rainfall. Where rain-fed cultivation is possible yields are often low and unstable and soil erosion poses a threat. These risks are illustrated in northern Syria and Iraq, where rapid expansion of mechanised farming in the 1950s was abruptly halted by the long drought of 1958–61, when much of the land reverted to desert. The significance of the climatic régime for the land tenure structure and for agricultural development cannot be overstressed. Here there are no large reserves of land which can be taken into cultivation at low cost with the prospect of stable yields (Iran is a possible exception). Shortage of water and irrigation potential conditions land use and employment, and water storage and irrigation schemes are highly capital intensive. Indeed the cost of such projects puts them not only beyond the scope of the individual small farmer but often beyond the reach of capital accumulation within the whole agricultural sector, and, occasionally, as with the Egyptian Aswan High Dam and the Syrian Euphrates Dam, beyond the entire country's financial resources. The underutilisation of labour, then, is conditioned by the underutilisation of water rather than of land as in the classic latifundian model, and the success or failure of structural reform hinges significantly on efficient provision and management of irrigation equipment.[1]

The second major unifying feature of the region is social geography. In all Middle East countries, except Israel, the Islamic religion prevails, and in most of them this is reinforced by the Arabic language. Spread from the Atlantic Ocean to the frontiers of the Far East, Islam is not just a religion: it is a way of life, strongly influencing social sctructure and landholding patterns.

Before Islam the inhabitants had no clear concept of landownership beyond the paying of tribute by settled farmers to the warlike nomadic tribes in return for protection of their fields from raiding. Islam legalised individual landownership in contrast to the tribal institution which made *hema* land common to all tribal members, and so introduced the Arabs to civilisation.[2] Although Islamic social policy stresses maximum productivity and efficiency, wide distribution of wealth, security for the underprivileged and the gaining of additional income only through work, various problems reflect basic economic contradictions. Banning of lending of money at interest encourages luxury consumption and hoarding, with a lack of capital for agricultural investment, while the principle of wide distribution of wealth has promoted extreme subdivision, which can conflict with technical efficiency.[3] Generally Islam favoured, wherever natural and social conditions allowed (and often they did not), individual ownership. But according to whether Islamisation was adopted voluntarily or under coercion, land tenure relations differ: if voluntarily the farmer paid only the standard moslem land tax; if not, he paid heavier taxes for only usufruct of the land. These two types of tenure, the individual and the estate, have been in great conflict. Other influences, such as features of the old Ottoman land code and the insertion of European colonial and estate tenures, make the contemporary landholding situation complex. The principal types are as follows:[4]

(1) Land held in full individual ownership is called *mulk*. Since the benefits of any improvements accrue solely to the owner, there is every incentive to develop the land. Unfortunately *mulk* land is not widespread.

(2) *Miri* land was originally state land which has been transferred to individuals (who often became absentee, feudal-type landlords) to reward services to the ruler. Sometimes full ownership was transferred, making the land equivalent to *mulk*; sometimes transfer was only for a prescribed period; and sometimes for payment like a conventional leasehold. Much Iraqi land has been in this last category (*miri sirf*). Short leases tend to encourage rapid exploitation without thought of long term improvements or maintenance of soil fertility.

(3) *Waqf* land (called *habous* in the Maghreb) is trust land whose revenues go to religious or charitable bodies. Individual title to the land thus vanishes, leaving only certain rights of use, which can be inherited, and therefore fragmented. Because many restrictions usually apply to *waqf* holdings and the plots are generally small, attempts at improvements by tenants are discouraged. Because *waqf* cannot be transferred, except by inheritance, it cannot be used as security for loans or mortgages. Originally the system was intended for security, but in practice it takes wealth out of circulation by freezing it.

(4) The fourth type is communally-owned property and in-

cludes several variations. In Iraq *matruka* denotes land used for public benefit such as government land, threshing floors etc, and is very small in extent. Elsewhere *matruka* means property of an entire community, either operated communally with the income divided, or allocated in shares to individual members. More usually *matruka* is communal grazing land, a widespread form in mountain areas and amongst pastoral nomads (for example, Kurdistan, Western Iran and Arabia). Another system, *masha*, involves communal ownership, with allocation amongst families of one share per male member, including children (thus emphasising the social inferiority of women in traditional Middle Eastern society). *Masha* holdings are commonest in eastern Syria, Jordan and parts of Libya.

The explanation of how such a poor resource base and unfavourable tenure structure nurtured such great civilisations lies partly in a complex and delicately-balanced adaptation to the environment, reflecting an ecological trilogy.[5] Middle Eastern society comprises three mutually dependent communities—urbanites, peasants and nomads—each with its own distinctive life-style, each operating in a different setting (the city, the village and the tribe) and each helping to support the other two and thereby to maintain the total cultural equilibrium. The common association of the traditional Middle East with bedouin and nomads and of the contemporary scene with oil obscures the fact that the village is the major unit of Middle Eastern society, now as in the past. Nearly 80 per cent of the region's population live in rural agrarian communities. Villagers form the majority in every Middle Eastern country except Saudi Arabia and some of the small Gulf oil states, and only the highest mountains and the cores of the great deserts are devoid of settled rural populations. These facts crystallize the fundamental and continuing importance of agriculture in these countries. In all of them, agriculture employs 50 to 90 per cent of the population. In all except trade-oriented Lebanon and a few sparsely-peopled oil countries (Libya, Kuwait, Saudi Arabia), agriculture is the largest single contributor to the GNP (30 to 60 per cent of the total) and to exports (50 to 90 per cent of the total).

The impact of oil on agricultural development, so often regarded unquestioningly as wholly beneficial, has not been entirely advantagous. The Middle East contains approximately two-thirds of the world's proven oil reserves. Saudi Arabia, Kuwait, Iran and Libya are major producers, but several other countries also produce appreciable quantities (Algeria, Egypt, Iraq, and the Persian Gulf Sheikhdoms). The problem is how to use oil revenues to maximise geographical and social spread effects to the national economy and society: while oil remains an enclave industry within the overall economy, its beneficial effects are limited. For the rural sector oil development provides high price markets for agricultural products, capital for investment in health, education and manpower training and such useful by-products as geological surveys, roads and other infrastructural services; it tends, however, to raise price levels, thus decreasing the competitive power of agriculture for factors of production, and to draw farmers into the cities and oilfields. This latter effect is detrimental if it causes wholesale land abandonment (as in Libya) and the collapse of agriculture, or beneficial if it reduces pressure on land just enough to enable rural incomes to rise and fragmented holdings to be consolidated—as in eastern Saudi Arabia, where oasis agriculture has abandoned dates to supply fresh fruit, vegetables and poultry to the oilfields. The greatest hope is that oil wealth will finance land redistribution (e.g. by reimbursing dispossessed landowners) and development schemes such as irrigation and nomad settlement projects. Finally, oil revenues in the oil-producing countries puts the others at an additional disadvantage: in these countries (such as Morocco, Yemen, Syria, Afghanistan) economic development essentially requires improving the terms of trade for the agricultural export crops and increasing the rate of capital formation in the rural sector.

But oil has not been alone in revolutionising the Middle East over recent decades. There have also been important sociopolitical changes. Until the end of the Second World War most of the countries were under foreign domination. Political independence since 1946 brought new governments; many of them, with markedly socialist leanings, have intervened vigorously in the private sector, and land reform has been an integral, sometimes the most important, part of this social and economic reshaping. Land reform in the Middle East started in Egypt in

1952, and 20 years later had embraced most, though not all, countries of the region to a greater or lesser extent. Land reforms have made a positive contribution toward breaking the yoke of feudalism and overcoming much of the insecurity characterising tenancy. Poverty and low socio-economic status still burden the peasantry, but a sense of dignity, at least, is spreading.[6] Two broad approaches to the land question have been followed. The first, as in Egypt in 1952, Syria and Iraq in 1958 and Iran in 1962, is the classic expropriation-redistribution type, often backed up by tenancy legislation. The second, as in Algeria and Tunisia, is the nationalisation of European-owned estates and farms, and their subsequent operation under various forms of state and communal management. The remaining countries include those like Morocco, Turkey, Lebanon and Afghanistan, which follow a basically laissez-faire approach, and those like Libya and South Yemen, which, with revolutionary changes of government more recent, are just embarking on radical reform schemes.

REFERENCES

1. D. Warriner: 'Employment and income aspects of recent agrarian reforms in the Middle East', *International Labour Review*, 101 (6), 1970, pp. 605–25.
2. A. Abd al-Kader: 'Land property and land tenure in Islam', *Islamic Quarterly*, 5 (1–2), 1959, pp. 4–12.
3. E. Gaballah: 'The significance of some aspects of Islamic culture for tenure adjustments: a comment', in K. H. Parsons, R. J. Penn and P. M. Raup (eds.): *Land Tenure* (Madison, University of Wisconsin, 1956), pp. 109–10.
4. W. B. Fisher: *The Middle East* (London, Methuen, 1971), pp. 194–202.
5. P. W. English: 'Urbanites, peasants and nomads: the Middle Eastern ecological trilogy', *Journal of Geography*, 66 (2), 1967, pp. 54–9.
6. F. Baali: 'Agrarian reform policies and development in the Arab World', *American Journal of Economics and Sociology*, 33 (2), 1974, pp. 161–74.

17

Egypt

As the earliest large-scale land reform in the Middle East and one of the most important of the non-communist world, the Egyptian land reform not only brought great improvements in Egyptian rural life but was a landmark in Middle East history, influencing other countries of the region.

Before 1952 the Egyptian peasants were among the most poverty-stricken, disease-ridden and socially oppressed in the world. Yet, because a landlord-dominated parliament effectively stifled incipient protest, the peasants made no coherently-formulated demand for land reform. Instead the Egyptian land reform was rushed through immediately after a revolutionary coup wrested power from King Farouk and his corrupt landlords. The new government, not of peasant origin (most members were young army officers), saw land reform as a means both of ousting the landlords and of establishing broad support for themselves amongst the 70 per cent of the country's population who worked on the land. For the revolutionaries the land reform was essential to the complete revitalisation of Egyptian life and economy, to break the institutional barriers to, and prepare the Egyptian peasants for, a complete restructuring of life along more dynamic, liberal and egalitarian lines.[1]

LAND TENURE AND SOCIAL STRUCTURE BEFORE THE REFORM

The Egyptian land tenure situation before 1952 had been continually worsening since the nineteenth century. The country's geography and demographic history go far towards explaining this. Human Egypt is a narrow green snake winding

through arid emptiness, a meandering strip of cultivation cling-
ing to its life-source—the Nile. Over 95 per cent of the population are concentrated in a narrow belt a few miles wide, totalling
only 3½ per cent of the country's surface area. With a virtually
fixed land resource (some extension of the cultivated area is
possible—but only at great cost), rapid population increase for
a century and a half had eroded the rural population's well-
being to a peneplain of abject poverty. The cultivated area of
just over 6 million feddans (1 feddan = 1·038 acres) had to support in 1952 20 million people, one of the highest rural densities
in the world. Although irrigation and drainage improvements,
particularly the Aswan Dam (1903) and the various barrages
effectively increased the cropped area by 37 per cent between
1897 and 1949 (perennial irrigation supporting two or even three
crops per year against only one under basin irrigation), population increase in that period was over 100 per cent (9·7 to 20
million). This demographic tidal wave reduced the average
cropped area per inhabitant from 0·83 feddans in 1897 to 0·47
in 1949, and the average size of holding, through the Islamic
law of inheritance, from 1·5 to 0·8 feddans per proprietor.[2]
Labour productivity was continually falling, apart from a brief
upturn in the early 1930s, and by mid-century underutilised
labour was estimated at 25 per cent.[3]

In 1952, just before the reform, the landownership pattern
was as follows.[4] 2119 large landowners (under 0·1 per cent of
total owners), owning over 200 feddans each, possessed 20 per
cent of the agricultural land; 199 of them owned 7·3 per cent of
the cultivated area in units of over 1000 feddans. Many such
large holdings dated from the campaigns of Mohamed Ali and
his successors in the nineteenth century. 2·8 million peasant proprietors owning less than 1 feddan constituted 72 per cent of
landowners, but held only 13 per cent of the total area. Around
1·5 million additional families were landless, living by casual
labour or sharecropping small areas of other people's land. Under mounting population pressure land was steadily priced out
of the small peasant's reach, with tenancy becoming increasingly widespread. In 1939 only 17 per cent of Egyptian farmland was tenanted: by 1949 the official figure was 61 per cent
and by 1952 it was estimated at 75 per cent. The average rent
per feddan meanwhile tripled, rising to absorb over 60 per cent

of a tenant's total annual expenses. Fragmentation worsened also, causing production losses estimated at 30 per cent of total output. *Waqf* land in 1950 covered 10 per cent of the cultivated area, inefficiently administered in large blocks by the Ministry of Waqfs.[5]

Rural social structure corresponded to the landholding system, with a small wealthy group above a broad base of poverty-stricken *fellahin* (peasants).[6] The *fellahin* were landless peasants and those with holdings, owned or rented, insufficient for subsistence, less than about 1 feddan. Although traditionally politically apathetic, during 1950–2 the *fellahin* were beginning acts of violence against the big landowners. Rising rents and increasing indebtedness were forcing the 'middle peasants' (with 1 to 5 feddans) to revolt alongside the proletariat. The privileged classes were those with more than 5 feddans, who regularly hired labour, and comprised: medium farmers with 5 to 20 feddans, the most traditional in outlook, often occupying local government offices such as mayor—at 150 000 this group was larger than in other Middle East countries; large farmers with 20 to 200 feddans, usually producing efficiently for export or regional demand; and the landed aristocracy owning over 200 feddans, usually absentee, lavish consumers and politically dominant. The tenure-based social structure also differentiated factor endowments in agriculture, which reinforced rural poverty amongst the majority. The major effect was excess of farm labour and shortage of capital. The Agricultural Bank of Egypt, founded as early as 1902, never succeeded in its objective of helping small farmers. The commercial banks were mostly foreign-owned and, agriculturally, mainly concerned with financing the principal export crop, cotton, by short-term loans to big landowners. Small farmers had to seek credit from village money-lenders at annual interest rates of 30 to 50 per cent.

THE REFORM LAWS

The 1952 Egyptian land reform laws authorised government requisitioning of private land above a 200 feddan ceiling over a five year period. Individuals with two or more children could retain up to an extra 100 feddans; other exemptions involved fallow and desert land, *waqf*, and land belonging to agricultural, industrial and scientific organisations. Landowners were compensated by state bonds bearing 3 per cent interest redeemable in 30 years, equivalent to 70 times the basic land tax, which averaged around £200 per feddan, with additional compensation for fixed capital equipment (buildings, irrigation works) and trees. The royal estates, 178 000 feddans, were expropriated in full without compensation, which greatly facilitated financing of the reform. The expropriated land was to be distributed in lots of 2 to 5 feddans (the average worked out at 2·4 feddans) to agricultural labourers, tenants and farmers possessing under 5 feddans, with preference to those actually working the relevant land. The recipients were to pay, in 30 annual instalments, the cost of the expropriated land, as calculated above, plus 3 per cent interest and 15 per cent for administrative costs (a 1958 amendment modified these figures to 40, 1½ per cent and 10 per cent respectively). These instalments commonly totalled about half the rent previously paid to the landlord, for frequently tenants gained ownership of land they previously rented. For tenants of landlords unaffected by expropriation, rents were fixed at seven times the land tax, and the landlord had to produce a written contract. Under sharecropping arrangements the landowner could not receive more than half the proceeds. Minimum daily wages were fixed for labourers not assigned a reform plot, but this was ineffective, labour being in excess supply. Finally, all reform beneficiaries had to join government-supervised co-operatives.

Expropriated orchard land, some 4280 feddans, requiring special standards and techniques of cultivation, was exempted from distribution to smallholders: such land would be assigned only to agricultural diploma holders, in lots of up to 20 feddans providing that the assignee did not already possess more than 10 feddans. Despite this selection of candidates, however, the arrangement failed because recipients seldom dwelt on their land, but stayed in the towns as absentee landlords. Orchard land ceased to be distributed in 1955 and was supervised by the land reform authorities. This failure to bring educated, middle class groups into the reform contrasts interestingly with the success of the small peasant reform holdings.[7]

With experience in operating the 1952 law and with the increasingly socialist character of the government, amendments were made to the original reform scheme. In 1961 the ceiling was reduced to 100 feddans (though *families* could still hold up to 300 feddans) and the amount a landlord could lease out was restricted to 50 feddans. In 1969 the landholding ceiling was further lowered to 50 feddans, with a maximum family holding of 100 feddans. *Waqf* land, initially exempted from reform, was now included. Beneficiary repayments were cut to a half in 1961 and to a quarter in 1964, when compensation to dispossessed landlords ceased and the bonds already issued were rendered worthless.

EFFECTS OF THE REFORM

By 1967 754 000 feddans of the 944 457 expropriated (79 per cent) had been distributed to 317 000 beneficiary families counting over a million and a half individuals. Redistribution jumped in 1953–4 (60 000 feddans per year) and during 1962–4 (100 000 annually), following the two main laws. An additional 180 000 feddans have been distributed from public domain land and reclaimed waste land.

In the changes Table 24 shows, however, the reform was assisted by other land transfer processes working in the same direction. The normal subdivision of property on inheritance continually increases the number of smallholdings and the land reform itself brought more land on to the market by its devaluation of land as a socio-economic good: in 1952 and 1953 (when the practice was outlawed) many large landowners hastily sold their land in excess of 200 feddans in small lots to local peasants to avoid direct expropriation—145 000 feddans of fertile land were sold in this way in a single year.[8]

The table shows that the impact of the land redistribution primarily affected the largest and the smallest landholders. Proprietors with under 5 feddans increased by 13 per cent and the land they owned by 74 per cent, while the largest estates (over 200 feddans) disappeared entirely and the average area of holdings of 100–200 feddans fell substantially. It was the need to remove from political power the landed aristocracy that initially led the revolutionaries to expropriate only those 2000-odd estates of over 200 feddans. Although Egypt is currently overwhelmingly socialist, the wide discrepancy between the ceiling levels (50–200 feddans) and the assigned plots (2–5 feddans) and the present landholding pattern (see the second half of the table) show the great inequalities still existing. Redistributed land re-

presents about 10 per cent of total Egyptian farmland, and
beneficiaries only 9 per cent of the rural population. The great-

TABLE 24

THE CHANGING PATTERN OF EGYPTIAN LANDOWNERSHIP, 1952–1965

Ownership Class (feddans)	Before land reform (1952)				After land reform (1965)			
	Owners		Area		Owners		Area	
	Number '000	per cent	feddans	per cent	Number '000	per cent	feddans	per cent
0–5	2 642	92·3	2 112	35·4	3 033	94·5	3 693	57·1
5–10	79	2·8	526	8·8	78	2·4	614	9·5
10–20	47	1·7	638	10·7	61	1·9	527	8·2
20–50	22	0·8	654	10·9	29	0·9	815	12·6
50–100	6	0·2	430	7·2	6	0·2	392	6·4
100–200	3	0·1	437	7·3	4	0·1	421	6·5
over 200	2	0·1	1 177	19·7	0	0·0	0	0·0
Total	2 802	100·0	5 984	100·0	3 211	100·0	6 462	100·0

Source: J. S. Oweis: 'The impact of land reform on Egyptian agriculture: 1952–
1965', *Intermountain Economic Review*, 2 (1), 1971, p. 49.

est beneficiaries were smallholders and tenants; the tenancy
laws, for example, affected 4 million tenants. Landless labourers, however, suffered; their numbers actually increased by 30
per cent between 1950 and 1966. Many employees of expropriated estates were displaced by the redistribution since the new
smallholders needed no hired labour; one estimate puts this
displacement at 11–22 000.[9]

The reform, then, had no profound effect on the country's
social structure. Some social reshuffling took place, some individuals gaining and others losing, but these changes, limited to
a few per cent of the population, occurred within a basically
unchanged social structure. Nationally, deposing the landed
aristocracy was a major political change, but in most villages
the status framework remained basically unaltered. A majority
of poor and land-hungry peasants and a privileged minority of
medium and large-scale farmers still remain: the only difference
is the increased weight of the medium landowners (20–50 feddans) within the privileged group.[10] The 20–50 feddan class increased 30 per cent by number and 25 per cent by area. Apart
from ordinary land purchases by this well-off group, many from
foreigners fleeing the country, this increase probably reflects the

splitting up of large estates among family members to avoid expropriation. Gadalla, having compared reform and non-reform villages in the Nile Delta, concluded that while the reform has created conditions favourable to social change the actual direct impact on social development has been very limited.[11]

The reform's economic effects, on incomes, employment and agricultural production, are more tangible. An immediate achievement was a considerable income redistribution from expropriated landowners to beneficiaries and tenants. Saab's detailed fieldwork revealed many signs of improved standards of living in reform regions.[12] Reform beneficiaries were considerably better off than those peasants not affected by the reform. Beneficiaries ate meat, for example, twice a week instead of once a month as before, sugar consumption had soared and clothing standards improved. Whereas before 1952 the landlords drained capital from rural areas and spent it on luxury living, the post-reform increase in peasant incomes is spent locally, increasing domestic trade and production of textiles, foodstuffs and household goods. Relatively little of the extra income was, however, invested in the farm.

According to Eshag and Kamal[13] income per feddan of all land now farmed by beneficiaries increased by nearly three times between 1953 and 1965; with the rise in cost of living allowed for the increase in real income was about 35 per cent. In Upper Egypt, where the peasants were relatively badly off before the reform, income increases up to 100 per cent have been recorded. Against this, however, those landless labourers not assigned plots were considerably worse off than before, with less work available on the reduced large estates and cost of living for basic staples rising steadily. A 1967 government estimate showed that the average agricultural wage worker was employed for only 180 days per year. Just how serious current rural unemployment is remains unclear although the estimate that the Aswan High Dam, with its Lake Nasser as big as England, will provide enough land and work for the rural population increase for only five to six years gives some idea of the implications of population increase. Land redistribution has provided only some temporary relief from the momentum of Egypt's population growth.

Production increases in Egyptian agriculture over the past

o

twenty years are well documented, but how much of these increases the reform generated and how much government agricultural policy and investment is not clear. The general indication is that the land reform effect was positive—a considerable achievement, for Egyptian agriculture with its intensive multi-crop régime is highly geared to certain institutional production factors such as irrigation and careful husbandry, and many thought that a sudden structural switch would be detrimental. Whereas before 1952 population was winning in the race with food production, now the latter has drawn slightly ahead. The incentives the reform created for small owners and tenants get official credit for average increases in crop yields between 1952 and 1967 of 17 per cent for unginned cotton, 33 per cent for wheat, 67 per cent for rice, 65 per cent for maize and 90 per cent for millet, figures generally supported by private investigations. Gadalla[14] compared yields on 300 sample beneficiary farms on three former estates with 300 farms on matched unexpropriated estates nearby and found that cotton yields increased more on reform than on non-reform farms (13·2 per cent against 2·6 per cent from 1948–52 to 1952–6), giving an average income differential of 20 per cent. Saab's investigation of various reform localities, too, shows usual yield increases between 1952 and 1959 of up to 50 per cent.[15] This yield and output information, however, refers to productivity of *land*. Little evidence exists of significant increases in *labour* productivity. According to Hansen and Marzouk[16] output per man increased only about 2 per cent per annum between 1950 and 1965—a relatively low figure, but better than the stationary or even declining labour productivity before 1950.

CO-OPERATION

Strong co-operatives were necessary to reduce the problems of smallholder farming and to provide the investment, credit and production organisation functions of the dispossessed landlords and their agents. Before the reform some 2000 agricultural credit co-operatives channelled funds for agricultural improvement, but had generally been taken over by large landowners, who borrowed most of the funds for their own use or for sublending to their tenants at inflated interest rates. Under the reform these co-operatives were freed from landowner control.

Their funding was substantially increased (interest-free loans were available after 1960), their functions widened to embrace many other services and their number increased to 3800, so that virtually every village had one. In reform zones cultivation and marketing of produce were organised by specially created state-supervised co-operatives; in 1966 they numbered 565, with 303 624 members. Membership of the supervised co-operatives was compulsory for the beneficiaries, and has since been thrown open to other small peasants. Each reform co-operative is theoretically run by an elected board led by a ministry-appointed supervisor, but in practice the supervisor, often an agronomy graduate, has the ultimate decision-making power. The degree of supervision suggests in practice a state rather than a co-operative system. State control of agriculture has increased further in recent years with obligatory quotas of certain crops (wheat, rice and onions) at fixed prices.[17] The authoritarian approach, initially adopted to ensure sound operation, appears now to have become permanent policy, thus stultifying the emergence of local peasant leadership, originally specified as a reform objective. Compulsory co-operative marketing of cotton, onions, rice and groundnuts does, however, guarantee market outlets for small farmers' produce and a fixed income. Bulk selling by the Egyptian Cotton Commission of cotton collected by co-operatives is reported to have gained 10–15 per cent additional income for the producers, though such organisations are still exposed to major external market variations.

Perhaps the most original aspect of the Egyptian reform has been the Unified Rotation Co-operatives. In land reform regions where large areas of expropriated land enabled rational field lay-outs to be established, each district is divided into three blocks, with each beneficiary possessing a parcel in each block, following a triennial cotton, wheat, clover rotation. Although this perpetuates a degree of farm fragmentation, it is at least controlled and rationalised. Farmers are responsible for cultivating their individual plots, but important operations, more effectively organised on a large scale, such as mechanised ploughing, irrigation and pest control, are entrusted to the co-operatives. Farms outside land reform areas have also followed this pattern by regrouping their holdings or exchanging produce to operate the same three-block rotation.

CONCLUSION

The stated objectives of the Egyptian reform were: (1) to distribute land to landless or semi-landless peasants to achieve a measure of social justice and political stability; (2) to increase incomes of the *fellahin*; and (3) to raise agricultural production. A fourth, covert, objective was to consolidate support for the revolutionary régime. The reform achieved some success in all four aims. It is still, after twenty years, an ongoing process, proliferating its effects on the country's life and economy. Negative aspects—the relative failure of legislation to control wages and rents, the generally small scale of intervention in the totality of Egyptian agriculture, the fact that reform did not initiate an immediate and fundamental social revolution—should not detract from what has been achieved in increased agricultural production, crop yields, rural incomes and the national balance of power. For the first time this century growth in food output exceeds population increase. These are important achievements, since Egypt before the revolution suffered not merely from poverty but from increasing poverty, and not merely from unemployment but from Malthusian overpopulation.

SYRIA: AN AMBITIOUS REFORM BUT MEAGRE RESULTS

The 1958 Syrian land reform resulted directly from the country's union earlier that year with Egypt in the United Arab Republic, and closely followed the Egyptian laws, but without clauses on tenancy and agricultural wages (which had proved difficult to enforce in Egypt). In Syria before 1958 big estates, numbering only 2 per cent of the properties, covered 45 per cent of the irrigated farmland and 30 per cent of rain-fed land. About two-thirds of these big landowners were merchants who had invested their commercial earnings in agricultural land, managed for them by agents. Property concentration was most serious in the districts of Aleppo, Euphrates and Jezirah. Private *mulk* land covered under 1 per cent of the total area (2·4 per cent of the farmed area). About 70 per cent of the rural population owned no land. Tenancy covered 75 per cent of the agricultural area. The tenants were heavily subservient to the landlords. Tenure conditions were imprecise, the agreements being verbal, short term and terminable at will by the landlord. High rents led to indebtedness, for interest rates of 50 per cent and more were charged on borrowed money.

The Syrian reform relative to the population and area of the country could have been considerably wider than the Egyptian. Although ceilings were set higher than in Egypt—80 hectares irrigated land, 300 rain-fed—Syrian extensiveness of land use made this a more stringent level. Official estimates put the expropriable area, from 3240 large landowners, at 1·5 million hectares, nearly 30 per cent of the country's agricultural area, which, with a further 1·5 million hectares of state domain land, would make the total available for redistribution 3 million hectares, 60 per cent of the total agricultural area. Land would be assigned to peasants in lots of up to 8 hectares irrigated or 30 hectares non-irrigated land, or a combination of the two in the ratio 1:3·75. By 1961, when a new government suspended the 1958 law, 670 000 hectares had been expropriated and 176 000 hectares, including 27 000 hectares of former state domains, had been allocated to about 15 000 peasant families. Co-operative societies, assigned major entrepreneurial responsibilities, including crop rotation, provision of seeds, fertilisers and pesticides, and well-drilling, numbered 134 in 1961.[18]

Initially the reform impressed by its vigour and comprehensiveness, but the three years of drought that coincided with the reform's period of operation make evaluation of its impact on production impossible. Syria was unusual among underdeveloped countries and contrasted with Egypt in that private enterprise, chiefly by the city-based merchant class, was rapidly improving agriculture before the reform (and this without an oil industry to provide capital for expansion of, or extra demand for, agricultural produce). Cotton production multiplied by ten between the 1930s and the 1950s. Grain production doubled between 1943 and 1953, compared with a population increase over the same decade of 33 per cent from 2·9 million to 3·9 million. These gains were made almost wholly by indigenous private enterprise, without government planning, foreign experts and capital, transport and other infrastructures or agrarian reform. Indeed, in 1956 Warriner[19] doubted the need for land reform, at least in some parts of the country.

Operationally, the greatest obstacle to land reform implementation has been the country's volatile politics. In its twenty-five years of independent existence the country has had some twenty military coups d'état. This political instability and the amendments and counteramendments to the reform laws make reliable data on the situation hard to find. A February 1962 law which relaxed the ceilings on land holdings was rapidly repealed when it was realised that beneficiaries were in danger of having their distributed land taken back by the landlords. Following this, and a working conference of central and regional reform administrators, the redistribution, which had lagged, gained momentum, with 92 000 hectares in 197 villages distributed to 6500 beneficiary families in one year. Some progress was also made in settling the underexploited Jezirah region in the north-east and in distributing state land to peasants.[20] Political domination by the Ba'athists in 1963 lowered ceilings on private property to a variable limit (recognising diversity in land quality across the country) of 15 to 55 hectares for irrigated land, 35 to 40 hectares for orchard land, and 80 to 300 hectares for rain-fed land, and made provision for state and collective farms where 'conditions favoured such an organisation.' In consequence, a further 1372 landowners lost land totalling 350 000 hectares. Although expropriation made considerable progress after 1963, up to 1967 relatively little land was actually distributed to peasants, the majority remaining in state hands. By 1969, however, with requisition of land nearly complete, distribution of land began to overtake expropriation. In 1968 official figures showed that, during the ten years of reform, a total of 1 341 359 hectares had been expropriated, of which 76 104 hectares was irrigated land, 1 025 959 rain-fed and 238 796 non-agricultural. About a third of the country's cultivable area was affected (but only 14 per cent of the irrigated area). Distributed land totalled 574 082 hectares, of which 45 434 was irrigated and 528 648 non-irrigated. Beneficiaries totalled 39 650 families, or 229 436 persons.[21]

REFERENCES

1.   K. B. Platt: 'Land reform in the U.A.R.', in Agency for International Development: *Spring Review of Land Reform* (Washington, Department of State, 1970), Vol. 8, pp. 1, 24–5, 27.

2.   G. S. Saab: *The Egyptian Agrarian Reform 1952–1962* (London, Oxford University Press, 1967), pp. 1, 9.

3. B. Hansen and G. Marzouk: *Development and Economic Policy in the U.A.R.* (Amsterdam, North Holland, 1965), pp. 46, 61.

4. M. M. El-Kammash: 'A note on the system of landownership in Egyptian agriculture 1800–1960', *Farm Economist*, 11 (7), 1963, pp. 263–80.

5. Saab: *op. cit.*, pp. 10–12.

6. C. Boeckx: 'Réforme agraire et structures sociales en Égypte nassérienne', *Civilisations*, 21 (4), 1971, pp. 373–93.

7. Saab: *op. cit.*, p. 32.

8. *Ibid*: pp. 20–1.

9. Platt: *op. cit.*, pp. 46, 50.

10. Boeckx: *op. cit.*, pp. 389–90.

11. S. M. Gadalla: *Land Reform in Relation to Social Development: Egypt* (Columbia, University of Missouri Press, 1962), pp. 62–7, 108.

12. Saab: *op. cit.*, pp. 120–5.

13. E. Eshag and M. A. Kamal: 'Agrarian reform in the U.A.R. (Egypt)', *Bulletin of the Oxford University Institute of Economics and Statistics*, 30 (2), 1968, pp. 73–104.

14. Gadalla: *op. cit.*

15. Saab: *op. cit.*, pp. 109–13.

16. Hansen and Marzouk: *op. cit.*, p. 79.

17. N. Saad: 'Structural changes and socialist transformation of agriculture in the U.A.R.', *Égypte Contemporaine*, 60, (337), 1969, pp. 263–95.

18. E. Garzouzi: 'Land reform in Syria', *Middle East Journal*, 17 (1–2), 1963, pp. 83–90

19. D. Warriner: *Land Reform and Development in the Middle East: Egypt, Syria and Iraq* (London, Oxford University Press, 1967), ch. 3.

20. I. El-Zaim: 'La réforme agraire en Syrie', *Tiers Monde*, 9 (34), 1968, pp. 508–17.

21. A. Ayoub: Réforme agraire et propriété rurale: le cas de la Syrie', *Options Méditerranéennes*, 8, 1971, pp. 55–61.

18

Iraq

Like Syria, Iraq had a major land reform in 1958, modelled on the Egyptian. Although the Iraq laws copied the Egyptian in most respects, the conditions in which the laws operated and the results they achieved differed considerably. The Iraqi law was more radical, more chaotic in implementation, and it reduced agricultural production.

On the face of it, the scope for land reform and development seemed much greater than in Egypt. Iraq had greatly under-utilised land resources, but oil brought the capital to develop them; and projects for water storage, control and irrigation on the Tigris and Euphrates rivers brought the water that, particularly in southern Iraq, had been lacking. Furthermore, Iraq in 1958 was stronger economically than Egypt in 1952. Grain production had doubled since 1945, outpacing population growth. Oil production was booming. In 1956 oil and agriculture were both contributing 25 per cent to GNP; but, while oil employed less than 1 per cent of the work force, some 80 per cent remained in agriculture. Today oil provides 60 per cent of national income and 90 per cent of export revenue.

Nonetheless, implementing reform in Iraq was fundamentally more difficult, since to raise agricultural incomes and achieve full employment required conversion to settled farming with stable yields of shifting cultivation with irregular yields and soil salinisation. In Egypt the environment is tightly controlled, resources are skilfully utilised, population densely settled, society quite highly evolved and the government stable; in Iraq the environment remains relatively uncontrolled, natural resources lie underdeveloped, population density is low, society is disaggregated and the politics are confused. Compared with Egypt's pressure-cooker tension, Iraq's agriculture is a low pressure vicious circle of extensive cultivation.[1] For a country which, as Mesopotania, probably saw the origins of settled cultivation, present-day agriculture is extremely primitive. Indeed, Iraq is virtually a new agricultural country, with three-quarters of the farmland brought under cultivation since 1918 and a third since 1945. In the north, rain-fed agriculture is possible, with barley, wheat and Mediterranean fruits, but periodic drought reduces yields drastically every few years. In the south irrigation is necessary, the main crops being barley, rice and dates (of which Iraq provides 80 per cent of world exports), but land use remains extensive, a patch of land being cropped until it is flooded or goes saline, and then abandoned. Half the country is desert or semi-desert, mostly in a broad belt across the south-west. About 25 to 30 per cent of Iraq is potentially cultivable, only half of which is actually cropped, the rest lying in disuse or periodic fallow.

Another reason for Iraq's backwardness in agriculture in the 1950s was the gap between the *fellahin* and the complex and conservative political nexus that ruled the country.[2] Rural social structure was too divided tribally, ethnically and religiously to organise any opposition, nor were the urban intelligentsia allowed to intervene on their behalf. Consequently the country's considerable economic development potential never diffused downwards from the privileged class. In the 1950s, development policy concentrated on purely technical aspects; water resources were developed but the people were not.

LAND TENURE BEFORE THE REFORM

The main features of land tenure in Iraq before 1958 were the great estates in the irrigated zone and the ill-defined and chaotic nature of landholding in general. Until the end of the Ottoman period (1918) the basis of landownership was the *dirah*, a large area over which a tribe exercised customary rights of occupation and use. From about 1900, however, tribal tenure has been weakening. Settlement for permanent cultivation, the opening up of markets, particularly for grain as steamship transport came to the Persian Gulf, the development of pump irrigation, a measure of political security (the Iraq state dates from 1918, though it did not become independent of Britain until 1932), all put pressure on the sheikhs for individual ownership. A 1932 law, designed to reduce the confusion in landownership by enforcing registration of title to land, allowed the sheikhs to appropriate the tribal lands, thus turning themselves into feudal overlords, with their former tribesmen turned into servile tenants and labourers, often tied to the land by indebtedness. There was probably no greater single cause of poverty in Iraq than this law; it legalised twentieth century feudalism. In southern Iraq, where this newly-constituted feudal structure was most dominant, the landowners' share of agricultural production averaged 70 per cent. In the north rents were lower (50 per cent), because population pressure was less and the stronger survival of the Ottoman land code prescribed splitting up of land on inheritance, which reduced the size of the large estates. Small, peasant-owned holdings characterised the Kurdish hill villages.

The few available pre-reform statistics give some indication of the maldistribution of land, identifying 272 holdings of over 10 000 donums (1 donum equals 0·25 hectares or 0·62 acres) and 3620 holdings of over 1000 donums, with 89 per cent of the peasants registered as landless.[3] Large properties were especially dominant in Amara, where four sheikhs possessed almost the whole of the cultivated area; these landlords reckoned their possessions in terms of pumps and people rather than in donums, for machines and cultivators were the real units of political and economic power here. The parlous state of the rural population in Amara province caused large scale outmigration to the shanty quarters of Baghdad and other large towns; in 1958 nearly half the migrants to urban areas were from this single small province.[4]

Following the 1932 Land Settlement Law four land tenure categories, *mulk*, *matruka*, *waqf* and *miri*, were recognised, which, although based on the old Ottoman land code of 1858, formed the land tenure classification until the 1958 reform. *Miri* land was much the most widespread and was subdivided: *miri tapu* land carried permanent tenure from the state with the holder able to sell, mortgage or will his tenure to others; *miri lazma*, instituted by the 1932 law, differed from *tapu* in that the state had power to veto its transferal; and *miri sirf* land belongs wholly to

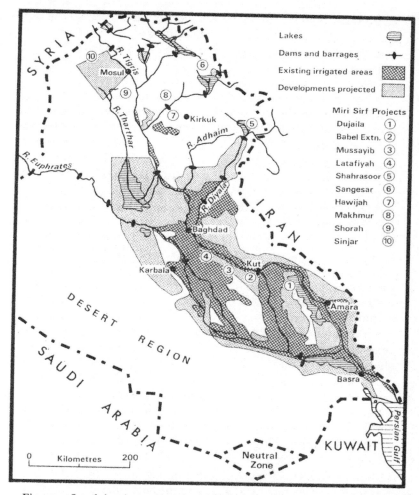

Fig. 12. Land development and *miri sirf* settlements in Iraq. *Sources:* W. B. Fisher: *The Middle East* (London, Methuen, 1971), p. 363; H. Treakle: 'Land reform in Iraq', in Agency for International Development: *Spring Review of Land Reform* (Washington, Department of State, 1970), Vol. 2, Fig. 2

the state even though in practice individuals enjoy undisturbed rights of occupation. In 1958 *mulk* constituted 0·8 per cent of the agricultural land, *matruka* 11·5 per cent, *waqf* 1·4 per cent, *miri tapu* 38·8 per cent, *miri lazma* 33 per cent and *miri sirf* 14·6 per cent.[5]

THE PRE-REVOLUTIONARY DECADE OF LAND REFORM[6]

While the sheikhs and large landowners held political power, no legislation restricting landlords' property rights could ever be enacted. Instead, the period between 1945 and 1958 featured schemes for settling underdeveloped state land. Under the *Miri Sirf* Land Development Law ten projects, mostly along the Tigris, distributed *miri sirf* land to settlers (Fig. 12). Since the state held large areas of land served by new irrigation schemes, small farmers could be settled without direct conflict with the large landowners. Colonisation was advocated as an effective, indirect, evolutionary way toward a general improvement in the *fellahin's* condition: apart from directly benefiting the settlers, the programme would theoretically reduce labour supply on the land and so induce landlords to improve their cultivators' conditions and rents.

Unfortunately results proved different. In the Dujaila Land Settlement project, the largest in the country, made possible by the opening of the Dujaila Canal, bringing abundant Tigris water, allocation to *fellahin* was in 100 donum lots, but nearly half of the best land was appropriated by the sheikhs themselves —apparently as their price for allowing the law through parliament the year previously. The government received some 50 000 applications for holdings, an indication of the latent demand for smallholder ownership, but only 1500 lots were assigned. Initially the settlement improved the standard of living of its 7400 residents, but its technical shortcomings included failure to install drainage schemes to circumvent salinisation, the curse of agriculture in southern Iraq.[7]

Because the Iraqi government refused to give the *Miri Sirf* schemes proper status and full support, there were too few projects to affect the social problems of rural Iraq significantly. At most, 20 000 farm families acquired holdings on these settlements. While the large landowners retained the political power, no measure would gain enough leverage to change the tenure structure. So Iraq in 1958 was ripe for revolution and for land reform. Malcontents had only to look to Egypt for inspiration. Without a revolution there could be no reform; with a revolution, reform was likely to be chaotic and inefficient—a dilemma not peculiar to Iraq.[8]

THE LAWS

In July 1958 a gory revolutionary coup brought Brigadier Kassim to the head of a new republic, the King, the crown prince and the prime minister being assassinated. Immediately, Kassim announced the intention of controlling land ownership, and two months later the reform laws were issued.

The Iraqi legislation duplicates the Egyptian in structure, so only some points of variance need mention. The personal maximum of landholding was fixed at 1000 donums for irrigated and 2000 donums for rain-fed land. All *miri tapu* and *lazma* land became state (i.e. *miri sirf*) land, seized without compensation if the landholder had not cultivated it himself during the three years before 1958 or during the year following the law. All land acquired by the state would be distributed to deserving peasants in lots of 30–60 donums irrigated or 60–120 dry land, with priority for those who had worked the land, followed by those supporting the largest families on the smallest incomes. In 1970 the ceiling on irrigated land was reduced to 300 donums of fertile, flow-irrigated land and 400 of pump-fed land, and these limits could be halved for land near urban markets.

PROGRESS OF THE REFORM

Expropriation, quickly and rigorously enforced with little evasion, was more drastic than in Egypt; even though the ceiling irrigated area was three times the Egyptian, it represented lower real income because of the lower land productivity. The compensation originally authorised was discontinued after a few token payments, and beneficiary repayments were not enforced.

The progress of the reform has been hampered by political instability. Kassim's government comprised three main factions, the Nationalists, the Ba'athists and the Communists. In 1959 a communist Minister of Agrarian Reform expelled Egyptian experts and brought in Russian. Requisitioning of land accelerated, but distribution of land and formation of co-operatives lagged, the intention being to collectivise the rapidly accumulating bank of undistributed land. Since, however, Kassim had won considerable support initially through his revolutionary pledge of land to the peasants, there was discontent at the communists' holding up distribution. Kassim broke with the communists in 1960 and the reform suffered through squabbles between communist and non-communist elements in the Agrarian Reform Ministry. Then in 1963, in the so-called Ramadan Revolution Kassim was murdered and the Ba'athists took over. The new reform minister favoured rapid redistribution of the land held by the government but the left-wing Ba'athists had by now embraced the collectivist ideal. Before any move either way could be made, however, in another revolution the army ousted the left-wing Ba'athists. Further political musical chairs renewed military dictatorships until 1968 since when the Ba'ath Socialists have provided relatively stable government.[9]

Accurate information on the reform's progress is scanty. Official figures maintain that by 1966 an area of 6·3 million donums had been requisitioned, 5·1 million of them from 2433 private landowners, who now retain little of their former properties. By July 1968 2·6 million donums had been distributed (i.e. assigned with provisional ownership contract) to 55 000 families. Of this, 1·7 million donums had been taken from private landowners, the remainder being state domain, including the pre-1958 *miri sirf* settlements. Families operating 'under temporary contract' numbered 250 835 in 1966, five times as many as had secured provisional ownership. Beneficiaries thus appear to total 300 000 or more, about half the 1958 agricultural population, but very little is known about land cultivated under temporary lease and the figures are almost certainly official exaggerations.[10] Abandonment of reform holdings seems to be fairly common, due socially to tribal links and economically to poor land productivity. Co-operative and credit schemes have not succeeded.[11] In the Shammar tribal lands near the Syrian border, the sheikhs, their lands having been expropriated and distributed, were known in 1964 to be taking up to 90 per cent of the crops of their former tribesmen, now the legal owners of the land, in return for mechanised cultivation.[12] Progress in Amara province has been slow because of the confused cadastral

situation and the numerous claims and counter-claims to land.
Migration to the Baghdad slums continues as before 1958. The
general conclusion is that the abolition of feudalism has largely
been achieved, but the socio-economic emancipation of the
fellahin has not.

PRODUCTION EFFECTS

How far the sharp fall (about 20 per cent) in output of the
main crops (wheat, barley, rice, cotton) that followed the reform
resulted from the reform itself is difficult to estimate, since serious drought from 1958 to 1961 would have reduced crop production in the rain-fed north anyway; but the reform certainly
had some adverse effect, for output also fell in the southern
irrigated zone, and the 1962–6 average grain production, when
the drought was over, remained about 10 per cent below the
pre-reform (1954–8) average. Rice production, however, recovered its deficit and by 1966 had doubled the mid 1950s
average; and cotton also, less important in terms of output, has
regained pre-reform production levels.[13]

Several factors are responsible for the relative economic failure of the Iraqi reform. Whatever its political pay-offs, pushing
ahead with expropriation while distribution lagged brought
great uncertainty into farming. Property owners due for expropriation fled the land, taking their capital with them (most of
this ending up in foreign banks), whilst the beneficiaries are
largely still cultivating under temporary tenures, with little incentive to invest for the future. The post-reform shortfall in
production, too, reflected the reform organisation's failure to
provide and administer the machinery and irrigation equipment
formerly maintained by the landlords. The reform laws, following those of Egypt, where irrigation is state controlled, made no
provision for maintaining pumps and canals and controlling
water distribution. In the north, tractor services were poorly
organised.[14]

Perhaps the fundamental reason for the post-reform production failures lay in the ecology of Iraqi agriculture.[15] Iraq's
traditional extensive agriculture, with much fallowing to allow
soil rejuvenation and combat salinity, although somewhat
wasteful of land, constituted a stable equilibrium. The tenant on
the large estate, where land was plentiful, rarely had to cultivate

land which needed its fallow period. Reform smallholders, however, were forced by the limitations of plot size to cultivate most of their land, including what should have been left periodically fallow. As the reform failed to prescribe soil-maintaining fertilisers or to institute effective drainage schemes, soil depletion and yield decreases resulted. Improving the ecological conditions for farming takes considerably longer than simple land distribution. Despite irrigation's long-acknowledged importance in Iraq the country still has no economically viable intensive irrigation project. The Al-Wahda land reform settlement project, started in 1964, 30 kilometres east of Baghdad, suffers similar shortcomings to the pre-1958 projects—poor administration, particularly of the irrigation facilities, failure to appreciate the role of co-operatives, shortage of trained and interested personnel, and lack of drainage to combat salinisation.[16] On the Lower Khalis Project north of Baghdad average farm income doubled from 1958 to 1970 mainly through a shift from cereals and cotton to vegetables, fruit and livestock production, but this is exceptional, and anyway the increased peasant income appears to be the complement of the sheikhs' misfortune and to have been absorbed by expanded peasant consumption.[17]

CONCLUSION

The revolutionary reform of 1958 achieved its political aim of breaking up the large estates but, in the continuing political turmoil, progress towards the reform's social and economic goals has been negligible. Iraq provides a prime land reform example of political leaders being compromised by the necessity, often self-imposed, to allow political ideology and short-run political gain to sabotage much needed long-run economic measures.[18] One aspect is the intrusion of foreign-inspired dogma into the arena of Iraq's agricultural development, the patterning of the Iraqi reform on the Egyptian. While some model may be better than no model at all, the gulf between Egyptian agriculture, the intensive cultivation of scarce land by an excessive yet stable and culturally evolved peasantry, and Iraqi agriculture, the extensive utilisation of abundant, underused land by people of low farming skills, received little recognition. Hostility between the urban administrator and the tribal peasant dates from antiquity and is still strong between the reform agency personnel and the beneficiaries; visits to villages accompanied by armed guards make proper evaluation of the reform by outsiders almost impossible. While this attitude persists, and while the political situation remains precarious, the acute land question will continue to exist.

REFERENCES

1. For an excellent account of the pre-reform period in Iraq see D. Warriner: *Land Reform and Development in the Middle East: Egypt, Syria and Iraq* (London, Oxford University Press, 1962), ch. 4.
2. *Ibid*: p. 116.
3. *Ibid*: pp. 141–2.
4. F. Baali: 'Social factors in Iraqi rural-urban migration', *American Journal of Economics and Sociology*, 25 (4), 1966, pp. 359–64.
5. H. C. Treakle: 'Land reform in Iraq', in Agency for International Development: *Spring Review of Land Reform* (Washington, Department of State, 1970), Vol. 8, pp. 20–1.
6. W. E. Adams: 'The pre-revolutionary decade of land reform in Iraq', *Economic Development and Cultural Change*, 11 (3), 1963, pp. 267–88.
7. Warriner: *op. cit.*, pp. 157–9, 162–9.
8. D. Warriner: *Land Reform in Principle and Practice* (Oxford, Clarendon, 1969), pp. 78–9.
9. *Ibid*: pp. 79–83. During 1958–65 the reform laws were amended 27 times.
10. *Ibid*: pp. 91–2.
11. M. M. A. Ahmed and J. A. Al-Jezzy: 'The role of supervised credit in land settlement: case studies of Mikdadiya and Kanaan, Iraq', *Land Reform, Land Settlement and Co-operatives*, 2, 1971, pp. 21–8.
12. Warriner: *Land Reform in Principle and Practice, op. cit.*, p. 89.
13. D. Warriner: 'Employment and income aspects of recent agrarian reforms in the Middle East', *International Labour Review*, 101 (6), 1970, pp. 605–25, esp. p. 618.
14. *Ibid*: p. 619.
15. R. A. Fernea: 'Land reform and ecology in postrevolutionary Iraq', *Economic Development and Cultural Change*, 17 (3), 1969, pp. 356–81.
16. M. M. A. Ahmed, A. Radha, A. Al-Dahin and J. A. Al-Jezzy: 'Land reform in Iraq: an economic evaluation of the Al-Wahda irrigation project', *Land Reform, Land Settlement and Co-operatives*, 1, 1970, pp. 62–77.
17. M. Adams: 'Lessons from agrarian reform in Iraq', *Land Reform, Land Settlement and Co-operatives*, 1, 1972, pp. 56–64.
18. M. Palmer: 'Some political determinants of economic reform: agrarian reform in Iraq', *Journal of Asian and African Studies*, 6 (3–4), 1971, pp. 169–78.

19

Iran

The Persian land reform is a most imaginative and original one. Several features are of special interest, but the complexity of successive waves of legislation, and of the country itself, and paucity of verifiable data make assessment difficult. Contrasts with Iraq, however, immediately appear, for the Persian reform is pro-peasant, liberal in conception and boldly original in strategy.[1] Although it was not the outcome of sudden governmental change, its effects have been moderately revolutionary and certainly more constructive, for it has reduced the power of the landlords and contributed towards creating an independent peasantry. Although deep-seated social and political pressures generated the forces making for reform, the Shah has supplied the vital continuity of purpose necessary for any reform's complete implementation.[2]

Variety and complexity are the keynotes of the country's agricultural geography. Persia is poised between east and west, yet isolated from both, and internally split by terrain and poor communications into remote regions with marked local character and self-sufficiency. Its peasants unmistakably derive from an ancient culture; their world is a world apart, but not a primitive world. Physically the country is largely an arid tableland ringed by high mountains with narrow lowland strips bordering the Persian Gulf and the Caspian Sea. Climate and ruggedness make about half the country desert and waste. Cropland represents only 10 per cent of the total area, and, apart from the fertile, well-watered Caspian provinces, is mostly fragmented in isolated mountain valleys fed by underground irrigation conduits (*qanats*). Yet this fragmented rural spatial structure has also had advantages: the recuperative power of agriculture and rural society from periodic foreign invasions and urban exploitation derives partly from the strong, semi-autonomous nature of the local communities. And one reason why land redistribution succeeded in maintaining production was that it satisfied a long-settled rural population with well-tried traditional skills and capable of acting as village communities.[3]

Towards the mid-twentieth century, however, this basic role of agriculture in the Persian economy and civilisation began to break down. Rapidly expanding oil revenues and an influx of American economic, technical and military assistance brought dramatically visible developments in Iran's landscape and economy. Numerous infrastructural and industrial projects were completed. Malaria and the locust scourge were controlled. Principal cities mushroomed with new construction, and transport improvements brought greater inter-regional movement. These developments made the stagnation of agriculture increasingly conspicuous. Iran brought to the twentieth century feudal land tenures and medieval agricultural technology. The 75 per cent of the total population still bound to the land and to primitive farming techniques increasingly failed to feed a growing nation's population. Many landowners had deserted rural areas, losing their managerial and technical skills in farming and ceasing to invest in much-needed improvements in land and water resources. Iran's plainly archaic agriculture needed to be changed before it strangled the national development. The crucial need for land reform therefore lay less in the villainy of the landlords, though this was not unimportant, than in the nature of Iranian economic and agricultural development.[4]

LAND TENURE AND EARLY ATTEMPTS AT REFORM

The complexity of tenures in Iran makes generalisation difficult. Land records are fragmentary and no accurate cadastral compilation exists. Although it was common knowledge that large absentee landowners held much land, the size of their estates was unknown; they reckoned their property in parts or numbers of villages, not in measured areas (Table 25). An official ministry study in 1957 showed over a quarter of the land held in units of more than one whole village, while over a third was owned in units of under one *dang*, a *dang* being a sixth of a village and a village anything from a few farmsteads to an agglomeration of several thousand people. Certain families reputedly owned as many as a hundred villages which together literally constituted a fiefdom. In the fertile Maragheh district some 300 villages, average size 400 hectares each, were held by only 12 landowners. By contrast, a 1958 study estimated that 65 per cent of cultivators owning land possessed under 1 hectare each.[5] Amongst the small peasants, however, ownership was exceptional. Perhaps 20 per cent of farmland was owned by smallholders before 1962. Tenancy covered an estimated 60 per cent of the cropland in 1958, with rental payment usually by crop-sharing. A common practice allotted a fifth of the product

TABLE 25

OWNERSHIP AND TENURE CHARACTERISTICS OF PERSIAN VILLAGES
BEFORE LAND REFORM

Category	No.	per cent
Villages owned by a single landlord	9 644	23·6
Villages owned by medium landlords[1]	5 009	12·2
Villages under small peasant ownership[2]	6 555	13·8
Domain villages	1 578	3·8
Villages owned by the crown[3]	801	2·0
Villages under *waqf*	758	1·8
Villages under mixed tenure	608	1·4
Ownership/tenure unknown	4 000	9·8
Total	40 756	100·0

Notes: 1 Villages with property units of less than a whole village and more than one *dang*
2 Villages with property units of less than one *dang*
3 Before the distribution of crown lands this figure was at one time much higher—about 2 100

Source: H. Malek: 'Après la réforme agraire iranienne', *Annales de Géographie*, 65 (409), 1966, p. 276.

to the provider of each of the five production factors—land, labour, water, livestock power and seed; if the peasant provided only his labour, 80 per cent of the crop went to the landlord. Written tenancy agreements were rare, and only along the

Caspian littoral, Iran's richest agricultural region, were cash or other fixed rentals common.

Lambton argued that the large landlords of pre-reform Persia were not an hereditary aristocracy of standard feudal type.[6] The so-called feudal features of the traditional Persian land system derived in fact not from feudalism but from the arbitrary nature of power. Although elements of the Persian land system stretch back over 2500 years, the Islamic inheritance code, recurrent anarchy and repeated dynastic changes made the transmission of complete estates down through the generations unlikely. Outside religious and tribal lands, landlords were either members of the ruling family and other civil and military elites, who had obtained their land by conquest, gift, inheritance or purchase, or a newer class of merchants, professionals, bureaucrats and bailiffs, who had invested in land. Most landlords were absentee; indeed an individual owning several villages widely scattered could not avoid being absentee. Political and social prestige motives of landholding gave most landowners preference for owning several villages in poor condition over one in good condition. Between landowner and peasant yawned a wide gulf of mistrust: seldom was there a sense of co-operation or of being engaged in a mutually profitable enterprise. Because of the 'root-rights' clause in Islamic land law (peasants could not be evicted as long as roots they had planted remained in the soil), landlords frequently prohibited their tenants from planting trees, grapes, alfalfa or other long-lived crops. Tenants were also rotated around plots to prevent them from establishing 'continuous use' rights on land. These two practices inevitably discouraged investment in land.

1900–60 saw little change in the land tenure situation, but several attempts at agrarian reform legislation, although either abortive or giving only small-scale results, form important background to the present reforms. In the 1930s Reza Shah attempted to break the power of certain tribal leaders by allotting tribal land to nomads in individual holdings, including large areas in Sistan province in eastern Iran, but sedentarisation had little success. In 1951 the present Shah began distributing the royal family's estates of some 2000 villages. After survey and cartographical division, the land was sold to peasants at approximately ten times its annual crop value, with payment in interest-free annual instalments over 25 years. Holdings assigned were limited to 30 hectares, but most were below 5 hectares. Peasants drew lots for the parcels. The Shah established the Bank of Development and Rural Co-operatives (Bank Omran) in 1951 to administer credit and co-operative aspects of the scheme, which was officially declared complete in 1963, with 11 000 farmers on the land. Excellent results were achieved in the Varamin Plains, 60 kilometres south-east of Tehran, where villages got much technical and financial assistance; elsewhere, however, the redistribution was criticised for its high cost, the small size of the assigned units, the lack of credit and the general indebtedness of the beneficiaries. The crown lands distribution was intended as an example for other landlords to follow, but, despite considerable peasant clamour, it found few emulators. Finally, a 1955 law prescribed the distribution of public domain land. By 1961 only 55 of the 1578 domain villages had been dealt with (due to lack of finance, administrative procrastination and the need to survey and classify all land before sale), but 1971 official figures gave 1536 villages distributed (63 per cent of them in Kurdistan) to 90 000 beneficiary families.[7]

THE LEGISLATION OF THE 1960s

An ill-conceived and badly-drafted reform law limiting property ownership to 400 hectares of irrigated land or 800 hectares of non-irrigated was introduced in 1960. Apart from the obvious impossibility of implementing such a provision in a country where no land measurement or registration had ever been accomplished, the landlords and religious leaders so emasculated the law in parliament that the ceilings became virtually meaningless. The overthrow of the landlord-dominated Eqbal administration in 1961 and the appointment of the dynamic Dr Hassan Arsanjani as Minister of Agriculture in the new reformist government revived concern for effective reform action. A 1962 law limited the land an individual could hold to one whole village (or six *dangs* in separate villages). Excluded from expropriation were orchards, tea plantations, groves, homesteads and mechanised holdings worked by wage labour. Landlords' compensation, based on their own tax returns, was payable over 10 years (later 15). A similar sum, plus 10 per cent for administrative costs, was payable over 15 years by the peasant beneficiaries.

Only members of a village co-operative were eligible for land, preference going to those who actually tilled the land in question and to those who previously provided more than just their labour in the sharecropping contract.

Lambton thought the 1962 law had a touch of genius.[8] It was simple in conception, and made rapid implementation possible despite the lack of a cadastral survey and a body of officials trained in land reform matters. It aimed at breaking the political and social influence of the landowners and at promoting an independent peasantry. The landlords had had, since 1959, warning of probable landownership limitation, and considerable transfer and division of land amongst family members occurred shortly before the reform. Large estate areas were hurriedly planted to orchard crops when it was realised that such land would be exempt. In Isfahan landowners hired tractors for the day the land reform officials arrived to administer the redistribution in the district (mechanised land was also exempted). But the conceptual and indeed historical importance of the Persian land reform overshadows these shortcomings; in Arsanjani's words it was the first step towards reversing the inequities of Persia's 2500 years of land tenure history.

Although the original objective of expropriating all the expropriable villages by the end of 1962 was not achieved, partly because of evasionary tactics by the landlords, Arsanjani decided to initiate the second stage of his reform master-plan, to give peasants security of tenure in villages unaffected by the original reform, especially villages the landlords retained as their single remaining possessions. The plan was to lower the landholding ceiling to a limit of 30 to 150 hectares (according to land quality and nearness to markets). 4700 representatives of the newly formed reform co-operatives assembled in Teheran in 1963 to hear and support Arsanjani's land reform philosophy and to vote their support for the Shah's 'White Revolution' six-point policy for development, which included land reform.

Arsanjani, however, was becoming too popular with the peasants, and the Shah and the government slowed down the pace of reform and brought about his resignation. The 'Amended Articles' of January 1963 (modified in 1964 but not applied till 1965) considerably altered Arsanjani's earlier proposals. Briefly, this legislation regulated large landholdings not affected by the 1962 law, or the villages residual to that law, and empowered the landowners concerned to choose one of five courses: (1) to rent for 30 years their land to the occupying peasants for a cash rent based on the average annual income of the land and subject to five yearly review; (2) to sell the land to the peasants by mutual agreement; (3) to divide the land held between landlord and peasant according to the shares of the previous tenancy agreement (e.g. if the peasant's share of the produce was two-fifths, then that proportion of the landlord's land should be sold to the peasants); (4) purchase by landowner of tenants' rights; (5) formation of an agricultural enterprise jointly operated by landlord and tenant. Provision was also made for 99 year leases to tenants on both privately and publicly endowed *waqf* land. In contrast to stage one, implementing this complex body of legislation was extremely protracted, quite apart from the doubtful benefits to the peasants of the various options. In fact, most landlords concerned in this phase leased their land according to (1) above (see Table 26).

Having about 70 per cent of the land still under tenancy failed the 'land to the tiller' ideal of the original law. Moreover, neither stage attempted to deal with sub-economic holdings and excessive fragmentation, which became the target of the 1968 legislation—the third stage—passed in January to establish agricultural corporations which would cover at least two villages each, and be directed primarily at abolishing fragmentation and developing irrigation and mechanisation. The corporations were initially to be run by the government, which invested considerable finance in them. But because the peasants had to exchange ownership of their land for shares in the corporation, they virtually became agricultural labourers, a complete reversal of the original reform. Considerable hostility exists among peasants to the corporation idea. Certainly the declared aim is to hand over the corporations eventually to the members, but a danger remains that they will become permanent managerial operations of the state. Despite the official intention of setting up farm corporations throughout the country, by 1972 only 27 had been instituted; they covered 102 700 hectares in 164 villages and had 9171 members.

The second, and more important, step under the third stage was the October 1968 law ordering either the sale to tenants of the land they rented or the division of landlords' property amongst tenants according to their sharecropping share, at a price 10 times the rent, paid back over 12 years. 'Farmers' Day',

TABLE 26

RESULTS OF THE THREE PHASES OF LAND REFORM IN IRAN, 1972

First Phase

1   17 344 villages transferred from landlords to 774 008 peasant families.

Second Phase

2   225 261 landowners let their lands to 1 227 950 tenant farmers.
3   3 280 landowners sold their holdings to 57 261 farmers.
4   Jointly-operated agricultural units set up in 4 411 villages.
5   25 824 landowners divided their land with 157 091 sharecroppers according to the traditional sharing proportions.
6   10 065 public endowment villages and farms were let to 135 631 farmers.
7   957 private endowment villages were let to 35 932 farmers.
8   6 392 landlords bought out their tenants.

Third Phase

9   123 678 landowners sold their land to 477 670 peasants.
10 4 839 landowners divided their holdings among 161 900 peasants. A further 101 300 similar transactions are being processed (August 1972).

Source: N. Khatibi: 'Land reform in Iran and its role in rural development', *Land Reform, Land Settlement and Co-operatives*, 2, 1972, p. 66.

22 September 1971, was declared the end of a 'decade of land reform'. If by then landowners had not arranged sale or division among their tenants, the rental payment thereafter would be regarded as instalments of the purchase price; the ministry would eventually ratify titles.

RESULTS

Detailed evaluation of the Persian reform is difficult. The legislation (apart from the original law) is complex, and the regional variations in nature and progress of the reform are wide. Generally the reform was most speedily and successfully accomplished in the more progressive northern provinces. In the south and south-east (Kirman and Baluchistan especially) progress was much slower, because of tribal and environmental problems.[9]

Official data on the reform are suspect. Table 26 gives the official statement on the results at 1972, but other studies clearly indicate that these figures exaggerate the real position.[10] For example, a village was officially 'reformed' even if only a small part of its land had been distributed. If one landlord sold part of a village, its entire population was classed as beneficiaries; if a second landlord in that village sold another fraction, then double counting occurred. Apparently only 3788 villages qualified for complete distribution under the original law; all other expropriable villages, over 10 000, were only partly affected. Probably only about 15 to 20 per cent of the villages (or whole village equivalents) and of the peasant population benefited from land reform.[11]

Exposing the falsity of official figures does not prove that the reform did not achieve much: it did. By any criterion, and certainly in comparison to many other countries surveyed in this book, the Persian reform is unique and successful. This success reflects three factors, oil revenues, dynamic leadership in the crucial initial phase, and support from the Shah and the government. The speed of implementation was vital and impressive: within a year over half the villages scheduled for wholesale expropriation under the original law had been processed—1988 villages distributed amongst 120 018 peasant farmers. Already in 1964 Lambton in her detailed field studies in the west of the country noted the greatly improved incomes, diet, living and farming standards of those peasants affected by the reform.[12] The great lesson of the Persian reform is that it is the first step that counts.[13]

In the absence of cadastral surveys, systematic figures on tenure structure and farm size distribution before and after the reform are not available. On production, the widespread attainment of landownership clearly had had some positive effect, security of expectation allowing a switch into alfalfa, orchards and profitable summer cash crops such as potatoes, tomatoes and peas, previously prohibited by the landlords because of root-rights and the difficulty of collecting the landowners' share of the product. An increase of 33 per cent was registered from

1962 to 1969 for total agricultural production, with vegetable production increasing 16 per cent annually.[14] There has been no production cutback, as in neighbouring Iraq, but the agricultural increase only just exceeds annual population growth (3·8 per cent as against 3·0 per cent). Whilst Iran successfully exemplifies old-fashioned land redistribution, without the modern trappings of 'integrated' reform, recognition of the limits to achievable improvements stimulated the recent policy switch to larger scale agricultural units. Joint-farming companies, co-operatives, modern technology large landowners' collectives and government sponsored 'agri-business' units are four approaches by which the many smallholdings created by the reform are being reintegrated after a period of temporarily 'dropping out' of the national economy.[15]

Co-operatives were important to the success of the reform, particularly given the local and regional isolation and the lack of extension workers (in 1970 Iran had only a tenth of Egypt's 10 000 extension workers to serve as big a rural population far more widely scattered). The original co-operative organisation of 1962–4, although meeting only some 15 to 20 per cent of potential credit demand, was effective to that extent because, not being run by government officials, it fostered peasant participation and confidence. Besides short-term credit, many societies provided seeds, fertilisers and household goods. Since 1966, however, the government has reduced support for the co-operative and credit movements, and incorporation of the co-operative federation within the land reform ministry in 1967 introduced a policy of more direct control. Peasant enthusiasm for the co-operatives has accordingly waned somewhat.[16]

The reform's impact on rural social structure has been slight. Rather than promoting equality for the poorer classes, the reform favoured the tenants and sharecroppers at the expense of the one million landless and casual labourer households, who, with no land, no gleaning rights, no minimum wage and no unemployment benefit, are worse off than before. One village study showed that the better-off beneficiaries now lend capital at high interest rates to their poorer fellows and so are replacing the land capitalism of the landlord with the 'oxen and cash capitalism' of the new system.[17] Perhaps the most important social effect of the reform, then, is the emergence of a petit bourgeois class based on money lending, general commerce and trading in the crops produced by the beneficiaries.[18] With the recent reorientation of co-operative and credit policy towards larger projects favouring the wealthier peasants, and with the current emphasis on mechanised production, this trend seems likely to continue.

REFERENCES

1. D. Warriner: *Land Reform in Principle and Practice* (Oxford, Clarendon, 1969), p. 109.
2. For an account which emphasises this point, but which is extremely biased in favour of the Shah, see D. R. Denman: *The King's Vista: A Land Reform which has Changed the Face of Persia* (Berkhamstead, Geographical Publications, 1973).
3. A. K. S. Lambton: *The Persian Land Reform 1962–1966* (Oxford, Clarendon, 1969), p. 19.
4. K. B. Platt: 'Land reform in Iran,' in Agency for International Development: *Spring Review of Land Reform* (Washington, Department of State, 1970), Vol. 2, pp. 2–4.
5. Q. West: *Agricultural Development Programs of Iran, Iraq and Sudan* (Washington, Department of Agriculture, Foreign Agriculture Report 112, 1958), p. 5.
6. A. K. S. Lambton: *Landlord and Peasant in Persia* (London, Oxford University Press, 1953), ch. 13.
7. Denman: *op. cit.*, pp. 80–2.
8. Lambton: *The Persian Land Reform, op. cit.*, p. 64.
9. *Ibid*: chs. 6–11.
10. N. Keddie: 'The Iranian village before and after land reform', *Journal of Contemporary History*, 3 (3), 1968, pp. 69–91; I. Ajami: 'Land reform and modernisation of the farming structure in Iran', *Oxford Agrarian Studies*, 2 (2), 1973, pp. 120–31; M. A. Katouzian: 'Land reform in Iran: a case study in the political economy of social engineering', *Journal of Peasant Studies*. 1 (2), 1974, pp. 220–39.
11. Keddie: *op. cit.*, p. 85; Ajami: *op. cit.*, p. 123; Katouzian: *op. cit.*, p. 229. Even estimates of the total number of Persian villages vary, from 41 000 to 71 000!
12. Lambton: *The Persian Land Reform, op. cit.*, p. 192.
13. Warriner: *op. cit.*, p. 134.
14. Platt: *op. cit.*, pp. 81–2.
15. U. Planck: 'Die Reintegrationsphase der iranischen Agrarreform', *Erdkunde*, 29 (1), 1975, pp. 1–9.
16. Lambton: *The Persian Land Reform, op. cit.*, pp. 291–346, 360–5.
17. W. Miller: 'Hosseinabad: a Persian village', *Middle East Journal*, 18 (4), 1964, pp. 483–98.
18. K. Khosrovi: 'La réforme agraire et l'apparition d'une nouvelle classe en Iran', *Études Rurales*, 34, 1969, pp. 122–6.

20

Tunisia

Tunisian agrarian reform, begun soon after independence in 1956, is still continuing. The post-independence government has never considered rural development a single problem to be solved by a once-for-all programme; rather the process has experienced phases as the new leaders sorted out their nation's destiny. One group of laws aimed at creating a stable, independent peasantry, another at establishing large, state-run co-operative farms. The co-operatives were part of a massive investment in agriculture. The Ten Year Plan 1962–71 directed 41 per cent of all investment to agriculture, and 80 per cent of total investment in agriculture was state administered. This was in a country with an investment rate averaging 25 per cent of the gross domestic product, among the highest in the developing world. Over half the Plan's investment came from foreign grants and loans, making Tunisia second only to Israel in foreign aid per capita. Yet despite this considerable capital input, the government's land strategies have not proved wise. State co-operatives foundered on inefficient management and unattained production levels, leaving the Tunisian *fellahin* probably worse off than before.

TRADITIONAL LAND TENURE AND COLONISATION

Tunisia's agricultural history is dominated by colonialism, chiefly French. Before the French Protectorate in 1881 Ottoman rule had crystallised the standard Islamic tenures of *mulk*, *miri* and *habous* (the Maghreb equivalent of *waqf*), and important expanses, chiefly in the arid south, of collective tribal land. These tenures continued, at least to the end of the colonial period, but French colonisation profoundly affected the landownership pattern. Between 1881 and 1891 the French acquired some 443 000 hectares, partly by speculative purchase and partly by official decrees which facilitated French acquisition of state, *habous* and loosely-tilled land at very low prices. Widespread climatic irregularity determined a rather feeble bond between peasant and land; *mulk* land before colonisation was extremely restricted and the colonists exploited the ill-defined tenure status of much land to their own advantage. Ninety-three per cent of this early land grab was acquired by 16 large owners, some of them finance companies. By 1911 Tunisia housed 2500 French settlers who farmed 725 000 hectares and 1270 Italian, mainly Sicilian, settlers who held 84 000 hectares. At independence the colonials numbered 6600 families. They managed some 815 000 hectares of land 615 000 of which they owned and 200 000 of which they rented from Tunisian landowners. Although the colons managed only 18 per cent of the agricultural area, the value added of their production represented over 40 per cent of agricultural income. Most of the best land was foreign owned, including the well-watered vine and citrus lands of the north coast and the Cape Bon peninsula and the fertile cereal land of the north-centre. In these zones up to 50 per cent of the land was in colon hands. The Tunisian *fellah* became either a landless labourer on the colon estates or a smallholder or sharecropper scratching a living in the eroded hill regions. In the north 5100 large landowners, mostly colons, 1·6 per cent of the total property owners, possessed 1 450 000 hectares, or 30 per cent of the land; 270 000 peasants, 80 per cent of the total landholders, owned no larger an area.[1]

The colonial system did much more than just create colonial estates. It unleashed a process which subsequently escaped its control, creating a mass of peasants with no land and no regular work. Landless groups—for example, the *khammes*, who received only a fifth of the product for working someone else's land—certainly existed in pre-colonial times, but these groups were numerically small. Before colonisation underemployment basically reflected archaic farming technology; after colonisation essentially the scarcity of cultivable land available to the indigenous peasants.[2]

EARLY PHASES OF LAND REFORM: THE MEDJERDA VALLEY SCHEME

In contrast to Egyptian and Iraqi, Tunisian independence was not followed by immediate and radical steps to reform agriculture. Although social reform was attacked through education and an improved legal system, economic policy aimed at preserving the status quo to avoid alienating local and foreign investors by overt socialism. Colon agricultural production still carried the economy, and the chief market, particularly for wine, whose consumption is forbidden to moslems, was still France. Manufacturing businesses, too, were almost entirely foreign-owned. Early land policy was therefore aimed at safe-guarding colon agricultural interests rather than at expropriating the colonial landlords, and the first phase of reform legislation, 1956–8, was concerned with promoting private rights to landholding. It included the establishment of small *cellules de mise en valeur* in underexploited, potentially irrigable blocks of land of 50 to 500 hectares in the centre and south, laws making *habous* land private property which could be bought and sold, laws abolishing collective land rights to permit survey of common land in the south and distribution of titles to tribal members. All rural debts contracted before 1953 were cancelled by edict.

The outstanding measure in this phase was the 1958 reform law governing the development of the Lower Medjerda Valley, between Tunis and Bizerta.[3] The zone was selected for its potential for intensive irrigated farming, a potential unrealised since Roman times, when numerous aqueducts, their remains still visible, fed the valley. The valley's location, adjoining the chief markets and ports, has both economic and political significance, for a successful development within almost daily view of much of the population, including the capital city, can strongly reinforce popular support of a central government. Because of its limited size—its 2800 square kilometres represents only 4 per cent of Tunisia's arable land and will absorb not more than 5 per cent of the country's farming population—the scheme has only a minor role in reforming national agriculture. Its value was as a pilot project to test a reform philosophy and as a precedent for what could be effected elsewhere.

The June 1958 reform law for the Medjerda Valley stated that: farmers in the development must raise irrigated crops on at least two-thirds of their land, on pain of fine or expropriation; owners of over 2 hectares must contribute to the amortisation of government funds used on their behalf at the estimated rate that the productivity of their holdings is increased by irrigation; holdings above 50 hectares would be expropriated and distributed to landless peasants (except where landowners had themselves irrigated their land). A special agency—*Office de la Mise en Valeur de la Basse Vallée de la Medjerda* (OMVVM) was to administer the programme. The principal objectives were land reform, irrigation, erosion control and industrial processing of the agricultural produce. Redistribution of land above the 50 hectare ceiling affected some 50 000 hectares, about 40 per cent of the land in the project area, but the 1964 nationalisation of foreign-owned land brought nearly 75 per cent of the project surface under state control. Irrigating 45 000 hectares will change land use from extensive cereal farming to intensive fruit, vegetable and dairy farming. Dams and reservoirs have been built, or are under construction, to supply irrigation water and provide electric power and drinking water for Tunis. Afforestation and terracing in the surrounding hill country control erosion and prevent the new reservoirs from silting.

Beneficiaries were carefully selected from the abundant landless labourers in north-east Tunisia (e.g. they had to be in good health, under forty years old, married with fewer than five children) and assigned plots varying with land quality from 5 to 12 hectares. Lots of 1 to 2 hectares (e.g. El Habibia, zone F) provided minimum subsistence areas for workers working part-time elsewhere. With title to the land retained by the state, the assignee became virtually the agent of the state, raising the crops prescribed by the extension authorities and attending evening classes on modern farming methods. He repays the cost of the holding in 25 annual instalments.

Table 27 shows the characteristics of the eleven settlement districts of the valley. Mabtouha and Utique are pastoral settlements with much larger lots. New settlement houses are either completely dispersed or clustered in small nuclei (Figs. 13 and 14); the physical appearance and planning of such settlements, indeed many aspects of the project, closely resemble the reform settlements in southern Italy completed a few years earlier. Little progress has yet been made in agricultural industry, ex-

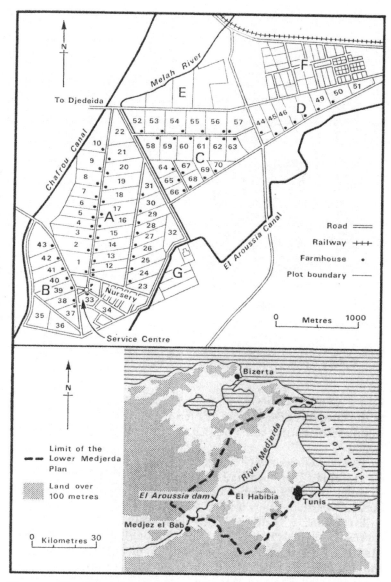

Fig. 13. The Lower Medjerda Valley Plan and El Habibia settlement,
Tunisia. *Sources:* E. Karabenick: 'The Medjerda Plan: a precedent to
agrarian reform in Tunisia', *Professional Geographer*, 19 (1), 1967, p. 18;
H. Mensching: 'Das Medjerda-Projekt in Tunisien: agrarlandschaftlicher
und sozialgeographischer Wandel in der Kulturlandschaft des Medjerda-
Tales', *Erde*, 93 (2), 1962, p. 134

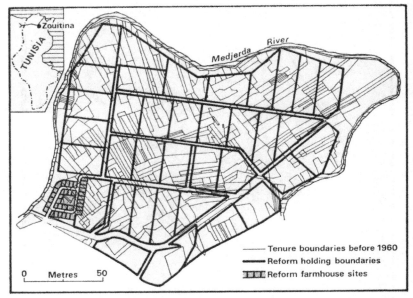

Fig. 14. Zouitina: an example of land tenure reform in the Lower Medjerda Valley. *Source:* E. Karabenick: 'Irrigation development in Tunisia', *Tijdschrift voor Economische en Sociale Geografie*, 60 (4), 1969, p. 364

cept a tomato-processing plant at El Habibia. Average incomes of the farmers in the scheme tripled between 1958 and 1965 and population density has doubled to a mean of one person per hectare.

The first co-operative settlement completed in the valley was El Habibia. The land had been parcelled, subsoiled, levelled, drained and irrigated before the co-operative opened in 1959. A whitewashed stone house, with kitchen and two or three utility rooms, a courtyard and stalls, was built on each plot, served by a new road (Fig. 13). Although the farmers of El Habibia own their plots and do their own cultivation, community effort is emphasised under the direction of OMVVM rural technicians. The agriculture comprises intensive production of fruits (chiefly apricots), vegetables (artichokes, tomatoes and peppers) and forage crops (maize, lucerne and berseem) for cattle (imported Dutch Friesians). The co-operative pro-

TABLE 27

REFORM SETTLEMENTS IN THE LOWER MEDJERDA VALLEY, TUNISIA

Name of Settlement	Date created	Area (hectares)	No. of lots	Av. size of lot	Predominant tenure origin
El Habibia	1959	815	135	6·0	Colonisation
El Moazzia	1960	168	30	5·6	Private habous
Sanhaja	1961	667	33	20·2	Public habous
El Mansoura	1961	724	126	5·7	Private habous
Sidi Thabet	1963	1 605	165	9·7	Colonisation
Sidi Daoud	1964	813	68	12·0	Remembrement
Mabtouha	1964	5 100	50	102·0	Colonisation
Zouitina	1965	235	35	6·7	Remembrement
Destour	1965	600	90	6·7	Colonisation
Bori Toum	1966	580	78	7·4	Colonisation
Utique	1966	3 100	129	24·0	Tunisian landlords

Source: M. El Aouani: 'Les lotissements de réforme agraire de la Basse Vallée de la Medjerda', Revue Tunisienne des Sciences Sociales, 5 (15), 1968, p. 80.

vides extension services and all necessary agricultural inputs: irrigation water, seed, fertiliser, machines for hire, marketing of principal crops and credit. It also provides important social services: school, mosque, post office and general shop. A social worker instructs the wives in domestic budgeting, child care, birth control, nutrition and hygiene. The whole enterprise received much publicity and became something of a symbol of Tunisian land reform and agricultural co-operation.

Despite the obvious landscape changes in the Lower Medjerda Valley since 1958, scathing criticisms of the project are heard. The 50 hectare ceiling has not been adhered to and only 30 per cent of the irrigated land is being wet-farmed.[4] Increased demands from Tunis and pressure for more irrigation water allocation in the upper valley pose serious problems of diminishing water supply.[5] Irrigation and drainage costs were twice as high as expected and present revenue barely covers operating costs, let alone the initial massive capital outlay. Studies of market gardening in the El Moazzia lotissement and of dairying in Destour show that individual farmers' incomes and yields of various crops mostly fall well below the levels prescribed by

OMVVM officials.[6] Salinity, reducing the choice of crops that will grow, is serious.

The pragmatism of Bourguiba's economic and land policies could not last indefinitely. Pressure, chiefly from Egypt and Algeria and from the Tunisian left wing, induced more vigorous action. The second phase was introduced by Ahmed ben Salah, the first Minister of Planning, in the Ten Year Plan of 1962–71, which clearly stressed the co-operatives' role in developing Tunisia. They became the symbol for economic progress and were to support an annual production growth of 5 per cent to feed, increasingly better, a population increasing at 2·3 per cent. Foreign ownership of land was declared contrary to Tunisian interests, and funds were provided to purchase foreign-owned assets. By 1964 the government had bought about 300 000 hectares, half the colon land, but in May 1964 Bourguiba suddenly nationalised the remaining colon land without compensation. Agreements with Italy in 1967 and France in 1968 endorsed part payment for it.

The 1956–64 period of co-operative evolution saw notably increased state involvement in co-operation and great variety in forms of co-operatives designed to modernise agriculture and to substitute for the disappearing French managers, for whom local replacements were lacking. Co-operative types included *unités co-opératives de production* for cereal farming, *unités de poly-culture* for mixed farming, *pré-co-opératives* for workers with little farming experience and the *cellules de mise en valeur* already mentioned for settling and controlling irrigated land in the south. The period 1964–9, beginning with the expropriation of remaining colon land, saw an intensified reliance on the co-operative-collective model, based partly on a questioning understanding of Yugoslav communal farming. By far the most important mode of agricultural production was the *unité*; although in theory a co-operative, in practice it was virtually a state farm. Over-reliance on this vehicle for agricultural reform and development, and the early 1969 spurt towards state control of all land, led to the later 1969 dramatic collapse of the system.

The *unités* took two forms. The first grouped a vacated colon estate with surrounding properties into a single operating unit of 1000–2000 hectares and 50–200 people. Combining traditional small-scale farms with modern ex-colon estates particularly marked the northern cereal-growing regions, where most good cereal land had long had foreign management. The other form of *unité* grouped smallholders without a colon estate. Neither form required the consent of the relevant landowners. Their tribal background and their faith in Bourguiba and the co-operative experiment made most peasants willingly accept this state autocracy, at least initially. Although landowners incorporated in a *unité* retained title to their land, they yielded management to a state-appointed bureaucracy. A crucial operational shortcoming is immediately apparent. Quite apart from Tunisia's scarcity of management resources (even the Planning Minister was qualified only to teach school Arabic and openly eschewed anything to do with economics), bureaucratic decision-making was far too cumbersome for the manifold day-to-day operating decisions necessary in farming.

The objectives of the co-operative programme were stated only vaguely. Co-operatives would provide for self improvement and social justice (*'promotion de l'homme'*) besides economic development and *mise en valeur* (literally, valorising underutilised land); the conflict between these goals was ignored, only to obtrude later. The prime immediate objective was to cushion the production collapse that would occur if the colons departed with nothing done to fill their managerial and capital-providing roles. The 1964 confiscation of colon farms made the state suddenly responsible for over 300 000 hectares of the country's richest land; overnight co-operation was required to grow and market some 40 per cent by value of the nation's agricultural produce. Not surprisingly they achieved only very modest success, especially with the handicaps of poor weather in the mid 1960s and the sudden restriction of the traditional French markets for wine and hard wheat. By August 1968, just before the final rapid expansion of state control in 1969, Tunisia had 478 *unités*, 337 of them in the north. They covered 805 000 hectares, nearly 38 per cent of the cultivable land (in the north over 60 per cent) and included 900 000 people, 30 per cent of total rural population. In January, 1969, came the sudden announcement of nationalisation of all land. Within eight months land under state control nearly tripled to include the entire cultivated area. In September the higher authorities prevented the Minister of Planning from implementing his grandiose scheme, and the policy of all-out co-operation collapsed when the Prime Minister announced that private holdings could be withdrawn from the co-operatives. By October only 13 per cent of Tunisian farmland was under co-operative management, chiefly former colon land. Politically the September move stepped back ten years to the first phase of land policy.

Most peasants and farm labourers in Tunisia wondered where the benefits of co-operation and independence were. Not only were they as poor in 1969 as in 1956, but many had less real income and the gap with the urban population had progressively widened since independence. Only a mixture of the patience born of fatalism, the visible advantage of the new schools and a reverence for Bourguiba prevented more marked alienation of the rural population.

The *unités* were dubbed co-operatives to appease both eastern and western aid sources; in fact they were state farms. The final attempt at state control of all land wrecked the whole system. The 5000 largest landlords in Tunisia argued directly with Bourguiba the case for retaining some private ownership, urging the inefficiency of the state farms and the bitterness of the dispossessed peasants and small commercial farmers. Numerous violent outbreaks, with several fatalities, greeted the decision to co-operativise the rich Sahel and Cape Bon orchard farmers. The richer farmers saw little possibility for improvement under nationalisation, and their political opposition forced Bourguiba to reverse his policy.[8] Considerable information is available concerning the co-operatives' effect on rural incomes, production and employment, although the evidence sometimes conflicts. The major constraint on state farm operation was the complete absence of management and accounting personnel. Enthusiasm could not compensate for lack of skill, and the government recruited no foreign help in these fields; instead it set its own political agents and technicians to teach the peasants modern farming. The dilemma was that self-management was considered impracticable because of the co-operators' illiteracy and lack of farming experience, but that state farming was also unworkable because of lack of qualified technicians and administrative personnel.

Another mistake was equating modernisation with mechanisation. Official figures for 1962, at the beginning of the co-operative drive, showed that out of 34 800 farms in northern Tunisia, 33 per cent used modern machinery on 1·2 million hectares or 72 per cent of the total agricultural area (mostly on cereal land) —a level hardly to be paralleled in any other Mediterranean or Middle Eastern country. The co-operative policy erroneously assumed, despite all the contrary evidence, that all land could be mechanised, without risk of peasant unemployment. The Kef region, with over three-quarters of the agricultural area under large, mechanised cereal co-operatives, had substantial unemployment, and land shortage for peasants outside direct benefit from the co-operatives.[9] Although the average co-operator-land ratio in northern *unités* was 1 per 10 to 15 hectares, in some cereal farms it reached 1 per 80 to 100 hectares, absurdly low for a country with a population density averaging 50 persons per square kilometre and with considerable possibility of agricultural intensification and diversification. 191 *unités* studied by a World Bank group (the World Bank had an interest, having lent the co-operative movement £13 million at 6 per cent per annum interest in 1967), had 17 530 active co-operators on 213 600 hectares of agricultural land (an average of 1 per 12 hectares), working on average 165 days per year; additionally 10 112 inactive co-operators had furnished land but got no work in return.[10] Zamiti cites co-operatives which could have functioned just as productively with half the members and puts 13 days per month as the average work load.[11] Those co-operative members who did get regular work throughout the year— the managerial and technical workers—also received higher daily rates of pay—400–500 millimes as against 350 per day worked for labourers. For a labourer working only part of the year this barely covered food expenses. A kilo of meat was ten times the daily wage, and eggs, the other main protein source, were often sold to buy more bread and oil. The average annual net income per co-operator was given in 1965 as 84 dinars (£65) but there were considerable regional contrasts. In the south, where co-operators averaged only a hundred days work per year, net income fell to £10; in Jendouba in the north, where most work was available, it was £95.[12]

Whether the Tunisian peasants would have been better off

without the whole co-operative experiment is a difficult, hypothetical question. A 1968 sample enquiry showing 30 per cent of the co-operators as previously unemployed and 55 per cent as landless labourers concluded that the position of this large group had not been worsened by the co-operatives because it was already beyond deterioration.[13] This may be true for the cereal zone landless, but peasants who had disposed of their land and livestock to join the co-operatives were left stranded when the movement folded. A peasant who, for example, had sold cattle at 15 dinars per head in the early 1960s found they now cost from 60 to 110 dinars to buy. The money economy based on monocultures and mechanisation the co-operatives introduced had broken down the old polycultural familial farming structure.

In production, too, the *unités* had little success beyond cushioning the potential cutback with the departure of the colons. Sufficiently complete accounts for colon and state farms do not exist. Global data for the chief crop, wheat, show little change in yields in this period, but a drop in area and total output of over 30 per cent, partly reflecting government sponsored orchard planting and conversion to industrial crops such as tomatoes. Livestock statistics, for cattle, sheep and goats, indicate a severe 1956–9 decrease, involving serious loss of revenue and food for many small peasants.

FUTURE PROSPECTS

The September 1969 turnabout gave the landowning classes new life and was rapturously welcomed. By mid 1970 only 218 *unités*, covering 203 000 hectares and containing 10 000 peasants, remained, chiefly on the colon land that could not be returned to its previous owners. Enormous agricultural problems remain, but increased investment and output have already followed denationalisation. New hybrid wheats, introduced in 1966, covered 50 000 hectares by 1969 and are expected to cover 500 000 hectares by 1980. Yields of 20 quintals per hectare, over twice as much as local strains, benefit mainly the richer, more knowledgeable farmers. If Tunisian co-operation is to succeed at a second attempt, it must display a more realistic concern for peasant welfare. Already the old free-association service co-operatives have revived unaided, and a new pilot co-operative project at Oued Meliz on the Algerian border concentrates on labour intensive methods and animal traction, but the current most important facet of Tunisian human geography is the population explosion, which any future development policy will have to cater for.[14]

REFERENCES

1. G. Duwaji: 'Land ownership in Tunisia: an obstacle to agricultural development', *Land Economics*, 44 (1), 1968, pp. 127-33.
2. A. Zghal: 'Changement de systèmes politiques et réformes des structures agraires en Tunisie', *Revue Tunisienne des Sciences Sociales*, 5 (12), 1968, pp. 9-32.
3. E. Karabenick: 'The Medjerda Plan: a precedent to agrarian reform in Tunisia', *Professional Geographer*, 19 (1), 1967, pp. 17-22.
4. J. L. Simmons: 'Land reform in Tunisia', in Agency for International Development: *Spring Review of Land Reform* (Washington, Department of State, 1970), Vol. 8, p. 71.
5. E. Karabenick: 'Irrigation development in Tunisia', *Tijdschrift voor Economische en Sociale Geografie*, 60 (6), 1969, pp. 360-8.
6. M. El Aouani: 'Les lotissements de la réforme agraire de la Basse Vallée de la Medjerda', *Revue Tunisienne des Sciences Sociales*, 5 (15), 1968, pp. 75-92.
7. This section is drawn largely from J. L. Simmons: 'Agricultural cooperatives and Tunisian development', *Middle East Journal*, 24 (4), 1970, pp. 455-65; 25 (1), 1971, pp. 45-57.
8. L. Rudebeck: 'Developmental pressure and political limits: a Tunisian example', *Journal of Modern African Studies*, 8 (2), 1970, pp. 173-98; J. L. Simmons: 'The political economy of land use: Tunisian private farmers', in R. Antoun and I. Harik (eds.): *Rural Politics and Social Change in the Middle East* (Bloomington, Indiana University Press, 1972), pp. 432-52.
9. J. Poncet: 'L'expérience des "unités co-opératives de production" dans la région du Kef', *Tiers Monde*, 7 (27), 1966, pp. 567-80.
10. R. Dumont: *Paysanneries aux Abois: Ceylan, Tunisie, Senegal* (Paris, Seuil, 1972), p. 138.
11. K. Zamiti: 'Les obstacles matériels et idéologiques à l'évolution sociale des campagnes tunisiennes: l'expérience de mise en co-opératives dans le governorat de Beja', *Revue Tunisienne des Sciences Sociales*, 7 (21), 1970, pp. 9-55.
12. M. P. Moore and M. S. Lewis: 'Agrarian reform and the development of agricultural co-operation in Tunisia', in M. Digby (ed.): *Yearbook of Agricultural Co-operation* (Oxford, Blackwell, 1968), pp. 29-52.
13. E. Makhlouf: 'Les co-opératives agricoles en Tunisie: structures et difficultés', *Revue Tunisienne des Sciences Sociales*, 8 (26), 1971, pp. 79-114.
14. Dumont: *op. cit.*, pp. 143, 154, 160-1, 167-8.

21

Algeria

As adjacent countries in North Africa, Tunisia and Algeria share many features of environment, agricultural development and colonial history. But whereas Tunisia's agrarian reform experience was instructive only in its failure, Algeria's policy may well give a more positive demonstration for developing socialist countries. It is still too soon to digest fully what the Algerians are doing, but their 'autogestion' or workers' self-management experiment is of exceptional interest.

Algeria's decolonisation problems were more massive yet more clear-cut than Tunisia's. The country is much larger (larger in fact than the whole of western Europe) and its population nearly three times Tunisia's. The French penetration lasted fifty years longer and was more complete; in fact Algeria was constitutionally a part of France. But the Algerian independence movement was immensely more powerful than the Tunisian. It succeeded after eight years of bloody fighting, with a million Algerians dead and 8000 villages destroyed. Algeria's novel experiment with socialism began in the agricultural sector, when landless labourers spontaneously occupied and started managing abandoned colon estates.

THE COLONIAL PERIOD

Colonial land was acquired mainly during the mid-nineteenth century. Two broad types of agricultural colonisation took place: private colonisation, by individual or commercial acquisition of land from local people; and official colonisation, by which the colonial government, by sale or grant, transferred public domain property to incoming colonists.[1] First to change hands were the large private estates (*azel*) of the old Turkish governors, who still held some political sway over the Tell region and who possessed some of the best land in Algeria. With Frenchmen replacing Turks, transfer of this land was straightforward and to be expected. Much less so, however, was the French sequestration of *habous* land from 1830 onwards. Although the amount of *habous* transferred to colons between 1830 and 1850 was only 16 250 hectares, it aroused more resentment than any other single aspect of the tenure changes the French enforced.[2] Other devious schemes catered for appropriation of *arch* land, the traditional tribal lands of semi-nomadic, tent-dwelling bedouin Arabs. One such scheme, *cantonnement*, assumed that a tribe could support itself on only part of its lands by cultivating more intensively; the land not considered necessary for the tribe was expropriated and given to French colonists.[3] The *mulk* land of the settled Berbers, located on marginal mountainsides and unsuited to colon commercial farming, remained largely in native hands.

At independence Algeria's 10 million cultivated hectares (virtually all in the north) were divided between 21 674 French holdings comprising 2·7 million hectares of the very best land, and over 630 000 peasant families whose farms covered 7·3 million hectares of mostly infertile, remote and eroded land. About a third of the colon holdings (6385) were over 100 hectares in size, totalling 87 per cent of the foreign-owned area, but 7342 under 10 hectares indicated substantial smallholder settlement. Nevertheless the average colon holding of 125 hectares contrasted markedly with the average native holding of 12 hectares. In fact two-thirds of the native farms were under 10 hectares. Colon land yielded on average three times the value of native land per hectare, and productivity per worker was five times as high. During a century of colonisation the indigenous rural population more than doubled, yet control of the best land and water resources by the colons reduced indegene cereal production by 20 per cent and livestock numbers by half.[4] The European farmers constituted 2 per cent of Algeria's rural population, yet possessed nearly a third of all tillable land and produced 60 per cent of the total crop production by value. As in Tunisia, colon land was chiefly geared to supplying France with wine, fruit and vegetables. Only 3 per cent of the produce was consumed domestically.

REVOLUTION AND AUTOGESTION

Algerian land reform is intimately linked with the nationalist revolution. The need for land reform was an underlying cause of revolution and the character of the new agrarian structure is a product of that revolution. Nationalisation came in three stages.[5] The first was in July and August, 1962, when the French colons in regions far from the coast with sparse European population abandoned their estates. These *bien vacants* were promptly occupied by the Algerian labourers to safeguard their livelihood. So was born the motivating force of the Algerian agrarian revolution and some 950 000 hectares, mostly cereal land, were incorporated into the socialist sector.

Unprepared for the chaos following the hasty departure of the French, in December 1962 the Algerian government enlisted René Dumont, the French agronomist sympathetic to the Algerian cause, to make recommendations for coping with the emergency.[6] Dumont considered the rapid re-establishment of government authority the most important single immediate requirement. To administer the abandoned estates a semi-autonomous organisation within the Ministry of Agriculture was established—the *Office National de la Réforme Agraire* (ONRA). For the long term Dumont suggested for the north, the replacing of wine grapes by table and raisin grapes and oranges, and for the high plains the emphasising of livestock farming, replacing the cereals-fallow régime with a forage rotation.

A rapidly deteriorating situation (damage by the departing French, hurried selling of machinery for scrap and of land) required urgent action. By the 'Decrees of March', 1963, the government regained control over the revolution and prevented the bourgeoisie from grabbing the vacated land by ratifying the spontaneous action of the Algerian estate workers.[7] It also introduced the second stage of agrarian reform by expropriating the largest French estates, which added another 800 000 hectares to the socialist sector. The third stage came in October 1963, when the remaining one million hectares of French land, including the most productive vineyards and citrus groves, were expropriated. Some 2·8 million hectares thus passed from the colons to the government, which, with small pieces of other state land, now holds 3000 self-managed units of around 1000 hectares each. Usually, one or more colon estates were transformed directly into a *grand domaine*, but some collectives amalgamated a large number of small colon farms. Although ONRA initially kept socialised farms to a limit of 1000 hectares, many in the cereals zone are now larger, and 22 exceed 5000 hectares.

ORGANISATION OF THE SOCIALISED FARMS[8]

The March Decrees aimed at combining strong central government direction with considerable local participation in farm decisions. In each estate the decision-making organs are the General Assembly of Workers, comprising all permanent working members over 18 years old, the Workers' Council, elected by the General Assembly, the Management Committee (3–11 members) elected by the Workers' Council, and the President nominated by the Management Committee. The President is essentially a figurehead. The Management Committee handles the daily running of the farm, including raw material purchase, sale of produce and authorisation of short term loans. The Workers' Council is responsible for membership decisions, purchase of equipment and long term borrowing, and the General Assembly is a forum for endorsing decisions made by the other bodies and for general debate. The Workers' Council works closely with the Director, appointed by ONRA to supervise the running of the farm in accordance with official policy.

The financial set-up is as follows. Revenue is defined as income less all costs except labour costs. The state gets part, the collective part, and the workers part. First come the state levies on the collective for (a) depreciation on its capital equipment (such capital being considered national property), (b) a national investment fund—by which agriculture contributes towards financing national economic development, and (c) the national employment fund (to supplement wages in poor regions and to finance employment-creating public works). Then come: (1) payment of non-permanent workers (chiefly seasonal labourers); (2) the members' basic wages; and (3) bonus schemes to members based on productivity successes. The Assembly or the

Workers' Council divides any surplus remaining among a farm investment reserve fund, a special housing and welfare reserve fund and the individual members themselves.

RESULTS OF AUTOGESTION

Land reform Algerian-style was approved by most Algerians: it seemed a logical way to offset the exodus of the European owner-managers, and it appealed to their sense of social justice, which, after eight years of bitter strife, was all-pervasive.[9] Official objectives behind the agricultural policy were: (1) a just distribution of income and wealth; (2) socialisation of the land; (3) increasing agricultural production; (4) maximising employment; (5) fully utilising existing capital and creating new capital; and (6) encouraging decision-making at farm level.[10] Some of these objectives conflict on the farm, and other objectives have emerged. Local jockeying for power within the system soon appeared and job security and advancement up the administrative hierarchy became the individual's aspirations. Two important goal conflicts have emerged: the national goal of maximum employment conflicts with the local goals of maximum farm profits and maximum individual income, and the national goal of increasing agricultural production can conflict with the local goal of maximum farm profits.[11] These problems reflect the national planners' desire to use the abundant semi-employed labour at the lowest wage possible to accumulate capital for economic development, and the local administrators' desire to maximise farm profits, even if they must limit the number of workers hired, while the individual workers are primarily interested in maximising their own incomes.

A prime difficulty has been to find capable directors. Sometimes one director has had to be responsible for up to five collective farms. As a temporary solution the ministry has appointed *chargés de gestion* ('managing officials'), but they are usually young and inexperienced. Lack of proper accounts procedures, too, makes economic decisions almost impossible to make. For good worker psychology, most socialised farms are probably too big.[12] The worker feels no individual identification with an estate of 1000 hectares; he cannot see his contribution making any difference to the income or profitability of the enterprise. Lack of initiative is thus widespread, and petty thievery common.

Produce is supposed to be collectively worked and marketed but illicit marketing of privately grown vegetables is common. Foster's case-study farm (Benkheira Abdellah, on the coast 80 kilometres west of Algiers) contained 90 squatter families enjoying free accommodation yet working outside the farm and intermittently cropping or grazing 'non-tillable' parts of the collective.[13] Many Algerian collectives show a sharp division between the permanent members and the seasonal workers, who are excluded from profit-sharing arrangements. Resulting resentment may undermine the co-operative spirit necessary for the socialist philosophy to succeed, and seasonal workers might be appropriately included in the share-outs, perhaps proportionately to the number of days worked on the farm.

While production problems are being solved, marketing remains a major difficulty. The state, which buys most of the socialist sector output, may be the most efficient organ in the Algerian situation, but state monopsony generates problems of quality, incentive and pricing. More important is the loss of the traditional French market for agricultural produce. Initially after 1962 France continued as Algeria's principal trading partner, but the closure of French outlets for Algerian wine—her most important agricultural product—has been cruelly felt; having bequeathed Algeria her great vineyards, France now excludes most of the produce. In 1970 and 1971 Russia imported most of the Algerian wine output very cheaply. Reduction of the vine-planted area, perhaps by a third, is recommended, and now taking place.

Wine apart, increased home consumption of agricultural produce is lessening the reliance on exports. In 1962 80 per cent of citrus fruit was exported, in 1965 57 per cent. Corresponding changes were 50 to 41 per cent for hard wheat, 80 to 67 per cent for soft.[14] Citrus fruit is now experiencing the same market squeeze as wine: western European demand is saturated, competition from a dozen other Mediterranean countries is fierce and Algeria is increasingly turning to Russia and the East European block. The other change to take place in Algeria's trade patterns is Saharan oil: in 1960 80 per cent of the country's exports were agricultural; in 1970 70 per cent was oil. In land use the autogestion farms, compared with their colonial performance, have increased cultivation of hard wheat, citrus and

TABLE 28

ALGERIA:

CHARACTERISTICS OF COLONIAL AND SOCIALIST AGRICULTURE

(A) CULTIVATED AREA

Crop	Colon land, 1950		Autogestion land, 1965		Socialist sector as percentage of national total by	
	Area (hectares)	per cent	Area (hectares)	per cent	Area	Value
Hard wheat	265 382	19·6	469 960	37·3	} 26·9	35·3
Soft wheat	246 118	18·2	238 060	18·9		
Barley	176 945	13·1	55 130	4·4		
Oats	130 858	9·7	14 455	1·1		
Other cereals	3 854	0·3	2 525	0·2		
Leguminous vegetables	47 658	3·5	24 540	2·0	30·1	22·5
Market gardening	20 559	1·5	21 160	1·7	32·9	45·0
Forage crops	39 776	2·9	28 340	2·3	not available	
Industrial crops	23 278	1·7	12 605	1·0	53·8	37·1
Vines	348 409	25·8	313 415	24·9	87·7	92·1
Citrus	22 577	1·7	40 735	3·2	88·7	91·7
Other fruits	27 468	2·0	38 760	3·0	22·6	25·5
Totals	1 352 882	100·0	1 259 685	100·0	33·8	58·8

(B) LIVESTOCK

	Colon land, 1950	Autogestion land, 1965
Cattle	113 290	10 725
Sheep	509 721	84 750
Goats	34 252	1 250

Source: H. Isnard: 'Les structures de l'autogestion agricole en Algérie', *Méditerranée*, 9 (2), 1968, pp. 143–5, 149.

other fruits, and decreased vines and other cereals (Table 28). Livestock numbers have fallen dramatically, but livestock farming is by peasants, who possess over half a million head of cattle and six million sheep.

Agricultural output in the socialist sector has maintained pre-independence levels but no more. Lack of data and climatic effects on yields make it difficult to be more precise. The first year of autogestion, 1963, saw the production of colon years equalled partly because of an exceptionally heavy harvest. Subsequently citrus and vegetable production held up better than vines. Cereal output suffers from climatic vagaries. For all crops combined, the production index (1957–9 average equalled 100) for the years 1963 to 1969 registered figures in the 90s, except for 1966, when there was a disastrous wheat harvest. The socialist sector, like the colon sector before it, covers a third of the total cultivated area and produces nearly 60 per cent of total output by value. Whilst these figures do not make Algerian socialised agriculture look any more productive than the previous system, socialisation undoubtedly prevented a production disaster after the skilled European managers left, and in that context was a success.

AUTOGESTION: AN EVALUATION

At a time when pressure for redistributing the fertile colon estates as small-sized plots was very strong, autogestion was a boldly original and on the whole fairly successful policy. It had several unique characteristics. It promulgated land reform solely for landless agricultural labourers, excluding all other peasant categories, and it concentrated on collectivising an already modernised sector, socialist-collectivist schemes elsewhere having concentrated on aggregating peasant smallholdings.

But do the autogestion farms represent workers' democracy or state capitalism? At least in the early stages autogestion veered sharply toward a collectivised capitalism, with each enterprise pitted against the others to achieve maximum profits.[15] The socialist sector now constitutes a privileged class of 1 million people, distinguished by extra wealth, improved living conditions and better security of employment; it contrasts sharply with the brooding, impoverished 6 million Algerian *fellahin* unaffected by autogestion. One kind of dualism has replaced another. The injustice is accentuated by the fact that the peasants, by their numbers, their toughness and their knowledge of the countryside, formed the backbone of the liberation army, whereas estate workers were little involved in the war. Concentration of autogestion in areas mostly densely settled by the French adds a geographical perspective to dualism. Five of the country's twelve *wilayate* or *departements* (Algiers, El Asnam, Mostaganem, Oran and Tlemcen), stretching along the coast

west of the capital, contain 64 per cent of the collectives.[16] Inland, the *bled*, the home of most *fellahin*, remains disinherited, a
huge denuded wasteland where rain is scarce and the wind can
erode a hundred hectares of soil a day. Traditional peasant
agriculture provides extremely low incomes and employment.
Average annual per capita income is £25 as against £55 for the
socialist sector, and estimates give 68 per cent of peasant labour
time as unemployed, with half the peasants working less than
100 days per year.[17]

Moreover, the private sector has its own inequalities. In the
sixties 20 000 landholders owned over a quarter of the arable
land in holdings of over 50 hectares, 147 000 holdings of 10 to
50 hectares covered another half, whilst the remaining land
(25 per cent) was under 424 000 holdings below 10 hectares
(310 000 below 5 hectares), most of which were inadequate as
family farms. A further 500 000 peasant families were landless.[18]
The larger landholders were mainly urban-based absentee
landlords who extracted rents equal to 10 per cent of total
private sector agricultural production.[19]

ALGERIA'S NEW LAND REFORM[20]

The long overdue reform of private land distribution, which
followed from Boumedienne's 'Charter of the Agrarian Revolution', announced in November 1971, was also boldly original in
conception. It is proceeding in two stages, the first virtually
complete, the second just started. Phase 1 concerned a rapid
census of public agricultural land, completed between March
and June 1972, and its distribution to peasants. Of 5 million
hectares of public land surveyed (including *habous*), 1 million
hectares were deemed agriculturally useful and parcelled out to
nearly 60 000 beneficiaries.

Stage 2, expropriation of privately-owned land from large
and absentee landholders, was more difficult. Basic information
was collected from all landowners in 1972–3, with local checks.
Landowners had to declare their place of residence, their sources of income and their properties. All absentee-owned land is
being expropriated, irrespective of size of holding. Ceilings for
private land, specified in August 1973, vary with land use,
availability of irrigation, and location. Ceilings on irrigated
cropland, for instance, varied from 1 hectare to 5 hectares, on

olive groves from 12 hectares to 45 hectares, and on vineyards from 4 hectares to 18 hectares. Limits on date holdings were expressed in numbers of trees, varying from 90 to 320 palms, according to variety, irrigation method and production. The guiding principle is that the retained holding should be sufficient to guarantee farm income of three times the wage of an autogestion worker. Landowners are indemnified proportionately to their previous land tax returns by $2\frac{1}{2}$ per cent state bonds redeemable over fifteen years. Land is distributed to landless peasants or to those with insufficient land, priority going to those who previously worked the land in question as tenants or labourers. Size of assigned lots is generally one-third of the ceiling limit. Beneficiaries do not receive title of ownership but permanent right of usufruct, hereditary in the male lineage, ownership being vested in the 'National Land Fund,' an organ created by the 'agrarian revolution'. Monthly cash payments of about £15, together with food grants, are provided for assignees until the first harvest.

Recipients of both public and private land are compulsorily grouped into production co-operatives, membership of which is open to other farmers. The first phase of the reform, dealing with public land, saw 1349 production co-operatives established. These co-operatives, along with private and autogestion farms, are being grouped into larger general service and marketing organisations called *Co-opératives Communales Polyvalentes de Services* (CAPCS); 600 CAPCS are planned, one in each rural commune. Each will require an office, storage barns, repair workshop and other buildings reflecting local agricultural specialisms. A target of 400 CAPCS for late 1973 was not reached because of shortage of iron and steel and lack of suitable cadres to run the organisations. A related settlement effect is the much publicised policy to construct 1000 new *villages socialistes* between 1972 and 1976. A first phase of 100 villages was planned for 1973, but at the end of the year only 2 had been handed over to beneficiaries for occupation, with a further 15 under construction.

Several years must elapse before results of the current land reform become clear. Prospects are reasonable given continued government support. Funds seem assured for land redistribution and the co-operatives; the longer term project of the thousand new villages is less certain. The phased operations of Algeria's agrarian reform seem better organised than the sweeping co-operative movement in Tunisia in 1969, but if a Tunisian-type reaction is to be avoided, the next few years must ensure the political defence of the reform. Long term success hinges on economic results; the reform must break the stagnation of Algerian agriculture (production fell by 1 per cent per year between 1969 and 1972). If it is intended to keep most peasants on the land, the farmed area must be expanded. The present reform, affecting an estimated 3 million hectares (2 million private, 1 million public), covers only about a third of the potential recipients of land.

REFERENCES

1. J. Ruedy: *Land Policy in Colonial Algeria* (Berkeley, University of California Middle Eastern Studies 10, 1967), p. vii.
2. *Ibid*: p. 67.
3. P. Foster: 'Land reform in Algeria', in Agency for International Development: *Spring Review of Land Reform* (Washington, Department of State, 1970), Vol. 8, pp. 10–11.
4. T. Tidafi: *L'Agriculture Algérienne* (Paris, Maspero, 1969), pp. 27–8.
5. K. B. Griffin: 'Algerian agriculture in transition', *Bulletin of the Oxford University Institute of Economics and Statistics*, 27 (4), 1965, pp. 229–52.
6. See R. Dumont: 'Des conditions de la réuissité de la réforme agraire en Algérie', in F. Perroux (ed.): *Problèmes de l'Algérie Indépendante* (Paris, Presses Universitaires de France Collection Tiers Monde, 1963), pp. 79–123.
7. For full translation and discussion of the Decrees see Foster: *op. cit.*, pp. 28–30, 63–76.
8. Based on Z. Reggam: 'Agrarian reform in Algeria', in M. R. El Ghonemy (ed.): *Land Policy in the Near East* (Rome, FAO for the Government of Libya, 1967), pp. 235–46.
9. Foster: *op. cit.*, p. 48.
10. *Ibid*: pp. 37–8.
11. *Ibid*: pp. 56–61.
12. Griffin: *op. cit.*, pp. 234–5.
13. Foster: *op. cit.*, p. 45.
14. Tidafi: *op. cit.*, pp. 51, 57.
15. T. L. Blair: *The Land to Those who Work it: Algeria's Experiment in Workers' Management* (New York, Doubleday, 1969), pp. 106–21.
16. H. Isnard: 'Les structures de l'autogestion agricole en Algérie', *Méditerranée*, 9 (2), 1968, pp. 139–63.
17. Griffin: *op. cit.*, p. 242.
18. Tidafi: *op. cit.*, pp. 131–5.

19. A. Prenant: 'La propriété foncière des citadins dans les régions de Tlemcen et Sidi-Bel-Abbes', *Annales Algériennes de Géographie*, 2 (3), 1967, pp. 2–94, esp. p. 79.

20. This account is based on K. Sutton: 'Agrarian reform in Algeria—the conversion of projects into action', *Afrika Spectrum*, 9 (1), 1974, pp. 50–68, and K. Schliephake: 'Changing the traditional sector of Algeria's agriculture', *Land Reform, Land Settlement and Co-operatives*, 1, 1973, pp. 19–28.

Index

Printed in Great Britain
by Amazon